Writing Marketing

Writing Marketing

Literary Lessons from
Academic Authorities

Stephen Brown

SAGE Publications
London ● Thousand Oaks ● New Delhi

SAGE Publications Ltd
1 Oliver's Yard
55 City Road
London EC1Y 1SP

SAGE Publications Inc.
2455 Teller Road
Thousand Oaks, California 91320

SAGE Publications India Pvt Ltd
B-42, Panchsheel Enclave
Post Box 4109
New Delhi 110 017

British Library Cataloguing in Publication data
A catalogue record for this book is available from the British Library

ISBN 1 4129 0265 7
ISBN 1 4129 0266 5 (pbk)

Library of Congress Control Number: 2005901827

Typeset by M Rules
Printed in India at Gopsons Papers Ltd, Noida

Contents

The ABCs of Writing Marketing

Writing is easy. All you do is sit staring at a blank sheet of paper until the drops of blood form on your forehead.

Gene Fowler[1]

Author, Author!

Marketing is myriad. Marketing is multifarious. Marketing, like Walt Whitman, is large and contains multiples. The marketing academy, akin to that legendary Biblical building, is a house of many mansions. Marketing scholars are nothing if not polymorphously perverse. Present company excepted, of course.

As a quick flick though the leading journals indicates, marketing is an extraordinarily diverse discipline. Academics study everything from the costs of globalization to the benefits of money-back guarantees.[2] Research methods range from structural equation modelling to 'netnography', a kind of online in-dwelling.[3] Philosophical perspectives stretch from prim and proper positivism to wild and woolly postmodernism.[4] The ultimate purpose of marketing scholarship is either descriptive or prescriptive (or both), depending on the axiological ambitions of the academic concerned.[5]

Despite this diversity, there is one thing that unites the various strands of marketing endeavour. And that is the written word. Whether they be quantitatively or qualitatively inclined, whether they be diligent data miners or factorial experiment finessers, whether they study the pupil dilation of supermarket shoppers or the relationship between macroeconomic cycles and retail institutional change, all marketing academics set out their arguments, postulates, hypotheses, findings, or whatever they choose to call them, in a written document. Articles, books, reports, dissertations, case studies, chapters, monographs, working papers, and analogous literary forms, are the principal output of the marketing academy.

There are, admittedly, several other salient forms of symbolic scholarly expression, such as pie charts, flow diagrams, scatter graphs and, increasingly, digital camera recordings.[6] Marketing academics, what is more, communicate their findings in many different ways, from student seminars and conference presentations to personal websites and television interviews. These variations, however, ultimately rest on the written word, the textual artefact, the published paper. Not only does the published article represent a distillation of several other textual phenomena – questionnaire surveys, interview transcripts, secondary data, literature reviews and so on – but it is arguable that research *doesn't actually exist* until, and unless, it appears in published form – ideally in a journal of record. Certainly, that is the view taken by most professorial tenure committees and university appointment-panels. Videos are nice and personal websites can be very impressive, but they don't help secure tenure or offers of employment, especially in our RAE-orientated times.

Whatever their philosophical, methodological or epistemological differences, then, all marketing academics are literary types. They write for a living. They publish or perish. They put words on the page, occasionally in the right order. Their careers are advanced, their employability is enhanced, and their professional standing is predicated on the written word.

Writing about writing, however, is conspicuous by its absence. There is very little published literature on the published literature. There are, I grant you, copious citation studies and innumerable ranking analyses of the leading journals.[7] Myriad self-help texts, how-to handbooks and best-practice primers on the mechanics of doing research, writing dissertations, getting into print and so on are also readily available.[8] Anthologies of classic articles, bibliographies of recommended readings, and comments and rejoinders on individual research papers are an equally important part of marketing's rich textual tapestry.[9] The reviewing process, in particular, has attracted much academic discussion and not a little disdain.[10]

All things considered, it is clear that marketing writing has not received the academic attention it deserves nor, indeed, its professional significance warrants. If professorial preferment depends on words on a page, then those words and those pages are a subject worthy of detailed investigation, if only for self-help or job-search purposes.

Applied Scientism

No doubt there are many deep-seated reasons for the marketing academy's reluctance to write about the written word, but scientism and pragmatism must figure prominently among them. For more than sixty years, marketing has been marketing itself as a science, as a Science with a capital 'S'.[11] It is positioned in the academic firmament as the scientific repository of the laws, axioms, and principles of the marketplace, such as they are. There has, of course, been a great deal of internal debate about the nature and extent of marketing's scientific standing.[12] Some say it is a science, some say it isn't. Some say it will become a science in the fullness of time, or when squadrons of porkers fly in formation over Cranfield Business School. Nevertheless, the aspiration to scientific status runs deep, even among those who subscribe to the interpretive research tradition, which by and large draws inspiration from the liberal arts. Thus our field's leading learned journal is emblazoned with the resonant by-line, 'advancing the practice and science of marketing', and the vast majority of academics, I strongly suspect, accepts this statement of scientific intent.[13]

Practice, indeed, is no less important. Marketing prides itself on being an applied discipline. It is not given over to high-falutin, namby-pamby, artsy-fartsy, fancy-pantsy flights of literary fancy.[14] It has little or no truck with pseudo-intellectual pretension and scholarly self-indulgence, let alone lounging about in libraries agonizing over split infinitives, dangling participles and errant apostrophes. It has demanding constituents to cater for – students, managers, policy-makers etc. – and doesn't have time for frivolity or anything that diverts attention from the bottom line. It is a serious business and it is in the business of being taken seriously. It focuses on the facts. Got that?

Although these assumptions and aspirations are debatable – marketing's scientific status is moot, as is its purported pragmatic imperative – most would agree that they are widely shared. Worrying about literary matters is considered trite, trivial and tangential to the real business of B-school scholars (when it is considered at all, that is). In the great marketing scheme of things, writing doesn't require much thought. Literary analysis is unnecessary, not to say narcissistic. Textual analysis has its place when the works of Shakespeare, Shelley, Emerson, Eliot and what have you are under investigation. But it is irrelevant to the academic marketing situation. It wastes valuable time that would be better spent disseminating the marketing message or investigating important practical issues such as retaining customers and increasing loyalty. Worse still, it sends out the wrong signals. In an era characterized by seriously socially responsible corporations, pedantically pondering literary matters seems, well, somewhat irresponsible.[15] At a time when marketing practitioners are under inordinate pressure to specify, justify and quantify their 'contribution', arguing over assonance, alliteration, allegories or adverbs appears almost obscene.[16] In a world where concerned citizen-activists are attacking marketing's record, condemning its practices and questioning its basic right to exist, rhapsodizing on rhetoric, rhythm and similar recherché concerns is a recipe for disciplinary disaster.[17] It is the ivory tower equivalent of fiddling while Rome burns, 'I'm all right Jack', or 'let them eat cake'.

The only problem with this line of argument is that it doesn't scan, much less resonate or rhyme. Marketing's hostility to literary matters, the presumption that it prevents marketing from being taken seriously, is belied by the fact that longer established academic disciplines see things differently. Literary considerations have been debated at length by adjacent subject areas, such as anthropology, economics, psychology and organization studies. Clifford Geertz, for example, has published a brilliant excursus on the writing styles of leading social anthropologists like Claude Lévi-Strauss, Bronisław Malinowski and Edward Evans-Pritchard.[18] Deirdre McCloskey has convincingly demonstrated that the 'dismal science' is anything but, in literary terms at least.[19] A.J. Soyland has portrayed the history of psychology as a cavalcade of constantly changing metaphors, from Freudian water closets via Skinnerian mazes to latter-day Lacanian mirrors.[20] And, contemporary organization studies is chock-a-block with analyses of narrative, irony, tragedy and all the writerly rest.[21]

The tragedy, for marketing, is that it continues to disavow its discursive roots in the hope that it will be taken seriously by the scholarly community in general and the social sciences in particular. The irony is that its apparent reluctance to address rhetorical issues is one of the very things that prevent it from being taken seriously by contiguous academic disciplines. The gnarled narrative that marketing is a science, and that science focuses on content not style, is negated by a recent upsurge in stylish scientific writing, writing that not only reaches big audiences but regularly bestrides the best-seller's list, thanks to Stephen Hawking, Stephen Pinker, Stephen Jay Gould and several others.[22] When was the last time a marketing scholar lurked in the literary charts, let alone topped them?

Similarly, the assumption that marketing academics are pragmatists in all but name, that they supply actionable insights for eternally grateful sales and advertising executives, is totally at odds with reality. The reality is that marketing executives and practitioners *don't* read the academic literature.[23] They get next to nothing from it. They regard the leading journals as vehicles for scholarly advancement rather than founts of eternal marketing wisdom. They turn to Jack Trout, not *JM*, to Tom Peters, not *JMR*, to Sergio Zyman, not *MS*, when they're looking for meaningful marketing insights. They ignore the alleged 'managerial implications' of our 2×2 experiments on 120 undergraduate students from a mid-western university, who receive course credit for their reflections on imaginary products and hypothetical marketing situations. And who can blame them?

The bottom line is that marketing's bottom line mentality – the belief that academics add value – is bereft. The notion that marketing executives regard academics as information providers of choice is nonsense.[24] The very fact that marketing can ignore literary matters when its intellectual elders and betters consider them worthy of detailed attention is clueless at best and cretinous at worst. Marketing likes to boast that it focuses on the facts, but the fact of the matter is that the facts don't speak for themselves. They are selected, shaped and spread by literary means. They are spun on a textual loom. Facts are textual constructs. They only exist on paper. They are entirely textually mediated. There is nothing untouched by text.[25]

Lit-crit It

If it is accepted that marketing scholarship is a literary matter, in a manner of speaking, and that writing is central to what marketing academics do for a living, then the treasures of literary theory and cultural criticism are available to us. For most people, admittedly, that prospect is less than alluring. Their memories of literary criticism are confined to painful classroom encounters with impossibly impenetrable poems and less than side-splitting Shakespearean comedies. Heroic couplets, iambic pentameters, metrical feet, ottava rima, spondees, trochees, dactyls, enjambment and equivalent prosodic utterances are all that remain, lodged in the interstices of remembrance like food in a broken tooth – their precise meanings long since forgotten.

There's much more to literary criticism than prosody, however. Lit-crit, in fact, is a long-established and extremely diverse intellectual endeavour. Although it is approximately the same age as marketing – both emerged as formal academic disciplines towards the end of the nineteenth century – it is, if anything, even more fragmented into subdisciplines, subject area specialisms and sneering scholarly splinter groups. As any introductory anthology attests, lit-crit is astonishingly eclectic (and getting more so with every passing year).[26] Its principal paradigms range from Reader Response and Russian Formalist to Feminist, Freudian and a veritable plethora of 'posts' (post-this, post-that, post-the-other). All of these theoretical approaches can be meaningfully adapted to marketing literature, as shall be demonstrated in due course.

But where to start? With the dominant paradigm, naturally! This is easier said than done, unfortunately, on account of lit-crit's inherent catholicism, not to say maddening mutability. Sixty years ago, when the so-called New Critics held literary studies in a vice-like grip, the choice was comparatively straightforward and the approved approaches easily itemized (detailed explication, close reading, seeking paradox, irony and ambiguity, as well as intentional or affective fallacies).[27] Nowadays, the decision is not so simple. The hegemony of Wimsatt, Brooks and Penn-Warren has long since dissipated, the clear-cut critical hierarchy has gone the way of the once inviolable canon, and an 'anything goes' ethos currently prevails.

Closer inspection, nevertheless, reveals that lit-crit does, indeed, possess a Lakatosian 'hard core', an essentially ideological stance that shapes its basic outlook.[28] And that stance, in a nutshell, is anti-marketing. Marketing, for the scribbling classes, is within spitting distance of the Devil Incarnate and a stone's throw from Hades HQ. The literati see themselves as last-ditch defenders of high culture, what Matthew Arnold famously deemed 'the best that has been known and said in the world'.[29] Marketing, selling, trade and the insidious imprecations of late capitalism are abhorrent to those who hail from the liberal arts end of the scholarly spectrum. Commerce is crass. Profit is poison. Money-grubbing is grotesque. Art is above such base concerns. Art for art's sake is the dominant mot juste. Art is everlasting, lucre is ludicrous . . . and filthy, furthermore.

The literati's anti-marketing mentality is very long established and can be traced from Plato to the present.[30] It is espoused, moreover, by authors and critics alike (though these two are often difficult to distinguish in practice, since many authors write criticism and vice versa). As a recent summary of literary representations of British business life reported:

> One is faced with a rather damning picture of prodigiously wasteful, yet Scrooge-like businessmen who are abnormal and antagonistic; corrupt, cunning and cynical; dishonest, disorderly, doltish, dumb and duplicitous; inhumane, insensitive and irresponsible; ruthless; unethical and unprincipled; and villainous to boot.[31]

Another, even more recent, assessment of the American situation concluded that, throughout the postwar period, literary types:

> have been straightforwardly antagonistic towards business. . . . It has rarely been the case that the explicit ideological objectives of business or businessmen have been ratified by literary culture in the United States. These writers have often been attracted instead to what, as early as the 1840s,

Henry David Thoreau was calling the 'lives of quiet desperation' that men lead in the face of a materialistic market society dominated by business. From the 'exhaustion' that Arthur Miller uses in his very first description of Willy Loman in *Death of a Salesman*, through the self-pitying melancholy of Bob Slocum in Joseph Heller's *Something Happened*, right up to Patrick Bateman's disregard for the human body in *American Psycho* inspired by the depthlessness of contemporary stock trading, there has existed a resentment for the pressures and strains business and its attendant culture imposes on the individual male.[32]

The same attitude, incidentally, is true of media representations generally. A US study of 200 episodes of 50 prime time TV programmes variously found that over half of all corporate chiefs commit illegal acts ranging from fraud to murder; 45 per cent of all business activities are portrayed as illegal; and only 3 per cent of television businessmen engage in socially or economically productive behaviour.[33] The prevailing picture is perfectly captured in the comments of best-selling author Jonathan Franzen (before he hit the big time with *The Corrections*, that is):

There's never been much love lost between literature and the marketplace. The consumer economy loves a product that sells at a premium, wears out quickly or is susceptible to regular improvement, and offers with each improvement some marginal gain in usefulness. To an economy like this, news that stays news is not merely an inferior product; it's an *antithetical* product. A classic work of literature is inexpensive, infinitely reusable, and, worst of all, unimprovable.[34]

All Changed, Changed Utterly

Although Franzen's market-phobic prejudices are still widely shared, there are at least some signs that this is beginning to change. The absolute disdain that characterized the high modernist era of literary experimentation has abated of late. Dramatic changes in the production (desktop developments), publication (multi-media conglomerates), distribution (online operations, mega bookshops) and reception of literature (reading groups, the Richard and Judy effect in Britain or Oprah's influence in the US), the increasingly customer-orientated ethos that has penetrated all but the most illiberal liberal arts colleges, and the sheer relentlessness of the commodification process, which can offer all sorts of rewards in return for author compliance, has led even the stoutest defenders of the faith to doubt their calling and bend their formerly absolute anti-marketing principles.[35]

While it would be incorrect to state that Culture has capitulated to Commerce – the recent counter-capitalist street protests suggest there's life in the old left yet[36] – things are certainly heading that way. In *Nobrow*, a twenty-first century reworking of hoary high-, medium- and low-brow cultural categories, John Seabrook argues that marketing has not simply been accepted by the arts, but it has absorbed the arts *tout court*.[37] Marketing isn't something that is applied to culture, culture is a component of the marketing–industrial complex that holds the entire developed world in its thrall.

A broadly similar case is made by David Brooks, who identifies a 'BoBo' propensity among contemporary consumers.[38] The traditional never-the-twain-shall-meet distinction between Bourgeois (business people in the main) and Bohemians (artistic types who renounce crass materialism) has pretty much disappeared. These days, he says, the bourgeois have bohemian inclinations and bohemians are bourgeois at heart. The counter-culture radicalism of the sixties has been combined with the 'greed-is-good' ethos of the eighties to produce the marketing-as-art mindset of the nineties and noughties.

Brooks and Seabrook are just the tip of the textual iceberg. In *High Pop*, Jim Collins contends that elite culture is being progressively popularized. That is, made palatable to mainstream, middle-brow taste via blockbuster museum exhibitions, superstar opera singers, art-house movie specialists like Miramax, design-led chain stores, such as Target, make-yourself-at-home mega bookstores, and so on.[39] A broadly similar adulteration process is identified by Curtis White, who despairs of the ever accelerating cultural debasement – epitomized, he argues, by Spielberg's execrable *Saving Private Ryan* – yet who can't help admiring multinational capital's chameleon-like ability to recast itself as 'creative', 'cool' and 'cultured'.[40] So brilliant is big business's ability to co-opt critique and subsequently resell it as radical chic, that White finally waves the white flag of surrender with the weary confession, 'we need to learn from capitalism'.[41]

Wire Hair Day

Needless to say, the latter-day commodification of culture has not gone unnoticed by the left-leaning, lapsed-radical rump of leading literary critics (memorably described by Tom Wolfe as 'bitter old Marxist academics with wire hair sprouting out of their ears'[42]). Comfortably ensconced in citadels of cerebration, far from the madding marketplace, this well-padded professoriat has responded in diverse ways. Some, such as Harold

Bloom and Stanley Fish, are happy to be given the Tom Clancy, John Grisham, Barbara Taylor Bradford treatment. Lit-crit superbrands, their books are piled high in mega bookstores and airport departure lounges worldwide, and they are content to counsel cultural capital-less capitalists from the hopelessly tainted pages of *HBR* or *WSJ*.

Others, like Fredric Jameson (the foremost Marxist literary critic in the US), prefer to rail against the dying of the light, while championing those few remaining exponents of 'authentic' cultural production that haven't been penetrated by the market. The only problem, as Delany demonstrates, is that these allegedly authentic offerings are brought to our attention and sold as such by the multi-media conglomerates that Jameson despises and, ironically, depends upon.[43] Fredric Jameson is the critical equivalent of Sprite, a bookish brand who is marketed on the basis of his anti-marketing stance. Image is nothing. Anti-image is everything.

Still, perhaps the most interesting response to this gradual melding of art and mart is that of Stephen Greenblatt and his fellow New Historicists, who attempt to have their critical cake and eat it.[44] On the one hand, they consistently articulate an implacably oppositional stance by exposing the machinations of capitalism in even the most disinterested cultural productions. On the other hand, their written works are replete with marketing-infused concepts and practices. Terms like 'exchange', 'negotiation', 'transaction', 'circulation' and suchlike litter their texts. The colonization and commercial exploitation of the new world by the old is a constantly recurring theme.[45] Greenblatt even acknowledges that the term 'New Historicism' was a deliberate branding exercise, an attempt to position his school of thought in the intellectual agora (though he has since abandoned the old New Historicism brand name for something more marketable, namely Cultural Poetics).[46] The New Historicists, in short, are openly complicit with what they ostentatiously condemn. And they have the gall to call marketers mendacious . . .

Marketing Ho!

Just as marketing is colonizing cloistered colleges and paternalistic publishing houses, so too the artistic temperament is making its presence felt in marketing. At a macro level, it is increasingly recognized that the cultural industries generally are one of the principal engines of the post-industrial economy. Richard Florida, for instance, makes a compelling case for arts-led regional development – exemplified by Bilbao's Guggenheim Museum – and regards cultural vibrancy as the key to effective place marketing.[47] Michael Wolf, likewise, argues that entertainment is an increasingly important feature of the contemporary corporate landscape and considers Hollywood, Bollywood, Silicon Valley and suchlike as harbingers of what the future has in store.[48] It's not so much that there's no business *like* show business as there's no business *without* show business. David James, moreover, maintains that the music industry offers a model for marketing in the twenty-first century, as do several other enthusiasts.[49] 'We live', says one, 'in a world where heavy industry has been superseded by heavy metal, where FMCG stands for Flagrantly Manufactured Chart-topping Groups, and where the legendary degeneracy of the music business is matched, possibly surpassed, by the degeneracy on Wall Street and executive suites worldwide'.[50]

At the micro, company-specific scale, meanwhile, recent years have seen a slew of marketing principles textbooks for art, culture and entertainment organizations, broadly defined, as well as executive education offerings predicated on literary classics. These range from the *Leadership Secrets of Shakespeare* and *Winnie the Pooh on Management*, to books like *Beautiful Corporations* and *Marketing Aesthetics*, which posit a liberal arts-inflected, rather than social science-driven, approach to marketing management.[51] A particularly good example of the genre is *Fictions of Business* by Robert Brawer, a former English literature professor and CEO of leading lingerie manufacturer Maidenform. By focusing on works of fiction that foreground business life – everything from Sinclair Lewis's *Babbitt* to David Mamet's *Glengarry Glen Ross* – Brawer is able to extract nuggets of eminently implementable management wisdom on matters as diverse as office politics, closing the sale and surviving in today's dog-eat-dog world.[52]

Impressive as this proliferation of practitioner-targeted texts undoubtedly is, the bookish turn doesn't stop there. The marketing academy has also been bitten by the literary bug. Not badly bitten, it has to be said, not bitten to the point of rabidity. But bitten sufficiently to break the skin and require a little scratching. This scratching takes two main forms. First, academics are culling works of literature, both classic and pulp, for meaningful marketing insights.[53] Jackie Collins's sex 'n' shopping novels, for example, provide windows on the world of compulsive consumption. *Bridget Jones's Diary* mirrors the manners, mores and marketing-saturated lifestyle of unmarried urbanite professionals. The fiction of Douglas Copeland and Jay McInerney encapsulates the aimless, amoral, anti-aspirational outlook that characterized the brand-savvy slacker decades of the late twentieth century. David Henscher's *The Gift* explores the dilemmas, difficulties, dismay and, indeed, dementia of buying something for someone who has everything. Nick Hornby's *High Fidelity*, furthermore, paints an unprepossessing picture of marketplace mavens – sad,

conversationally challenged, prematurely middle-aged men who spend inordinate amounts of time in record stores, used bookshops, loitering with content on the internet and, naturally, cataloguing their compendious collections. Not that I know anyone like that.

Such studies, in short, are predicated on the premise that creative writers can better articulate the essence of everyday experience – the consumer condition, if you will – than any number of questionnaire surveys, focus groups or ethnographic safaris into the precast canyons of the concrete jungle. 'Art,' as cult novelist Chuck Palahnuik (paraphrasing Picasso) rightly observes, 'is a big pumped-up operatic version of real life; it's the lie that tells the truth better than the truth does.'[54] For literary critics, Young and Caveney, 'Fiction is now the closest we're likely to come to truth and as such it should be loved and cherished.'[55] 'Culture', according to Jen Webb et al., 'makes the invisible visible, and brings into material form the unexpressed conditions of being'.[56]

Text Messages

The second form of scholarly scratching involves applying the tools and techniques of literary theory to marketing phenomena such as shopping centres, supermarkets, service encounters, brandscapes and, above all, advertisements. For the purposes of analysis, these artefacts are treated as 'texts' and interpreted accordingly. In a series of pioneering studies, Barbara B. Stern has parsed a variety of ads from a variety of theoretical standpoints. This commenced with a New Critical explication of prominent advertising slogans, continued with commercials' appropriation of allegory, symbol, personae, and similar literary devices, culminated in a delightful Derridean deconstruction of cigarette advertising in general and Joe Camel in particular, and carried on with studies of Frye's topos of narrative types, feminist readings of the macho Marlboro Man and many others besides.[57] More than almost anyone before or since, Stern has forged literary criticism into a legitimate marketing research method.

Stern, moreover, is not alone. Her approach has spawned a small (but perfectly formed) school of marketing thought. To list but a few examples, Linda Scott has applied Reader-Response theory to commercial messages, as has Lorna Stevens in her feminist interpretation of women's magazine consumption.[58] Edward McQuarrie and David Mick have highlighted the importance of rhetoric and resonance – that is, the use of puns, wordplay and the like – in marketing communication.[59] Benôit Heilbrunn has drawn upon the narratological theories of Vladimir Propp to conceptualize the

brand-buyer dyad.[60] Jean-Marie Floch has adapted Greimas's semiotic square to all sorts of martefacts, including hypermarkets, corporate logos and the Paris Metro.[61] Stephanie O'Donohoe has picked up on Kristeva's notion of intertextuality and applied it to young consumers' relationship with television adverts.[62] And Brown et al. have variously examined heritage parks through the admittedly opaque lens of Jameson's postmodern historicism, studied a carnivalesque Moët et Chandon magazine ad from a Bakhtinian perspective, and read the recent rapid rise of retro branding in relation to the aphoristic literary theories of Walter Benjamin.[63]

The above, it must be stressed, is but a smattering of the academic studies that are currently available. The literature on metaphor – and, to a lesser extent, storytelling – is particularly voluminous.[64] It even forms the basis of a trademarked, pat-pending, mega money-spinning, intellectual-property-protected, and doubtless ravenous-Rottweiler-guarded research method ZMET (Zaltman Metaphor Elicitation Technique).[65] True, the procedure has been described as the mutant methodological lovechild of Ernest Dichter and Walt Disney. Nevertheless, its evident popularity, plus the powerful imprimatur of Harvard Business School, stands testament to the latter-day penetration of literature-led research methods.

Welcome though this textual transformation is, marketing's embrace of things literary doesn't extend to marketing literature. Although academics are happy to engage with *metaphorical* marketing texts – as the 'readings' of advertisements, supermarkets and brand extensions bear witness – they remain strangely reluctant to interrogate *literal* marketing texts, the writings of their fellow researchers. There are, needless to say, several noteworthy exceptions to this ludicrous rule. Barbara B. Stern has considered the publications of Ernest Dichter from a literary perspective, as has Jeff Durgee.[66] Craig Thompson published an hermeneutic analysis of the vituperative Realism versus Relativism debate of the early eighties.[67] Daragh O'Reilly demolished the rich brew of mixed metaphors pressed between the precious pages of Hamel and Prahalad.[68] Avi Shankar and Maurice Patterson have applied narratological methods to the rise of the interpretive research tradition, creatively construing it as a series of crises, climaxes and resolutions.[69] More recently, Chris Hackley has deconstructed the ideological arguments that inhere in introductory textbooks of the Lancaster and Massingham stripe.[70]

Such studies, however, are not only few in number, they are preoccupied with writing wrongs. That is, they focus on the disagreeable, the confrontational, the belligerent, the aberrant side of marketing scholarship. Aberrance, admittedly, isn't always abhorrent. The deviant are advantaged, according to management gurus Mathews and Wacker.[71] The 'bad guy' role is inherently appealing, as actors and audiences readily attest. It is perhaps not surprising, therefore, that initial literary analyses

of the marketing literature should deal with 'dark side' concerns. But if literary criticism is to be considered a force for the good, as an intellectual redeemer, as something that every scholar and student should be thoroughly versed in, then a more upbeat approach is called for. Indeed, if we wish to increase our marketing word-power, in classic *Reader's Digest* fashion, it may be wise to start with the masters of marketing's literary art. And masters there are.

Although we're sometimes reluctant to admit it, presumably because it might detract from our serious scientific credentials, the simple fact of the matter is that there are several very able writers in the marketing academy and not a few first-class poets. John Sherry's essay on NikeTown, for example, is a tour de force.[72] Russ Belk's paean to a pair of plastic glasses is as powerful as they come.[73] Beth Hirschman's autobiographical accounts of her manifold addictions are straight from the heart.[74] Craig Thompson is blessed with a turn of phrase that places him on a par with Pulitzer prize-winners, or *The Simpsons'* scriptwriters at least.[75] Hope Schau, Anthony Patterson and Bob Grafton Small are equally gifted, albeit less well known than the foregoing literary foursome.[76]

An upbeat approach to marketing poetics is sorely needed and long overdue. Surely it is time to celebrate the marketing literati and learn from their achievements, their publications, their textual practices. It is time to overcome marketing manuscript myopia. It is time to deny our denial of what we do day and daily. It is time to put things *write*. That's what this book is about.

Beware, Bullet-point Breakout

Clearly, there are many ways of reading the writings of marketing academics:

- content analyses of the leading journals – noting their principal themes and underpinning ideology;
- citation studies of scholarly influence and/or intra-disciplinary interpersonal networks;
- historical overviews of the rise and fall of various schools of marketing thought, such as institutionalism or functionalism;
- critical cogitations on the generic character of published articles, their standardized structure, rhetorical devices, and stylistic tics; and
- comparative mappings of marketing's literary landscape, with salient features marked, major hazards identified and topological variations recorded.

All of these are perfectly legitimate approaches to the marketing literature. However, they are not particularly literary. They comprise somewhat cold, calculating and unnecessarily 'scientific' approaches to what is an artistic or proto-artistic pursuit. Writing is an artistic endeavour, not something that can be captured in an equation, or involves following a formula, or boils down to a boxes-and-arrows diagram. Writing is an art, a craft, a knack, if you will, that even the hardest of hard marketing scientists must acquire.

Literary theorists, I grant you, have occasionally wrapped themselves in the mantle of science. The New Critics firmly believed that their rigorous methods of textual explication were placing literature on a solid scientific footing. The pioneering narratological analyses of Vladimir Propp involve elaborate 'formulae' for folk-tales and fairy stories. A.J. Greimas's semiotic square is not a million miles away from marketing by matrix. As Valentine Cunningham cogently explains, however, such exercises diminish literature.[77] They detract from rather than add to the compelling power of the written word. Literature is singular. It is not about averages, or eigenvalues, or, heaven help us, autocorrelation. It is about the unique, the inimitable, the sublime, the apotheosis, the Nietzschean lightning flash that illuminates for an instant, an unforgettable instant.

Pretentiousness is an occupational hazard of literary types. And I apologise in advance. Yet despite the clear and present danger that inheres in stylistic overkill, the present volume will adopt an unashamedly literary approach to the marketing literature. Scientistic studies of marketing scholarship undoubtedly have their place. But not in the chapters to follow. Accordingly, *Writing Marketing* interrogates the published works of five influential marketing academics; academics who are renowned for their writing and whose writing has helped shape the development of the marketing discipline in the modern, postwar era. Using the tools and techniques of literary criticism – one 'school' per author – their corpuses will be examined in fine detail and appropriate literary lessons duly derived.

The aims of *Writing Marketing* are thus threefold: (i) to identify the practical lessons can be learned from past masters of the marketing article; (ii) to provide an introduction to literary theory with worked examples drawn from marketing writings rather than metaphorical 'texts' like advertisements and service encounters; and (iii) to move beyond the normative analyses of 'how to' guidebooks (this is what you *should do* if you want to get published) and focus instead on positive approaches to writing marketing (this is what great writers *actually do* in their published articles).

The text is structured as follows: Chapter 2 will tackle Theodore Levitt, using Reader-Response theory as a conceptual template; Chapter 3 considers Philip Kotler from a Marxian perspective; Chapter 4 is a Deconstructive take on Shelby D. Hunt; Chapter 5 adopts a Biopoetic approach to the writings of Wroe Alderson; Chapter 6 places Morris Holbrook on the couch of Psychoanalytical literary criticism; and Chapter 7 will attempt to show how writing marketing can help right marketing.

Although the individual chapters stand alone and can be read without reference to the overall argument, each contains the same basic elements: an introduction to the academic in question, a summary of the lit-crit stance and an interrogation of the selected author's oeuvre. The balance and sequencing of these elements, however, varies from chapter to chapter. What's more, some of the critiques are trait-based – that is, they examine the scholar's writings against salient theoretical themes – whereas others are in the classic compare-and-contrast tradition, usually in relation to another critical figure. The schools of criticism increase in intricacy as the book progresses, though the text also loops back on itself, eventually returning to the practicalities of writing in the final chapter. If not quite a 'writerly' text, in the poststructuralist tradition, it isn't exactly a 'readerly' text either.

The ABCs of Writing Marketing

It almost goes without saying that these overall objectives invite several obvious objections about the *Academics* and *Approaches*, *Basis* and *Beliefs*, and *Contents* and *Concepts* of the present book. With regard to Academics and Approaches, perhaps the paramount issue is why Levitt et al. and why Reader-Response theory etc.? How can my choices of scholarly exemplars and lit-crit perspectives be justified? As with most matters literary, there is no single compelling reason why some writers are scrutinized and not others. The same is true of the various schools of critical thought. Many other prominent marketing academics *could* have been chosen – George Day, Sid Levy, Russ Belk, Beth Hirschman, to name but a few – and the ones that have been selected *could* be approached from all sorts of alternative theoretical directions. A feminist reading of Ted Levitt might be illuminating, as might a neo-Aristotelian analysis of Shelby Hunt. My choice is motivated partly by a desire to cover most of the major marketing constituencies and schools of lit-crit (practitioner-orientated, educator-directed, scholarship-led, reader-response, post-structuralist etc.); partly by wanting to provide a spread of literary styles and marketing subject matters (extravagant, restrained, industrial, consumer, macro, micro); and partly by a need to encompass the entire 'modern' marketing epoch (from academics active in the 1950s to those making their mark in the twenty-first century).

These decisions are challengeable, needless to say, but ultimately they're the critic's call. Indeed, the critic's task is to ensure that the final analysis justifies the initial decision. Justification is posterior to, not an anterior requirement of, the interpretation. It comes afterwards not beforehand. In other words, it is *my* task, as a critic, to convince *you*, the reader, that our exemplars are well chosen but you'll only be able to decide when you've read what I've got to say about them.[78]

Be that as it may, most would agree that the individuals selected rank among the most influential, the most cited and the most widely read in the marketing discipline. They are the giants of our field, on whose shoulders the rest of us struggle to stand. More pertinently perhaps, they are all blessed with striking writing styles and owe at least some of their eminence to the words they set down on the page. True, the 'literariness' of their styles varies considerably, but few would deny that they are nothing if not stylish. Like fine wines, or mature cheeses, or piquant perfumes, their textual output is instantly recognizable, totally unique and unfailingly unforgettable. They are the master craftsmen of the marketing discipline.

In this regard, Michel Foucault's famous essay 'What is an Author?' makes an important distinction between authors who merely write books or articles and authors who write a theory, a tradition, a discipline, a paradigm.[79] The latter are 'founders of discursivity', insofar as they set the terms of the ensuing debate. Their writings spawn other writings, both pro and anti, and subsequent contributors are in effect forced to work within the discursive framework that they have established.

An equally evocative distinction is made by Foucault's celebrated contemporary, Roland Barthes. In an arresting 1960 article, '*Écrivains et écrivants*', he separates 'authors' from 'writers'.[80] The former perform a singularly important function, the latter undertake a prosaic, if necessary, activity. Authors are the shamans of society, the high priesthood of prose, larger-than-life figures who make things happen and change the world, or our perception of it at least, writers are clerks, drones, commissionaires, literal pen-pushers, mere conveyers of the facts. Bibliographic beancounters, so to speak.

More recondite still is Harold Bloom's anxiety of influence thesis, his agonistic conception of succeeding generations of 'strong' poets, who struggle manfully with each other for pre-eminence and a place in the poetic pantheon.[81] The outcome of this mano-a-mano set-to is that the intergenerational combatants stand head-and-shoulders above their contemporaries, like mountaintops protruding through the mist.

Although Foucault's, Barthes's and Bloom's conceptions of authorship have been much debated, there's no doubt that certain people set the scholarly agenda, rearrange the intellectual furniture and, with apologies for my metaphor mangling, plough up the prairies of knowledge. For example, Philip Kotler's pioneering textbook, *Marketing Management*, effectively established the template for subsequent principles primers, as the clatter of Kotler clones clearly demonstrates. His unavoidable authorial presence not only determines what can and can't be said about marketing management but affects the very way in which it is presented. Wroe Alderson, likewise, may have lacked literary finesse, or so the legend goes, but his newsletters and annual conferences certainly made things happen in marketing. Ted Levitt, meantime, turned a single, innocent word, 'myopia', into the ultimate expression of marketing opprobrium. Shelby Hunt all but expunged the term 'positivism' from the academic marketing lexicon, which is no mean achievement. And Morris Holbrook is currently reinventing the very character of the marketing article, content-wise, style-wise, every-which-wise.

In short, all five of the scholars featured in the present text are authors rather than writers, founders of discursivity rather than producers of articles, strong poets who move the discipline forward by the power of their prose, albeit in very different ways.

The Clause that Refreshes

Alongside the Academics and Approaches in the chapters to follow, the Basis and Beliefs of *Writing Marketing* require justification. How can you, dear reader, believe in, rely on, or indeed trust the interpretations to follow? How, conversely, can I make general statements about writing marketing on the basis of five – that's right, *five* – authors? Call that a sample, Stephen?

At the risk of begging the question, my justification derives from the basic approach adopted by the liberal arts. Whereas the social sciences, and wannabe social sciences such as marketing, place great emphasis on rigour, rectitude, reliability, replication and representativeness, the opposite is the case with most schools of literary criticism.[82] In fact, the whole point about literary analyses per se is that they are not 'scientific', that they cannot be 'proven' as such and that they shouldn't be judged by 'normal' evaluative criteria. The reader's trust is not gained through hard evidence, concrete proofs, carefully-conducted experiments, statistically-significant confidence levels, or impeccably-drawn representative samples. It is attained through imaginative, arresting, compelling, breathtaking writing – the awe-inspiring power of the written word. It is not a question of whether the analysis is right or wrong, true or false, confirmatory or contradictory, but whether it is interesting, whether it is insightful, whether it is intriguing, whether it is incredible, whether it is inconceivable beforehand, but afterwards inescapable, indisputable, self-evident to the point of banality. The best works of lit-crit, as Christopher Norris adroitly observes, push up against the 'giddy limit' of absurdity, where everything we know, or think we know, is suspended, set aside and no longer taken for granted, if only for a moment.[83]

Absurdity may seem like a strange ambition, yet the absurd, the odd, the bewildering have their place. According to Harold Bloom, the one thing that distinguishes literary giants from mere mortals – the thing that makes them *and only them* worth studying – is strangeness. The titans articulate 'a mode of originality that either cannot be assimilated or that so assimilates us that we cease to think of it as strange'.[84] When you read a canonical work for the first time, he goes on to say 'you encounter a stranger, an uncanny startlement rather than a fulfilment of expectations'.[85] What icons have in common, Bloom concludes, is uncanniness, the unsettling ability to make us feel strange at home. This is the notion of 'defamiliarization' beloved by Russian Formalists, most notably Viktor Shklovsky. Poetic language, they argued, is what estranges us from the everyday. It transcends what has become stale, banal, clichéd or hackneyed through overuse.[86] The leviathans of literature are those who supply the clause that refreshes.

Note, great writers are not necessarily those whose prose is extravagant, ornate, or totally OTT, though some write in a look-at-me manner. Great writers are not necessarily those whose plangent pearls of limpid pellucidity evacuate the text of their unavoidable authorial presence, though some certainly do. Great writers, rather, are those who emancipate us from the past by describing old things anew, by helping us see the world from a different angle, by showing us that what we thought we knew is what we thought we thought we knew.

This process of reframing the familiar is not without cost. Greatness is often accompanied by complexity. One of the key differences between mediocre art and great art is difficulty. Or, as White puts it:

> The difference between a simple folk melody or a hymn and the work of art that a Bach or Beethoven will then make of this tune is simply that the artwork is vastly more complex. Both the folk tune and the Beethoven sonata ultimately confirm the same laws of tonality and harmonics of the diatonic. The difference is that Beethoven will test the limits of the diatonic, or work against the expectations of the diatonic for dramatic effect, or even leave that confine for brief and startling moments. We admire Beethoven and his fellow adventurers for this, and hold them to be 'great', in part because our

culture admires the performance of difficult feats. But we also admire such complexity because it seems to be telling us something both truer and more complete about the world in which we live. . . . This is not to say that there is anything wrong with or lacking in the folk tune, but it is to say that Beethoven's rendering and extending of its premises is much more emotionally and intellectually rich. Beethoven's version seeks to be larger and more encompassing. It is more ambitious.[87]

As great writers one and all, Ted Levitt, Phil Kotler, Shelby Hunt, Wroe Alderson and Morris Holbrook are ambitious, encompassing, brilliant, complex, difficult. They are not 'representative' in any crude statistical sense. They do not constitute a sample of modern marketing scholarship. They are the summit of modern marketing scholarship. They simultaneously create and convey, guide and goad, amuse and bemuse, infatuate and infuriate. They are representative of the best in our business and that's representative enough for the rest of us – the mediocre majority – the likes of you and me.

In this regard, it is normal in literary analysis to identify iconic works, or artists, or groups of works and artists that somehow express the bigger picture. Analysis proceeds on this 'sample of one', since the emblematic object expresses everything of significance that needs to be said – and then some. Akin to William Blake's 'World in a grain of sand / And a heaven in a wild flower', literary criticism is largely predicted on the classic, the canonical, the masterpiece, the magnum opus. True, the lit-crit community is perennially embroiled in futile debates about the works that qualify as masterpieces; about the existence and character of the canon, and about the relationship between the grain of cultural sand and the wider world as it were.[88]

All sorts of different terminologies, moreover, are used to describe this extrapolative technique or process. Erich Auerbach, for instance, refers to *azantpunkt*, the point of departure within an individual artwork, the tiny detail that provides the key to its overall meaning.[89] Walter Benjamin argues for *micrological* thinking, a procedure that focuses on the fragment, the artefact or the small-scale object, with a view to revealing its large-scale, universally-applicable, *macrological* secrets.[90] Roland Barthes distinguishes between *studium*, essentially rational, linear understanding of textual meaning, and *punctum*, the electrifying fragment that seizes and ravishes the reader's imagination.[91] The part not only stands for the whole, it overwhelms, transcends and swallows the whole. It is all-consuming. It is a law unto itself. It is both unique and universal. It is like a fractal or strand of DNA, the something that is in everything. If, as they say, Dublin were to be completely obliterated by flood, meteorite or the wrath of a vengeful God – or, these days, a God who enjoys a cigarette with his pint of Guinness – it could be reconstructed circa 1904 on the basis of Leopold Bloom's peregrinations in James Joyce's *Ulysses*.[92]

As the populist philosopher A.C. Grayling appropriately notes about Jane Austen's incomparable *Emma*:

> On her 'two square inches of ivory' Jane Austen painted an inexhaustibly large universe. In the narrow round of country life as lived by the Georgian gentry, in the interesting but even narrower margin of that epoch in the lives of young ladies when they are looking about them for a husband, she finds what is immutable and eternal in human experience. With brushstrokes as fine as a scalpel's cut, and with an unsurpassed delicacy of irony, humour, and penetration, she gives us a portrait of one important kind of human truth.[93]

The essential point, then, is that this microcosm-in-the-macrocosm model permeates literary criticism. Even the most 'scientific' critics subscribe to some variant thereof. Northrop Frye, the famous Canadian scholar who dominated the discipline from the mid-1950s to the mid-1960s, and who strove manfully to move the field beyond a 'tutti-frutti collection' of individual prejudices, subscribed to the grain-of-sand school of thought.[94] Despite his lifelong attempts to place the subject on a systematic, semi-scientific footing, he openly acknowledged that the arts are characterized not by improvement or progress, but by 'classics and exemplars', revelatory moments of exceptional impact that seem to express the 'very essence' of music or poetry or literature or whatever:

> Occasionally we feel that what we are listening to epitomizes, so to speak, our whole musical experience with special clarity: our profoundest response to the B Minor Mass or the Jupiter Symphony is not 'this is beautiful music', but something more like 'this is the voice of music'; this is what music is all about. . . . In the greatest moments of Dante and Shakespeare, in, say, *The Tempest* or the climax of the *Purgatorio*, we have a feeling of converging significance, the feeling that here we are close to seeing what our whole literary experience has been about, the feeling that we have moved into the still center of the order of words.[95]

The Write Stuff

Although the Academics and Approaches, and the Basis and Beliefs of *Writing Marketing* are defensible from a theoretical perspective, many readers may be wondering about its Contents and Concepts. Why is it necessary, some might say, to study the contents of our exemplars' corpuses in such inordinate length? What is the point of such fine-grained readings, especially when we can (a) simply ask them how they do it and (b) invite them to give us some advice on best writing practice? Aren't we employing a lit-crit sledgehammer to crack an academic marketing nut? Is it really relevant to the practicalities of penning a paper about two-for-one price promotions or the sales patter of second-hand car dealers? Do we have to go through all this literary palaver when the great authors themselves are an email away?

These are perfectly legitimate (and understandable) questions. However, they raise several significant literary issues, both practical and theoretical, which necessitate a brief summary of some key concepts. From a purely practical perspective, one of our chosen few is dead (Wroe Alderson), another is unwell and sadly incommunicado (Ted Levitt). We could, of course, confine our discussion to living authors, though if such a policy were applied throughout literary criticism, the bulk of the discipline would turn instantly to dust. As some of the most interesting marketing writing dates from the pre-modern period, it seems unnecessarily Draconian to deem those responsible off-limits, especially as doing so would reinforce the frequently made accusation that marketing scholarship has no respect for its past.

Happily, the majority of *Writing Marketing*'s roster is still academically active and long may this continue. However, asking them to comment on what they do and how they do it is not the answer either. Studies of creative artists often show that they themselves don't know how they do it. It's a gift – a curse, in some cases – which doesn't repay close examination, since analysis can cause paralysis.[96] As Ernest Hemingway observes in *Old School*, Tobias Wolff's wonderful novel about coming of age and learning to write:

> Don't talk about your writing. If you talk about your writing you will touch something you shouldn't touch and it will fall apart and you will have nothing.[97]

Analogously, is Morris Holbrook *aware* that he makes incessant use of the 'in general . . . in particular' construction? Does Phil Kotler *know* just how many 'spectres' stalk the perilous pages of his trembling texts? Is Shelby Hunt *cognizant* of his figurative fixation with impotence or did Wroe Alderson *realize* that he was obsessed with size in general and big numbers in particular? When Ted Levitt described marketing as a 'stepchild' did he *imagine* how readers might react to that term forty-five years later?

The answer, I suspect, is: no, they don't know. Or didn't know. Had they known about, or been aware of, their stylistic tics, they'd surely have taken steps to use the repetitious construction less often, or expunge the incriminating image completely. Authors aren't the best judges of their own work. They are often blind to what others find in their writings. If you want to know what a work of literature means, or how an effect was achieved, asking the author isn't the best way to go about it, let alone the best place to start.

The relationship of an author to his or her own work also raises a couple of salient theoretical issues. For those untutored in literary theory – that is, most of us – the natural assumption to make is that 'the author knows best'. The creator's opinions of their poems, novels, articles, short stories, stage plays, or pieces of music are privileged, sacrosanct, the final word. Thus, when we read a poem we wonder what the author meant and, if we're lucky, we'll get out of the piece what the wonderful wordsmith put into it.

Although this interpretive strategy seems eminently sensible, it is anathema to literary critics, who term it the 'intentional fallacy'.[98] The idea that the author's intentions are inviolable, or somehow authorized, is unacceptable to literary theorists and has been for fifty or sixty years. The New Critics, Wimsatt and Beardsley especially, contended that the value and meaning of each literary work resided solely in the autonomous text. Its author's intentions are interesting but they are utterly irrelevant for critical purposes, which must focus on the work's language, imagery, wordplay and what have you, rather than the mindset, or personal situation, or historical circumstances of the living, breathing author. Typically forthright, Northrop Frye puts it thus:

> The absurd quantum formula of criticism, the assertion that the critic should confine himself to 'getting out' of a poem exactly what the poet may vaguely be assumed to have been aware of 'putting in', is one of the many slovenly illiteracies that the absence of systematic criticism has allowed to grow up. . . . That is, the critic is assumed to have no conceptual framework: it is simply his job to take a poem into which a poet has diligently stuffed a specific number of beauties or effects, and complacently extract them one by one, like his prototype Little Jack Horner.[99]

Let Us Go Then, You and I

If the New Critics basically *displaced* the author, the poststructuralists effectively *replaced* the author. Roland Barthes, in particular, famously announced the 'death of the author', no less.[100] By this he means that authors don't have the freedom of expression that we, in our ignorance, conventionally imagine. Their writings, rather, are shaped by pre-existing (albeit unstable) structures of language. Language permits and, in many respects, determines what can and can't be said on any subject. The author doesn't write but is written by language, counter-intuitive though this notion may seem. Barthes thus eschews the long-standing humanist view that authors are the origin or creators of texts and the source or fountain-head of their meaning. Authors, he avers, simply reassemble existing texts. They are the products not the producers of language. All works of litera-ture are 'a multidimensional space in which a variety of writings, none of them original, blend and clash'.[101]

This euthanasian take on authorship is undeniably extreme, not least because the eulogy was written by such a singular literary stylist. Barthes's obituary, nevertheless, cannot fail to strike a chord with most marketing academics. Who, after all, actually writes our articles, books and all the rest? They typically go through several rounds of R 'n' R (revise and resubmit). We try to take on board the comments and cavils of reviewers, editors, associate editors and so on, to say nothing of the avun-cular advice of our colleagues, associates and other third parties, who foolishly agreed to cast an eye over our grisly first draft. We follow the manuscript submission guidelines laid down by the journal or publisher concerned and, when the work is finally accepted, enter into a lengthy dia-logue with in-house or freelance copy editors, which is an experience in itself.[102] True, they turn our illiterate inanities into something resembling proper English (while no doubt regaling their horrified friends with the unspeakable barbarities they're forced to work with in order to earn an honest crust), but they also turn the manuscript into something that we, the authors, don't recognize as our own. Did I really write that? Can I call this work my own? Is that what I meant to say?

Above and beyond editorial input, there's the not inconsequential matter of co-authorship. It seems to me that most academic articles in mar-keting are co-authored and, while there are many different modes of co-creation (some authors sit in the same room and compose together, others write separately and swap files back and forth, etc.), the fact that it happens at all poses problems for literary criticism. In this regard, every one of our marketing greats is beset by authorship issues. Several of Wroe Alderson's best-known works, most notably *Dynamic Marketing Behavior*, were assembled by others after his untimely death. So, who is the author here? Ted Levitt is a literary loner, by and large, but he published a lot in *Harvard Business Review*, which employs teams of ace copy editors who ensure that every paper adheres to the organ's distinctive house style. Again, who is the author here? Both Shelby Hunt and Morris Holbrook work with co-authors quite often, sometimes with three, four or more scholarly sidekicks. Who are the authors on these collegial occasions?

Philip Kotler's best-selling textbooks are produced by dragoons of dedicated copywriters, fact checkers, graphic designers, case-study compilers and, for the various international issues, a veritable standing army of co-contributors. So, where's Phil in all this? Has anyone here seen Kotler?

Authorial attribution, however, is much less difficult in practice than it is in principle. In addition to their co-authored endeavours, each of our famous five has published sufficient solo-authored work to facilitate ready identification of their signature-stylistic foibles. Once one gets a sense of their personal style, which can only come from systematic reading and rereading of their entire corpus, near enough, it's comparatively easy to pick out what they actually wrote, or when another author is involved, or where the text has been tweaked during the publication process. Lone-wolf Levitt, admittedly, is more of a problem, but luckily he is such a distinctive stylist that even the massed jewel polishers of Cambridge, MA, can't take the shine off his literary lustre.

As you're about to discover, dear reader.

The Antinomies of Theodore Levitt

> The sole purpose of
> Marketing is to create
> And keep customers.
>
> *HBR* haiku (after Ted Levitt)[1]

Hold the Front Page

Not many marketing articles attract fulsome newspaper coverage. Fewer still attract fulsome newspaper coverage because the article is mistaken. But only one, surely, has attracted fulsome newspaper coverage of its mistakes a full twenty years after it first appeared.

That one is 'The Globalization of Markets' by the inimitable Theodore Levitt, marketing's foremost man of letters and, word for word, perhaps its premier literary stylist.[2] In May 2003, the twentieth anniversary of Ted's seminal *HBR* article, it was commemorated by a full-page tribute in the *Financial Times*. Written by distinguished columnist Richard Tompkins, the pungent opinion piece noted how Levitt's bold, early-eighties' claim, that the age of the global corporation is upon us, had failed to stand the test of time.[3] The great Harvardian's confident assertions about cultural and corporate convergence, with all the associated economies of scale in production, distribution, marketing and management, turned out to be erroneous. Thinking local, acting local and managing local is the order of the twenty-first century day. The homogenization of consumer behaviour, and the attendant standardization of marketing offerings, has not come to pass as the prodigious professor predicted.

So there!

Needless to say, Tompkins's tart attack on Ted Levitt was tartly attacked in turn. *Marketing Week* columnist and would-be guru Alan Mitchell robustly defended the sainted scholar's sadly sullied reputation.[4] In a thousand words of textual ecstasy that would make a New Labour spin doctor blush, Mitchell maintained that Levitt was right all along. Hitherto inaccessible markets have indeed opened up since 1983; consumer behaviour has indeed converged to a brand-bedecked, gold card-carrying global mean; economies of scale have indeed been reaped, thanks largely to the information technology revolution; and identically marketed multinational mega-brands have indeed become ever more ubiquitous. True, the process hasn't transpired as fast as Levitt originally anticipated. What's more, a countervailing trend towards localization has been set in train by the onward march of globalization. But, all things considered, the marketing guru is being accused unfairly and criticized for things he never said in the first place. The charges are unfounded. Acquittal is called for and costs awarded against his adversaries. Release the professorial prisoner forthwith.

A rather more measured deposition appeared in the august pages of the August issue of *HBR*, which called an expert witness to mark the anniversary of Levitt's landmark piece.[5] According to John Quelch, Harvard's head honcho in marketing matters, his colleague's thesis unfolded as anticipated in the 1980s and 1990s, when American munificence penetrated numerous hitherto inaccessible or underdeveloped markets such as Eastern Europe, South America and South-east Asia. However, today's stalling global economy, coupled with a rising tide of anti-Americanism, has interrupted the product-market imperialism of MTV, Marlboro, McDonald's and the rest of the big brand battalions. But only temporarily. Once the world economy picks up again and, more significantly, once China emerges as a cheap and cheerful countervailing power to American marketing monoculture, Levitt's thesis will be back on track. A cyclical or dialectical pattern of globalization/localization thus obtains.

Regardless of the ins and outs of this intractable argument, it is remarkable that a marketing article, written by a university-based academic, should continue to polarize the press twenty years after it was published. Rather less remarkable, if no less noteworthy, is the fact that latter-day contributors to the pro- and anti-Levitt debate acknowledged that the article's impact was as much due to its author's writing style as to the content of the paper itself. For Mitchell, Levitt is 'still the best read there is'.[6] Quelch considers it a 'provocative classic that seemed irresistible to executives'.[7] Tompkins too concedes that the article is still enormously influential, largely on account of its 'bold assertions, colourfully described'.[8]

The Ted Zone

Although most authorities agree that Levitt's lyricism is second to none, many scholarly sober-sides are inclined to dismiss him as a mere rhetori-cian, a representative of the style over content school of writing, the marketing equivalent of a big-budget, blockbuster, crash-bang-wallop, cast-of-thousands movie. As Bartels notes in his decidedly straightlaced *History of Marketing Thought*, Ted Levitt's eminence is largely due to his 'attention-catching titles and phrases . . . [and] . . . not narrowing his focus by deeper probing'.[9] A back-handed compliment if ever there was one!

Nitpickers notwithstanding, there is some truth in this assessment. It can legitimately be argued that Theodore Levitt is the Jerry Bruckheimer of business education, a master of writerly razzmatazz, a special effects-led, superlatives-stuffed, sock-it-to-em schlockmeister, who gives the public what they want. And then some. In literary terms, Ted Levitt's the Tom Clancy-cum-Jackie Collins of marketing discourse, with just a soupçon of Stephen King.

Characteristically, however, the great man *agrees* with his critics. When discussing his astonishing academic achievements, Levitt unfailingly attributes them to his ability to string pithy, punchy, pacy phrases, para-graphs and papers together.[10] In fact, he frequently presents himself as a humble wordsmith, someone who takes the arcane ideas of others – others much more learned than he – and renders their recondite ruminations and recherché researches into readable prose, something that everyone can understand. As he modestly observes in his retrospective commentary on 'Marketing Myopia', the only paper to surpass 'Globalization of Markets' in terms of initial impact and continuing popularity:

> My contribution . . . appears merely to have been a simple, brief, and useful way of communicating an existing way of thinking. I tried to do it in a very direct, but responsible, fashion, knowing that few readers (customers), espe-cially managers and leaders, could stand much equivocation or hesitation. I also knew that the colorful and lightly documented affirmation works better than the tortuously reasoned explanation.[11]

Equally characteristically, Levitt doesn't stop there. He maintains that his function as a communicator of ideas is, in many respects, *more* important than that of the composer of ideas. He is a marketer not a manufacturer of knowledge and, as everyone knows, marketing is everything. Or near enough. Far from being a 'mere' rhetorician, the guru's guru regards his 'rhetorician' designation as high praise, since 'the things which are most easily believed are those which are most fetchingly presented'.[12] He is cognisant that style may not be more important than content, but it comes pretty close and marketers, of all people, should appreciate this throbbing reality of writerly life. Those blessed with literary flair, he further avers, should be praised not patronized, celebrated not criticized, lionized not lacerated. Or, as he puts it in his panegyric postscript to 'Marketing Myopia', unquestionably the great man's greatest hit and by all accounts the best-selling *HBR* reprint of all time:

> But why the enormous popularity of what was actually such a simple pre-existing idea? Why its appeal throughout the world to resolutely restrained scholars, implacably temperate managers and high government officials, all accustomed to balanced and thoughtful calculation? Is it that concrete examples, joined to illustrate a simple idea and presented with some attention to literacy, communicate better than massive analytical reasoning that reads as though it were translated from the German? Is it that provocative assertions are more memorable and persuasive than restrained and balanced explanations, no matter who the audience? Is it that the character of the message is as much the message as its content? Or was mine not simply a different tune, but a new symphony?[13]

Symphonic or not, Levitt's list of rhetorical questions is very revealing. They say a great deal about the (implied) author. The most striking thing about them, when read cold and out of context, is that they are somewhat high-and-mighty, to put it mildly. Far from being a simple scribe or humble hack, Levitt comes across as an individual untroubled by low self-esteem. Bearing in mind that this passage appears immediately after an abject apology to those academics whose ideas he admits to having adopted, adapted and advanced as his own, it sends decidedly ambivalent signals. The man, clearly, has hidden depths. There's more to him than meets the (presumably myopic) eye. This is not a hewer of wood and drawer of water, but a scholar with heft, an intriguing hybrid of hauteur and humility, an immodest man with much to be immodest about.

Never Knowingly Understated

Still, if there is a single literary concept that encapsulates the quixotic character of Professor Theodore Levitt, that concept is *antinomy*. Antinomy is the formal term for contrasting ideas, images, insights or interpretations that continue to make sense even though they contradict one another.[14] Part of the oxymoron family, alongside antithesis and paradox, antinomies are common in the poems of, say, John Donne ('Death, thou shalt die'), John Milton ('the darkness visible'), William Blake ('a Heaven in Hell's despair') and William Wordsworth ('The stationary blasts of waterfalls').

Antinomies are also closely associated with Walter Benjamin, the celebrated cultural critic of the Weimar Republic, who expounded at length on the pleasures and pains of tragedies and comedies respectively, as well as the religious aura of original artworks when reproduced by profane mechanical means like film and photography.[15] What is more, in his magnum opus, Benjamin ruminated on the curious combination of old and new, individuality and communality, technology and tradition, which come together in enclosed shopping arcades.[16] And, as if that weren't enough, he further forged a method of literary criticism based on an amalgam of Messianic Judaism and neo-Marxist critical theory. Holy Karl!

A more recent, marketing related example of antinomous reasoning is found in the novel *Savage Girl*, by Alex Shakar.[17] Set in a cool-hunting research agency, Tomorrow Inc., the book affords all sorts of creative insights into twenty-first century consumer behaviour, perhaps the most striking of which pertain to 'paradessence'. This is the paradoxical 'promise', 'offer', 'value', 'deliverable', 'USP' – or whatever you want to call it – that lies at the heart of all successful products and brands. Thus, ice cream combines innocence and eroticism; theme parks provide terror and reassurance; Levi's jeans meld youth and heritage; Nike sneakers integrate athleticism and relaxation; and Starbucks stands for expensive coffee and a cheap treat.[18]

Ted Levitt is the Savage Girl of marketing scholarship, insofar as his approach is essentially paradessential. Just as great brands are built on antinomies, so too Levitt's literary style rests on a congeries of incongruities, oxymorons, paradoxes. His writing is full of quixotic quips, quotes, quirks and quibbles. He observes that, 'we are all continually faced with a series of great opportunities brilliantly disguised as insoluble problems'. He announces that marketing requires 'the passion of the scientist and the precision of the artist'. He opines that 'when people don't want to come, nothing in the world will stop them'. He intimates that management is 'not about doing things right but doing the right things'. He notes that 'forecasting is difficult, especially with respect to the future'. He posits that 'not everything that can be learned can be taught'. And, when all is said and done, he claims that 'after all is said and done, mostly all that's done is said'.

The Oxymoronic Inferno

Alongside the oxymorons a-go-go, Professor Levitt is nothing if not contrarian. Throughout his career, he has consistently argued against the prevailing management orthodoxy. For example, he defended the dignity of marketing at a time when those of a hidden persuaders persuasion considered it immoral at best and iniquitous at worst. He made the case for constancy when change was the catchphrase du jour. He stressed the importance of imitation when innovation was the word on everyone's lips. He championed the second-in-command when leadership was being loudly lauded. He articulated the advantages of large firms when small businesses were all the rage. He challenged the cult of creativity when creative was the accolade of choice. He sang the praises of slowness when the chorus was chanting con brio. He even saw the good in greed when Boesky-baiting was a popular spectator sport.[19]

This congenital contrariness, it must be stressed, is not an academic affectation. To the contrary, it reflects Levitt's background and upbringing. Born in Vollmerz, Germany, he emigrated to the United States in 1935, studied an eclectic mix of subjects at Ohio State, and taught economics in North Dakota before his 1959 move to Harvard.[20] He is not a marketer by training. He is an intellectual outsider, somewhat akin to the industry-transforming misfits and mavericks he immortalizes in his manifold immortal articles. Theodore Levitt may be a lion of Harvard Yard, or the Business School at least; he may be the author of nine best-selling books, such as *The Marketing Imagination* and *Thinking About Marketing*.[21] He may have garnered innumerable garlands including the John Hancock Award, the George Gallup Award, the Charles Coolidge Parlin Award and the Paul D. Converse Award; he may have had more articles published in *HBR* than any other management guru, winning four best paper awards along the way,[22] but he is also the much-needed grit in the marketing oyster. He is a conceptual catalyst, an outspoken zinger-slinger, a self-appointed apostate who is always prepared to challenge convention, repudiate received wisdom, and say nay to the naysayers.

Levitt's overall approach, what is more, is driven by opposites, antitheses and, above all, absences. He often implies that things are not what they seem, that we are missing something important, obvious or hidden. People don't buy ⅜-inch drills, they buy holes. Ladies don't buy lipstick, they buy hope. Gasoline is a tax that people pay to continue driving. Successful leaders understand what subordinates aren't saying. Effective differentiation involves doing what competitors don't do. Consumers' detestation of advertising is proof that it's working. The existence of private labels demonstrates that branding is worthwhile. The rise of segmentation is evidence of globalization. Market research doesn't lead to better decisions, but more indecision. The surest sign of a deteriorating customer relationship is the lack of complaints from one's customers. In order to be marketing orientated, organizations must limit their marketing orientation. Nothing is more wasteful than doing what should not be done at all. The less there seems the more there is. Absence of evidence is not evidence of absence.

The marketing magus's modus operandi, in sum, is intrinsically dialectical. It is predicated on the premise 'think opposite'.[23] It works on the presumption that the existence of something precipitates the appearance of its antithesis, the opposite, an opportunity. 'In marketing,' he sagely observes, 'sound strategy often consists not in doing a better job of what competitors are doing but in doing what they are *not* doing'.[24]

Exploit the Levitt Write Cycle

To be sure, Levitt's antinomous inclinations are not confined to corporate contrariness, quirky one-liners or ironic inversions like 'Innovative Imitation', 'Fast History' and 'you can observe a lot by watching'. The basic structure of his publications runs counter to generic conventions. He resolutely refuses to follow the standard scholarly storyboard of stolid Introduction, followed by Literature Review, followed by Methodology, followed by Findings, followed by Implications, followed by Further Research, followed by – phew! – tentative Conclusions.

So unorthodox, indeed, is the great writer's approach that a casual reader might conclude there's no overarching structure at all. The majority of his papers flit from topic to topic, often at a very rapid pace; there aren't any results being reported, as a rule, though exemplars and mini case studies abound; the section headings are reliably unreliable, since they rarely refer to what the ensuing section actually contains; and when the individual essays are anthologized, as Levitt's articles invariably are, the resulting volume is itself given only the most perfunctory formal organization.[25]

Yet for all the ostensible disorder, Professor Levitt's papers are rigidly structured. Very rigidly structured. Rigidly structured to the point of formulaic. The formula, however, owes little to the conventions of social science scholarship. Its wellsprings, rather, are those of the short story, the literary essay or Tom Wolfe's 'new journalism', which famously applied fictional modes of writing to weighty factual matters.[26] And, reluctant as I am to reveal Ted's trade secrets, his writing recipe involves seven sequential steps:

1   A succinct, striking, stop-right-there opening statement, which runs counter to conventional wisdom or the management fad of the moment ('Advertising works', 'Greed is boring', 'Never leave well enough alone').

2   An elaboration of this arresting assertion, judiciously interlarded with exceptions, qualifications, and minor rhetorical retreats, which are unfailingly signalled by the trusty weasel words 'Of course'.

3   A series of vivid case studies drawn from a variety of manufacturing and service sectors, involving a judicious mix of household names (for example, Sears), little known organizations (Hooker Chemicals), and long-forgotten favourites (American Wind Engines).

4   An autobiographical anecdote, imagined conversation, expropriated aphorism, 'unscientific' survey of executives or some other method of signalling his hard-headed, horny-handed marketing credentials ('When my son broke a finger in a hockey game, I went with him to the hospital where . . .').

5   An ironic sideswipe at one or more of the multitudinous, money-grubbing miscreants who blow smoke where the corporate sun don't shine – motivation researchers, management gurus, rogue economists, pontificating pundits et al. ('sweaty evangelists', 'devout acquisitors', 'imprecise and artless').

6   A checklist; or two, or three, or more; sometimes numbered, often bullet-pointed, always semi-colon separated; swiftly followed by a critique of those who listlessly rely on checklists ('ritualized substitutes for thought and substance').

7   An imperiously emphatic, decidedly dogmatic, tantamount to pedantic conclusion, which may not actually include the economist's acronym of choice, QED, but certainly implies it ('All else is mere administration', 'All other truths on this subject are merely derivative', 'All distortion is, finally, disabling').

Levitt's literary blueprint, however, never quite becomes boilerplate, or lapses into caricature, largely on account of the seer's extraordinarily vivid prose – prose that isn't so much purple as indigo:

In the year 1900 the American Wind Engine and Pump Company was a magnificently thriving enterprise. Its majestic windmills stood like powerful giants astride the farms of America's vast prairies.[27]

In Brazil thousands of eager migrants from the preindustrial Bahian wilderness swarm daily into the exploding coastal cities, quickly to install television sets in crowded corrugated-iron huts before which, next to battered Volkswagens, they make sacrificial candlelight offerings of fruit and fresh-killed chickens to the Macumban spirits.[28]

As these excerpts indicate, the exhilarating sweep of Levitt's rattling writing is almost entirely attributable to astonishing adjectival abundance and abject adverbial overkill. It sometimes seems that every noun comes complete with a numinous aureole of adjectives and every verb surmounted by a tottering cairn of accompanying adverbs. Or, as he himself puts it, in an aphorism attributed to the late great piano-playing showman Liberace, 'too much of a good thing is just the right amount'.[29]

> The world's aspirations now level simultaneously outward and upward, with increasingly larger portions of its population greedily wanting the modernity to which they are so constantly exposed.[30]

> No explanation of America's enormous economic achievements is so spurious as the one that attributes them simply to the munificence of its natural resources, the vastness of its geography, the enormity of its markets, the balanced equitableness of its climate, the salubrious absence of pre-existing social barriers, and the facilitating absence of restrictive laws.[31]

Levitt Be

Set against this literary effulgence, which serves to screen the standard structural scaffolding, our serial antinomian is strangely partial to the platitude, the truism, the chestnut. He has published a list of own-brand aphorisms and he recycles them incessantly ('What's new?', 'Familiarity breeds', 'Customer creating value satisfactions', 'What has to happen for that to happen?'). His all time favourite, of course, is 'the purpose of marketing is to get and keep a customer,' which not only pervades his entire corpus, from first to last, but comes as close to an *HBR* haiku as makes no difference. It is the academic equivalent of a comedian's catchphrase, a goldsmith's hallmark, a corporate mission statement, a time-grooved advertising slogan. It's a Ted Thing. Every Levitt Helps. The Ultimate Writing Machine.

Levitt's overall aim, it sometimes seems, is to synthesize everything there is to be said about business into a single, all-encompassing statement or saying, what he calls 'the simple essence of things'.[32] The closest he comes, admittedly, is his much chanted marketing mantra of getting and keeping customers, but other one-liners have a gnomic, Zen-like, almost Orphic sense of simultaneously stating the obvious and unveiling a universal truth ('people like what they like and don't what they don't', 'the future comes from the present but it occurs in the future', 'the primary business of any business is to stay in business', 'a customer usually doesn't know what he's getting till he doesn't'). As the superlative scholar repeatedly observes, 'man does not live by bread alone, but mostly by catchphrases'.[33]

To be sure, statements like 'what is happening has already happened', 'the purpose of a large organization is to achieve its larger purpose', or 'without the organizing presence of the organization, there would be no organization', contain more than a modicum of mysticism, voodoo, counter-cultural dippy-hippiedom, the very thing that Professor Theodore Levitt, the realer than realist, rails against on numerous occasions. Following the guru's own logic, however, the very fact that he abjures such practices and constantly stresses his no-nonsense credentials, is positive proof that spirituality, religiosity and ethereal other-worldliness are an integral part of his conceptual cosmos. Indeed, one of the most striking things about the seer's body of work is its consistently mystical character. Aside from the obvious thaumaturgy of personified phenomena – from myopic organizations to living, breathing brands – religious citations are one of his favourite textual utensils. Few articles fail to name-check an Old Testament prophet, or mention a biblical incident, or draw parallels with a spiritual parable, or simply quote a quotable theological passage. Isaiah, Daniel, Joshua, St Peter, St Paul, Job, Noah and numerous others are permanent fixtures in Father Ted's evangelical prose:

> Things are little different than when God told Noah to build an ark so that he, his family, and all the species of the earth could survive the flood he'd let loose in two weeks. Shocked, Noah said, 'Two weeks? God, do you know how long it takes to build an ark?' And God replied, 'Noah, how long can you tread water?' It got done in two weeks.[34]

Above and beyond the marketing magus's repeated reliance on pietistic parlance, as well as direct devotional citation, there is an implacably providential quality to his utterances and commandments. Levitt's writing is not only biblical in its inalienability, but positively Abrahaminian in its tone. The Almighty has spoken. The Word of Ted is all of the Law. Levitt is the Way, the Truth and the Light:

> The marketing concept is closely related in origin and purpose to mores and the Ten Commandments, which represent an attempt to enforce civilization – i.e. goal congruence. The marketing concept is the civilizing consequence of the large business organization. It asserts a goal and advocates supporting strategies designed to consolidate a large organization behind a single purpose.[35]

A general rule can be laid down about predictions regarding the shape of business conditions in the distant future: Beware of the fluent expert. The answer man is always provocative and inspirational, owing his success to the same wonder-working evangelical talents as the itinerant soul saver in a tent. But inspirational answers are seldom prescriptive answers.[36]

Reading Theo(ry)

For all the hellfire and damnation, however, the thing that lifts Theodore Levitt's books and articles above the quotidian, the mediocre, the ho-hum, is his downright writing ability, his talent for timeless turns of phrase, his peerless gift for placing sublime words on the page. Whatever else he is, Professor Levitt's a wonderful writer. Everyone says so. And 'everyone' is always right. Right?

Wrong!

The crucial point about the laudatory Levitt literature is that it is largely written by fellow scribes and would-be communicators. Academics, consultants, copywriters, jobbing journalists and, of course, the man himself are the principal commentators on the marketing guru's oeuvre. The feelings of *real* readers, those with the warm armpits that Levitt occasionally valorizes, are rarely reported on. Sales figures, the fact that his articles are *HBR*'s best-selling offprints by far, are considered a reasonable surrogate for customer satisfaction. If it sells it must be good, or so marketing ideology maintains. When coupled with the admiring comments of his fellow wordsmiths in the locution foundry, the prevailing assumption is that Levitt is the last word, as it were, on forging phrases together.

This may be so, but it raises an interesting issue that has attracted the attention of many latter-day literary theorists. As noted in Chapter 1, literary criticism originally focused on the intentions of authors (what is the poet trying to tell us?) and, during the lengthy New Criticism interlude, on the form, function, structure and significance of the poem itself (regardless of the author's aims and objectives).[37] Literary criticism in the postwar epoch has witnessed the rise and demise of innumerable schools of thought, but many of these foreground readers' reactions to the text under consideration. That is, how *real world* readers respond to a writer's words of wisdom.[38]

Reader-Response Criticism, as it is commonly called, comes in all manner of hybrids, offshoots and miscegenations, as do most major schools of literary theory.[39] However, they all focus on readers' subjective experiences, the fact that poems, essays or novels are essentially inert until readers read them and breathe life into them. They don't exist, as such, in bookstores or libraries, let alone Amazon.com's central warehouse. They only exist in the act of reading. Books happen. And what happens while books happen is the primary concern of the reader-response contingent. In place of narrative, plot, character, style and so forth, the textual features that preoccupy traditional literary critics, reader-response affiliates attend to the expectations, hesitations, alterations, vacillations, self-corrections and suchlike that accompany the flow of the individual reader's reading experience. Most reader-response critics, moreover, concede that as the 'meaning' of any text is co-created by its author and reader, there is no single correct, definitive, final, or ultimate meaning, message or lesson that can be extracted from a work of literature. That said, this proliferation of possible meanings does *not* mean that every single reading is idiosyncratic or that all readings are created equal. Some readings are more equal than others.

These points of commonality, however, are overshadowed by the differences between reader-response critics. Drawing upon Freudian psychology, for example, Norman Holland maintains that readers respond to texts in accordance with a limited number of personal identity 'themes' which are activated by their encounters with the work in question.[40] David Bleich, by contrast, contends that 'classroom consensus' determines the meanings, or acceptable range of meanings, that are ordinarily permissible.[41] Stanley Fish, similarly, suggests that the relevant, 'interpretive community' of scholars – professors, students, researchers, critics, etc. – not only shapes the repertoire of responses to literary texts but also their very status as texts that are suitable for literary study in the first place.[42]

Just as some readings are more equal than others, so too certain works are more readable than the lugubrious rest. In this regard, author assassin Roland Barthes distinguishes between readerly (*lisible*) texts and writerly (*scriptable*) texts.[43] The former rely on literary conventions, are easily understood and assimilated, and leave little scope for meaning-creation on the reader's part. Writerly texts, conversely, violate literary conventions, are difficult to understand and assimilate, and therefore leave considerable scope for reader intervention and interpretation. An analogous distinction between 'open' and 'closed' texts is made by Umberto Eco, though the unconventional definitions he gives to his key terms – closed texts are open to all sorts of interpretations, whereas open texts are closed to multiple meaning generation – has done little to propagate or disseminate this taxonomic dichotomy.[44]

Much more popular is Wolfgang Iser's intimation that literary texts are simultaneously open and closed.[45] Readers' responses are constrained and in part controlled by the author's intentional acts – the words on the page – but all texts, especially 'modernist' texts, contain gaps, aphoria, indeterminacies and spaces that are filled in by the reader's creative participation. This participation, in turn, is affected by the reader's background, experience, personality, social class, ethnicity, gender, emotional equipoise and what have you, which ensure a multiplicity of possible meanings, even when the texts are ostensibly transparent and seemingly straightforward.

Meanings are not only co-created between writer and reader – 'concretized', in Iser's terminology[46] – they are also time-bound. When de Sade's *Justine* first appeared in 1791, it was widely regarded as an egregious affront to bourgeois sensibility, as indeed were Flaubert's *Madame Bovary* in 1857 and Houellebecq's *Atomised* in 1999. Nowadays, *Justine* is considered an anarchic classic, *Madame Bovary* the high watermark of nineteenth century naturalism, and as for *Atomised*, well, time will doubtless tell. The reception and meaning of literary works change through time[47] – and these changes form the basis of Hans Robert Jauss's *Rezeptionasthetik* (reception theory), a strand of reader-response criticism that is particularly pertinent to Professor Levitt.[48] As noted earlier, 'The Globalization of Markets' means something very different to twenty-first century readers, as do Levitt's occasionally androcentric quips of the misogynistic mid-sixties.

Moreover, 'Marketing Myopia' may be a seminal publication, reproduced to this very day in anthologies of marketing classics, but what do today's readers get from it, more than forty years after it hit the streets?

In order to find out, 208 marketing researchers were asked to read 'Marketing Myopia' and write extended introspective essays on their reactions to the article. Approximately half the 'sample' were in employment and the remainder were full-time students. Most were Irish; ages ranged from early-twenties to mid-fifties; 57 per cent were female; and none had previously read anything by Levitt, though some had heard of him. No restrictions were placed on the length of their essay or what was considered an 'acceptable' response. The researchers were simply asked to read, record, reflect on and write up their reactions to Levitt's much-lauded marketing classic. They were required, in effect, to interview themselves about their reading experience and set out their considered response in extended essay format.[49] Difficult as this sounds when baldly described, it's much less onerous in practice than in principle. Enjoyable even. In the event, the introspective essays averaged 2,500 words, with a maximum of 6,000 and a minimum of 1,200. More importantly perhaps, the richness of the responses accords with Elizabeth A. Flynn's contention that, as written reactions to literary works tend to be more considered than interpersonal discussions, they typically reveal deeper understandings of, and interpretive insights into, the work in question.[50]

The Ultimate Writing Machine?

So, what do my readers think? 'So what?', in the main. The overwhelming reaction to Marketing Myopia is one of 'we covered this already', 'tell us something we don't know', 'been there, done that, bought the Ted-shirt', so to speak. As marketing researchers, with several years of study behind them, the contents of 'Marketing Myopia' tell the readers nothing new. They've been hearing about customer orientation for some time now – almost to the point of interminability – and, while it is nice to go back to the fountainhead of customer focus, so to speak, most readers are unmoved, unenlightened, unimpressed, unenthusiastic:

> Reading this article today, I am not moved to instigate the next wave of the customer-oriented revolution, because it is nothing new to me. Although his points, to some extent, remain valid, it is not the first time I have encountered the ideology of the customer-oriented approach to marketing. Everything that Levitt has had to say in this article has been paraphrased time and time again in textbooks and journal articles alike. Although a breakthrough piece of literature in its day, it is now accepted as a given.[51]

> From reading the article I cannot say that I have taken a great deal from it. As it was written 42 years ago, most of the marketing theory which was suggested then is now seen as basic marketing theory which has been drilled into my head over the past 8 years. Therefore, I did not gain any intellectual experience from reading Marketing Myopia.[52]

To be sure, the very fact that 'Marketing Myopia' is preaching to the converted is a testament to its impact. The ideas it contains, ideas that were decidedly revolutionary and somewhat shocking in their time, are now part of marketing's received wisdom. They are fixtures of first chapters of fundamentals of marketing textbooks, the Holy Writ of our field. Just as Joyce's *Ulysses* shocked all and sundry when it burst on to the scene in 1922, only to be absorbed and apotheosized, so too the concepts in Levitt's 1960 classic have been canonized and commodified. Indeed, just as *Ulysses* is still hard going, the burgeoning Leopold Bloom business notwithstanding, so too 'Marketing Myopia' remains heavy sledding for twenty-first century readers.

Professor Levitt may be regarded as one of our discipline's foremost literary stylists, but my ample sample thinks otherwise. Tedious, tiresome, repetitious, rambling, interminable and, as often as not, 'a sure-fire cure for insomnia' are just some of the less than enthusiastic expressions routinely employed by the essayists:

Well to be honest, the first couple of times I read Marketing Myopia thoughts of boredom, confusion and 'this man needs to get a life', crept into my head. I had a box of matches beside my bed to keep my eyes open and I found I was tending to pick it up late at night to put me to sleep. Who needs hot cocoa and a sleeping tablet – just read Marketing Myopia and it will have the same effect but at half the price. Ted Levitt could market this as a revolutionary new insomnia cure – 'Marketing Myopia – makes you sleep in minutes'.[53]

To begin with, I could safely say that Mr Levitt's article is far too long-winded. It seems to go on forever, taking ages to get the point across, bringing in too many issues and companies, and comparing each of them. He also seems to refer back to things a lot, maybe to a point he made six pages back, which I would have forgotten about. I felt that when I eventually reached the end of the article, which felt like a lifetime, that I still hadn't got the point.[54]

Not every reader feels this way, of course. Some find themselves ravished by Ted's recondite writing, others deem it trite tripe, and yet others consider his tone unnecessarily negative:

His use of the English language is fantastic when he refers to a leader having to have a 'vision of grandeur'. Indeed, Levitt's main weapon is the way that he can communicate with the reader to coerce them into believing his viewpoint. He should have been a politician![55]

I really felt the tone of the article [was] very downbeat and depressing. Apart from the examples he gives of the nylon, glass and aluminium industries, it appears that no other industry or company within an industry has performed as they should have done. He even goes on to say, referring to the railroad industry, that they lack 'managerial imaginativeness and audacity'.[56]

However, the overwhelming consensus is that the article is heavy going in places and even heavier going in the places in between. Far from being 'simple, brief, and useful', as Levitt claims in his retrospective commentary of 1975[57] – a remark numerous readers find highly amusing – 'Marketing Myopia' is believed to be boring, bordering on baffling:

I think that its effectiveness lies in the way that the article is written and perhaps some of the content. Perhaps it's because I was never any good at English and big words (uncultured child that I am) or my inability to actually keep track and understand what was being said, but I just totally fail to truly appreciate this piece of work. For me, the structure of the article was confusing because although Levitt said that he would write about 4 main themes, I had a hard time trying to find where they started and ended. I had to have a 'wee chuckle' to myself when I was reading the 1975 retrospective commentary when Levitt says that his contribution was 'simple, brief . . . ' and that he tried to write the article 'in a very direct way'. I would hate to see an article of Levitt's that wasn't so direct or simple. It's 12 pages long with long-winded examples and explanations and he thinks this is brief? I don't think so.[58]

Dude, Where's My Concept?

Readers' adverse reactions to Levitt's alleged classic – this is our literary lion, remember – is not only unexpected, it is intriguing. Is it a manifestation of the 'dumbing down' that supposedly afflicts today's debased society? Certainly, the fact that so many had to look up the word 'myopia' suggests that average vocabularies are not what they were:

> Being one of those very intelligent students, I had to reach for my Collins dictionary to look up the meaning of 'myopia'. Finding out that it meant 'an inability to see clearly things that are far away' made me both more confused and intrigued as to what the article might be about and encouraged me to read on.[59]

Is it a side-effect of our so-called 'sound-bite culture', where 12 pages of purple prose – even Ted Levitt's peerless purple prose – is way, way too much? Certainly, the widespread belief that the paper's message could've been boiled down to five pages max, seems to indicate that attention spans are diminishing:

> Throughout this essay I have been rather harsh on Mr Levitt and his article. It's not that I disagree entirely with what he says. However, I don't think it was necessary for him to spend 12 pages getting his message across.[60]

Is it a reflection of rising visual literacy, the article's very lack of four-colour figures, flashy sidebars, and boxes-and-arrows diagrams, that readers increasingly expect in texts, journals and even *HBR* these days? Certainly, lots were put off by the all-text, no-illustrations look of the piece, long before they started reading it:

> It seemed that the fates were against me, the article was twelve sides long, there were no diagrams and the writing was a tiny size eight font. Reading

this would be no mean feat for the truly myopic amongst us! Wondering if Levitt's goal was in fact to *create* myopic marketers with this optical assault, I bravely began to read . . .[61]

Is it due to the latter-day triumph of marketing, our happy-clappy twenty-first century state, where every organization is customer-led or claims to be? Certainly, many feel that hyperbolic, customer-orientated histrionics are totally uncalled for, not to say utterly unnecessary, in this day and age:

> Ted to me is a genius. He's light years ahead of his time. However, he could be a bit repetitive – customer orientated, customer orientated, customer ori- entated, that's all he goes on about. I actually felt a bit pissed off he went on about it so much, but if you look at today's marketplace it's full of com- panies being customer orientated for Christ's sake. When's it all going to end?[62]

Is it a consequence of Levitt's nonchalant scholarship, the paucity of supporting citations, the 'casual survey' of executives, the complete lack of hard empirical evidence? Certainly, more than a few readers find them- selves thrown by his Herculean extrapolations – to every industry, no less – on the basis of a few 'lightly documented' case studies:

> My initial reaction to Marketing Myopia was one founded on mystification. The wealth and depth of the article was immense and yet, with all the so- called craze surrounding it, I felt the need to ask myself – why the big deal? My major concern throughout Levitt's article was his lack of referencing. Regularly he arrived at several conclusions, based on industry insights and apparent 'true stories' and yet there is no referencing other than to second- ary pieces of work. Likewise Levitt concluded his findings on the entire oil industry based on one article. How could he make such a wealth of con- clusions based on one article?[63]

Is it a function of Levitt's failed futurology, the prognostications that failed to come to pass as confidently predicted? Certainly, copious com- mentators are critical of the seer's maladroit soothsaying and consider it a significant contributor to their overall scepticism:

> Until I read this article I had never heard of these advanced powerful chem- ical fuel cells that would sit in a cupboard below the stairs. Maybe this was where J.K. Rowling got her initial idea for Harry Potter. A mystical magical force silently ticking from the depths of a dwelling.[64]

Unless it has been hidden from me for the past 20 years I haven't seen too many rocket-powered cars cruising down the motorway, unless they have been going so quick that my retina isn't picking them up. But I doubt it![65]

Or is it simply due to the fact that Levitt's case studies – railroads, petrochemicals, electricity – are redolent of the fast-disappearing smokestack epoch, with little appeal for today's post-industrial populace? Certainly, several readers wish he'd elaborated on the Hollywood exemplar and find themselves wondering, furthermore, what on earth 'buggy-whips' are:

> The examples used in the article are very sound if somewhat old-fashioned and fusty. I find it very hard to relate to them and I would have been more interested had the products been a bit more glamorous, say, clothes, beauty products etc. That just shows my level of interest; I get very easily bored, but hey come on, dry-cleaning and grocery stores, it's hardly gripping stuff unless you are into it.[66]

> I have to say he confused me slightly with the 'buggy whip'. What? I sat and thought as to what this could be. Was it a new range in Ann Summers, a new pram in which if parents are not going fast enough, the children crack a whip?[67]

Show Me The Antinomy

Regardless of the underlying reasons, readers' unsettled reaction to the word of Ted is contrary to expectation. Nevertheless, it is consonant with the congenitally-contradictory character of his corpus. The contradictions, what is more, don't end with readers' somnambulant appreciation of the scholar's somewhat circuitous writing style. Many find the content contradictory and, appropriately antinomously, many respond to these contradictions in a contradictory manner:

> Above are some aspects of the article that I wanted to highlight because as I was reading it they were areas that particularly jumped out at me because they were contradictory. However, what surprised me was that when I sat down to really think about Levitt's emphasis on customer orientation and its relevance to today's marketplace, I found that my own view is indeed also contradictory. Organizations are as product-oriented as the 1960s, yet more customer-oriented that ever before. I will now explain how I reached this bizarre conclusion.[68]

Numerous readers, for instance, consider Levitt's assertions about 'growth industries' both inconsistent and irreconcilable. His treatment of the marketing–selling dichotomy is also deemed incongruous, as is his wavering position on R&D:

> The most obvious example of his inconsistency is his use of the phrase 'growth industry'. At the beginning of the article Levitt stated that it is impossible to mention a single major industry that did not at one time qualify for the magic appellation of 'growth industry'. However, later on in the article, he stated that there is in fact no such thing as a growth industry, instead there are only companies which capitalize on growth opportunities. Surely this is a clear contradiction of his earlier statement.[69]

> Levitt argues that selling and marketing are different. However in his article he says that marketing is 'a tightly integrated effort to discover, create, arouse, and satisfy customer needs'. It is the word create that bothers me, surely this is more in keeping with a product orientation (selling) not a customer orientation; as a true customer orientation would advocate creating the product to fulfil the needs of the customer, not creating customers to sell the product to. Little incongruities like this crop up throughout the article.[70]

> Levitt once again contradicts himself. He claims the oil industry did not do enough research and development towards finding a substitute for their product in the event that it should become obsolete. He later goes on to condemn the electronics industry for spending too much time and money on research and development.[71]

Many more find themselves contradicting the great scholar's basic contention that customer orientation is all and that organizations should define themselves more broadly. True, they often preface their critiques with carefully worded apologia (for example, 'as a humble marketing student', 'who am I to disagree with a guru?', 'we are not worthy') or, alternatively, with condescending comments concerning the ancient days when the sage was presumably putting quill-pen to parchment ('that may have been so in 1960', 'OK for it's time, I suppose', 'things have moved on since then' etc.). But the prevailing view is damning. Defining the business too broadly is dangerous. Total customer orientation can prove fatal. Core corporate competencies have to be considered. Consumers don't know what they want. Marketing isn't everything. Whither competition?

> I feel that there are some flaws in Levitt's argument, particularly in the examples he used to illustrate his point. I don't feel that management short-sightedness could independently lead to as drastic an outcome as the

downfall of the industry. For example, the railways. I would have serious difficulties believing that the numerous problems the railroads were experiencing were all associated with marketing errors and errors in defining their industry too narrowly. Competition, like the increasing popularity of cars and aeroplanes, I'm sure had a lot to do with it, and it is doubtful that these problems of stiff competition could be overcome through redefining the industry. I am also somewhat confused as to what Levitt thinks can be achieved by merely defining your business in broader terms – I assume that Levitt is speaking partly about diversifying into other markets – yet resources would not always permit this. The outcome of broader defining of the industry could lead the management of the business to spread its resources too thinly. It is my opinion that it is usually a combination of factors that lead to the downturn of an industry. I would therefore estimate that Levitt can at times be guilty of over-simplification and perhaps exaggeration in favour of marketing. Although the marketing concept is almost taken for granted today, Levitt's huge emphasis on customer orientation in this article was probably a revelation at the time. The concern I have about Levitt's argument in this area was that he almost over-emphasized its importance, at the risk of neglecting other areas of management that are equally as important in achieving success. For example, a business could spend all its time finding out what the customer wants through researching the area thoroughly, they could then start to develop the product according to the specifications obtained from the customers, but if distribution then suffers and the product is not accessible to the market then it will not be successful. Therefore I feel that although clearly the customer should be at the center of all activities carried out by the organization, and marketing is essential, it is vital that other functions in the organization area not neglected as a consequence.[72]

Yet, irrespective of the ambiguities, a sizeable number of readers find themselves *agreeing* with Levitt. Agreeing with Levitt, despite themselves. Yes, they admit, the article is consistently inconsistent. Yes, they accept, it has bigger holes in it than the ozone layer. Yes, they acknowledge, it is longer than the proverbial piece of string. Yes, they argue, the scholarship is somewhat lackadaisical, a veritable citation-free zone. Yes, they aver, Levitt is no seer, much less marketing's Mystic Meg. But for all that, many organizations *are* manifestly myopic. For all its 40-odd years before the marketing mast, Levitt's lesson hasn't been fully taken on board. For all its faults and failings, the basic message of 'Marketing Myopia' remains very relevant. For all its terminal verbosity, the article continues to convince. For all its rambling repetitiousness, the rhetoric still resonates. For all its orotund Orphism, the snappy sound-bites retain their elasticity. Almost half a century on, Father Ted's swelling prose sweeps all before it:

When I first looked at Marketing Myopia my initial thoughts began with 'Oh shit', how do I do this when I don't even understand what the bloody thing means? and what's more 'Where on earth will I find the energy, and the will, to read and comprehend this 12-page piece of 1960 ancient history?' Well, I surprised myself! With a dictionary in tow, I began to read it. Surprisingly, I actually enjoyed his loose representation as it gave me something to think about. During my entire university life I have been preached to about how marketing is about giving the customer what they want, when they want it, where they want it, how they want it, all at the right price. So to read an opposing article that explored marketing short-sightedness in a way that many companies and marketing students could relate to was like a railroad track bringing me away from the norm. And, I like that.[73]

Interestingly, lots of the readers attribute their ambivalent reaction to the literary ability of our textual titan. Even as they complain bitterly about the eyelid overload, the sheer boredom, the long-windedness, the opinionated arrogance and downright dogmatism of the man – to say nothing of his obvious attitude problem with the railroads and oil industry in particular – they find themselves falling under his spell, quoting a quotable quip or two, succumbing to his stentorian self-assurance, acceding to his insidious arguments or, indeed, being taken aback by an unexpected approach to a hackneyed topic (Henry Ford, marketing genius, in particular). On occasion, the incomparable professor is lauded and lambasted in the same sentence. Antinomian first, last and always, it seems that Levitt induces antinomy among his admirers and antagonists alike. He infuriates in one paragraph and infatuates in the next:

So, what do I think about Levitt's article? Overall I would have to say that Marketing Myopia feels a bit dated, I would go as far as saying I even find it dull in places. Most annoyingly for me personally, the article lacked depth, fair enough there was extensive use of examples but little conclusive theory was provided. I personally would argue with some of Levitt's points, not that they are wrong but that perhaps they are too black and white. But having said all that I liked the article for one reason – it made me think.[74]

When I set out to read this article while lying in bed my intention was to read half the article and then read the other half the next day. Instead I read the article in its entirety and went to bed feeling I had received a lesson from the master of marketing. From the opening sentence my interest was immediately kindled and the desire to read on in anticipation for something great kept driving me from paragraph to paragraph in awe of the genius I had before me. However, on closer reading I realized that my initial favourable response to the article was undoubtedly a result of my own myopic marketing mindset.

I wanted to believe that Levitt was right and up to a certain point the article is very helpful in articulating what marketing is about. But on reflection I found that the basis for some of Levitt's arguments is dubious.[75]

You Don't Have to be CEO to Love Levitt's

Commonplace though it is, this for and against stance is unevenly spread throughout the essayists. There are several noteworthy variations in reader-response to 'Marketing Myopia'. Generally speaking, those who are in employment as marketers or have considerable experience of working life, maintain that Levitt is definitely on to something. They are aware that organizations can be extremely short-sighted and that customer orientation is more often honoured in the breach than the observance. They have seen myopia for themselves, as it were, and often wonder whether there is an organizational optician in the house:

> While reading this article I had to keep reminding myself that it was written over forty years ago, as I feel it is still as applicable today as then. The companies and industries may have changed since then, but they are still facing the same problems. Many have altered their approach to business, but too many are still blinded by their own success, until it is too late.[76]

> Given that Theodore Levitt's article on Marketing Myopia was written in the 1960s his words in my opinion can still ring true in today's culture. Organisations are in many respects still not responding to the changing needs of customers and are letting their organizations go down the pan due to the short-sightedness of their managers. Quite possibly I agree with him on this because I myself work within retail and am of the opinion that my company is (as I can only describe it) in the Dark Ages. In my opinion Theodore Levitt has hit the nail on the head and I can't help feeling that if more attention had been paid to his article, many businesses would not be in trouble today.[77]

The same people, curiously enough, also tend to be more tolerant of Levitt's rococo writing style. Many consider 'Marketing Myopia' more appealing than the usual scholarly waffle, though even these readers sometimes wish the blue pencil had been used more liberally – much more liberally:

> Although I have made many criticisms of Levitt's article, I also feel that he outlined an incredible marketing theory on customer orientation. . . . It

shows true genius potential. I feel that this is why it was such a highly regarded article. However, I feel that Marketing Myopia was too long to read. Levitt did not need to provide as many examples as he did, especially as he seemed to have very limited factual information on the industries. My view is that he should have condensed the paper into a theory-based article with few examples.[78]

Marketing students, by contrast, as well as those younger essayists with their professional careers largely ahead of them, are inclined to be more critical of the guru's generalizations and rather less tolerant of the longueurs, the repetitions, the meanderings, the imperiousness, the bah-humbuggery. They are aware, from their extensive studies – studies unblemished by collision with the real world, let it be said – that narrowness of strategic vision has advantages, that corporate failure can occur despite top management's best efforts, and that, therefore, the basic message of 'Marketing Myopia' is debatable at best and dubious at worst. As children of the postmodern world, what is more, they are less prepared to accept sweeping generalizations or universally-applicable statements like 'every industry was once a growth industry'.

Mr Levitt, whether by nature or through my interpretation of his work, appears to look at things in a negative way. I really don't know why I got that impression. It was as if he failed to notice just how successful some industries really were running things their way and making a good job of it. He also seemed to 'tar everyone with the same brush', in that he seems to generalize a lot. In the first paragraph he uses 'every' twice when he talks about growth industries and how they have failed to grow because of management failure. Surely all industries must be looked at individually. Each will have their own individual market with a different customer base and they are all there to make a profit in whatever way they see fit at the time. I know the paper was written over forty years ago but even then I am sure that strategies were drawn up and followed and that complacency was not on the agenda. Mr Levitt seems, to me anyway, to suggest that *all* industries fail for the same reasons, that is, they do not recognize which market they are in. Perhaps there might be other factors such as over-expansion, bad management, or lack of resources that have caused the problems.[79]

Another factor that influences reader-response is gender. As a rule, men and women react differently to 'Marketing Myopia'. This difference, however, is not solely due to the sexes' divergent attitudes towards the article's contents, or indeed its author's efflorescent writing style. True, some female readers find our alpha academic's tone overbearing and sexist. More than a few, furthermore, are appalled by his throwaway remark about marketing's 'stepchild' status. But by and large, those favourably disposed and antagonistically inclined towards Levitt – in terms of either style or content or both – are reasonably well spread across the genders:

> The more I stewed over this paper the more I felt that I did not like Mr Levitt's way of looking at this topic. I have never met, nor am I ever likely to meet Mr Levitt, but he came across to me as a man who expects to be right, and that his way was the best and only way to behave, act, think or whatever. Not the type of man who would or could compromise, rather sees issues in either black or white with definitely no grey areas.[80]

> I also found the article offensive in that he is sexist throughout by constantly referring to businessmen. What about women, are they not allowed to work? Maybe in the period he wrote the article a woman's place was in the home, but this is not the case in today's society.[81]

> I thought Levitt was quite cruel and blunt when it came to his choice of words on certain topics. He makes three references to 'stepchild treatment' when he spoke about the oil industry. He came across as heartless as he described marketing as a stepchild as – 'recognized as existing, having to be taken care of, but not worth very much real thought or of dedicated attention'. This is quite a controversial thing to say and indeed quite hurtful if you were actually a stepchild.[82]

The crucial difference, rather, lies in the way they have structured their responses. In accordance with feminist literary theory, which argues that men and women write differently – male linear, female circular – many male readers structured their essays in a strictly sequential fashion.[83] They discussed Ted's paper item by item and topic by topic in the exact order that the article was originally written, often using the same section and sub-section headings to organize their essays. Female readers, conversely, adopted a much less structured, much more selective, near enough synoptic stance on our modern marketing classic. To be sure, these gendered distinctions aren't absolute, which indicates that we are dealing with 'masculine' and 'feminine' writing styles as opposed to some kind of genetic, biologically preordained predilection. Yet, interpenetration notwithstanding, it is fair to infer that, when it comes to writing, 'females' tend to shuttle back and forth, whereas 'males' are inclined to march straight ahead. One beats about the bush, the other gets right down to it. Such is the joy of text.

Hope Springs

Fascinating as they are, gender factors and work experience are far from the most significant shapers of reader-response to Levitt's masterwork.[84] That honour belongs to prior expectations. Those who were dreading reading the article, for fear it might be outdated or too theoretical, often found themselves very pleasantly surprised by its style and content:

> When asked to write a piece on Marketing Myopia by Theodore Levitt I felt like those seafaring explorers who approached the new land in trepidation, gripped by fear and apprehension. I sat for days, sword in hand (or pen) waiting for inspiration, eager to launch the opening attack on Levitt and his drastically flawed paper. Because of course that is what it had to be, the mother of all marketing battles, between Old Ted – the Ivor the Engine of Marketing, with his outdated and cumbersome concepts – and myself, the twenty-first century Stealth Bomber, with my finely tuned theories and sharp original marketing concepts. The old boy didn't stand a chance. However, as the days drew into weeks and the blank canvas spread before me was, for the want of a better word, BLANK, I began to realize that a problem may be presenting itself. The point being that I had nothing to say, my sword was blunted, my jet plane had no fuel. It was at this point in time that I reached a critical decision, one that in hindsight was unavoidable but had, nevertheless, up to that point escaped me – I was going to have to read the paper!
>
> Alright, so I've done that thing, read the piece from cover to cover, thrice in fact and I still have a problem, albeit a different problem, but a problem nonetheless. Apparently Theo's got a point, that is to say, he's off the hook. His credentials as a great marketing guru are no longer under threat. It would seem that this dude knows what he's talking about, at least I think he does and if he doesn't, then truth be told I may not even notice. You see, Levitt wrote this paper in 1960 and it still stands up today as being at the very least relevant and at most nothing less than biblical in marketing terms.[85]

However, those who were looking forward to imbibing a best-selling, award-winning, cool-refreshing draft of marketing wisdom were frequently disappointed by its dreary repetitiveness, high-handed tone and apparent paucity of innovative insights:

> After studying marketing modules for the past three years, I was all too familiar with the name Theodore Levitt. I was aware of the standing that Levitt had in the marketing community and was therefore looking forward

to reading what the 'guru' of marketing had to say. Upon initial reading of the article I was in no way surprised by the clarity of his argument. However, as it was necessary to read the article a number of times to complete this essay, I have to say I was quite taken aback by the inconsistencies of some of his observations. Levitt did raise a number of valid points but there were a number of flaws with the article too. I was expecting a literary masterpiece, this unfortunately did not happen.[86]

Meanwhile, those who were fairly neutral beforehand – that is, those who tried to approach the piece without predispositions or priming of any kind (perusing secondary literature, attending to peer chatter, etc.) generally considered it somewhat analogous to the legendary curate's egg – good in parts. Or, alternatively, found their appreciation increasing with each additional reading:

> On my first few readings of the article I had to force myself to stay awake (and that wasn't because I'd been out partying the night before). I found the article extremely boring and difficult to understand, at times having to use a dictionary to translate many of the words. After reading the article for the fifth, sixth, seventh . . . time I began to realize that Levitt was making some very good points. The article was highlighting things that I as a business studies student have never given much thought to.[87]

Almost inadvertently, then, our scrutineers concur with Jauss's *Rezeptionasthetik*, his contention that reader-response is primarily determined by the 'horizon of expectations', historicized presuppositions that are challenged, confirmed, refuted or reformulated by the features and contents of the text itself.[88] However, the present essays reveal an interesting wrinkle, a twenty-first century quirk that Jauss didn't anticipate.

Perhaps the most remarkable thing about our 208 insurrectionists' reaction to the guru's guru is the high degree of self-consciousness the essays exhibit. Readers not only responded to 'Marketing Myopia', they responded to their responses, often wondering why this interminable, antiquated, 42-year-old article, chock-a-block with erroneous predictions, hyperbolic exhortations and superannuated concepts, still manages to make them think, make them smile, make them challenge their convictions:

> I had always thought of Research and Development (R&D) as being beneficial to any business. When the idea of focusing too much attention on R&D was put across, it caused me to think twice. Is that why so many people believe in Levitt?[89]

Come to think of it, it is probably Mr Levitt's fault that we are so customer orientated now, with his big ideas and his 'it's the only way to survive or sustain growth' attitude. It's his fault I get all this junk mail, people phoning me to tell me of their latest deals, filling all sorts of questionnaires in. Starting to get really annoyed, feel myself getting emotional and starting to boil inside. He better hope I don't get hold of him. He's made my life a misery. Where did that come from? Years of built-up hatred towards junk mail, or is it the fact that nobody writes to me and if it wasn't for the junk mail the postman wouldn't call to my house at all? SOB, SOB. My overall view of Ted's article was that it actually made me think. Now that is extraordinary, especially for me.[90]

Although it is tempting to attribute this readerly reflexivity to the zeitgeist – our age is nothing if not self-conscious – it is an integral part of the introspective method. Remarkably, however, a number of readers have taken it one stage further by second-guessing the author of the article, as well as themselves, the readers. Some, for example, describe Levitt and his award-winning opinion piece as 'myopic':

One of the attractions of Levitt's argument was his industrial examples, they served to clearly illustrate his point and added credence to his argument. Subsequently and rather ironically, Levitt's examples were also one of the major flaws of the piece. Arguably, some of the examples used by Levitt in this article show a 'myopia' on his part, in that the industries he had predicted as 'doomed for demise' turned out to be completely wrong. It is quite ironic actually that in an article about short-sightedness, the author could be accused of suffering from the same weakness.[92]

Some think 'Marketing Myopia', akin to the stricken growth industries it describes, has had its day:

Has the Marketing Myopia article run its course, is it in effect obsolete, is it still about like the oil industry only because it is being saved by outside forces like lecturers, resolutely restrained scholars, implacably temperate managers? Perhaps I should try to write a new article about not pandering to the customer's needs. After all everything has a substitute, even TED LEVITT. So, let's hear it for the title of my new article, THEODORE LEVITT'S MYOPIA.[92]

Some wish – in keeping with Ted's advice to 'start backwards' – that they had read 'Marketing Myopia' in reverse, since the conclusion contains by far the clearest statement of the paper's overall argument:

Within the conclusion of the article, Theodore Levitt includes a commentary by Isaac Bashevis Singer. This man mentions more industries in one conclusion than Levitt has in the whole article, but it makes more sense. All in all, Isaac has showed exactly what Marketing Myopia is in two paragraphs, where Levitt has taken twelve pages to get his point across. Perhaps I should have adopted his theory of working backwards, I would have understood the concept of Marketing Myopia more quickly.[93]

Some see clear parallels between Levitt's case for 'creative destruction' and the creative destruction of the original article itself, which was clearly designed to shock, unsettle and irritate its complacent readers:

I don't believe Ted has been entirely honest about his motives behind writing this article. In 1960 when the article was written, marketing was a relatively new concept. What better way to raise its profile (and that of its author) than by singling out the major industries, prophesying their doom, and explaining why they will fail? But wait, do as Mr Levitt says and all will be well.[94]

Some, it also has to be said, are less than impressed by the author's questionable 'retrospective commentary', inasmuch as it attempts to distance the author from the impact of his message. After all, the 'marketing mania' he describes (and loudly denounces) is partly attributable to Levitt's ability to sell the idea of customer orientation in the first place, as well as his supremely confident assertion that the principles apply to *every* industry *at all times*. To turn round 15 years later and describe it as a 'manifesto not a prescription', or contend that 'an idea is not responsible for who believes in it', is a tad disingenuous, to put it politely:

If the article was not meant to be a 'balanced position', why did Levitt not make this clear? Was his objective to 'tie marketing to the inner orbit of business policy'? If so, why did he not state this? It would have been more impressive to have stated this and highlighted the limitations and bias in his article. It begs the question was Levitt happy to be a semi-fictional rogue playing games or a responsible academic dedicating his work to the world of business for the greater good? Harvard's award and the consolation of Archy the Cockroach's words ('an idea is not responsible for those who believe in it'), suggest that there is a place for this type of colourful, flamboyant approach in the academic arena. The article publicized and benefited Levitt. I'm not sure it displayed someone who was customer orientated. Did Levitt listen carefully and produce something that was expressly of benefit to his customers? In some ways it abused this relationship. It got Levitt fame and publicity and boosted his career but if the business world in general is accepted as customers of the university, as they must be, then Levitt let them down.[95]

The ultimate antinomy, then, is that for many of today's readers the supposed strengths of the original paper are now considered its principal weaknesses. What was once deemed succinct, accessible, readable and strikingly original, is widely regarded as rambling, inaccessible, unreadable and singularly unoriginal. The seeming pragmatism of the original piece – its palpable sense of speaking from the horse's mouth – cuts no ice with today's readers, partly on account of its lack of solid supporting evidence and partly because of its unrealistic recommendations, such as beating buggy-whips into fan belts. Similarly, and inconveniently for Levitt's less than compelling case, most of its calamitous case studies, such as Hollywood, electricity, dry-cleaners and so on, are still going strong, despite their continuing, congenital myopia:

> The oil industry is cited as proof positive of Levitt's theory – an industry too narrowly defined (as being in the oil industry and not the energy business). Product rather than consumer orientation is a recipe for disaster. Yet the oil industry stands firm, car ownership continues to grow and cars are powered by petrol and diesel and not electricity and gas as Levitt prophesied. The strength of the industry today makes Levitt's shortcomings clear to even the most short-sighted. Also, Levitt's portrayal of Hollywood as a myopic institution stumbling into disaster because it dares see itself in the movie business and not the entertainment one is clearly defective. Hollywood still sees itself in the movie business and the nine-letter line in the hill remains a living landmark. In defiance of Levitt's theory Hollywood has survived without branching out into general entertainment and is still in the business of movies and not circus acts, stand-up comedy or even Gilbert and Sullivan.[96]

Over the last forty years computers have practically taken over the world; Ford no longer make cars of 'any colour as long as it's black'; and the customer is more educated and marketing-savvy than ever before. It is a wonder that any article still rings true considering the amount of change the marketing world has encountered, and this can only be of credit to Levitt. Having said that, I did not like the article. It was repetitive, the industries used to illustrate his examples were of no real interest to me, and the whole thing smacked of a Sunday morning sermon.[97]

The Blind Reading the Blind

There is, however, an ultra-ultimate antinomy, a kind of anti-antinomy, and that is this: readers' ambivalent responses to 'Marketing Myopia' – the boredom, the irritation, the dislike, the wry reflexivity, the extraction of quotable nuggets, the reluctant admission that he's saying something important, despite everything – *are exactly what we should expect from great literature*. Great writing, as noted in Chapter 1, can be difficult, knotty, puzzling.[98] And 'Marketing Myopia' bears this out. It grows on us. We have to work at it. It reveals its secrets slowly. Instant it isn't:

> At first, I didn't find this paper interesting but once I got into it and got a feel for what Mr Levitt was portraying then interest grew. To think that great successful industries such as the railroads could crumble by narrow-mindedness is just amazing.[99]

> It was only after reading Marketing Myopia a number of times that I began to feel Levitt was asking more than the obvious, there was an underlying message in the text. To me, he was asking that we look at things differently, depart from the norm, take an alternative route, be creative, modernize and change. . . . Can't his words be related to the way we live our lives. Is he not perhaps suggesting that there is no satisfaction in simple survival . . . the world in which we live offers us the opportunity to live our lives gallantly, a unique gift which is all too often wasted.[100]

According to the earliest work of reader-response criticism, St Augustine's *On Christian Doctrine*, 'no one doubts that what is sought with difficulty is discovered with more pleasure'.[101] The scriptures are written as they are (with the divine meaning eternally inscrutable) 'in order to discourage those who read casually'.[102] It follows, therefore, that the greatness of Father Ted's writing doesn't inhere in his flashy turns of phrase or the superabundance of adjectives, though it has plenty of those. The greatness, furthermore, doesn't come from the content of his articles, since Levitt openly admits to appropriating others' ideas. It comes, rather, from counter-intuitiveness. It comes from confounding prior understandings. It comes from unexpected twists and turns. It comes from uncertainties, paradoxes, antinomies. It comes from hidden depths.

How myopic of us not to see that Myopia isn't myopic, after all.

The Spectres of Philip Kotler

A spectre is stalking Europe, the spectre of Kotlerism.

Alan Smithee (after Marx and Engels)[1]

Kotler & Me

There's a scene in *Roger & Me*, Michael Moore's breakthrough documen-
tary, where the movie-maker finally gets to meet his corporate quarry.
Having pursued the CEO of General Motors, Roger Smith, for the best
part of a year and having been rebuffed at every turn, the camera-toting
crusader eventually catches GM's main man in Chicago, on Christmas
Eve. Moved by Smith's stirring speech on the corporate lessons to be
learned from Charles Dickens's *A Christmas Carol*, Moore seizes the
moment, collars the CEO and invites him to visit Flint, Michigan, the
hometown of the movie-maker, where General Motors had just closed its
factory throwing thousands of people out of work. The CEO blows him
off, however, and the end credits roll . . .

When I look back on my admittedly modest career, there's an element
of Kotler & Me about it. Like many academics of my generation, I am a
child of Kotler. I was raised on the fourth edition of his pioneering textbook, *Marketing Management*; I grew up to the strains of *The New
Competition* and *High Visibility*, his seminal mid-eighties analyses of Japan
and celebrity respectively; and even as a sagacious marketing professor –
come on, grant me some literary licence here – I am in awe of his continuing ability to crank out best-sellers like *Marketing Moves*, *Marketing
Insights* and *Ten Deadly Marketing Sins*.[2] Indeed, if I were asked to identify

a marketing role model, someone that other scholars should endeavour to emulate, I would unquestionably plump for Professor Philip Kotler.

The reasons speak for themselves. Recently ranked tenth in a list of leading management visionaries, alongside Nelson Mandela, Alan Greenspan and Bill Gates, Kotler is one of only two marketing academics included in the American Management Association's *Ultimate Book of Business Gurus*.[3] He was voted the first Leader in Marketing Thought by members of the American Marketing Association and is the recipient of the Paul D. Converse Award, the Steuart Henderson Britt Award, the Distinguished Marketing Educator Award, the Charles Coolidge Parlin Marketing Award and the Marketing Educator of the Year Award, among many others. He holds seven honorary doctorates; he defined 'Marketing and Merchandising' for the *Encyclopaedia Britannica*; he has written seventeen multiple-edition, multiple-language, multiple million-selling textbooks; and, to top it all, he is the only three times winner of the annual Alpha Kappa Psi Award for the best article published in *JM*. Philip Kotler 'is the world's leading authority on marketing', according to Carol Kennedy's *Guide to the Management Gurus*, and few would disagree with her assessment.[4] He is, quite simply, the founder of 'modern' marketing, the framer of our discourse, the father of our field.

Children, of course, rebel against their parents and, as insubordination is my middle name, I have made one or two untoward remarks about the S.C. Johnson & Son Distinguished Professor of International Marketing at Kellogg School of Management, Northwestern University. More than a decade ago, for example, I took a cudgel to *Marketing Places* and gave it a pretty brutal beating in the precious pages of the *Irish Marketing Review*.[5] As you might expect, the rant eventually found its way to Kotler's crenellated citadel in Kellogg and, even though I'd slandered *Marketing Places* from here to Timbuktu (and back again), the sagacious scholar responded as a true titan should: 'You'll have to be a lot more abusive than that if you want to upset me, sonny'. The perfect riposte. A squelch and a half.

So, with a challenge like that, what else could I do but raise the stakes! I dashed off an article called 'Kotler is Dead' and shamelessly used my influence (as special issue editor) to get it published in the *European Journal of Marketing*.[6] Naturally, I wrote it under a pseudonym – the one and only Alan Smithee – and, although it upset numerous worthy but dull marketing academics, several of whom penned letters of complaint to *EJM*'s editor-in-chief, Kotler himself loved it. Scholarly superstar that he is, Philip wanted to reprint part of the piece in one of his books and asked *me* for permission. Needless to say, I denied any knowledge of the author or the article in question. Integrity is my other middle name.

Anyway, akin to Michael Moore in *Roger & Me*, I finally got to meet the venerable Phil when I spent most of 2001 in Northwestern. Our first meeting was, well, nothing if not memorable. Singularly appropriate too. I'd been in Kellogg for a couple of months but hadn't actually encountered the superstar scholar. Then, one happy day, while I was idly chatting to the departmental secretary, the door of his corner office suddenly opened and the peerless professor appeared – in person. He was looking for a telephone directory, which just happened to be sitting on a little, low table immediately in front of me. He bent over to pick up the book and presented his posterior to your humble scribe. I didn't know whether to kiss his ass or kick his ass. However, I considered his gesture deeply symbolic. There was no need for me to speak with him thereafter. He had said all he needed to say to me. And said it most eloquently.

Despite this Roger Smith moment, we did eventually make contact, when Kotler kindly allowed me to interview him about his life, work and career. I have described this meeting, and its memorable aftermath, elsewhere.[7] Suffice it to say that his answers confirmed what I already suspected; namely, that *Philip Kotler and Karl Marx are indistinguishable*. That's right, indistinguishable, interchangeable, inseparable. They are cerebral clones, scholarly synonyms, intellectually identical. There are biographical parallels also.

Now, I appreciate that this suggestion is a tad wild and woolly. Some of you may consider it utterly preposterous, not to say laughably absurd. Apart from the one hundred year gap between the publication of *Das Kapital* (1867) and *Marketing Management* (1967), marxism and marketing are inherently and indefatigably antithetical.[8] Aren't they?

They are indeed. But there are two extenuating circumstances that need to be taken into consideration. First, antithesis is an integral part of marxian analysis and the very fact that marxism and marketing are deemed antithetical is prima facie evidence that a marxian interpretation of the Kotlerite corpus may prove worthwhile, preposterous though it appears. Second, preposterousness is not necessarily a bad thing from the standpoint of literary criticism, as we noted in Chapter 1. In fact, the aim of marxian literary analyses, according to leading left-leaning critic Fredric Jameson, is to induce moments of 'dialectic shock', where readers are forced into a new perception by the preposterous juxtapositions or iconoclastic inversions of the essayist. The most successful of these, he goes on, stimulate a 'sense of breathlessness, of admiration for the brilliance of the performance, but yet bewilderment, at the conclusion of the essay, from which one seems to emerge with empty hands – without ideas and interpretations to carry away with us'.[9]

Hold your breath, boys and girls, bewilderment beckons . . .

Karl Marx, Marketing Man

Karl Marx is renowned for many things – revolutionary fervour, dialectical materialism, scientific socialism, irreligious religiosity – but contributions to the marketing cause are not among them.[10] On the contrary, as the bête noire of the bourgeoisie, he had nothing but disdain for hucksters, barkers and parasitic middlemen of all kinds. True, he was not averse to dabbling on the London Stock Exchange and he had several capitalist skeletons in the extended family cupboard (an uncle helped establish the Philips' electrical empire). In the main, however, he regarded marketing intermediaries as little more than bloodsucking leeches, as did his ample followers.[11] So marked was their anathema for the 'vampire-like' trading classes that some maintain marketing and marxism are intellectually irreconcilable polar opposites. They are the chalk and cheese, night and day, east and west, communist and capitalist of a conceptual Cold War.[12] Marxian precepts have of course been successfully introduced into marketing thought by a number of admirably ecumenical thinkers, especially in the aestheticized neo-marxian forms associated with postmodernism, feminism and critical theory.[13] The burgeoning sociological, anthropological and cultural studies literature on marketplace phenomena also employs marxism as its principal point of departure.[14] But compared to its penetration in cognate disciplines like history, politics, economics or even organization studies (that B-school sump of downsized sociologists), marketing must be regarded as a marxian-free zone.

And rightly so, many might say. Aside from the anti-marketing rhetoric of the hirsute one's fellow travellers, who continue to portray marketers as exploitative bloodsuckers when it is well known that marketing has the customer's interests at heart, marxism itself has been weighed in the balance and found wanting.[15] The dramatic collapse of 'actually existing' communist regimes in eastern Europe and elsewhere, effectively undermined what little intellectual credence marxism previously enjoyed. A marxian critique of the marketing system or the literary juxtaposition of Karl and Kotler may have had some curiosity value fifteen or twenty years ago. However, the triumph of capitalism, as ostentatiously announced by Francis Fukuyama in *The End of History*, has rendered redundant any such investigation.[16]

Or not, as the case might be. Although the implosion of the Soviet Empire dealt a severe blow to the scholarly cachet of 'tenured radicals',[17] it would be rash to conclude that communism has been consigned to the trashcan of history. The anti-globalization riots of recent years are positive proof that the spectre of communism still haunts the marketing mansion.[18] Not only are the counter-capitalist protests intellectually underpinned by the so-called *Das Kapital* of the twenty-first century – *No Logo* – but the marketing activities of mega-brand corporations, such as Nike, McDonald's and Starbucks, are one of the primary causes of contemporary anti-capital confrontations and the riots are performed, as often as not, in the vicinity of their flagship stores. It seems that Adbusting, Nike-nobbling, Starbucks-stiffing and McDonalds-McMangling are the extreme sports of Generation ®, as someone once described them.[19]

More to the point perhaps, Marx has been recuperated by the very bourgeois apparatchiks he once railed against and, of all things, finally outed as a pre-modern marketing man. From the attention-grabbing misdemeanours of his rambunctious youth to the shameless promotional stunts that surrounded the publication of *Capital* (he penned anonymous newspaper reviews of his masterpiece and 'persuaded' Engels to do likewise), there is more than a touch of P.T. Barnum about Karl Marx.[20] According to a recent biographer, he cunningly exploited the cupidity of the media, the curiosity of the public and the cavils of his competitors to promote a brand of counter-capitalism that still enjoys a substantial market share more than one hundred and fifty years after its launch, in China and Cuba especially.[21] Indeed, in the fateful winter of 1852, four years after publishing *The Communist Manifesto*, the penurious prophet seriously considered going into the hardware business, by acquiring the rights to a new and improved furniture polish. Regrettably, his Marx and Stains Remover never made it past the drawing board.

Philip Kotler, Marxist Agitator

Just as Karl Marx can be considered a marketing man *avant la lettre*, so too Philip Kotler is moved by the spirit of marxism. In more ways than one. The first and perhaps most obvious point to make is that Kotler was, and is, directly influenced by marxian dogma. As the eldest son of a Russian immigrant, who was raised during the Great Depression, Kellogg's finest is a lifelong liberal, which is a code word for 'socialist' in the US. He studied sociology, under David Riesman, at the University of Chicago. His PhD dissertation dealt with labour productivity in the developing world. And Marx is specifically cited in a couple of his early, reputation-establishing publications, most notably the famous four-category shopper typology, where he notes Thorstein Veblen's indebtedness to Highgate Cemetery's finest.[22] To be sure, youthful infatuation with the socialist values of Karl Marx is not unusual and, in this regard, Kotler is little different from many other aspiring intellectuals. What's more, as an assistant professor in the sixties, when radical chic was at its height, he could hardly have avoided being affected by the communistic mindset of his flower-powered peers and pupils.[23] Professor Kotler, however, maintained his interest in Marx even when the radicalism of that never to be forgotten decade – a decade many couldn't remember in the first place – was forgotten by all and sundry. And sundry's stoner siblings.

In a 1987 anthology, co-edited by two of marketing's foremost marxian aficionados, former students A. Fuat Firat and Nikhilesh Dholakia, the great thinker posited what can only be described as a quasi-communist vision of commercial life where all traces of exploitative materialism are eradicated and peace and harmony reign.[24] Granted, he doesn't actually refer to Marx in that particular piece but several editions of *Marketing Management* specifically cite the Teutonic thinker with approval.[25] More recently, *The Marketing of Nations* goes out of its way to laud marxian lines of thought and even his eponymous best-seller, *Kotler on Marketing*, notes that 'Technology is the ultimate shaper not only of the material substructure of society but also of human thought patterns'.[26] This statement is about as close as one can get to Karl Marx without the use of quotation marks.

Above and beyond Kotler's direct reliance on Marx, there are several intriguing parallels in their overall intellectual undertakings. Both devoted their lives to describing the big picture about big business and wrote voluminously to that effect. Both based their arguments in firmly established economic principles but adapted the abstruse theories of their academic brethren to pressing practical problems. Both were brilliantly persuasive popularizers of extant ideas rather than original thinkers, as they both openly admitted. Both were blessed with unfailingly creative collaborators, though they were equally eminently capable of virtuoso solo performances. Both were committed to a cause (a communist vision of society in Marx's case, a social vision of commerce in Kotler's case) which they pursued with assiduous enthusiasm despite the denigration of doubters, detractors and debunkers. Both became embroiled in bitter internecine wrangling and were not reluctant to castigate their intellectual antagonists when the occasion called for it, as it often did. Both were misrepresented by their manifold opponents and deified by overenthusiastic supporters.[27] Both were remarkably prescient – Marx anticipated the 1848 revolutions and Paris Commune of 1871, whereas Kotler was demarketing in a socially conscious manner before the 1973 Oil Crisis – albeit their reputations as runes readers may have had more to do with good fortune than good foresight. Both were activists in a class struggle, be it Marx's putative 'dictatorship of the proletariat' or Kotler's counter-revolutionary vision of marketing-dominated organizations and a managerially-orientated academic discipline. The 'dictatorship of the marketariat', so to speak.

Although both thinkers were determined, in Marx's famous

formulation, to change the world, not merely understand it, there is more to the Karl Marx–Philip Kotler analogue than prodigious productivity, biographical parallels, breadth of vision, will to power and a penchant for praxis. The *conceptual content* and *rhetorical form* of their published writings also reveal a number of striking similarities.

Conceptual Content

The collected works of Karl Marx run to approximately a hundred voluminous volumes. Commentaries on and extrapolations of these writings are almost beyond number and an entire science of marxology, with all the attendant academic apparatus, developed in the erstwhile communist regimes of eastern Europe and elsewhere.[28] A scholarly exegesis of the extant literature is humanly impossible but, for the appreciative purposes of the present chapter, seven key Kotler–Marxian conceptual congruities can be tentatively identified.

Mode of Production: As is well known, Karl Marx identified five successive modes of production, from the Asiatic in the dim and distant past, to the Communist in the very near future.[29] These socio-economic configurations are made up of two elements, the *relations of production* and the *forces of production*. The latter refers, in the main, to the prevailing technology (water wheels, steam engines, and analogous means of production), as well as the raw materials and labour power that form part of the production process. The former recognizes that production of any kind is an unavoidably social process, involving various types of economic and non-economic relationships between individuals and their associated institutions (for example, employer and employee, serf and nobleman, tenant and landowner). According to Marx, competition-driven changes in the forces of production precipitate crises, conflict and eventual change in the relations of production – one social class rises as another social class falls – all of which inevitably lead to the emergence of a new and improved mode of production. These evolutionary mechanisms, of course, have been endlessly debated by marxian scholars,[30] but the essential point is that just as capitalism usurped feudalism in the aftermath of the agricultural and industrial revolutions, so too the inherent contradictions of capitalism would eventually bring it down, a communist mode of production would prevail, and 'with this social development, the prehistory of society ends'.

At no point in Philip Kotler's compendious corpus does he dissect relations, forces or modes of production. What he does do, however, is provide a detailed description of the contemporary *Mode of Consumption*.

That is to say, he itemizes the various means of consumption (such as department stores, supermarkets and credit cards), outlines the tools and techniques that engineer consumption (the 4Ps, STP, SWOT analyses and so on) and highlights the labour power that underpins the forces of consumption (salespersons, market researchers, strategic planners). What's more, he opines at great length on the relations of consumption (with suppliers, customers, stockholders, the media and so on), as well as the institutions that embody these relations (advertising agencies, channel members, legislative bodies and suchlike).[31]

Indeed, Kotler frequently contends that changes in the forces of consumption (the internet and e-commerce) will fundamentally alter the relations of consumption (between increasingly empowered consumers and increasingly disempowered organizations), which will give rise to a new mode of consumption in the impending 'Age of Information Democracy'.[32] Professor Kotler, of course, isn't the only scholar who addresses the mode of consumption. Most introductory marketing textbooks cover pretty much the same ground. Nor was he the first to deal with the forces and relations of consumption. The institutional and commodity schools of marketing thought had long-predated the managerial paradigm, after all.[33] However, as the innumerable editions of his bestselling textbooks amply testify, Kotler has dealt with them more often and at greater length than almost anyone else.

Base and Superstructure: Although Marx trained as a philosopher, and earned his doctorate on the difference between the natural philosophy of Democritus and Epicurus, he was a self-taught economist whose account of the evolving class struggle is predicated on the economic base (that is, the foregoing forces, relations and modes of production). So marked was his economism, in fact, that in the famous Preface to *A Contribution to the Critique of Political Economy*, he contends that the character of superstructural institutions – politics, law, education, art, literature, etc. – is determined by the economic base:

> In the social production of their life, men enter into definite relations that are indispensable and independent of their will; these relations of production correspond to a definite stage of development of their material forces of production. The sum total of these relations of production constitutes the economic structure of society – the real foundation on which rises a legal and political superstructure and to which correspond definite forms of social consciousness. The mode of production of material life determines the social, political and intellectual life process in general. It is not the consciousness of men that determines their social being, but, on the contrary, their social being that determines their consciousness.[34]

This passage is admittedly ambivalent, inasmuch as the words 'correspond', 'constitutes', and 'determines', suggest subtly different degrees of determinism.[35] It also loses a lot in translation, according to Fredric Jameson, since it is actually a railroads metaphor that has been consistently mistaken for an architectural allusion.[36] Be that as it may, there is no doubt that Marx is extending his economistic analysis to broader cultural matters, arguing that the economic base somehow produces the cultural superstructure. He broadened the concept of production.

Among the cognoscenti of the marketing concept, Philip Kotler is celebrated for many reasons, from his early avocation of mathematical models to his latter-day analysis of networked organizations.[37] However, he is best known, by his own admission, for 'broadening the concept' of marketing. Kotler's keystone scholarly achievement involved extending the scope of marketing from its base in business organizations to the superstructure of non-business, not-for-profit institutions in the fields of government, education and politics, as well as to charities, museums and the performing arts. In fact, it is not unreasonable to contend that the bulk of his academic career has been devoted to cashing out the ideas contained in his classic, award-winning 1969 paper on broadening.[38] The ensuing torrent of full-length texts has been almost entirely concerned with the superstructural domains identified in this his first Alpha Kappa Psi winning article – hospitals, churches, places, professional services, academic institutions and so on.[39] As in Marx's case, moreover, the theoretical building blocks are the same from context to context (the forces, relations and means of consumption), but their systematic application to a very diverse range of non-business sectors is a truly astonishing academic achievement, one that may never be surpassed, let alone equalled.[40]

Mediation: Kotler's majestic application of basal concepts to superstructural institutions inevitably brings up an intractable marxian matter known as 'mediation'. Marx's insistence that the superstructure somehow reflects the base proved extremely controversial. So much so, that it has been discussed, dissected and, as often as not, dismissed by generations of Western marxist intellectuals, such as Adorno, Althusser and Lukács, who largely devoted their scholarly careers to aesthetic issues and cultural concerns.[41] Rejecting the reductionism of the master's original formulation, which essentially argues that the base *determines* the superstructure and thereby precludes the eminently plausible possibility of a reverse flow – the life imitating art option, as it were – Marx's philosophical progeny scoured the *Schriften* to extract the notion of mediation. This accepts that the economic base and cultural superstructure are interrelated but the influence is neither direct nor one-way. On the contrary, it is mediated by the entire social formation. That is to say, the superstructure and base are situated within and refracted through a broader social milieu of mores, meanings, beliefs, assumptions and ideas. Each sphere of socio-economic activity is separate from, yet affected by, the others and it is the interactions between them that create 'conditions of possibility' for change.

Just as Marx's base-superstructure framework stimulated a great deal of scholarly discussion, so too Kotler's broadened concept of marketing was mercilessly attacked for ill-advised ambition, for going too far, for applying the marketing model in contexts, such as religion, education or the arts, where it was totally inappropriate.[42] And, just as the marxians found a mediating mechanism, in the shape of social formations, so too Kotler came up with the social marketing concept. In the second of his classic Alpha Kappa Psi-winning articles, social marketing is specifically presented as a mediator, 'a bridging mechanism', between social scientists' knowledge of human behaviour and its socially useful implementation.[43] This may be so, but by suggesting that marketing is applicable to ideas, beliefs and causes, the social concept spans the business/non-business divide, blurs the base/superstructure boundary, and helps reduce the reductionism of the broadened concept. Ideas and causes are promulgated by profit and not-for-profit organizations alike. The former may issue non-pecuniary messages, as in the case of automobile manufacturers advocating safe driving, whereas the latter can help further the purchasing process, for example when AIDS charities promote the use of condoms. Thus, by shifting the focus from organization to idea, Kellogg's prodigious professor found a way of mediating between economic base and cultural superstructure. In doing so, he made the intellectual case for, and helped realize, his socialist vision of the marketing discipline – a vision wherein marketing serves the interests of society as a whole. Kotler's societal marketing concept is analogous to Engels's celebrated assertion that the superstructure is determined by the base 'in the final instance'. An instance, as Althusser observed, that never actually transpires.

Reification: Interestingly, Phil's seminal social marketing article commences with a discussion of politicians and this application of the marketing concept to individuals raises the spectre of 'reification'. Within the marxian canon, reification (*Versachlichung*) is usually regarded as a special form of alienation, the existential experience of dehumanized and disempowered desperation that characterizes all societies at all times but is especially strongly marked under the capitalist mode of production.[44] More specifically, reification refers to the transformation of human beings into thing-like entities, which act according to the dictates of the market-place rather than in a recognizably human way. Under capitalism, labour is exchanged for a subsistence wage; it is bought and sold like any other commodity; and, as a consequence, working people are estranged from the fruits of their labour, while the bourgeoisie reap the financial rewards. According to Lukács, indeed, reification is the defining feature of contemporary capitalist society, where every conceivable sphere of human activity is objectified, commodified, marketized and perverted. For Marx, however, the real perversion is that in addition to reifying human activity, capitalism endows inanimate objects with person-like qualities. *Versachlichung* begets *Personifizierung* (personification), as his celebrated discussion of commodity fetishism ('and the secret thereof') in the first chapter of *Capital* eloquently testifies:

> A commodity appears, at first sight, a very trivial thing, and easily understood. Its analysis shows that it is, in reality, a very queer thing, abounding in metaphysical subtleties and theological niceties. So far as it has a value in use, there is nothing mysterious about it, whether we consider it from the point of view that by its properties it is capable of satisfying human wants, or from the point that those properties are the product of human labour. It is as clear as noon-day, that man, by his industry, changes the forms of the materials furnished by nature, in such a way as to make them useful to him. The form of wood, for instance, is altered by making a table out of it. Yet, for all that the table continues to be that common, every-day thing, wood. But, so soon as it steps forth as a commodity, it is changed into something transcendent. It not only stands with its feet on the ground, but, in relation to all other commodities, it stands on its head, and evolves out of its wooden brain grotesque ideas, far more wonderful than if it were to start dancing of its own accord.[45]

Now, no-one would consider accusing Professor Philip Kotler of perversion, let alone fetishism – not even the late, lamented Alan Smithee – but there is no doubt that he has a penchant for personification. The corporations, concepts, products, places, institutions and ideas that punctuate his corpus are unfailingly portrayed as living beings, semi-human entities animated by the life force of marketing. As he points out, 'Everything about an organization talks'.[46] He also points out that:

> Most executives will see a physician at least once a year to check on their health but will let their product mix go unchecked until a crisis develops. During this time, many products lie infirm in the mix until they fade away or are suddenly massively ejected in a crisis-inspired housecleaning.[47]

At the same time, the imperishable professor is particularly partial to reification. In *High Visibility*, for example, Kotler and his co-authors contend that the principles of marketing are as applicable to individuals as they are to detergents, deodorants, dog foods and diet colas.[48] If fame and fortune are one's ultimate objective – and surely everyone is entitled to their fifteen minutes' worth, or a New York minute at least – then the tools and techniques of marketing science, such as market research, targeting, segmentation and positioning, strategic planning and competitor analysis, are readily available and easily adaptable to every imaginable high visibility scenario. From a traditional marxian perspective, admittedly, this celebrity-creation process is a travesty of human relations, the reductio ad absurdum of reification, but for Kotler et al. it is only a foretaste of things to come, when the random 'discovery' model of high celebritude is replaced with deliberate 'breeding'. Marketing has the technology to transform 'unknown aspirants into high visibles in much the same way that sumo wrestlers are grown in Japan, or ballerinas built in the Soviet Union'.[49]

Ideology: Nowadays, of course, self-marketing is widely regarded as perfectly normal. There are any number of personal development texts, such as Tom Peters's *The Brand You* or Rachel Greenwald's *The Program*, which exhort everyone to treat themselves as brands, while disbursing advice on how best to manage, develop and capitalize on 'own' brand equity, as well as differentiate one's brand in the crowded marketplace of ambitious individuals.[50] Such is the nature of ideology. In the Marxist cosmos, ideology refers to the social class or interest-group based system of beliefs, ideas and assumptions that influence how people understand the world and affect how they act on a daily basis, yet are rendered invisible by their natural, self-evident and seemingly 'common-sense' character.[51] The idea of ideology did not originate with Marx and, in actual fact, he employed the term in at least six different ways. However, it is indissolubly associated with marxian thought. In *The German Ideology*, he treated it as an inverted, topsy-turvy, contradictory worldview that blinds the oppressed to the oppression of their oppressors.[52] By presenting their ideas as universal, rational, objective and shared by society as a whole, the dominant class is able to pursue its own interests, perpetuate its position and persuade the dominated class to accept, as incontestable or inevitable, actions that are not in its best interest. As Gramsci subsequently noted, the hegemony of the ruling class is insidiously achieved through a combination of coercion and consent, where the dominant ideology is internalized and the conditioned collude in their own conditioning.[53]

Most would agree that marketing is the dominant ideology of our time. Thanks in no small measure to Philip Kotler's contention that the marketing concept is applicable in every conceivable situation, in every imaginable sphere of human activity, marketing is well-nigh hegemonic. What's more, it is Kotler's managerial, exchange-based, customer-centric conceptualization that holds irrevocable sway. Not only is it perpetuated through consent and coercion (textbooks, curricula, professional associations, journal review processes and so on), but in keeping with Marx's original formulation, it also involves a classic 'inversion' from non-market facing to market facing organizations. True, many empirical studies show that the marketing function is held in comparatively low esteem by CEOs, nevertheless the marketing concept itself – the idea of customer orientation – is all but unassailable.[54] Patients, pupils, visitors, voters, audiences, admirers, donors, distributors, clients, congregations and many, many more have all been transmuted into 'customers' and treated accordingly, in principle if not in practice. Even the artistic superstructure, which for many Western Marxists represents a site of ideological unveiling and resistance, has succumbed to the Kotlerite message articulated in *Standing Room Only*, *Museum Strategies and Marketing* and several others.[55] Some commentators maintain that the traditional highbrow/lowbrow divide has collapsed and only 'middle-mind' marketability matters any more.[56] Certainly, many cutting-edge artists like Jeff Koons, Damien Hirst and Traccy Emin openly boast of their marketing prowess.[57] Art for mart's sake is the order of the day. Or so it seems.

Historicism: To be sure, the hegemony of marketing did not transpire instantaneously. On the contrary, it has been a long, slow process of accumulation, a process encapsulated in that stalwart of introductory textbooks, the 'three eras schema'. Although it was Keith, not Kotler, who formulated the production-era, sales-era, marketing-era model, the latter has not been reluctant to refer to it.[58] The very first chapter in the first edition of *Marketing Management* alludes to the Dark Ages when the false consciousness of production-orientation and sales-orientation held sway. Kotler, however, does not rest on his temporal laurels by claiming that the current era – the marketing era – represents the culmination of this evolutionary process and that (marketing) history has ended. His teleological consummation, rather, is positioned at a point in the near future. It has been positioned there, furthermore, throughout our seer's academic career. In Kotler's works, a new marketing dawn is constantly breaking, though the terminology he uses to describe this perpetually impending epoch has changed considerably down the decades. In 1967, it was a new marketing era, pure and simple; in 1971, it was a societal marketing milieu of socially responsible behaviour; and in 2003, it became a 'lateral marketing' era predicated on outside-the-box, de-Bono-or-bust thinking about marketing matters.[59] Countless variations of this schema punctuate Kotler's corpus but they all posit the present as a threshold to a new and improved marketing dispensation.

In this regard, of course, Kotler is aping Karl Marx's classic model of historical materialism. Subsequently described by Engels as one of the stupendous thinker's two great scientific discoveries, historical materialism posits five stages in the evolution of modes of production: primitive communism, slave state, feudal state, capitalist system and, eventually, socialist or communist society.[60] Marx's model, admittedly, has a couple more stages than its marketing equivalent, albeit the first two aren't actually discussed, and stage-type schemata long pre-dated the rambunctious revolutionary. The important point, however, is that both prophets predict the dawning of a new day and, by implication, that they hold the key to 'Tomorrowland'. Such teleological trajectories, I grant you, are anathema to many traditionally-minded historians, who cleave to the view that there are no discernible patterns, trends or cycles in history. Karl Popper, in particular, launched a ferocious attack on historicist models of development and inadvertently impugned an established research procedure that traded under the same name.[61] But the cavils of idiographically-minded historians notwithstanding, stage-type models are a permanent feature of the social sciences and few are more influential than Marx's and Kotler's.[62]

Value: The other scientific discovery alluded to in Engels's famous graveside oration appertains to value, our final Kotler–Marxian conceptual parallel. Although the labour theory of value has not stood the test of time – even as Marx was developing it, he was being marginalized by the marginalists – it generated and continues to generate a prodigious amount of academic discussion.[63] The theory, in essence, attempts to explain why the capitalist mode of production leads not to the progressive improvement of the labourer's lot, as the astonishing achievements of the Industrial Revolution might lead us to expect, but to inexorably increasing immiseration and alienation. To this end, Marx argues that labour is a commodity, like any other, which is bought and sold in the marketplace. Every commodity has a use value, the function performed for its possessor (coats keep us warm, beer imparts conviviality) and an exchange value (the amount of money or equivalent goods that the commodity can command on the open market). As a commodity, labour is exchanged for its market value – a subsistence wage – and, as a commodity, it is exploited by the capitalist, who sweats the asset, extracts the maximum amount of output for the minimum outlay and expropriates any surplus value thereby obtained. Workers, in other words, add value to the goods they produce, but only receive a small proportion of that value in return. The rest is appropriated by the owner.

Although Professor Kotler alludes to the labour theory of value on one – and only one – occasion, he doesn't discuss it at length.[64] As always, however, the spectre of Marxian thought hovers over his learned analyses of exchange and value. Indeed, if there is one point Kotler has consistently stressed throughout his academic career, it is that *exchange* is central to the marketing concept and that marketing delivers *value* to organizations, their customers and society at large. Neither Phil Kotler nor Karl Marx was the first to grapple with these constructs, it should be said. Adam Smith and David Ricardo got there long beforehand.[65] Nor do our dilatory duo employ the terms in the same way, or even in a consistent manner, come to think of it. Nevertheless, it is arguable that Kotler's single, greatest achievement, as a conceptual capitalist, has been to extract surplus value from existing notions of exchange and value. By extending their reach far beyond physical exchange (to ideas, causes, beliefs, attitudes, etc.) and monetary values (to things such as charitable feelings, aesthetic uplift and a sense of social responsibility), our discipline's premier thinker has increased their use value to marketers and academics who are able to apply marketing principles to ever wider spheres of activity, and thereby accelerate the circulation of conceptual capital. In *Kotler on Marketing*, he pulls off the ultimate meta-marxian trick of demonstrating that the exchange value of use value exceeds the use value of exchange value:

> The marketer, here IBM, should not just focus on selling superior *purchase value* [that is, exchange value] to the bank. IBM must also take responsibility for selling superior *use value*. IBM should view this not as a one-time *transaction* but as a continuing *relationship* aimed at generating superior customer value at every point.[66]

The upshot of this extension, however, is the commodification of the marketing concept itself, its reduction to a formulaic 4Ps framework, which serves to disguise the true nature of marketplace relations (consider the inherent contradiction of Nike-wearing protesters attacking NikeTown, Seattle). Worse still, just as the capitalist is compelled by competitive pressures to squeeze every ounce of surplus value from the workforce, thereby increasing its destitution and propensity to revolt, so too the Kotlerite model of marketing is compelled to expand into ever-widening domains, no matter how inappropriate or tangential they appear. (A colleague of mine used to expound on the 4Ps of pre-stressed concrete.) It will only be stopped when the immiseration of the professorial proletariat is complete, a crisis of conceptual accumulation transpires and the expropriator of 'exchange' and 'value' is expropriated.

And with this marketing development, the prehistory of Kotlerism ends.

Rhetorical Form

Striking as they are, the conceptual parallels between Marx and Kotler are a mere bagatelle compared to their stylistic similarities. There are, of course, vast differences between the two, insofar as the actual textual contents (the examples, the organizations, the people, the technology, the countries, the socio-economic circumstances and so on) refer to the nineteenth and twentieth centuries respectively. Surface appearances, however, belie underlying essences, as both Marx and Kotler are at pains to point out, and when the sub-textual structures of their bodies of work are examined, seven intriguing analogues arise, spectre-like, from their compendious corpuses.

1. The first of these relates to science. Both Marx and Kotler go to great lengths to emphasize that they are engaged in serious scientific research and that the written output of their rigorous ruminations is science, no more, no less. Thus Marx modestly claimed to have identified 'the law of all history hitherto' in his 1875 *Critique of the Gotha Programme*. His Labour Theory of Value cleared up a problem that had defeated all previous authorities, including celebrated economic scientists like Smith and Ricardo, and, whereas competing commentators on communist society were idle utopian speculators, he presciently presented a suitably scientific scenario for the impending proletarian paradise:

> The question then arises: what transformation will the state undergo in communist society? In other words, what social functions will remain in existence there that are analogous to present state functions? This question can only be answered scientifically, and one does not get a flea-hop nearer to the problem by a thousandfold combination of the word people with the word state.
>
> Between capitalist and communist society lies the period of the revolutionary transformation of one into the other. Corresponding to this is also a political transition period in which the state can be nothing but *the revolutionary dictatorship of the proletariat*.[67]

Kotler too repeatedly stresses his scientific affiliations, ambitions and achievements. In the preface to the first edition of *Marketing Management*, for example, he emphasizes that the book eschews descriptive material in favour of analytical content; he contends that intuitive marketing must make way for '*more* theory and analysis'; and, just to make sure his readers get the rigour-is-right message, he notes that the book 'relies heavily on the basic disciplines of economics, behavioural science and mathematics'.[68] Thirtysomething years later, in the preface to *Kotler on Marketing*, he attributes his unparalleled academic success to the fact that prior studies of marketplace phenomena were 'basically descriptive'. The sage, it seems, was not only determined to put 'marketing decision making on a more scientific basis', but clearly believes he succeeded:

> In subsequent years it has been gratifying to witness substantial advances in the body of scientific literature in marketing – both explanatory and normative – contributed by a generation of talented marketing scholars bent on improving our understanding of how markets work.[69]

Now, science is a slippery construct, as decades of inconclusive marketing debate on the 'art or science' issue attests.[70] But even the most generous interpretation of scientific endeavour would be hard pressed to find room for our illustrious duo's collected works. There are no laws of history, the Labour Theory of Value is valueless scientifically, and, despite Philip's 700-page book on marketing models, few if any of these can be considered 'proven' in a scientific sense, let alone 'refuted' in accordance with proper Popper precept. Analogously, the four 'axioms' in Kotler's classic 'Generic Concept' paper are anything but – maxims possibly – and while Marxian 'science' can be massaged with reference to the German *Wissenschaft* tradition (where science refers to systematic thinking rather than formal methods and hypothesis testing, as such), that is not how he saw it. On the contrary, Marx maintained that he had achieved in the sphere of economic history what Darwin accomplished in natural history. Indeed, he famously sent Darwin a complimentary copy of *Das Kapital*, though the great biologist remained famously unmoved by Marx's remarks on the origin of specie.

To be sure, the fact that the works of Marx and Kotler fail to qualify as science is neither here nor there. And to condemn them for shortcomings on the scientific front is to miss the rhetorical point completely. Espousing a scientific approach, championing the inexorable advance of science and claiming to have scientific support for one's findings serve an important rhetorical purpose. It endows the author's arguments with an incontestable, almost inalienable authority that they wouldn't otherwise possess. Within the Western intellectual tradition, 'science' is regarded as the most esteemed, arguably the only acceptable, approach to scholarly understanding, and by wrapping themselves in the flag of science our sagacious arbiters legitimized their intellectual agendas. The scientific status of their research is irrelevant. Just as the preliminary 'methodological' chapters of *Das Kapital*, all twenty-six of them, convey a powerful impression of scientific rectitude – after all that, how can the findings possibly be doubted? – so too the 700 pages of *Marketing Decision Making* send a this-is-serious-stuff message. This was Kotler's first book (albeit the second to be published) and it did much to position him as a champion of the scientific cause, something the sage of Evanston has never completely lost. According to Kennedy, he 'applied a scientific rigour, with models and statistical analysis, to what had up till then been largely a seat-of-the-pants practice'.[71] Or as he put it himself when describing his own brand positioning:

> In examining the existing marketing textbooks, I felt that they lacked the tight analytical quality of economics textbooks. They contained many lists (such as the advantages and disadvantages of wholesalers, etc.) and hardly any theory. Little was reported in the way of research findings and method-ologies from the social, economic and quantitative sciences. As a result, I decided around 1964 to write my own marketing textbook. The original draft was highly quantitative and my publisher advised me to 'tone down the math' and 'beef up the prose and stories'. The result was *Marketing Management*, published in 1967. I saved the 'expurgated material' and extended and published it in 1971 as *Marketing Decision Making: A Model-Building Approach*.[72]

2. If Marx and Kotler fail to qualify as fully-paid-up scientists, they more than compensate with their astonishing literary talents. Simply put, they are great writers and it is arguable that their reputations owe as much to outright writing ability as they do to anything else. True, neither Kotler nor Marx is ordinarily regarded as a literary type, though the fact that they successfully passed themselves off as 'scientists' says much for their powers of persuasion. To the contrary, their weighty tomes are often considered heavy going at best and well-nigh unreadable at worst. Marx himself recommended that readers skip the twenty-six methodological chapters of *Capital*, while the USP of *Marketing Management*'s 'Millennium Edition' is that it has 'fewer chapters' than previous versions![73] It is necessary to appreciate, however, that 'weightiness' itself performs an important rhetorical function, especially when a work aspires to definitive status. Few writers, furthermore, are capable of sustaining the reader's interest over 700 pages, at least not without recourse to melodramatic plot twists or gratuitous sex and violence, both of which are sadly absent from mainstream marketing textbooks and the secondary literature on Marxism.

Yet for all the heavy sledding, particularly in *Capital* and *Marketing Decision Making*, Marx and Kotler are as one in their ability to craft an aphorism that encapsulates and energizes simultaneously. Marx, in particular, composed a crock of catchphrases that call down the years like none other: 'Workers of the World Unite!', 'The Opium of the people', 'A spectre is stalking Europe, the spectre of Communism', 'From each according to his ability, to each according to his needs', 'History repeats itself . . . the first time as tragedy, the second time as farce', 'Philosophers have only *interpreted* the world in various ways; the point is to *change* it', 'The history of all hitherto existing society is the history of class struggles', and so on and so forth.

Kotler, similarly, is no slouch with sound bites and snappy one-liners: 'Marketing takes a day to learn and a lifetime to master', 'Good companies meet needs, great companies create markets', 'The answers of yesterday lead to the errors of today', 'Without a top line there will be no bottom line', 'If you are not talking customers, you are not talking', 'The chief cause of problems is solutions', 'Advertising is what you pay for, public relations is what you pray for', 'Pick apples not lemons', 'There are riches in niches', 'Markets are pitiless' and many, many more. Most of the latter, admittedly, have yet to be inducted into dictionaries of dicta, anthologies of aphorisms and encyclopedias of epigrams, but surely is it only a matter of time before Phil joins the quip-coining immortals, the pantheon of phrasemakers, the proverbial Hall of Fame.

More epigrammatic yet is their terminological capacity. That is to say, Marx and Kotler's shared ability to concoct terms, words, phrases, expressions or neologisms that take on a life of their own (pardon my personification) and become the focus of subsequent attention, discussion and scholarly investigation. 'False consciousness', 'classless society', 'commodity fetishism', 'dialectical materialism', 'revolutionary socialism', 'petty bourgeois', 'mode of production', and 'class struggle' are just some of Karl's lexical creations, while locutions such as 'alienation', 'capitalist', 'communism', 'proletariat', 'expropriation' and, not least, 'exchange' were invigorated under his auspices.[74]

In a similar vein, Kellogg's kingpin has minted a wealth of conceptual coinages ('metamarketing', 'megamarketing', 'demarketing', 'turbo-marketing', 'neanderthal marketing') and codified countless others ('prosumers', 'social marketing', 'societal marketing', 'reverse marketing', 'new marketing'). That said, many of his neologisms have failed to stand the test of time. Who now employs 'synchromarketing', 'counter-marketing', 'remarketing', 'metamediaries', 'birth-dearthness', 'decisioning', 'upselling', or, for that matter, remembers the 'memory channel'? However, no one would gainsay Philip Kotler's prodigious New Phrase Development facility.

For some people, of course, this catchword creating capacity is undoubtedly cute, unquestionably clever, but ultimately inconsequential. For other people, such as the marxist literary critic Walter Benjamin or the marketing wordmonger Alex Frankel, naming is of paramount philosophical importance.[75] As our understanding of the world can only be expressed in language or similar symbolic systems, word making is world creating. Where, after all, would Marxian thought be without 'hegemony', 'praxis', 'accumulation' or 'emancipation'? Where would business and management be without grisly gerundives like 'downsizing', 'de-layering', 're-engineering' or 'customerizing'? Where, for that matter, would consumers be without marketing locutions like Linux, Dasani, Prozac or Accenture? In the beginning was the word.

3. In addition to their maxim-manufacturing acumen and phrase-producing prowess, Marx and Kotler are masters of metaphor. As might be expected, the former makes repeated use of railroads, telegraphs, steam engines, cameras obscura and similar examples of nineteenth century industrial technology, to say nothing of standard architectural tropes such as base/superstructure, military metaphors pertaining to the impending proletarian revolution, and commonplace biological conceits like evolution, survival of the fittest and so forth. Thus, in the *Economico-Philosophical Manuscripts of 1844*, he memorably describes low paid workers as 'a mere appendage of flesh on a machine of iron'. In the *Communist Manifesto* they are 'privates of the industrial army . . . enslaved by the machine . . . instruments of labour . . . training to act as a machine'. And in *Capital* the entire social system is 'a pumper-out of surplus labour and exploiter of labour power'.

Kotler too is not averse to biological, architectural, martial and technological allusions.[76] He variously describes marketing as a jungle, a garden and a life or death struggle; he explicates all sorts of militaristic manoeuvres in *The New Competition* and elsewhere; he includes countless figures of building blocks in his lavishly illustrated textbooks; and, at one time or another, compares marketing to a computer, a toolkit, an automobile, the atom bomb, a space ship, an airline dashboard, satellite navigation equipment, a 'resource conversion' machine and a 'gigantic apparatus' of cogwheels, crankshafts, dials, gears and ratchets. In 'Broadening the Concept', to cite but a single celebrated example, he avers that marketing is 'customer satisfaction engineering', and sets out to itemize the 'multitude of tools' in the marketer's lavishly-appointed conceptual knapsack.

Technological tropes, admittedly, are fairly common figures of speech, though few use them with felicity. The same is true of architectural conceits, biological similes and military metaphors. Where Marx and Kotler stand out from the figurative crowd, however, is in their passion for the paranormal and similar symbols of the supernatural. Such an analogical predilection might seem somewhat strange coming from self-professed 'scientists', but it is no less evident for all that. Marx, of course, is well known for his spectres, ghosts and apparitions, as the book by poststructuralist philosopher Jacques Derrida almost makes clear.[77] Indeed, the repertoire of his otherworldly allusions is quite staggering. These include:

Witchcraft, animism, tribal religions, spiritualism, magic, monsters, ghosts, wizardry and the cabala, mysterious hieroglyphics, werewolves, the soul, alchemists and alchemy, deism, unnatural metamorphoses, raising of the dead, metempsychosis and transmigration of souls, creation *ex nihilo*, miracles, conjuring tricks, levitation and perpetual motion machines ... God the Father, God the Son, the Lamb of God, the Garden of Eden, the Holy Grail, the beast of the apocalypse, the whore of Babylon, the incarnation, baptism, transubstantiation ... phenomena that are invisible, concealed or veiled, that are symbols, secrets, fantasies, enigmas, illusions or riddles, that are mysterious and in need of deciphering. ... Marx's vision of capitalism is a kind of unholy Chartres Cathedral where Christian iconography mingles with nightmarish creatures and pagan practices.[78]

Philip Kotler is equally partial to the paranormal, albeit in a less overt, more ethereal, somewhat shadowy manner. He specifically refers to 'spectres' on several occasions – the Bomb, the Japanese, the new economy, natural resource depletion, 'product overpopulation' and more besides. He gives space to spectral, bump-in-the-night behaviours, as well as 'scarifications', 'presences', 'uncontrollable forces' and 'chills down the spines' of executives. He reports sufficient 'visions', 'spirits', 'miracles', 'icons', 'images', 'signs and wonders', 'Days of Judgement', 'pacts with the Devil' and 'deadly sins' to put the sainthood to shame. He mentions magic, mysticism, mythology, meditation, soothsaying, foretelling, rebirthing, pyramidology, alchemy, time travel, good luck charms and maintains a 'seething cauldron' of magical elixirs, potions and panaceas. He describes his latter-day research method as Zen. He refers to all sorts of otherworldly figures including trolls, leprechauns, giants, ghosts, ogres, aliens and missing links. Indeed, the geographical ghoul that hovers between life and death in the opening pages of *Marketing Places* is not the sort of spatial spectre you would want to meet in a dark alley, late at night, with only the 4Ps for protection.[79] He also exhibits a conspiracy culture-immersed interest in brainwashing, mind control, subliminal messages and secret societies, which is the twentieth century equivalent of the nineteenth century's fascination with the occult, the esoteric and the unknown. Likewise, his virtual obsession with threesomes – the first edition of *Marketing Management* contains 135 three-category classifications, typologies and explications of marketplace phenomena and he has concocted countless conceptual three-fers since – has its ultimate origins in the orphic, cabalistic, hermetic side of Western civilization, a shadowy side that scientific rationality has sought unsuccessfully to suppress.[80]

For the most part, however, the spectres that stalk Kotler's pages are unmentioned, unobtrusive, invisible, intangible. They are the spectres of failure, of bankruptcy, of technological change, of foreign competition, of unplanned strategies, of uncoordinated activities, of dysfunctional supplier relationships, of outdated market intelligence, of wasted advertising spending, of pointless promotional stunts, of dubious distribution channels, of inadequate control systems, of mistaken mix manipulation, of irresponsible executives, of old-fashioned thinking, of standing still despite the rapidity of change and of what will happen if managers refuse to act *right away*. They are the ghosts of marketing past, the bogeymen of production- and sales-orientation, the infernal demons of customer disquiet, dismay and dissatisfaction. They are the spectres, in short, of consumerism.

4. Metaphors are the precious stones of literary endeavour – the diamonds, rubies and emeralds that catch the reader's eye. But the setting is no less important, as is the craftsmanship that goes into its construction. In addition to their remarkable metaphor cutting facility, both Marx and Kotler are blessed with very distinctive writing styles and strikingly similar modes of expression. They both impart an air of *urgency* by means of emphatic rhetorical devices like italicization, capitalization, overstatement, understatement, exclamation marks, adjectival accumulation and incessant use of normative imperatives, superlatives and gerundives ('must', 'ought', 'essential', 'vital', 'increasingly', 'accelerating', 'unprecedented', 'rapidly advancing'). This sense of semi-apocalyptic drama is heightened by eschewing the past tense, passive voice of standard scholarly prose and relying on the active voice, present tense beloved by revolutionaries, demagogues and tabloid newspaper editors (the future tense figures prominently as well). However, they take care not to alienate the masses unnecessarily by frequently employing the first person plural ('we', 'us', 'our'), which is less imperious than the first person singular ('I', 'me', 'my') and conveys a sense of conspiratorial solidarity between implied writer and reader, despite vast real world differences in professional, educational and socio-economic circumstances. This egalitarian ethos is underpinned with appropriately demotic expressions (there is an astonishing amount of slang in Kotler and Marx alike), amenable adverbs ('clearly', 'obviously', 'naturally') and congenial conjunctions ('thus', 'therefore', 'hence'), which combine to communicate self-evident straightforwardness – almost irrefutability – to what might otherwise be deemed decidedly dubious assertions.

5. Another rhetorical stratagem that helps them stand out from the crowd is repetition, *anaphora* and *antimetabole* in particular. Anaphora is the technical term for starting several successive sentences, clauses or paragraphs with the same word or words, and both Marx and Kotler employ it repeatedly. In the *Communist Manifesto*, for instance, Marx commences twelve sequential paragraphs with those anti-capitalist swear words 'the bourgeoisie' and he is no slouch at intra-paragraph anaphora either:

The bourgeoisie, wherever it has got the upper hand, has put an end to all feudal, patriarchal, idyllic relations. It has pitilessly torn asunder the motley feudal ties that bound man to his 'natural superiors', and has left no other nexus between man and man than naked self-interest, than callous 'cash payment'. It has drowned the most heavenly ecstasies of religious fervor, of chivalrous enthusiasm, of philistine sentimentalism, in the icy water of egotistical calculation. It has resolved personal worth into exchange value, and in place of the numberless indefeasible chartered freedoms, has set up that single, unconscionable freedom – Free Trade.[81]

Few writers can compare with such orgiastic anaphoric acumen and Kotler is no exception. Anaphora, however, is one of his most frequent rhetorical manoeuvres and what he lacks in anaphoric power – three-sentence sequences are the norm, though it can rise to seven or more – he makes up for in frequency:

There is often sentiment about the former heavyweight products which have passed their prime. There is a valid concern about the effect of dropping products on internal organizational morale and external customer and supplier relations. There is uncertainty about whether the product is chronically weak or only pausing before the next sales spurt. There is confusion about the right standards to apply in choosing products for deletion. There is a lack of predictable models and precedents for conducting periodic product reviews.[82]

Every organization must perform a financial function insofar as money must be raised, managed, and budgeted according to sound business principles. Every organization must perform a production function in that it must conceive of the best way of arranging inputs to produce the outputs of the organization. Every organization must perform a personnel function in that people must be hired, trained, assigned, and promoted in the course of the organization's work. Every organization must perform a purchasing function in that it must acquire materials in an efficient way through comparing and selecting sources of supply.[83]

Smart marketing companies are improving their customer knowledge, customer connection technologies, and understanding of customer economics. They are inviting customers to co-design the product. They are ready to make flexible market offerings. They are using more targeted media and integrating their marketing communications to deliver a consistent message through every customer contact. They are utilizing more technologies such as video conferencing, sales automation, software, Internet web pages, and Intranets and Extranets. They are reachable seven days a week, twenty-four hours a day at their 1–800 customer telephone number or by e-mail. They are better able to identify the more profitable customers and set up different levels of service. They see their distribution channels as being partners, not adversaries.[84]

If Kotler's oeuvre is epitomized by anaphora, Marx is antimetabole minded. Antimetabole is similar to anaphora, inasmuch as it involves repetition, usually within the same sentence. However, the grammatical sequence is reversed, as in John F. Kennedy's famous aphorism, 'ask not what your country can do for you, but what you can do for your country'. In literary criticism circles, Karl Marx is justifiably celebrated for his antimetabolic ability. 'The weapon of criticism cannot replace the criticism of weapons', 'It is not the consciousness of men that determines their being, but their being that determines their consciousness', 'The serious buffoon who no longer sees world history as a comedy but takes his comedy for world history' and 'Philosophy can only be realized by the abolition of the proletariat, and the proletariat can only be abolished by the realization of philosophy' are just a few of his many arresting antimetaboles. Their meaning, admittedly, is sometimes vague – clearly they're done for rhetorical effect rather than clarity of expression – nevertheless, they are copybook examples of the literary form.

Kotler is no less amenable to antimetabole, occasionally in its classic variant where the grammatical sequence is reversed ('If you fail to plan, you are planning to fail'). In the main, however, the marketing magus prefers *chiasmus*, a slightly looser form of antimetabole, which also involves intra-sentence inversion but not necessarily in the same grammatical sequence. For example: 'The sales department isn't the whole company, but the whole company better be the sales department'; 'The question is not whether to go into e-business, but rather how soon and with what sequence of steps'; 'If they spend too little on advertising, they may be spending too much'; 'It is production for the sake of consumption, not consumption for the sake of production'; 'The proposal's main weakness was not that it went too far but that it did not go far enough'; and, of course, the classic concluding sentences of 'Broadening the Concept':

> The choice facing those who manage non-business organizations is not whether to market or not to market, for no organization can avoid marketing. The choice is whether to do it well or poorly, and on this necessity the case for organizational marketing is basically founded.[85]

6. Reversal is central to two final rhetorical devices that are common in both Kotler and Karl. The first of these is *humour*, which famously works by upending the audience's expectations.[86] Marx wrote an (unpublished) comic novel in the picaresque manner of Laurence Sterne and sarcasm was his middle name, as innumerable incandescent passages in his pyrotechnic pamphlets, philippics and newspaper articles bear witness. *The Eighteenth Brumaire of Louis Bonaparte* still drips with ironic invective more than one hundred and fifty years after its composition. It has even been suggested, in all seriousness, that the first 26 chapters of *Das Kapital* were written ironically, as a parodic comment on the theory and methods of economics.[87] Some cynics have said the same thing about Kotler's literary corpus, though this is to overlook his fondness for one-liners, wry anecdotes, endearing self-deprecation and, in some early volumes, heavy-handed humour of the funny-foreigners-honey-I'm-home variety, much of which would be unacceptable today:

> Only one Frenchman out of three brushes his teeth, and only one German out of five changes his shirt more often than once a week. Clearly, the markets for dental products and laundry detergents, respectively, are not as good as the size and incomes of the respective populations in these countries would indicate.[88]

> If a housekeeper is paid for domestic services, this is a market transaction; if she is one's wife, this is a non-market transaction.[89]

Irony also figures prominently, as in the fictional case of the Arno Shoe Company, which allows the author to indulge in all sorts of straight-faced, footwear-related wordplay, and the latter-day critique of one-line formulas flogged by get-rich-quick consultants, which is a bit rich coming from a master manufacturer of one-liners. In the main, however, Kotler relies on the back-slapping, boiler room bonhomie of the smile-and-a-shoeshine super-salesperson.[90]

> *How do you make love to a porcupine?*
> *Very carefully!* [91]

> Banks used to be open from nine to three and closed all weekend. Banks followed the 3–6–3 rule: borrow money at 3 percent, loan it out at 6 percent, and get to the golf course by 3 p.m.[92]

7. Set against their humorous asides, both Marx and Kotler are inclined to proceed by *negation*. That is to say, they typically articulate a position, only to show that it is incorrect or, more usually, contradictory. Such an approach, to be sure, is an integral aspect of dialectical materialism, Marx's adaptation of Hegel's idealist philosophical procedures (thesis/

antithesis/synthesis) to real world, materialist concerns (the class strug-gle).[93] However, it completely permeates his writing. Not only does he spend an inordinate amount of time explaining the error of his antago-nists' ways, most notably in *The Communist Manifesto, Contribution to the Critique of Hegel's Philosophy of Right*, and *Critique of the Gotha Programme*, but even his aforementioned fondness for anaphora and antimetabole is a micro-level manifestation of this macro-level manoeuvre:

> The more the worker produces, the less he has to consume; the more values he creates, the less value, the less dignity, he has; the better shaped his prod-uct, the more mis-shapen the worker; the more civilized the object, the more barbaric the worker; the more powerful the work, the more powerless the worker; the more intelligent the work, the more witless the worker, the more he becomes a slave of nature.[94]

Negation is equally integral to Kotler's corpus (consider the constella-tion of coinages with 'de', 'dis', 'un', 'anti' and 'counter' prefixes). In many ways, indeed, it is his signature rhetorical stratagem, inasmuch as he incessantly posits positions and then proceeds to refute them. These posi-tions, moreover, are often expressed negatively prior to his negation of the negation, as in this powerful antimetabolic anaphora:

> The ad cannot adapt the message to the particular buyer; the salesman can. The ad cannot go into much detail; the salesman can. The ad cannot close the sale; the salesman can. The ad cannot give the company any feedback; the salesman can. The ad may not be noticed; the salesman will be.[95]

In a similar vein, he repeatedly rails against mistaken beliefs about mar-keting, whether it be the general public's perception that marketing is exploitative (not so!), top management's conception that marketing is advertising (wrong again!), or academics' erroneous assumption that his broadened concept of marketing is adversely affecting the discipline (no way!). His most recent best-seller, *Ten Deadly Marketing Sins*, isn't so much a 'how to' as a 'how not to' book.[96] He is especially fond, furthermore, of rhetorical constructions of the it-seems-to-be-but-it-is-not-so variety. Consider, for example, the very first paragraph in the first edition of *Marketing Management*:

> Surely among the most difficult business decisions are those that have to do with marketing. The variables in a marketing problem do not generally exhibit the neat quantitative properties of many of the problems in production, accounting, or finance. . . . Marketing decisions must be made

in the context of insufficient information about processes that are dynamic, nonlinear, lagged, stochastic, interactive, and downright difficult. These characteristics could serve as an argument for intuitive marketing decision making. Yet to this author and to many colleagues and marketing executives they suggest quite the opposite: they suggest the need for *more* theory and analysis in marketing, not less.[97]

Clearly, Kotler's 'negative capability' owes much to his hypothesis-testing training in economics.[98] However, the marketing maestro's innate feel for dialectical-style negation is evinced by his emphasis on the *contradictions* that inhere in the opponent's position – in the fact, for example, that not-for-profit organizations already use marketing tools, though they don't use them effectively; in the fact that opponents of his position are engaged in the very activity they are attacking, such as the luckless David Luck, who was severely chastised on several occasions; and in the fact that Japan's triumph in the marketplace is based on the self-same ideas that US managers have failed to embrace. The Kotlerite marketing concept, to be exact.

Are You Now, or Have You Ever Been, a Kotlerist?

It is evident, then, that Kotler's oeuvre is indebted to, or rather draws indirect sustenance from, all manner of Marxian precepts. Like Marx's dialectical materialism, Kotler's exchange-based model of marketing (dialectical mercantilism, perhaps?) sucks everything in, leaves nothing out, and forges connections between ostensibly antithetical elements (profit and not-for-profit, practice and philosophy, universal and local, art and science). So much so, that Kamenka's apt description of the marxian project could just as easily be applied to the Kotlerian corpus: 'The outstanding thing about his career as a thinker was the powerful logical thrust lying at the center of his work, the way in which he expanded his views, assimilating the most diverse materials and remoulding them to suit his system and his purposes'.[99]

Now some of you, I suspect, might be tempted to challenge the foregoing comparisons and pick holes in my argument. Most educated people have been influenced by Karl Marx to some degree, whether they're aware of it or not. His concepts, like those of Freud, are part of the pedagogic furniture. Karl Marx may not have been a Marxist, as he once made perfectly clear, but everyone else is – Kotler included. This counter-argument, of course, is incontestable. As Manuel observes about Marx's theory of historical materialism:

> Viewed in retrospect, his tableau of world history has come to occupy a
> place alongside the Four Monarchies doctrine . . . and Concorcet's ten-stage
> outline of rational progress, as one of the three most influential frames
> within which Western man has attempted to encompass historical experi-
> ence. Of all Marx's theories, this historical schema has been the most
> enthralling; the Western mind has hardly begun to awaken from its narcotic
> effects.[100]

Likewise, some sceptics may be moved to challenge the specific
Marx–Kotler comparisons made in this chapter. Thus, for every biographical parallel, a counter-example could be cited (Marx was ignored in his
time, Kotler has been feted; Marx was a great committee man, Kotler has
avoided organizational entanglements). For every conceptual analogue, a
non-analogous issue can be identified (Marx wrote at length about suicide,
but not even the broadest interpreters of our field consider suicide a form
of consumer behaviour).[101] For every rhetorical equivalent, furthermore,
a contrasting stylistic quirk is clearly discernible (Marx rarely employs
alliteration, whereas Kotler is full of it and variations thereof, such as
acronyms and acrostics). For every plausible plus, in other words, an
implausible minus might be mobilized.

But to dismiss my comparisons as 'unproven' or 'absurd' or 'idiotic' or
whatever is once again to miss the point completely. The purpose of literary criticism is not to prove or disprove a point or come to some
irrefutable conclusion. Textual evidence can always be interpreted in
another way or tackled from an alternative theoretical perspective. When
it comes to literary criticism, there is no right or wrong, just greater or
lesser degrees of insight, inventiveness and, indeed, necessary idiocy.

Yet, regardless of your reaction to this admittedly extravagant comparison, there are four final things that our two superlative movers and
shakers share, above and beyond the biographical, the conceptual, the
rhetorical. Despite their ceaseless assertions of scientific detachment,
scholarly propriety and, on occasion, artisanal indifference, both thinkers
are extraordinarily *passionate* about their work, which they pursue with
unrelenting zeal. The sheer volume of their output is testimony to this irre-
pressibly evangelical ethos. As a result, both thinkers are extremely
persuasive. They truly believe in the credo they're promulgating, whether
it be revolutionary socialism or marketing orientation, and it is this belief
that imbues their writings with such plausibility, such potency, such
power. Both men, moreover, believe in exactly the same thing; namely, the
desirability, possibility and indeed inevitability of *progress*. True, their
ideas of what constitutes progress are very different, virtually antithetical.
But both firmly believe that progress is attainable, given sufficient will,
total commitment and fierce determination. As Kotler says: 'I operate on

the assumption that 'progress' is possible, even in the face of much contradictory evidence. I prefer to believe that human beings can improve
their condition by applying collective intelligence to solving shared
problems'.[102]

In this regard, of course, both Marx and Kotler can be dismissed as
out-and-out utopians, as true believers in and eloquent spokespersons for
an impossibly perfect world, a communist and consumerist *paradise*
respectively. Marx and Kotler, to be sure, might take exception to this
suggestion. The former frequently denounced utopianism (as derogatory
epithets go, 'utopia' is the 'myopia' of marxism) and the latter generally
avoids firm predictions about the shape of things to come (though Kotler,
like Marx, occasionally indulges in time-travelling thought experiments).
The fact of the matter, however, is that they *are* utopians. They *do* believe
in paradise and there's nothing wrong with that. As Frank and Fritzie
Manuel make clear, utopianism is a recurring and deep-seated feature of
human thought, a vitally necessary fiction.[103] Marketing is and always has
been utopian and our discipline is fortunate to be blessed with a
Passionate, Persuasive, Progressive Paradisian of Professor Philip Kotler's
stature.

Twenty years ago, Professor Kotler was awarded the inaugural A.M.A.
Distinguished Marketing Educator Award. On accepting the honour, he
sagely observed, in a paradisiacal passage that encapsulates many of his
thematic preoccupations and stylistic quirks:

> Marketing is not the art of finding clever ways to dispose of what you make.
> Marketing is the art of creating genuine customer value. Marketing is the art
> of helping your customers become better off. The marketer's watchwords
> are quality, service and value. Can you imagine what the world would be
> like if the marketing concept became a universal principle?[104]

Philip Kotler, perhaps more than anyone, has articulated this paradisiacal
possibility for us. While the details of his marketing vision may – indeed
should – be challenged, his visionary ability is unquestionable, unsurpassed and uncanny. The ultimate issue, then, is not whether Kotlerism is
a spectre or not a spectre, for the spectre of Kotlerism cannot be avoided.
The issue is whether it is a good spectre or a bad spectre and on this neces-
sity the case for Kotlerism is basically founded.

4

The Deconstruction of Shelby D. Hunt

Something there is that doesn't love a wall . . .
The work of hunters is another thing

Robert Frost[1]

As opening sentences go, 'Assume competition' is not simply first among
equals, it is first by a long shot, a distance, a light year or several. It is the
'Marley is dead' of marketing discourse. Compared to 'Assume competition', Ted Levitt's 'Every industry was once a growth industry' is, well,
somewhat wordy, leaden, pedestrian, prosaic. And, as for the spectral
apparition at the start of *Marketing Places*, it should be passed over in silence,
I fear. If the palm for academic marketing rhetoric were being awarded,
the author of 'Assume competition' would be on a short list of one.

The brilliance of 'Assume competition' has nothing to do with its
brevity or boldness, though it possesses both in abundance. Indeed, it is
akin to 'Eureka!' in its declamatory audacity. Its brilliance lies in what it
does *not* say, yet succeeds in saying all the same. What the sentence really
says is 'Assume rhetoric', because only a rhetorician of the first order
would begin a book with the two-word sentence 'Assume competition'.[2]

The brilliance doesn't end there, moreover. There is another twist in the
rhetorical tale. To whit, that the rhetorician responsible disavows his
rhetorical ability and dismisses the use of rhetorical ploys in marketing's
academic conversation.[3] Rhetoric, however, is all the more powerful when
it comes from someone who champions straight talking, who stands for
rigour and rectitude, who subscribes to the sacred scientific ideals of objectivity, truth and dispassion, who has no time for scholarly sophistry,
literary legerdemain, or weasel wordplay.

Plastics!

Our reticent rhetorician, of course, is none other than Shelby D. Hunt, the Jerry S. Rawls and P.W. Horn Professor of Marketing at Texas Tech University, Lubbock, TX. Esteemed author of several enormously influential books on marketing theory, SDH is one of the 250 most cited scholars in business and economics, the winner of three Harold H. Maynard Awards for articles published in *JM* – a record number – and the distinguished recipient of innumerable disciplinary laurels, encomia and accolades, including the Charles C. Slater Award, the Paul D. Converse Award, the 1987 AMS Outstanding Marketing Educator Award, the 1992 AMA Distinguished Marketing Educator Award and the 2002 Society for Marketing Advances Distinguished Scholar Award.

In truth, SDH's achievements are all the more remarkable given the academic disadvantages he has overcome. That is to say, whereas the other marketing literati in this book are based in elite institutions, with all the unspoken yet undoubted advantages that Harvard, Northwestern, Wharton and Columbia bestow, SDH hails from a less than stellar school (Texas Tech), earned his scholarly stripes on a middling doctoral program (Michigan State University), and unlike many of *Writing Marketing*'s illustrious line-up, actually knows what it's like to make cold-calls, do a deal, close the sale and fight alongside the footsoldiers in marketing's sweaty trenches. SDH sold plastics for four years before entering the sylvan groves of academe.[4]

It's a long way from selling plastics to the editorship of *JM*, much less multiple Maynard Award-winning performances.[5] But SDH's staggering scholarly achievements cannot be denied. So eminent is he, that as far back as 1982 SDH was voted second only to Wroe Alderson as the greatest marketing theorist of all time.[6] At that stage, moreover, he had only completed the first phase of his intellectual arc, which was largely devoted to demarking marketing's domain, assessing its 'scientific' credentials, and developing a classification of core marketing foci, the celebrated 'Three Dichotomies Model'.[7] Post 1982, SDH played a starring role in the 'paradigm wars' of the mid- to late-eighties (aka the 'realism versus relativism' controversy)[8] and, having roundly defeated all comers, thereafter turned his dextrous hands to theory-building, most notably the Resource-Advantage Theory of Competition (or RAT, as it is occasionally irreverently known).[9] No doubt there are many more outstanding academic achievements to come, but there is equally no doubt that if the 1982 survey were repeated today, SDH would be No. 1 with a bullet. With an RPG, come to think of it.

SDH, then, began as a taxonomist, turned into an epistemologist and eventually became a blue-chip marketing theorist. These cerebral shifts, nevertheless, can't disguise the fact that SDH is a penman nonpareil, a scholarly scribbler of unparalleled power and persuasiveness. True, SDH trained as a mechanical engineer; his writings are widely regarded as mechanistic at best and dry-as-dust at worst;[10] he presents himself as a hard-headed, no-nonsense, straight-talking spokesperson for marketing science, intellectual rectitude and anti-obscurantism ('I would rather be found wrong than obtuse'); and his academic brand image is as the scourge of sloppy thinking, an incumbent of the scholarly Supreme Court, who lays down the law on what is acceptable as marketing research and whose sentences are suffused with legal allusions ('evidentiary support', 'fiduciary agents', 'jury of peers', 'I plead guilty to the charge').

Actually, magisterial is the word that best describes SDH's literary style. The repeated use of rhetorical questions; the pro and con arguments; the careful cross-examination of opponents' unfailingly flimsy cases; the systematic enumeration of (1) points, (2) sub-points, (3) sub-sub-points etc.; and, above all, the superb summing-up statements that simultaneously dismiss objections, make the case for the prosecution, and leave the final decision in the capable hands of the men and women of the marketing jury, are mini masterpieces of scholarly advocacy:

> In his 'Theory of Social Initiative', Robert Bartels states, 'Society, not the business entrepreneur, is the basic undertaker of all activity.' [39, p.32] Is this analytic or synthetic? Would it pass or fail the empirical content criterion for lawlikeness? As previously illustrated, the key depends on how certain terms (such as *basic undertaker*) are defined and, unfortunately, Bartels provides no definitions. However, since innumerable 'basic activities' do seem to be undertaken by business entrepreneurs, *if* the statement is intended to be synthetic, it is probably false. Therefore, there would probably be a strong temptation to define the term *basic undertaker* in such a way that the truth content of the statement would be assured. Consequently, to the extent that the statement is synthetic, it is probably false. And to the extent that the statement is analytic, it will fail the empirical content criterion. In either case, the statement should not be considered lawlike.[11]

This textual persona, however, is precisely that, a textual persona. It is a creation, an artefact, an outcome of the author's literary ability. A written role, if you will. SDH conveys the impression of forensic fearlessness and Solomonic even-handedness through his books, articles and especially his manifold comments and rejoinders on philosophical matters.[12] In this regard, it is important to appreciate that dry-as-dust is itself a literary style, a styleless style, a style that is perfect for those who want to present themselves as stolid scientists, as serious thinkers, as judiciously judicial weighers of the evidence. It implies that the author isn't glib, garrulous or given to unnecessary self-glorification. Crash, bang, wallop may be right for Theodore Levitt, since it says in effect 'I'm an iconoclast, I am', but it isn't right for those who wrap themselves in the mantle of science, as SDH has done throughout his dazzling academic career.

That said, just because someone claims to be a scientist, or a spokesperson for marketing science, or, as Blair and Zinkhan put it, 'teach . . . Sales Management in a white lab coat rather than white shoes and belt',[13] doesn't mean that they are accredited. Karl Marx claimed to be a scientist, as we have seen, as did Sigmund Freud, as did many modernist poets, artists and critics, such as T.S. Eliot, Ezra Pound, Wassily Kandinsky and Northrop Frye, and indeed so many postmodernists, who ally their inchoate outpourings to Gödel's uncertainty theorem, quantum mechanics, complexity theory or whatever.[14]

Domain Man

Now, drawing a line between science and non-science is extremely difficult, well-nigh impossible, as SDH cogently explains.[15] Yet, regardless of whether his scholarly corpus qualifies as science when set against the demarcation criteria that he himself sets out – and the jury's undecided[16] – it is my contention that his academic eminence is as much due to his literary ability as his scientific acumen. More so, in actual fact. It is surely no accident that many of the criticisms of RAT centre on its prosodic underpinnings ('too literary . . . much like a folk narrative . . . a dictionary of language without sentences')[17] and it is no accident that, from the very start of his academic career, SDH has pronounced on literary matters ('Many authors preface their theoretical structures with such statements as "toward a theory of marketing . . ." or "foundations for a theory of . . ."').[18]

However, perhaps the most obvious way in which SDH betrays his literary bent is in periodic purplish passages, such as the one cited at the start of this chapter.[19] Actually, 'Assume competition' is fairly mild compared to some of the theorist's textual eruptions. True, these volcanic utterances tend to come at the end of his often prosaic papers. They build and build and suddenly blow their top, so to speak. But these bombast bombardments, when they appear, are brilliant to behold. Their impact, indeed, is all the more powerful because of the coagulated passages that precede them. A kind of figure/ground effect is in operation, whereby the bland, boilerplate background throws the bright figures of speech into sharp rhetorical relief:

The prime directive for scholarly research in marketing is the same as for all sciences: *to seek knowledge*. The knowledge must be intersubjectively certifiable and capable of describing, explaining and predicting phenomena. Sometimes the knowledge will assist marketing managers in making decisions. Other times the knowledge will guide legislators in drafting laws to regulate marketing activities. At still other times the knowledge may assist the general public in understanding the functions that marketing activities provide society. Finally, at the risk of 'waxing philosophical', the knowledge may simply assist marketing scholars in *knowing*, a not inconsequential objective.[20]

Interestingly, the incandescent dynamics of SDH's colourful prose – from deepest purple to lightest lilac – accord exactly with the advice of Gerald Graff, a leading commentator on literary composition.[21] The key to successful scholarly communication, he contends, is a combination of exhaustive exegesis and snappy sound bites. SDH is not only a master of both, he is even better yet, inasmuch as his climactic statements often contain what crime novelist Elizabeth George calls, 'the bang within the bang',[22] an extra rhetorical twist that lifts the heightened excitement to an even higher level:

The edifice of general equilibrium theory, with its base of perfect competition theory, is elegant, mathematically formalized, and aesthetically pleasing. It is deeply embedded within a discipline that is large and influential, especially when compared with marketing. Neoclassical economics has enormous sunk costs in perfect competition. Indeed, all evidence of the theoretical, predictive, explanatory, and normative deficiencies of the set of beliefs that has perfect competition at its core has always been summarily dismissed. Perfect competition is unshakable, immutable, and impregnable. Nothing can be done.

Then again, Ptolemaic astronomy had all the preceding going for it plus the imprimatur of the Church. Hmm . . .[23]

In addition to occasional outbreaks of textual thermo-luminescence, our prodigious theorist's ordinarily tenebrous prose glimmers with inklings of the literary light beneath his scientistic bushel. His penchant for resonant epigraphs (as many as three in a single article); his fondness for fulsome footnotes (SDH is the David Foster Wallace of marketing research); his lucubratious lapses into alliteration, abbreviation, assonance, acronyms and analogous literary licks ('ZH', 'EF', 'KMV', 'imperfectly imitable', 'demean and damage', 'naïve, naughty and nefarious'); his use of calculated colloquialisms, compacted contractions and first person pronouns ('Hmm', 'Let's get started', 'I, for one, cannot'); and his ready recourse to high-impact, stop-right-there, one- or two-word sentences ('Why?', 'No.', 'Plenty.', 'Beg pardon?', 'Fair enough', 'Firms differ.'), all bespeak someone who is as far from a literary illiterate as it is possible to be:

> The realism I advocate defends only human reason, its use in academic discourse, its application to evidence, and its potential for helping us understand the world we inhabit. The twin pillars of the university, at least as a Western societal institution, are the tolerance of alternative views and the conviction that all views must be subjected to an evaluation that is civilly reasoned. Therefore, though all views merit civil assessment, not all views are meritorious when civilly assessed. So it is with the view labeled 'relativism/constructionism.'[24]

The above, to be sure, are liable to be found in the oeuvres of many prolific professors, provided one looks hard enough. In SDH's case, however, they are not only found in unusual abundance, but clearly mean a great deal to the author. His carefully-chosen epigraphs, for example, are frequently referred to, both within the body of the article concerned and in the end-of-chapter questions that pepper his textbooks. Indeed, on discovering that prefatory quotes are actually called 'epigraphs', not 'headnotes', he changed every single reference to the term between the third and fourth editions of his bulky volume on marketing philosophy.[25]

Perfectionist perhaps, obsessive undoubtedly, but this trait indicates that words are *extremely important* to SDH. He often refers to etymological matters (the linguistic roots of 'science', 'philosophy', 'skepticism', 'metaphor'); he reflects sagely on synonyms, tautologies and such ('Incommensurability ... is used as a synonym for "different"', 'Tautologies are true by linguistic convention', 'at best a non sequitur and at worst an oxymoron'), he is ready, willing and able to concoct neologisms, though these are fairly rare ('maloglops', 'contra-resource', 'heterodoxical', 'ism-ism'); and, as if that weren't enough, he even draws ostentatious attention to alternative spellings of individual words:

> (5) *Constructionism* (alternatively spelled 'constructivism') is the same thing as *reality relativism*.[26]

> Unless it is a direct quote, I adopt what appears to be becoming the dominant convention in the literature that the plural of competence is *competences*, rather than *competencies*.[27]

What is more, he constantly edits and tweaks his prose. Chapter titles are changed, article titles are altered, more suitable words are substituted between editions and, not to be outdone, his General Theory of Competition got renamed on several occasions (it started as Competitive Advantage Theory and evolved into Resource Advantage Theory).[28] Admittedly, his eye for potential acronymic embarrassment means that he refers to the latter as R-A theory, rather than RAT. And CAT, when it was extant, was spelt out in full. This pernicketiness, nevertheless, illustrates that SDH is someone who chooses words very carefully and expects others to do likewise:

> Changing the first part of the first sentence in the definition to read: 'marketing research is the function *within the firm* that links the consumer, . . . ' would succinctly accomplish this objective.[29]

> One of the problems with the entire demarcation issue in science is the word 'demarcation' itself. This unfortunate choice of words (by Popper) tends to suggest (connote) that an *unequivocal* judgment can be made in all cases using a single, simple criterion (like 'falsifiability').[30]

Words not only mean a lot to SDH, the meaning of words means a lot to SDH. It is fair to say that semantic matters are central to this marketing magus's conceptual cosmology. Much space is devoted to what many might mistakenly assume are trivial textual matters and unnecessarily subtle shades of linguistic meaning ('note the pejorative tone to the labels "monopolistic" and "oligopolistic"'). The denotation and connotation, the overtones and undertones, the implications and explications, the high redefinition and low redefinition of individual words, such as 'truth', 'objectivity', 'reason', 'realism', 'power' and 'competition', comprise the core of his corpus, the key to his academic achievements, the battleground where he bests his intellectual adversaries:

> To see this, compare the meaning of 'utopian goal' with that of 'visionary goal.' Both are denotative synonyms (Morehead, 1985), implying an aim that is probably unrealizable, yet 'utopian' connotes images such as 'impractical', 'hopeless', 'foolish', or 'quixotic' whereas 'visionary' connotes 'lofty', 'exalted', or 'highly desirable'.[31]

So attuned is SDH to semantic considerations, that he sometimes expounds on the 'strength' or 'weight' of words ('"reject" is probably much too strong a term to be used to describe the scientific realist position'). Their precise meaning, apparently, isn't enough for him. Their specific gravity also has to be taken into consideration. SDH is no less alert to rhetorical and metaphorical matters.[32] He has commented at length on rhetoricians' siren-like ability to befuddle innocent seekers after truth, reason and all the rest, though the following arrestingly written excerpt suggests that it takes a scholarly siren to know one:

> Academic integrity is worth safeguarding. Words have meaning. Rhetoric has consequences. Communities of academic researchers have fiduciary responsibilities to their colleagues, to other academics, to students, and to society at large. The price paid for historically false rhetoric is the potential destruction of trust. . . . This price, I suggest, is too high – it is also a price that it is unnecessary to pay.[33]

What is more, he has published one of the most insightful papers on marketing metaphors, a paper that goes beyond the standard banalities of 'metaphors are good, we need more of them', to a considered assessment of useful and useless metaphorical contributions, as well as their theoretical potential.[34] Interestingly, SDH rarely employs metaphorical devices in his own prose – he tends to stick to anthropomorphic similes – and when he does their non-literal status is usually marked by quotation marks ('Industry is the "tail" of competition; the firm is the "dog"'). The reason for this is quite simple: metaphors aren't just literary flourishes in themselves, they signal that the author is a literary type, something that our 24-carat marketing scientist is hesitant to reveal. Metaphors work by connotation, insofar as something stands for something else, but using metaphors connotes something too: the writer's metaphorical acumen. Only acute literary sensibilities are sensitive to such acute literary sensibilities.

In fairness, SDH sometimes wears his literary heart on his scientific sleeve. He alludes to the work of Lewis Carroll, H.G. Wells, Hans Christian Andersen, W.B. Yeats and William Shakespeare, among others. He refers to George Orwell as well. In 1984, at the height of the 'realism versus relativism' contretemps, our incognito artiste concluded a shattering scholarly salvo with the deathless words, 'For marketing science to turn toward relativism in the year 1984 would be Orwellian irony incarnate'.[35] Five years later, he elaborated on his characteristically combative climax, contending that Orwell's dystopian vision brilliantly anticipated the scholarly shenanigans and sheer sophistry of social constructionists, renegade relativists and marketing malcontents:

> The Orwellian society of Big Brother found it imperative to adopt a relativist perspective on reality in order to maintain control of its citizens through 'doublethink', which was the practice of holding 'two contradictory beliefs in one's mind simultaneously, and accepting both of them' (Orwell 1949,

p. 215). Doublethink was necessary 'to deny the existence of objective reality and all the while to take account of the reality one desires' (p. 216). Thus, it is remarkably similar to the incoherence, unintelligibility, and sophistry found in today's relativism.[36]

This passage perfectly illustrates SDH's literary leanings, as does his astute use of Robert Frost's pellucid poem, 'Mending Wall', to trump marketing's ace aesthete, Morris Holbrook.[37] They also reveal his unerring flair for the apt quotation. Without doubt, one of SDH's greatest gifts is his capacity to pick the perfect excerpt, the citation that best supports his case or subverts a critic. The mistake that many of his intellectual antagonists make is that they think they're dealing with a philosopher, whereas they're actually fighting a philologist, someone with a way with words and a way with the words of others with a way with words:

> As Durant eloquently puts it: 'The glory that had been Greece faded now in the dawn of the Roman sun; and the grandeur that was Rome was the pomp of power rather than the light of thought. Then that grandeur decayed, that little light almost went out. For a thousand years darkness brooded over the face of Europe. All the world awaited the resurrection of philosophy.'[38]

There's more to it than that, of course, since scintillating cites add sparkle to otherwise pedestrian prose (which is unavoidable when considering theoretical concerns), their contents can be denied or disowned if a challenge arises (since one was simply quoting, not expressing a personal opinion) and they can say what the author can't say for fear of reader disapprobation (such as the unfortunate syllogism, taken from Carnap, about blacks imbibing scotch whisky).[39] While it would be incorrect, and indeed crass, to intimate that SDH's texts are mere tissues of quotes – the construction of an argument from the words of others is a rare skill, as is the seemingly simple act of assembling, assessing and arranging the raw material – there's no doubt that the superlative scholar's philosophical fortress is built on prefabricated textual foundations. He is, in A.S. Byatt's cogent encapsulation of F.R. Leavis, 'a quoter of genius'.[40]

Above and beyond his eye for the killer quote, there's a meta-literary level to SDH's scholarly discourse. He doesn't confine himself to matters of cerebral substance, but is happy to expatiate on the exquisite literary styles of leading luminaries (like Larry Laudan, Michael Porter and Sir Francis Bacon) and the execrable writing endeavours of others (Wroe Alderson, J.M. Keynes, Ludwig Wittgenstein). What's more, he considers himself something of an expert on aesthetic matters, as his comments on Heidegger's 'bad' poetry attest, and he's not reluctant to make mock of the maladroit, the literally afflicted (in *Modern Marketing Theory*, he holds up lengthy passages by Francis Bradley, and other idealist philosophers, for the reader to ridicule).[41]

SDH also has a critic's characteristically colophonic obsession with the number of pages, illustrations and editions of the text he's explicating ('His 500-page 1961 book – having not a single differential equation or geometrical representation'). He frequently comments on the possibility of getting published in top-tier academic organs ('The results . . . would in general not be publishable in journals like the *Journal of Marketing* or the *Journal of Marketing Research*'), on the inordinate length of his lists of references ('Even for an academic book, approximately six hundred references are a lot'), on the difficulties facing readers, and publishers, of his words of wisdom ('I ask readers' indulgence for the extensive review of traditions'), and on the minutiae of academic article submissions, revisions, acceptances and so on ('Essentially, the process of evaluating manuscripts for a scholarly journal involves answering three questions').

In classic metaleptic fashion, he's quite prepared to 'step outside' the text and address his readership ('Try it!', 'By now most readers are probably thoroughly confused', 'I invite the reader to go through Table 1 line by line'). He's partial to reflexive phraseology ('perfect competition is perfect', 'marketing marketing to non-marketers', 'what is "strong" about the "strong" thesis?'). He's even inclined to quote others quoting himself. Thus he cites Hodgson's statement that there's much more work to be done on RAT, itself an excerpt from SDH (and an implicit endorsement to boot, since, hey, a leading economic historian said it!).[42]

Oh No, PoMo

All things considered, SDH's modus operandi is reminiscent of Watkins' much-quoted quote about postmodernism: 'something that seems to entail buildings constructed of Lego from designs commissioned by the Mayor of Toytown and novels about novelists experiencing difficulty writing novels'.[43] Our prodigious professor, admittedly, might contest this contention. He has no time whatsoever for philosophers of a postmodern persuasion and, despite his oft-stated adherence to the genteel norms of civilized scholarly discussion, is quite prepared to denounce them as 'epistobabblers', 'dogmatists', 'obscurantists', 'obfuscators', 'nihilists' and every conceivable combination thereof. Yet SDH is closer to the 'postmodernist epistobabblers' than he lets on. Aside from their somewhat similar scholarly worldview – antipathy to excessive mathematization, rejection of base managerialism, fondness for qualitative research methods (such as historical analysis), interest in figurative language, metaphor, rhetoric and 'unpacking' the arguments of others – the look, tone and sheer cite-heavy literary character of SDH's singularly stylish articles are more akin to the preoccupations of postmodern marketers than the bullet-pointed, ball-busting, bottom-line orientated ethos of the marketing mainstream.

The postmodern connection doesn't stop at surface sheen, similar concerns and striking turns of phrase, however. SDH's corpus contains all the characteristic features of postmodernism and then some. There are, I grant you, almost as many versions of postmodernism as there are postmodernists, a point SDH appositely makes about realism (and quantum mechanics). But, for the purposes of the present chapter, we will focus on five key features: *fragmentation, de-differentiation, retrospection, hyperreality* and *pastiche*.[44] All are evident in our poetic champion's scholarly compositions.

Fragmentation refers to the seeming disintegration of former certitudes – geo-political stability, guaranteed employment, economic growth, reliable knowledge, social stratification, the unified self, mass media, mass production, mass marketing and so on – and the relentless proliferation of choice, possibilities, options, alternatives, worldviews, selves, identities, products, competitors, television channels, advertising opportunities, management consultancy fads, and so forth. At first blush, such freneticism seems a world away from SDH, who has been nothing if not consistent throughout his academic career. He has focused on a fairly narrow range of topics pertaining to marketing's philosophical underpinnings and has held fast to his 'unfashionable' opinions despite the vilification of opponents, lamentations of learned colleagues and occasional cries of 'uncle' from anguished reviewers.[45] What's more, he places enormous store by consistency, since its absence is a sure-fire signifier of sophistry, sharp practice, sleight of hand ('One test for the presence of sophistry is whether people behave consistently with their stated beliefs').[46]

Yet, for all its consistency of content, the form of SDH's prose is fantastically fragmented, unbelievably so. His writing is riddled with enumerations, abbreviations, recapitulations, digressions, quotation marks, inverted commas, question marks, parenthetical statements, parenthesised parenthetical statements and dash delimited asides. These, in turn, are interspersed with very heavy scholarly citation, which further contributes to the congeries of commas, bevy of brackets, plethora of publication dates and profusion of page numbers:

> Why the strong relationships between economic freedom, productivity, and economic growth? Gwartney, Lawson and Block (1996) cite the works of

> Kirzner (1973) – see Section 2.2 – and North (1990) – see Sections 4.2 and
> 9.2.1 – and argue . . . [181-word quote follows]. . . . In conclusion, the works
> of Gwartney, Lawson, and Block (1996) and Gwartney and Lawson (1997)
> on economic freedom support R-A theory's emphasis on packages of insti-
> tutions for promoting vigorous competition and economic growth. Indeed,
> R-A theory – alone among extant theories of competition – can explain their
> findings: formal institutions promoting economic freedom promote R-A
> competition, which, in turn, promotes efficiency, effectiveness, and the inno-
> vations that drive economic growth.[47]

He over-punctuates, what is more, often adding unnecessary commas, a
condition Lynne Truss calls 'commaphilia'.[48] He is particularly partial to
conjunctions, which may bespeak logic and inevitability but, when used
in sentence after sentence, seriously disrupt the flow of his argument:

> First, R-A theory specifically recognizes that institutions can be independ-
> ent variables in analyses of competition. That is, societal institutions
> influence the process of competition (see Figure 6.1). Therefore, R-A theory
> can explain how societal institutions that promote trust contribute to wealth
> creation (see Section 9.3.3).
>
> Second, both economic sociology and R-A theory agree that embedded
> social relations constitute a resource only contingently. Indeed, for R-A
> theory, *all* entities constitute a resource only contingently. Again, recall that
> R-A theory views resources as the tangible and intangible entities available
> to the firm that enable it to produce efficiently and/or effectively a market
> offering that has value to some market segment(s). Thus, for example, a
> strategic alliance between two firms can be a resource for both, yet it is
> *owned* by neither.[49]

His prose also exhibits a curious, quasi-catechismal call-and-response quality, inasmuch as a rhetorical question is often followed by a reply that
restates part of the question ('how do formal language systems differ from
natural languages? Formal language systems differ from natural languages
in that they . . .'). Of late, furthermore, he has adopted a quirky stylistic tic,
whereby a statement and its (parenthesized) opposite are included in the
same sentence, thereby saying two antonymical things at once:

> Specifically, when firms have a comparative advantage (or disadvantage) in
> resources, they will occupy marketplace positions of competitive advantage
> (or disadvantage), as shown in Figure 6.1, and further explicated in the nine
> marketplace positions in Figure 6.2. Marketplace positions of competitive
> advantage (or disadvantage) then result in superior (or inferior) financial
> performance.[50]

As if that weren't enough, SDH is enamoured, shall we say, with *emphasis*. Every other sentence contains an italicized word. Or *several*. He *stresses* his point, just to *make sure* readers *get it*. He is not reluctant to use CAPITAL LETTERS in order to draw attention to SOMETHING PARTICULARLY IMPORTANT. He also interlards his argument with emphatic expressions and qualifiers ('note that', 'definitely not', 'most assuredly', 'most emphatically', 'most assuredly and emphatically', 'to say the very least', 'what is done, though regrettable, is done', 'nothing could be further from the truth', etc.).[51]

The upshot of this blizzard of brackets, swarm of commas and what can only be described as *stress fractures*, is a literary style that is rugged at best and ragged at worst. One only has to read SDH's articles aloud to realize just how jarring, jumpy, jerky and jagged they are:

> Firms do indeed take actions; they do indeed take note of financial indicators; and they do indeed make causal attributions between actions and indicators. But even if – and this is a big if – managers have good reason to claim to know that actions previously taken have led (or will lead) to increases in financial performance, they cannot know (or warrentedly claim to know) that some alternative action or set of actions (identified or not identified) would not have produced (or will not produce) even higher returns. Therefore, *superior* financial performance, not maximum performance, better describes the firm's primary objective.[52]

His writing, in short, has a spasmodic, syncopated, somewhat stumbling quality, a quality that is reinforced by his extreme lexical fluctuation, which alternates unevenly between learned cogitation and lamentable colloquialism ('goons', 'bum rap', 'loaded dice', 'kick in', 'no contest', 'slippery slope', 'confusion reigns', 'time immemorial', 'first among equals', 'wither on the vine', 'changing horses in midstream', 'throwing out the baby with the bathwater', 'downright shameful', 'just plain squandered', 'or just plain inappropriate'). The latter are particularly incongruous, not to say unsettling, since SDH's demotic discourse is so obviously clichéd that it's hard to decide whether this is a high-brow trying, and failing, to pass himself off as a man of the people, or a literary genius who is deliberately deploying low-brow banalities for insidious rhetorical effect.

The latter, I suspect, is closer to the mark, inasmuch as it's important to appreciate that a jerky, juddering, stilted, stammering style isn't necessarily a bad thing. On the contrary, the Huntian stutter is ideally suited to the basic message he's endeavouring to convey. Namely, *trust me*; I'm telling the truth about marketing thought; this is the real deal, straight from the horse's mouth; I may be somewhat inarticulate and prone to hokum, but I've got evidence to support my case. Too ostentatious a literary style is inappropriate for his target audience (serious academics by and large) who don't take kindly to the 'flash Harry', 'look ma, no verbs', chuck-another-adjective-on-the-barbie school of writing. SDH's stylistic stammering, his literary epilepsy, is a persuasive prosodic pose. It's his greatest strength. It carries everyman-ish connotations. SDH is the James Stewart of marketing scholarship. He comes across as an earnest, honest and diligent individual, whose stuttering utterances can be relied upon. Moreover, like *Mr Smith Goes to Washington*[53] his scholarly conscience forces him to fight, and fight fairly, the follies, sophistries and iniquities of fellow academics who have fallen from the path of truth, justice and the American marketing way.

Comma Chameleon

De-Differentiation is the blurring of formerly clear-cut entities, such as high and low culture, science and religion, education and training, politics and showbusiness, bourgeois and bohemian, philosophy and literature, art and commerce, etc. It is a postmodern characteristic that is particularly strongly marked in the marketing sphere, where recent years have witnessed the melding of, among others, producer and consumer, competitor and supplier, advertisement and editorial, and haute couture and street fashion, as well as the collapse of seemingly sacrosanct product-market categories (for example, supermarkets selling cars, bookstores with coffee bars and museum shops in shopping malls).[54]

Once again, this PoMo propensity appears inimical to SDH, who is not only regarded as a scholarly slicer and dicer, but someone whose slice-o-matic is set on extra, extra thin.[55] His corpus is replete with fine distinctions, carefully drawn. Thus he distinguishes between 'perfect' and '*perfect*', 'truth' and 'TRUTH', 'label' and 'epithet', 'procedures' and 'techniques', 'objectivity' and 'objectivism', 'market research' and 'marketing research', 'rare resources' and 'scarce resources', 'rival theories' and 'replacement theories', 'theory free' and 'theory neutral', 'synthetic theory' and 'composite theory', 'a general theory' and 'the general theory', 'general theory in marketing' and 'general theory of marketing', 'positive theory with normative implications' and 'normative theory grounded in positive assumptions' and, many, many more. He even ruminates on the meanings of 'meaning', our understanding of 'understanding' and what we see in 'see'.

Indeed, one suspects that if he were ever accused of hair-splitting – perish the thought – SDH would respond by (a) noting the long-standing difference between hair-splitting and hair-slicing; (b) convincingly demonstrating that he falls into the latter category; (c) inferring therefore that he is not and never has been a hair-splitter; and (d) regrettably concluding that his accusers fail to grasp the salient subtleties of tonsorial thought, which renders their arguments both incoherent and irrelevant, and leads inexorably to irrationalism, nihilism, comb-overs and the mullet.

Closer examination, however, reveals that SDH is a de-differentiator extraordinary. It is noteworthy, for example, that he deals directly with several of the disciplinary issues that are deemed emblematic of postmodern de-differentiation: strategic alliances, relationship marketing, companies that cooperate to compete, and the increasingly indistinct distinctions between distribution channel members. He established his academic reputation by integrating the 'nature' and 'scope' of marketing debates, which had previously been considered separately. His stated philosophical position, scientific realism, is a bespoke blend of several strands of realism, an especially fragmented philosophy of science, and his 'general theory of competition' is equally eclectic, a synthesis (but not a composite) of eleven separate research traditions.

More generally, he often denounces the 'false dichotomy' between marketing theory and marketing practice ('the notion that *theoretical* and *practical* are at opposite ends of a continuum is nonsense'); makes a case for classifications that are blurred rather than clear-cut ('*Most, if not all, genuine and useful categorizational schemata have borderline cases*'); and not only acknowledges the benefits of intellectual ambivalence ('One characteristic of the scientifically immature mind is to be uncomfortable in the presence of uncertainty'), but also treats 'causal ambiguity' as an important organizational resource that can help sustain competitive advantage in the marketplace ('sources of causal ambiguity . . . can create great uncertainty and thus render ineffective attempts to neutralize a competitor's comparative advantage').

Thus, far from being the authoritarian absolutist of legend, SDH is admirably ambivalent at times. So much so, that he has latterly been criticized for 'semantic confusion', 'vague constructs' and 'a loose argumentation style'.[56] These are not the kind of accusations that should be levelled at someone who adroitly differentiates between 'saying different things' and 'saying things differently' and who probably regards Bill Clinton's famous comments on 'is' as unforgivably imprecise. Be that as it may, anyone who has been pilloried for both absolutism and ambiguity is clearly a de-differentiator of outstanding ability.

When all is said and done, the academic achievement for which SDH is best known and most lauded, and for which he won two Maynard awards, is the melding of marketing and philosophy. *Modern Marketing Theory* is a tour de force of disciplinary de-differentiation. As he explains in a recent retrospective on his exemplary career:

[I]n the summer of 1973 I began working on a monograph with the aim of integrating the philosophy of science with marketing theory and research. The book was not to be on the philosophy of science, or about it, but rather to use philosophy of science to illuminate issues in marketing theory. . . . I adopted an eclectic blend of logical empiricism and realism, which I referred to as 'contemporary empiricism.' Two years' labor resulted in 'The Nature and Scope of Marketing' (Hunt, 1976b) and the first edition of *Marketing Theory* (Hunt, 1976a).[57]

Stylistically too SDH is a de-differentiator de luxe. A conflation inclination is apparent throughout his oeuvre. The penchant for acronymic abbreviations (C-S-S, HST, N-H-I, *P&P*); the overlapping Hemingwayesque sentences, previously noted ('what is the scope of marketing? The scope of marketing is unquestionably broad'); the incessant use of conjunctions in the titles of his articles (the combinatorial 'and' much more so than the divisive 'or'); and, not least, his high-brow hybrid of marketing speak and philosophical discourse, combine to create a singular literary style that is simultaneously scintillating and sibylline ('retreating into purposely encapsulated, purportedly incommensurate, semantical cocoons', 'In ethical theory terms, deontological considerations constrain teleological considerations'). It's perfectly postmodern, in point of fact.

Another way in which SDH successfully segues between seemingly sacrosanct categories is in his command of connotation. Part of his ability to persuade third parties – marketing academics unversed in the profound philosophical choices facing them – is due to the semantic overtones of the positions he posits. Although 'realism', 'truth', 'trust', 'reason' and so forth are quasi-technical terms within philosophy and, accordingly, subject to much debate and disputation, they also carry everyday meanings, meanings that any 'reasonable person' is sure to be sympathetic towards. They are what Whyte terms 'hooray words' – ideas or notions that almost everyone agrees with.[58] They are the 'peace', 'equality', 'tolerance', 'democracy' and 'mom's apple pie' of epistemology. Neutrals, undecideds and those who prefer empirical action to philosophical talk are more inclined, *ceteris paribus*, to cheer for hooray words and jeer at 'boo words' such as relativism, subjectivism or antirealism, to say nothing of closely-related (according to SDH) scholarly stances like 'nihilism', 'solipsism', 'irrationalism' and, naturally, 'postmodernist epistobabble'.[59]

You Must Remember This

Retrospection, for many, is the most characteristic feature of postmodernism and few would deny that it is an integral part of postmodern marketing. The astonishing 'nostalgia boom' of recent years bears witness to this retrospective propensity. So popular is retromarketing these days, that consumers must be getting nostalgic for the good old days before retro goods and services were all around, the days when eight out of ten ads claimed that eight out of ten consumers preferred their product and Brand X was enjoying its maximum market share.[60]

SDH is marketing's pre-eminent postmodern historian, though that hardly counts as a scholarly accolade, since the field is less than crowded. Marketing history, admittedly, is a healthy sub-discipline, with its own associations, conferences and analogous academic paraphernalia. However, most of its exponents are devotees of traditional historical methods, where facts are facts and the archive is all.[61] Although SDH has links to marketing's historical establishment (Stanley Hollander, the doyen of marketing history, was on his PhD dissertation committee), he is not part of it primarily because his swashbuckling, storytelling style is regarded as retrograde by the historical mainstream. This is nowhere better illustrated than in his insouciant contribution to Hollander's *Festschrift*, where he employed the Product Life Cycle to explain the rise and fall of the functionalist approach to marketing thought, which dominated our field prior to 1960.[62] Albeit much-loved by postmodernists, cyclical models of change are anathema to modern marketing historians, since they hark back to Arnold Toynbee, Oswald Spengler, Karl Marx and 'impositional' modes of historical explanation.[63]

Now, 'proper' marketing historians may turn up their noses at SDH's retrospective ruminations, but his corpus is replete with historical analyses, broadly defined. The bulk of his work, in actual fact, consists of summaries (and critiques) of traditions of thought, whether it be marketing's hoary art or science debate, the history of Western philosophy from Plato to post-relativism, or the eleven venerable schools of (predominantly) economic scholarship that undergird CAT, RAT and GTC. SDH, similarly, often sermonizes on the need for an historical approach to marketing research. He is not averse to dismissing others' assertions as 'historically inaccurate', 'ahistorical', 'unhistorical', 'historically false', 'uninformed by history', etc. And, it is fair to say that his tough-love approach to marketing's 'crisis literature', the rebarbative philosophical debates of the mid-1980s, rested on the relativists' basic lack of historical knowledge, particularly their patent ignorance of the antecedents of logical positivism:

> The crisis literature continues in marketing. The examples discussed in this
> article show at least some progress is being made toward meaningful eval-
> uation of the philosophical foundations of marketing inquiry. Unfortunately,
> however, although these articles push us one step forward, they then take
> two leaps backward. There is much to criticize about the current status of
> marketing inquiry. But until the crisis literature adopts a more historically
> informed, factually accurate, carefully reasoned approach, significant
> progress in addressing substantive issues will be thwarted.[64]

Steeped in history though he is, SDH's historical method is never made
fully explicit. He rarely cites marketing historians, much less history's
methodologists, and his basic guiding principle appears to be little more
than 'remain true to the integrity of the past'.[65] It is, nevertheless, possible to extract the great man's method and that method revolves around
great men. Hunt's history is curiously old-fashioned, a stirring chronicle
of scholarly dynasties and pretenders to the throne, their mighty battles
and internecine conflicts, their rampaging rise and hubristic fall. It's
fantastic stuff. It's pure Walter Scott – *Ivanhoe* for intellectuals – or Gibbon-
oid at least. It's very much in keeping with the storytelling propensity in
postmodern history, such as that espoused by Hayden White and
Dominick LaCapra:[66]

> The firestorm of German idealism swept through the Western philosophi-
> cal world and completely dominated it from 1850 to 1900. Even that bastion
> of empiricism, the British Isles, fell under the idealistic onslaught. The
> empiricism of Galileo, Bacon, Locke, Hume, Mill, and Newton was consid-
> ered so much rubbish to be swept from the idealist house of intellect.[67]

It's also somewhat Whiggish – this led to that and that led to the other,
which eventually led to us – not to say downright teleological ('deter-
ministic theory is an ideal toward which marketing is moving in a
natural fashion'). CAT, for example, is presented as the putative consummation of strategic marketing theory ('Our central thesis is that the
strategy dialogue . . . is evolving toward a new theory of competition').
Scientific realism is regarded as 'the next most reasonable step for philosophy of science' after logical positivism and logical empiricism, and
a consequence of the relativist debacle to boot ('After the repudiation of
Kuhnian relativism in the 1970s, the philosophy of science turned
sharply toward a *realist* orientation'). Likewise, Lakatos's Methodology
of Scientific Research Programmes is portrayed as a post-relativistic
response to the lunatic ululations of Kuhn and the like, which would
surely come as a surprise to Lakatos (if he were around to appreciate it)
who positioned his construct as a compromise between Popper and

Kuhn (the concepts were contemporaneous, not sequential, as Fuller artfully shows).[68]

As if the stupendous sweep of SDH's just-so stories were not enough, an anachronistic vocabulary perfectly complements our celebrated scholar's chronicles of philosophical derring-do. It is hard not to read SDH without being struck by the fustiness of the language – 'admonish', 'stricture', 'thwart', 'proffer', 'assuage', 'chastise', 'portend', 'trammel', 'aplenty', 'reprobate', 'abrogate', 'promulgate', 'adumbrate', 'vitiate', 'sedulous', 'copula', 'desideratum', 'explanandum', 'appellation', 'abjure', 'alas' and – get this – 'thusly'. It's not so much Macauley-lite as translated from the Latin. At one point in a twenty-first century publication he actually nays (as in 'the right to expect, nay insist, that our assertions'), a locution guaranteed to give gentle readers an attack of the vapours or instigate a search for one's discarded doublet and hose. It is the codpiece of scholarship. The hey-nonny-nonny of academic discourse. The marketing equivalent of a newly-opened ye olde curiosity shoppe.[69] In fairness, SDH often interjects calculated colloquialisms and demi-demotic expressions but, idiomatic slumming aside, his scholarly patois is patinated to the point of implausibility ('put forth', 'presumptively nefarious', 'not altogether unambiguous', 'full panoply of conditions requisite for perfect competition', 'Unfortunately, the phrase "high level of abstraction" does not have perfect antecedent clarity'). Actually, it verges on the embarrassing, a prosodic version of that frisson of momentary mortification induced by the sight of your parents gyrating on the dance floor or uttering hip expressions that have long been abandoned. Yeah, baby, yeah.

SDH may be the Austin Powers of marketing discourse, however he makes use of one retrospective device that is staggering in its rhetorical genius. Retrospection, remember, is not just another word for antiquarianism, the love of the past. Retro, rather, combines past and present, as in the relaunched VW Beetle (old look, new spec.) or the Harry Potter phenomenon (a contemporary take on *Tom Brown's Schooldays*).[70] SDH performs a prosodic version of this in his lengthy literature reviews, when he utilizes the present tense to summarize past publications. Whereas most tyro academics use the past tense to review the literature (so-and-so said such-and-such, A.N. Other argued otherwise), our incomparable literature reviewer often employs the present tense (so-and-so says such and such, A.N. Other argues otherwise), which gives his writing an immediacy, and indeed believability, that is lacking in all too many literature reviews, such as yours and mine:

> Alderson (1957) views functionalism as 'that approach to science which begins by identifying a system of action, and then tries to determine how

and why it works as it does' (p.16) . . . Extending Chamberlin's (1933) view
that intra-industry demand is substantially heterogeneous, he notes that the
particular assortment of goods that is viewed as meaningful or desirable by
any one household is likely to differ greatly from that of others.[71]

Tenacious D

Hyperreality refers to postmodernism's fascination with the fake, the fantastic, the recreation, the reproduction, the inauthentic, the imaginary.
Formally defined by Firat and Venkatesh as the becoming real of what
began as a simulation, hyperreality is epitomized by computer games, the
music video, virtual reality, the world wide web, the IMAC movie experience and, above all, by the theming phenomenon, whereby hotels, pubs,
restaurants, shopping centres, casinos, retail stores, museums, amusement
parks and suchlike are kitted out in a style plucked from a smorgasbord
of pre-digested national, temporal and recreational stereotypes.[72]

Hyperreality, in fact, is the only postmodern 'trait' specifically mentioned, and made use of, by SDH.[73] Adapting Baudrillard's contention
that hyperreality involves the separation of linguistic signifiers from their
original referents, which are then allowed to float free and attach themselves to new targets, SDH contends that postmodern marketing
researchers have done exactly that with positivism. The proper, precise
and historically accurate meanings of the term – that is, an approach to the
philosophy of science associated with the Vienna Circle of the 1930s, albeit
with antecedents going back to the 'positive sociology' of Auguste
Comte – has been stripped away and replaced with just about anything
anti-positivist marketing scholars wish to condemn: number-crunching,
model-building, hypothesis-testing, truth-seeking, cause and effect-iden-
tifying and so on:

> Thus construed, 'positivism' becomes a pejorative term of rhetorical abuse
> that can effectively stifle discussion and critique. If one's work is subjected
> to critical evaluation, rather than defending the research on its merits, one
> can shut down all discussion by retorting: 'You're just using outmoded pos-
> itivistic criteria to evaluate my post-positivistic, postmodern study'.[74]

Regardless of whether this statement represents a fair summary of the
postmodern position, it is a perfect encapsulation of SDH's position on
postmodernism. It is, actually, a perfect encapsulation of 'middle period'
SDH, when he took up the epistemological cudgel and set about the
'misses' ('*mis*conceptions, *mis*understandings, *mis*representations, and

*mis*characterizations')[75] of those who misapplied the philosophy of marketing science in general and misconstrued positivism in particular. Viewed in this light, hyperreality was the making of SDH, since he owes his stupendous scholarly reputation to his heroic performance during the paradigm wars of the 1980s. By showing all and sundry that the relativists, principally Paul Anderson, Jerry Olsen and J. Paul Peter, failed to comprehend the character of the very thing they were ostentatiously condemning, SDH did much damage to marketing's 'mischief makers', as he mischievously describes them.

So successful was SDH's rout of the relativists, that the term 'positivism' and its cognates have been effectively excised from marketing's scholarly vocabulary. Whereas positivism is still widely used in adjacent academic disciplines to refer to what Agger[76] calls 'Midwestern Empiricism' – the hypothetico, quantificatory, varimaxed, conjointed, Lisrelised, experimentissimo, big-science-or-bust mindset – it no longer means that in marketing. Thanks to SDH, 'positivism' rarely makes an appearance in contemporary marketing discourse, except when safely ensconced in quotation marks, the shrink-wrap of scholarship, or when accompanied by a protective prefix like 'neo-', the asbestos gloves of academe. Just as Baudrillard's hyperreality involves replacing one set of meanings with another, SDH has replaced the colloquial meanings of positivism with the original meaning. Like Disney's Main Street USA, SDH's positivism is a postmodern simulacrum of itself, not so much a bygone world as a bygone word. It is the intellectual equivalent of insisting that 'gay' means 'light-hearted', which is not so much hyperreal as phantasmagorical.

The hyperreal phantasm doesn't stop there, moreover, since SDH's prose hovers between ostensible fact and seeming fiction. On the one hand, he is incredibly precise about his sources, often quoting them at length and taking great care to ensure that the cites come complete with pertinent page numbers and what have you. On the other hand, he constantly invents – or rather constructs – anonymous commentators and informants, people who speak to him and give vent to their intellectual frustrations. Examples include the nameless well-wishers who urged him to include 'feminism' and 'postmodernism' in The Truth Continuum 'as examples of dogmatic skepticism'; his unspecified, if precocious, student who once said that 'The analysis of relativism, constructionism, and subjectivism is totally unnecessary'; the unknown marketing foot soldiers who demand action rather than thought ('tell me what factors that I control can influence attitude!'); the Professor John Does who employ terms like 'economic rents', 'abnormal profits' and 'assume a competitive market' in their marketing articles; the bewildered research assistant who 'has just been instructed to observe and record all data *relevant* to the problem of brand loyalty'; the even more bewildered conference delegate who purportedly turned to SDH and said 'Over the last two days I have heard people use the term paradigm in at least eight different ways. How am I supposed to understand what is going on here?'; or, indeed, the scholarly straw men that he sets up – or accuses himself of setting up – only to knock them over by the power of his persuasive prose.[77] There are more straw men in Shelby Hunt than red herrings in Raymond Chandler.

The inevitable upshot of the above is that our titanic thinker's prose has a somewhat unreal, almost otherworldly, tenor. The comparative lack of empirical material (the vast bulk of SDH's published output is untainted by hard data), the seeming hair-splitting over apparent trivialities (such as the meaning of the word 'because'), the incessant invocation of absences and, especially, 'space limitations' ('there is no market for shoes', 'dangerously close to an empty set', 'an article's method section in a research report should always be blank'), the fact that Copernicus gets mentioned more often than Coca-Cola, Newton more often than Nokia, Einstein more often than Exxon, Kuhn more often than K-Mart, Feyerabend more often than Ford (I could go on . . .), all somehow contribute to a strange sense that 'it's marketing, SDH, but not as we know it'.[78]

This sensation is especially strongly marked in RAT, which seems to have suffered a marketectomy. The theory, especially in its book-length treatment in *General Theory of Competition*, is a mélange of manifold schools of (mainly) economic thought. Marketing, as a number of reviewers note, has been all-but excised from the framework.[79] Indeed, reading *General Theory of Competition* is a decidedly disorientating experience, inasmuch as the book presumes that readers are already familiar with RAT and when the much-touted, ground-breaking, general equilibrium-eviscerating theory eventually materializes, after five lengthy chapters, it consists of a nine-cell matrix and a boxes-and-arrows diagram. Is that it?, is one's immediate reaction. What does this have to do with marketing? is the instant follow-up. Is this 'the return of the marketing repressed', a twenty-first century reversion to marketing's academic roots as an offshoot of economics? Is this, in fact, the end of marketing, a marketing-less form of marketing, akin to those fabulously hyperreal products like de-caffeinated coffee, colourless cola, alcohol-free alcohol and *I Can't Believe It's Not Butter*?

That'll Be the Day

Pastiche pertains to postmodernism's pick 'n' mix propensity, the (mis)quotation, (mis)appropriation and (mis)matching of disparate cultural forms, often in a knowing, ironic, tongue-in-cheek manner.[80] Postmodern architecture juxtaposes different styles, eras and building materials. Postmodern fashions throw together contrasting looks from preppy to urban. Postmodern novels teeter self-consciously between truth and lies. Postmodern music samples and mixes a medley of genres – rap and metal, classical and punk, world and garage, opera and electronica – and rips and burns them for good measure. Postmodern advertising tips a wink at other cultural forms, such as soap opera, reality TV, music videos and blockbuster movies. It also casts a wry eye on itself. Ads set in advertising agencies, where executives agonize over the advertising campaign we're actually watching, are so common these days that it's as clichéd as the eight-out-of-ten-consumers commercials of yore.

SDH is a postmodern pastischeur extraordinaire. His texts are massive patchwork quilts of quotations, excerpts, enjambments, and reworkings of extant material. They are scholarly collages, theoretical tapestries, cut-and-pastes of others' writings and, as often as not, *his own*. One of the most striking things about SDH's published articles, and the books even more so, is that they echo his earlier work – reproduce rather. He constantly drags and drops entire passages from one publication to another. The six-point 'refutation' of relativism has been published on at least six occasions. The three elements of marketing theory – a systematically related set of statements, including law-like generalizations, that is empirically testable – are reprinted three times in every mid-period paper, near enough. The Copernican revolution has been recycled so often that Copernicus must be turning in his grave. The three-dichotomies model of 1976 is the seventies revival night of marketing scholarship, the platform shoes of prose, and CAT, lest we forget, has had considerably more than nine lives. Considerably more.[81]

In fairness, SDH's prosodic reprocessing facility is partly a consequence of the countless marketing controversies he finds himself involved in, accidentally or otherwise.[82] There can't be anyone in marketing who has been in quite so many incandescent intellectual exchanges. Every single phase of his career has been punctuated with comments, responses, comments on the responses, responses to the comments on the responses, comments on the responses to the comments on the responses, and responses to the comments on the responses to the comments on the responses. Or perhaps it just seems that way.

The slightly repetitive, somewhat ramshackle air of SDH's writing, especially in the books, should not be confused with befuddlement. On the contrary, he is exceptionally sharp, unfailingly incisive and, above all, a superlative summarizer of others' arguments. One of his signature stylistic devices is to quote the contrasting views of different commentators on a certain topic – relationship marketing, scientific method, realist philosophies, functionalist explanations, etc. – and then compress them into a compelling conceptual précis. His powers of synthesis are second to none. His adroit overviews of, say, the Boston matrix or Chamberlin's monopolistic competition theory are models of coherence, compaction and lucidity. Anyone who has ever struggled to make sense of industrial economics or the philosophy of science literature, as I have, will concede that SDH's encapsulations are quite superb. Not only is the content cogent, but the style is correct too – a perfect pastiche of the original. SDH is a wonderful mimic, a conceptual caricaturist, an intellectual vent act, no less.

The irony, of course, is that SDH goes out of his way to denounce slick summaries and glib abridgements, what the New Critics aptly termed 'the heresy of paraphrase'.[83] He consistently stresses the need to quote authors at length – and he certainly can't be admonished on that score – even though reviewing, synthesizing and critiquing the literature is perhaps his principal talent. The irony doesn't stop there, moreover. If inverted commas are the hallmark of our ironic postmodern times, then SDH is postmodern marketing's poster boy. His writing is chock-a-block with the literary equivalent of that 'now popular gesture of wagging the first two fingers of each hand beside one's ears like a demented rabbit'.[84] When added to the copious quotations that striate his texts, the result is akin to a rabbit warren – a rabbit warren suffering a collective anxiety attack.

For many of his antagonists, SDH is the myxomatosis of marketing thought. Such ill-mannered insinuations, however, conveniently overlook our hero's wry side, his tongue-in-cheek tendencies, his occasional recourse to eyebrow-raising, his 'is that a blink or a wink?' moments. Thus he makes irreverent remarks about abominable snowmen, is suitably sarcastic when Congress gets a mention, beards an antagonist with a hyperbolic tale about Hostess Twinkies, cracks that old Kotlerite joke about porcupines making love, claims that the only quants in his books are the page numbers, extracts a quirky quip from set theory (which is no mean achievement) throws in a zinger about the theory of gravity's role in sending rockets to the moon, mercilessly mocks marketing academics with a 'stick to the facts' mindset, wistfully wonders if such people 'just like to read telephone books or census data' and, RAT notwithstanding, actually takes a pot-shot at boxes-and-arrows diagrams. Best of all, he adapts a line from Jerry Lee Lewis to send up self-satisfied scholars who fail to publish and refuse to perish ('there must be a whole lot of perishing going on').[85]

Humour, I grant you, is not something most people associate with the best thing to come out of Lubbock since Buddy Holly. Hen's teeth, several cynics might venture, are more numerous than thigh-slapping side-split-ters in *Modern Marketing Theory*. Poultry orthodontists, as well. But they'd be wrong. Superlative writer that he is, SDH leavens his prose when necessary. Given the heaviness of his subject matter, and the weight of the words he wrestles with, he goes to great lengths to lighten the literary load.

In addition to these amusing academic interludes, our incomparable ironist makes all sorts of flagrantly outrageous statements, statements that can only be interpreted as deliberate attempts to provoke, to unsettle, to take the mickey out of other marketing researchers. He declares that America is the most successful alliance that the world has ever known (Holy Roman Empire, anyone?). He announces that the single, most important macroeconomic event of the twentieth century was the collapse of the communist command economies (Great Depression, possibly?). He presents Adam Smith versus Karl Marx as 'the greatest natural experiment in recorded history' (get a grip, Shelby!). He states, and constantly restates, that 'the concept of "certainty" belongs to theology, not science' (how can he be so certain, unless SDH is waxing theological?). He denounces relativists *tout court* for the 'certitudes' of their 'sweeping generalizations', a generalized sweeping certitude if ever there was one. He trumpets that *General Theory of Competition* subsumes General Equilibrium Theory, beloved by neoclassical economists, and confines the critter to one – yes, one – of RAT's nine cells. He even has the gall to call one of his chapters 'The Wealth of Nations'. Now that's what I call cojones.

Indeed, such is his command of marketing thought that SDH makes minute mistakes, presumably deliberately, to see if his rivals pick up on them. Lacking SDH's incomparable close reading skills, they don't. Thus he cites papers that aren't listed in his references. He fails to close parentheses and quotation marks. He kindly shortens the word 'queues' to 'ques' (shorter queues are always better, are they not). He misinforms readers about the contents of his books' numbered sub-sections, the placement of epigraphs and, of all things, his (non)use of italics. He confuses commodity fetishism and commoditization, and misrepresents the dialectic for good measure. He misspells Auguste Conte (*sic*), Edward E. Evans-Pritcherd (*sic*), Jacques Barzum (*sic*) and, incredibly, Issac (*sic*) Newton. He misattributes the Big Bang theory to Steven (*sic*) Hawking. He mislabels his own RAT matrix on one gloriously self-abnegating occasion. He critiques German idealists for their obfuscatory term 'entelechy', a philosophical concept that goes all the way back to Aristotle. He even, in one deathless abstract in the *Journal of Marketing*, purports to be positing 'scientific relativism', a scholarly stance that doubtless regards 'science' as whatever societies, cultures or scholarly communities choose to call science. Paul Anderson's position, in short. J. Paul Peter's too.[86]

Now, some may regard the above as tiny typographical transgressions. But they are exactly the sorts of linguistic or logical infelicities that, when made by his opponents, SDH picks up on, proceeds to unpick and subsequently stitches together for the delectation of his readership. These marketing matters, as he frequently makes clear, are not inconsequential ('the issue here is not simply a slip of the pen . . . [or] . . . trivial semantics'). Researchers, he further argues, should focus on how people behave, not what they believe, or say they believe ('the beliefs of people are to be inferred from examining their actions. For example, if an individual in fact believes that a water-well contains no poison, the person should be willing to drink from the well'). Actions may speak louder than words, but as a close reader of unparalleled ability, SDH is aware that ill-chosen words are eloquent as well. Like the slips of the tongue studied by Freud, it is the itty-bitty errors that give the game away. And most would agree that SDH has an incredible eye for the indiscretions of others. Indeed, at the risk of indulging in postmodernist epistobabble, it is possible, just possible, that SDH secretly *wants us* to discover *his own* tiny mistakes, the philosophical parapraxes that reveal him as an inveterate ironist, a postmodern pastiche artist and, dare I say it, someone with professorial performance anxieties ('moral impotence', 'ethical impotence', 'explanatorially impotent', 'predictively impotent', 'heuristically impotent', 'impotent explanations', 'impotent and void of explanatory power').

Goodness, gracious, great balls of fire.

Frère Jacques

Although SDH exemplifies the five key features of postmodernism, there is one final word that pertains to this much commended and criticized academic. Deconstruction. Formulated by French philosopher-cum-literary critic Jacques Derrida, deconstruction is the proprietary method of postmodernism, an anti-method method, which seeks to interrogate texts and expose their inconsistencies, ambiguities and unstated self-contradictions.[87] It shows, as Norris notes, 'that texts cannot mean what they say . . . or say what they mean'.[88] During the 1980s, indeed, it was the litcrit method of the moment, thanks largely to the proselytizing endeavours of the so-called Yale School of boa-deconstructors (though the term has since seeped into popular consciousness where it is taken to mean something like 'critique', 'exposé' or 'analysis'). Appropriately for an approach that focuses on ambiguities, it too has become incorrigibly ambiguous.[89]

Irrespective of how the term is actually employed – colloquial, Derridean or Yale School – SDH qualifies as our discipline's deconstructor-in-chief. The bulk of his published work consists of critiques of others' published work. To cite but a few examples, he succinctly disassembles

Robert Bartels's general theory of marketing, Robert D. Buzzell's much-vaunted evaluation of marketing science, the Engel-Kollat-Blackwell and Howard-Sheth models of consumer behaviour, the Product Life Cycle and Wheel of Retailing theories, the official AMA definitions of marketing and marketing research, the philosophical premises of relativists/constructivists, the compendious competitive strategy literature, and everything from Goodman's 'grue paradox' (don't ask) to Wittgenstein's picture theory of language (definitely don't ask!).

À la Derrida, SDH is a critic rather than a creator. Despite his high hopes that RAT will precipitate a paradigm shift in economics, he is more likely to be remembered as a theoretical theorist (a commentator on theory) than a practising theorist (a constructor of new theoretical concepts).

À la Derrida, SDH employs an anti-method method – his philosophical publications rarely include 'methods' sections – which basically involves latching on to the terminological and linguistic inexactitudes of those he's critiquing, such as the misusers of 'positivism' or 'reification', which are then used to show how the terminological abusers contradict themselves, undermine their own arguments and, as often as not, are actually positing a position that is the complete opposite of what they imagine:

> Antipositivist claims to the contrary, the positivists did not search for causal explanations or causal linkages; they did not adopt, nor hold that science should adopt, the machine metaphor; they did not have a realist view with respect to scientific theories; and they could not possibly have been guilty of reification. Phillips . . . compares the views of social science antipositivists with the actual positions of the positivists and concludes that 'some of the most boisterous celebrants at positivism's wake are actually more positivistic than they realize, or have more in common with the positivists than they would care to admit'. As we shall see, a similar situation prevails in the consumer research literature.[90]

> Did the positivists engage in reification? That is, did the positivists improperly treat abstract concepts as having a real existence in the sense that a 'thing' has existence? Most assuredly, they did not. Their Humean skepticism and revulsion toward metaphysics led them to insist that theories must contain only observables, that is, labels for 'things'. . . . Therefore, the claim that positivist researchers engage in reification – in the philosophy of science sense of reification – is historically false.[91]

À la Derrida, he goes through the texts of those he's critiquing with a fine-tooth comb. He reads their sources, scours their footnotes, checks their indexes and, as in the classic case of Chalmers' philosophy of science primer (cited as support by Paul Anderson), showed how the author of *What is This Thing Called Science?* changed his mind between the first and second editions ('like Kuhn before him, Chalmers repudiated his 1976 views on objectivity, truth, and science').[92]

À la Derrida, he addresses the often uneasy relationship between word and world ('Such a set of optimal semantic rules of interpretation would thus achieve a kind of *isomorphism* or "one to one correspondence" between the marks on paper of the theory and the real world'). Indeed, in one immortal endnote, he describes a position that is almost identical to Derrida's war-cry: 'There is nothing outside the text' ('language is a self-contained system with no contact with the world it is presumably about').

À la Derrida, he makes frequent reference to what postmodern theorists term the syntagmatic and paradigmatic dimensions of language, the precise positioning of words in a sentence and the effect on meaning when one word is substituted for another:

> The meaning of an English sentence with a *not* depends crucially on where the *not* is placed. Rather than 'firms are universally not opportunistic', we actually state, 'universal opportunism is not assumed.'[93]

> Note that Feyerabend does *not* say there 'may' exist, he states *there exists*. Note also that he does *not* say an alternative 'may' be as good, but will be 'at least as good, or even better.'[94]

> His idiosyncratic definition, by using the words 'are not', rather than 'cannot', either rewrites or ignores the entire history of the incommensurability debate.[95]

À la Derrida, he appreciates that the search for solid, absolute foundations of knowledge – logocentrism, in Derrida's lexicon – is futile and ultimately rests on convention rather than certainty:[96]

> Infinite regress poses the major problem with the coherence theory of truth. That is, if statement A is to be justified as true by statement B, and statement B is to be justified by statement C, and statement C is to be justified by statement D, and so on, what is the justification for the statement at the end of the justificatory chain? Sometimes the last statement in the chain is justified by correspondence, as in the correspondence theory of truth. Sometimes the last statement in the chain is justified as a 'necessary truth' (true in all possible worlds). . . . Finally, the last statement in the justificatory chain might, simply, be assumed to be true by stipulation or convention.[97]

À la Derrida, his agenda is driven by difference, not simply in the sense that 'differentiation' is the key to competitive success in SDH's strategic cosmos, or indeed the dynamics of deferral that drive the leapfrogging process integral to RAT, but also in his belief that linguistic meaning is unstable, imprecise, contingent and context-bound. In several places, he articulates something akin to what Derrideans describe as the 'dictionary test', cogently summarized by Terry Eagleton thusly:

'Cat' may mean a furry four-legged creature, a malicious person, a knotted whip, an American, a horizontal beam for raising a ship's anchor, a six-legged tripod, a short tapered stick, [a theory of competitive advantage!] and so on. But even when it just means a furry four-legged animal, this meaning will never quite stay the same from context to context: the signified will be altered by the various chains of signifiers in which it is entangled.[98]

À la Derrida, SDH is an arch opponent of metaphysics, he rejects base utilitarianism, he is a controversial figure, who is loved and loathed in equal measure, he writes in a style that is not dissimilar to Hartman's apt description of Derrida, 'elegant opacity', and he makes frequent use of the term 'trace', which evokes both origin and overlay. SDH is obsessed with origins, as is Derrida, and his work is akin to a palimpsest, a tracing of others' arguments:

Although vigorous debate concerning the basic nature of marketing has alternately waxed and waned since the early 1900s, the most recent controversy probably traces back to a position paper by the marketing staff of the Ohio State University in 1965.[99]

I decided to trace the historical development of the fundamental tenets of logical positivism, logical empiricism, historical relativism, historical empiricism and scientific realism. However, I found it difficult to explain these 'isms' without at least briefly discussing classical realism and Hegelian idealism. Unfortunately, I could find no way to enable readers to comprehend Hegelian idealism without discussing classical rationalism and classical empiricism. At last, I recognized that I might as well start at 'the beginning' of Western philosophy – Platonism.[100]

À la Derrida, he has placed marketing thought sous-RATure, under erasure, where every claim is suspended, challenged, crossed out, wrapped in quotation marks and ripe for critique, *including his own*. SDH is not only a deconstructor, he is a self-deconstructor. He is *aware* of most of the points made in this chapter and admits them, what's more. Thus, he confesses that the purpose of RAT is to provoke. He notes that 'skillful rhetoricians' can make 'obviously implausible or even bizarre' philosophies seem reasonable. He recognizes that researchers should 'exercise caution' when borrowing concepts that have 'pejorative connotations'. He knows that 'Those who are skilled in rhetoric have long known that their normative views are often more persuasive when disguised as declarative, positive assertions'. He is cognizant of 'the literary devices that modern irrationalists use to seduce even highly trained philosophers (not to mention unwary, casual readers) into the relativistic thesis'. He is conscious that disingenuous arguments can be 'persuasive to one's audience', though he'd never dream of such heinous behaviours himself. He realizes, furthermore, that 'There are many ways to bias the results of a survey by choosing particular wordings of the questions'. Lucky, then, he does so little empirical research . . .

I jest, your honour.

5

The Biopoetics of Wroe Alderson

> Not many people can write well enough to produce material worthy of publication.
>
> Wroe Alderson[1]

Hell's Bells!

In June 1955, a party of six American Quakers paid a goodwill visit to the USSR. The purpose of their trip was to forge friendly relations with Soviet Societies of Friends – the precious few who were permitted to follow the faith in that singularly secular society – and to report back on their rushed Russian experience. Among the Puritan party's number was one Wroe Alderson, a self-styled 'marketing economist', who was charged with making sense of the communist socio-economic system. A co-authored account of the month-long visit, *Meeting the Russians*, was written on the Quakers' safe return and much publicized by means of radio, television and, naturally, the Kingdom Hall network.[2] Alderson contributed a chapter, archly entitled 'Main Street USSR' (Disneyland had opened a few months before the trip), which contains the following evocative description of Penza, a small town 400 miles south-east of Moscow:

> Despite its size, in atmosphere it reminded us of a typical American country town of the early 1920s with a tenth of Penza's population. The stores held much the same goods as those of the showy sort in Moscow, and at the same fixed prices. The leading department store was always crowded; and as we walked through its aisles and looked at the arrangement of its goods, several of us were carried back in memory to the general country stores of

our childhood. The unpainted log houses that marked the older part of town were reminiscent, too, of an earlier American era . . .

The main street of Penza, called Moscow Street, was a never-ending source of interest to us. The shady side of the street was crowded with leisurely throngs of pedestrians all day long (Penza summers are hot), and both sides were crowded throughout the evening. Motor traffic was light and, apart from the very good system of trolley-busses, consisted chiefly of trucks. Horse-drawn wagons were practically as numerous as passenger cars and reminded us of Penza's role in the agricultural life of the province. Three funerals on three successive days marched down Moscow Street past our hotel windows, with flowers and banners preceding an open casket and a dignified brass band bringing up the rear. A milk store across the street served a line of women each morning, turning away at least once the last few customers, their half-gallon pails empty, and closing its doors long before noon.[3]

In addition to this powerful passage on Penza and several sly yarns on Russian consumers' astonished reaction to his new-fangled Polaroid camera, the pamphlet contains an excerpt from Alderson's personal field notes:

We landed in Leningrad on an early evening plane, six American Quakers. There were the usual formalities, with unusual dispatch; a form to fill out but no examination of luggage. In the midst of this procedure, expedited by the Russian government travel agency Intourist, a tall, bearded, distinguished-looking man approached us with what was to become a familiar, warm greeting. He was Pastor Orlov, superintending pastor of the Leningrad district of the Baptist Church. He rather hesitatingly told us that a service was just about to begin at his church and asked whether we would like to attend and bring greetings. . . . It will be impossible to recapture the full drama of what we found. The service began at seven o'clock. It was now eight-thirty. Every square inch of the room was packed. No notice of our coming had been given. So, although the whole audience was singing, it was not difficult to see them say to themselves as we squeezed our way in, 'What's happening?' I shall never forget the effort on my part to suppress an outburst of emotion as we elbowed our way up the aisle. For I had consented to give a greeting to these waiting souls, obviously hungry for words of hope and consolation. And when the minister announced who we were, my task was made no easier. For through that whole congregation, estimated at 1,500 people, went a spontaneous audible wave of welcome, accompanied by tears of joy from literally scores of eyes. One was seeing a scene from an early Christian church when miracles happened. Here was the Book of Acts re-enacted in Leningrad in 1955.[4]

As these excerpts indicate, Wroe Alderson was a very stylish writer. Yet within the marketing academy, he is widely regarded as someone somewhat lacking in literary éclat.[5] Almost every commentator on the Aldersonian corpus, including most of the wordsmiths gathered herein,[6] regards reading Wroe's work as the nearest thing to hell this side of the grave. His writings, some say, are imposed as penances upon backsliding PhD students. They are the fiery furnace of marketing thought or the three-pronged fork at least.

These assessments, it has to be said, are not entirely inaccurate. Alderson's academic articles are indeed fiendishly difficult, bordering on diabolical. As Hostiuck and Kurtz rightly observe, 'even recognized scholars of marketing groan at the mere mention of Alderson and intimate that they never really understood him'.[7] However, the material in 'Main Street USSR' – written at the apogee of his prodigious intellectual powers – suggests that Wroe *chose* to compose in an irredeemably Mephistophelian manner. Unlike his radiant Russian reportage, the bulk of Alderson's scholarly work is devoid of poetic flourishes, evocative descriptions or amusing anecdotes. It is, rather, almost Puritanical in its eschewal of stylistic excess, resistance to rhetorical temptation and avoidance of literary élan.

Élan, nevertheless, is a particularly appropriate word when applied to Wroe Alderson, the Ur-guru of marketing thought.[8] Although he came late to academic life, having previously worked for the US military, the Department of Commerce, the renowned research department of Curtis Publishing Company and the wartime Office of Price Administration (under J.K. Galbraith), this lightly-educated, horny-handed farm-boy from Palouse County, eastern Washington was a veritable intellectual dynamo. More than almost anyone in the early postwar period, he recharged the flat battery of marketing research and restored power to a discipline drained by the shortages of an era when 'all goods were scarce and consumers asked few questions'.[9] In a comparatively short publishing career, which spanned approximately twenty years – compared, say, to the forty-plus years of Phil Kotler and Ted Levitt[10] – Alderson produced a string of groundbreaking articles in a host of learned journals, from *Philosophy of Science* to the *Annals of Business History*. What's more, he co-edited several pioneering volumes on marketing thought, organized a long-running series of annual, by-invitation-only theory conferences, and issued a regular, theoretically-informed newsletter from his highly successful consultancy firm, Alderson and Sessions. He also held high office in many professional societies, including the AMA presidency in 1948, received all manner of richly-deserved accolades, such as the prestigious Parlin and Converse Awards in 1954 and 1955 respectively, and was instrumental in the establishment of the Marketing Science Institute during his time at Wharton School of Finance and Commerce.

Most importantly perhaps, Wroe Alderson published two solo-authored books, *Marketing Behavior and Executive Action* and *Dynamic Marketing Behavior*, which are widely regarded as landmarks in the history of marketing scholarship.[11] The first of these is hailed by Robert Bartels as 'unquestionably the most fully developed theoretical exposition of marketing up to that time';[12] it represents the single most important 'breakthrough' in the history of marketing thought, says Ben Wooliscroft;[13] and, for professor emeritus Paul Green, it contains concepts that are 'as fresh today as when they first appeared'.[14] *Dynamic Marketing Behavior*, by contrast, is much less original than its predecessor – if rather more readable – and it is chiefly remembered for the famous final chapter of '150 testable hypotheses'.[15] Be that as it may, the two books effectively bracketed Alderson's formal academic career – which lasted from 1959, when he joined the University of Pennsylvania faculty, to his sudden death from heart failure in 1965[16] – and contain the most complete explanation of 'functionalism', the great guru's signature scholarly framework.

Function Juncture

Functionalism involves a total systems approach to marketing.[17] Unlike the so-called 'functional' school of thought, which concentrates on the specific activities or functions that form part of everyday marketing practice (breaking bulk, monetary exchange, transfer of title, etc.),[18] Alderson's 'functionalism' focuses on the entire marketing system or process, from initial production to ultimate consumption. More specifically, Aldersonian functionalism encompasses the relationship between the marketing system – and its constituent subsystems – and the surrounding environment, from which it draws inputs and delivers outputs of energy, information, materials and suchlike. Functionalism, in short, treats the marketing system as an organic whole, an organism almost, that can only be fully understood and effectively managed as a totality. It is, as one of Alderson's early explicants explained: 'an all-encompassing, integrating perspective of marketing entities *and* their interrelations'.[19]

Wroe Alderson, of course, wasn't the first academic to adopt an ecological approach to marketing matters, nor has he been the last.[20] However, in addition to his biologically-based 'systematics', Alderson's functionalist paradigm contains a number of well-known subordinate concepts – *transvection, differential advantage, organized behaviour systems, heterogeneity,* and *sorting* – which require only the briefest of summaries.[21]

Considered by Sheth et al. to be the richest of all Wroe's notions, *transvection* is a group name for a series of individual exchanges or

transactions.[22] In many ways, the marketing equivalent of a herd of buf-
faloes or pride of lions, transvections are the basic unit of marketing
activity.[23] The term refers to the process by which, say, a pair of gloves
makes its way into (and onto) the hands of the consumer, from initial
manufacture to ultimate acquisition. It includes not only the transfer of
goods and title, but all the inter-firm negotiations, personal communications, physical transformations and geographical relocations along the
way. If, in other words, the transaction is the part, a convergence of buyers
and sellers in immediate contact, the transvection is the whole, a conceptual encapsulation of the complete marketing process.

Transvections may be the elementary unit of marketing action, but they
do not operate entirely independently. On the contrary, 'the law of the
jungle'[24] obtains as businesses and organizations constantly struggle for
sustenance, status, stability and, ultimately, survival in an ever-changing
marketplace. *Differential advantage* is the means by which competitive marketing organizations stand out from the crowd and rise above the herd.
Every organization, like every individual, is unique in some way – either
in terms of its location, or the products it sells, or the way in which it operates, or with regard to the customer segments it serves – and in order to
maintain its position in the market, it exploits this uniqueness to its best
long-term advantage. Such advantages, however, are subject to neutral-
ization by rival firms and, inevitably, countervailing attempts to restore an
organization's initial competitive edge. Hence the inherent dynamism of
the marketing system.

Firms, of course, are but one of the two key *organized behaviour systems*
that loom large in the functionalist paradigm. The other is the household.
Defined as 'entities which operate in the marketing environment',[25] organized behaviour systems comprise coherent groups of individuals
conjoined by the expectation that they have more to gain by grouping
together than operating independently. Granted, the boundaries of the
group may be ill-defined, but such entities are characterized by interaction
with the surrounding environment, they compete and cooperate with
nearby behaviour systems, they have rules and rituals for determining
membership, duties and status, they have controls for evaluating the
inputs and outputs appertaining to the system; and, given occasional rein-
forcement, they tend to persist over time, since members appreciate that
their group-based gains can only be preserved if the organization itself
survives.

Clearly, the existence of highly differentiated, inherently dynamic
organised behaviour systems has significant implications for economists'
traditional notion of perfectly homogeneous markets. And, to this end,
Alderson posited the diametrically opposed notion of perfectly heterogeneous markets. As each firm's offerings are different and each family's

demands are different, it follows that markets are different to the point of radical *heterogeneity*. In such circumstances, the role of marketing is to successfully match heterogeneous demand and heterogeneous supply. In practice, the matching process is somewhat patchy and prone to failure, largely on account of imperfect information exchange. The inevitable upshot is that some goods remain unsold and certain consumers' wants are unsatisfied, albeit these discrepancies represent opportunities for marketing innovation (new products) and improved communication (promotional campaigns).

Market clearance, in Alderson's cosmology, is a theoretical possibility that never transpires in practice, on account of environmental turbulence, technological development and discrepancies between buyer and seller. Nevertheless, marketing's principal function is to make meaning out of meaninglessness by bringing together disparate demand and miscellaneous supply. This is achieved through a *sorting* procedure which involves both the assembly of offerings from sundry sources of supply and the delivery of these assemblies to diverse centres of demand, as well as any attendant physical or spatial transformations. This building up and breaking down process is further subdivided, on the basis of initial homogeneity or heterogeneity, to furnish a four-category classification of *allocation, assortment, sorting out* and *assembly*. The last of these is most important from a marketing perspective, since it refers to the final consumer's acquisition of heterogeneous goods and services from the heterogeneous offerings of the marketplace. [26]

Assembly may be most significant from a marketing perspective, but *sorting out* is most salient from the standpoint of literary theory. It is salient in the sense that 'sorting out', unlike the other categories in Alderson's classification, does not begin with the letter 'A'. Given that many obvious A-words could quite easily have been employed – Assignment, Accumulation, Apportion, Aggregation – it is evident that this gifted writer deliberately resisted the alliterative opportunity. He chose *not* to display his literary facility, and while such linguistic choices may be inconsequential from the standpoint of 'marketing science', they are of profound importance from an 'art of marketing' perspective.

Buying Biopoetics

Now art and science, as we've noted several times already, are often regarded as antithetical. Ever since the celebrated 'Two Cultures' debate, when the practising physicist and sometime novelist C.P. Snow identified the warring factions, it has been widely accepted that never the twain shall meet.[27] In reality, however, the two cultures co-exist, sometimes clashing, occasionally combining. Numerous physical scientists, for example, attest to the essentially aesthetic character of scientific research and discovery, as Nils Bohr's contention that 'scientists should think like poets' eloquently avers. Conversely, the history of the arts reveals that cultural endeavour is deeply affected by the scientific wonders of the day, be it Darwinian biology, Einsteinian astrophysics or the discovery of DNA.[28]

Indeed, the scientific wonders of recent times, such as cybernetics, complexity theory and the human genome project, have given rise to renewed interest in and a burst of theorizing around the art–science interface. A number of makeshift monikers have been mooted for this still emerging school of literary-cum-cultural criticism – ecopoetics, bioaesthetics, evolutionary aesthetics and so on – but the inaugural anthology was called *Biopoetics* and the term is starting to stick.[29] As the editors observe, the greatest obstacle to evolutionary analysis of art is the lack of an agreed name, since scholars in different fields are working in isolation, unaware of neighbouring developments and conceptual commonalities. The biopoeticists, however, are making up for lost time and all sorts of variations on the putative paradigm – defined as 'the science of at least one art'[30] – are already discernible. These include Rabkin's Darwinesque reflections on the 'descent of fantasy'[31], Kroeber's critique of nineteenth century nature poets' 'protoecological' inclinations[32] and Slethhaug's metatheoretical attempt to show how chaos theory can be applied to American novelists like John Barth, Michael Crichton and Don DeLillo, who incorporate aspects of chaotics into their own works of fiction.[33]

If the contemporary intellectual ecosystem is already replete with random variations on and mutations of the biopoetic gene, the origin of this scholarly species is firmly established. In 1975, the controversial entomologist Edward O. Wilson contended in his inflammatory book *Sociobiology* that the social behaviour of human beings is adaptive, a biological relic of our hunting and gathering ancestors on the pre-palaeolithic savannahs of east Africa.[34] These adaptive behaviours include altruism, aggression, reciprocity, courtship rituals, mating displays, incest avoidance and, not least, the making and appreciation of art. For Wilson, humankind's artistic impulse is shaped by natural selection, is to some degree inheritable, and exhibits evidence of universals or near-universals (archetypes, serpent imagery, ubiquitous narratives like the Oedipal triangle etc.). Accordingly, it is amenable to scientific study and Wilson's subsequent publications have sought to cash out this contention, most notably in *Concilience*, an admittedly ambitious attempt to unify all forms of knowledge, including 'The Arts and their Interpretation'.[35]

Whilst Wilson recognizes that science and art are very different in execution – the former seeks general principles, the latter transmits individual experience – he argues that they are convergent in what they reveal about human behaviour. The two vocations draw from the same primal wellsprings and depend upon similar stories, structures and images.[36] In both cases the primitive brain seeks eloquence, pattern, parsimony, geometry and novelty. Humankind is genetically predisposed to respond positively to certain shapes, sounds, smells and proportions, such as the Golden Mean, or the Three Unities in drama. More fundamentally perhaps, humankind's aesthetic instincts are an aid to reproduction and survival. Not only do they help make sense of a frightening and inscrutable universe but they are also a means of attracting mates and thereby ensuring the continued existence of *homo aestheticus*.

The arts may be the peacock feathers of our species, but Wilson's claim that even the greatest works of art are explicable in biological terms has not gone unchallenged.[37] Apart from the ferocious attacks of fellow physical scientists – the late, great Stephen Jay Gould dismisses Sociobiology and its latter-day avatar, Environmental Psychology, as a series of purite parables[38] – the aspirant conciliator has felt the wrath of neo-marxist and poststructuralist literary critics, who accuse him of anthropomorphism, reductionism, racism, sexism, homophobia and all sorts of politically incorrect inaccuracies, to say nothing of suspiciously marketing-orientated inclinations.[39] Is there no limit to his depravity?

Yet regardless of these critiques, it cannot be denied that many latter-day literary critics are drawing inspiration from developments in the natural sciences, broadly defined.[40] To cite but a few more examples: former deconstructionist J. Hillis Miller is currently engaged in a search for the literary equivalent of black holes and considers such astronomical entities a perfect metaphor for the lamentable lack of luminosity in today's hopelessly McDonaldized, utterly unenlightened universities;[41] Daniel Rancour-Laferrier regards memetics, biologist Richard Dawkins's much-discussed cultural equivalent of genetics, as the humanities' royal road to renewal and relevance, though there is a question mark over the precise memetic status of genres, plots, poems, metaphors and half-remembered quotations;[42] N. Katherine Hayles has applied the principles of emergence – the fact that complex systems embody deep structures of order – to scientific texts and literary classics alike, albeit her enthusiastic endeavours have received short shrift from practising physicists;[43] and Joseph Carroll, a leading conspirator in the putative biopoetic putsch, commences his revolutionary tract with the scintillating syllogism, 'In this study, I argue for the view that knowledge is a biological phenomenon, that literature is a form of knowledge and that literature is thus itself a biological phenomenon'.[44]

However, by far the most ambitious attempt by a literary theorist to meld the physical sciences and liberal arts is found in the works of

Frederick Turner.[45] In a series of powerful volumes, he maintains that aesthetic appreciation, our love of beauty, is not only hard-wired into the mammalian cerebellum, but it is reinforced by reflexivity, a cultural feedback loop that leads to increasingly successful actions, choices and decisions, all of which help humankind to become better adapted to its environment. Aesthetic appreciation, in other words, is a superior form of cognition that enables its possessors to appraise a situation with greater efficiency. Better yet, it is in tune with 'the deepest theme or tendency' in the cosmos itself, where 'the smaller parts of the universe often resemble in shape and structure the larger parts of which they are components, and those larger parts in turn resemble the still larger systems that contain them'.[46] Just as the three-line stanza of Dante's *Divine Comedy* parallels the tripartite structure of the poem as a whole, so too snowflakes, ferns and the fractal geometry of coral reefs echo the natural world's most elemental theme. And this, Turner concludes, is *reflexivity*, the self-reflecting feedback loop of organized behaviour systems, be they animal, vegetable or mineral.[47]

Reading Wroe Reflexively

If, as Turner contends, reflexivity is the essence of biopoetics – the secret of the universe, no less – then it follows that a biopoetic approach to Wroe Alderson's literary corpus should adopt a reflexive perspective. That is to say, it should take a functionalist approach to Alderson's functionalism. It should ask, in keeping with the founder's own injunction, how his system of scholarly action works. It should show, by close reading of Wroe's prose, what purpose his inscrutable literary style serves. It should apply, as the burgeoning literature on reflexive social science suggests, Alderson's principles to himself.[48]

It should, in short, offer an ecological reading of the textual ecology of an ecology-espousing scholar.[49] Granted, there is no guarantee that order will emerge from the complexities of Alderson's oeuvre, but the biopoetics of *Theoretical Transvection*, *Discursive Differentiation*, *Disorganized Belief System*, *Heterogeneous Hypotheses* and *Scholarly Sorting* may introduce a modicum of textual variation into marketing's intellectual gene pool. Or, to put it in Aldersonian terms, it may increase the potency of his cerebral assortment.

Theoretical Transvection: The transvection, Wroe Alderson's proprietary neologism for the series of marketing transactions that transpire between producer and consumer, is generally regarded as his conceptual crowning glory. He personally considered it something special and in *Dynamic Marketing Systems* bends over backwards to establish its provenance and etymology:

> The problems of competitive adjustment and of channel coordination call for a more powerful concept than the transaction. This is the concept of the transvection, a term invented by the author in 1958 for lack of an established English word with the same meaning. The word comes from the Latin roots *trans* and *vehere*. From its etymology the word is meant to convey the idea of *flowing through*, with special reference to something which flows through a marketing system. . . . The choice of a word which would sound something like the word transaction was deliberate since the two ideas were obviously closely related.[50]

Not everyone, it has to be said, was so enamoured with Wroe's transvectional notion – the Ur-guru's mentor Reavis Cox dismissed it as a fancy word for channels of distribution[51] – but most commentators concur with Sheth et al., who conclude that 'the concept of the transvection is the richest of those brought forth by Alderson'.[52]

Richness aside, the creator's contention that transvections provide a central organizing concept for marketing is entirely appropriate, since he himself was something of a theoretical transvectioneer. He was a theoretical transvectioneer insofar as his primary function in the organized behaviour system, that is marketing scholarship, was as a manufacturer and distributor of theory. Read today, one of the most striking things about the Aldersonian corpus is the sheer wealth of concepts it contains. In addition to the five core constructs under consideration, Alderson's intellectual biomass includes a sizeable fringe of theoretical forms including 'core and fringe', 'monostasy and systasy', 'proximate' and 'ultimate' environments, 'subrationality and pseudorationality', 'vicarious search', 'random pairing', 'extinction mode', 'conditional value', 'waiting power', 'promotional pricing', 'behavioural drift', 'consumer sweep rates', 'radius of power', 'principle of precession', 'constellation', 'prenegotiation', 'footing', 'blaze', 'potency', 'discrepancy', 'hedonomics' and many more besides. In biopoetic terms, a kind of conceptual hypertrophy clearly prevails in the Aldersonian ecosystem and, while the resultant theoretical thicket is somewhat impenetrable, the academic abundance of Wroe's rain forest cannot be denied.

Although Alderson's conceptual cultivating capacity is incontestable, he is chiefly remembered as an intellectual intermediary who scoured the scholarly universe for tradeable theories, which were subsequently sold in the academic marketplace.[53] He was a marketing middleman, in other words, a kind of educational entrepôt or conceptual clearing-house. The former farm boy's greatest gift, in many ways, was his remarkable ability to harvest a host of academic specialisms (economics, anthropology, sociology, psychology, mathematics, cybernetics, political science, military history, operations research and so on), and process the resultant scholarly crop.

That said, Alderson's success as a pre-modern theorem trucker is attributable, in no small measure, to his control over a fleet of concept-delivery vehicles. These comprise his annual seminars in marketing theory, which commenced in 1951 (and attendance at which was by Aldersonian fiat); his pioneering co-edited texts on marketing theory (in the second of these, Reavis Cox identifies Wroe as 'the dominant force keeping us to the task of working out an effective body of theory');[54] and, most importantly of all, his bi-monthly pro-theory newsletter, *Cost and Profit Outlook* (which was published under the auspices of Alderson's consulting firm and, according to Lusch,[55] was not only widely circulated amongst the academic community but was regularly discussed in lectures and seminars).

More than almost anything else, then, Wroe Alderson can be considered a conceptual channel captain, whose function was to convey the conjectures of conglomerate academic disciplines, control the output of marketing's theoretical utilities and do everything in his power to expand the market for marketing theory. Viewed in retrospect, Alderson is a sort of scholarly sales representative whose principal product is marketing principles, who sells the idea of ideas on selling and flogs the functionalist framework for all he is worth:

> The underlying viewpoint is the viewpoint of functionalism, which is likely to become the unifying thread in all the behavioural sciences. Functionalism has held a prominent place in sociology, psychology and anthropology. Several leading economists can broadly be classified as members of the functionalist school. . . . From his reading in the behavioural sciences this author has long been aware that functionalism is the only school of thought which provides a common thread in all these various fields.[56]

Above and beyond marketing marketing, Alderson is a middleman in another important way. He is a literary middleman, a stylistic distributor. As previously noted, the thinker's thinker could write – really write. Unlike many marketing academics and contra those who consider him unreadable, Wroe had a wonderful way with words, as the following 'ecological' extract from a private letter indicates:

> We have just had a week of golden October days beside the Chesapeake, with Heaven waiting in every sunset.

The hoarse cry of the wild goose is like a brute reaction to beauty too bright to be borne. A world in flames, over land and water, re-enacts the ancient and tragic mystery of Death-in-Life and Life-in-Death.

The dogwood leaves are dying in a burst of battle red. Oak and maple strew the lane with the vivid hues of passion and the soft shades of memory. And soaring there on a high stark limb is the scarlet banner of ivy.

On the water, where life first found its home, life is still harvesting life; a fisherman out in the chilly dawn; the sails of the oyster-men at noon; a belated woman crabber poling her skiff through the ripples along the shore. Underneath the surface the living still feeds on the living – or faces death in the stab of the heron or the swoop of the osprey.[57]

Yet, for all his literary abilities, Alderson's textual transvection – the words on the page that convey his ideas to a concept-consuming clientele – is decidedly flat, deliberately downbeat and largely devoid of ostentatious literary devices. Just as marketing is concerned with getting goods quickly and efficiently to market, so too Alderson's professional writing, particularly in his early articles, is straight to the point. Adjectives are rare, exclamation marks rarer still, alliteration is expressly eschewed, even when it is the obvious stylistic option, an impersonal tone prevails at all times (the first person singular is uncommon compared to self-identifying locutions, for example 'this author', 'the present writer', or 'the senior author') and, not least, his prose has a curiously telegraphic character, a strangely detached air that comes from an addiction to asyndeton (the excision of definite and indefinite articles). On many occasions, it is like reading a memorandum, an agenda, a bullet-pointed bulletin board with the bullet-points removed ('Number of firms engaged in wholesaling increased 50 per cent between 1939 and 1948 according to new official estimates').

True, Wroe's theoretical telegrams sometimes find room for literary flourishes, especially in his later works, but by and large Alderson's textual transvection is an uncluttered communications medium that gets his concepts to market with the minimum of fuss ('It is surprising how many words we can do without when writing a telegram'). Any stylistic curlicues, arabesques or flights of fancy that the first draft may have contained are largely expunged by the time the conceptual merchandise leaves Wroe's writing factory. It seems that his goods were graded and ground down before they entered the cerebral distribution channel:

He is acquiring the right to exploit the footing a firm occupies. He has his own reasons for wishing to acquire the opportunity that another is giving up. He may believe that he can operate a concern more successfully than his predecessor. He may be willing to accept a smaller return on his investment. He may be acquiring the business at a much lower figure than the original cost.[58]

Discursive Differentiation: The foregoing quote also illustrates a fundamental aim of Alderson's functionalism: namely, to establish marketing's
differential advantage or 'footing' in the academic scheme of things. A
functionalist interpretation of competition starts from the premise that
every successful firm or organized behaviour system is unique in some
way. Its offering is different from every other extant organism and firms
compete by making the most of their uniqueness. In doing so, they establish a special, ideally unassailable, niche or footing in the marketplace.
Differential advantage, however, is often fleeting, since rival firms strive
to denude, neutralize or in some way offset the competitive positioning of
the opposition. In a free, high-level economy, which sets great store by
innovation and improvement, something better, newer or cheaper – or,
most importantly, *different* – is always in the offing.

Just as the practice of marketing is 'embodied in the myth of
Prometheus',[59] so too its principles are guided by the precepts of differential advantage. Alderson's original aim, in a nutshell, was to
differentiate marketing from its academic rivals, to demonstrate that it is
a unique, specialized, stand-alone field of study.[60] Prior to Wroe's decisive
intervention, as Goodman explains, marketing was largely regarded as a
branch of applied economics, a view shared by many marketing academicians who were trained in the dismal science.[61] Alderson, by contrast,
contended that extant economic theory is inadequate for marketing's purposes. The unrealistic assumptions of economics – perfect competition,
perfect information, perfect decision-taking, etc. – simply do not square
with the everyday realities of the marketplace and the ever-present difficulties of organizing the orderly flow of manufactured goods from
producer to consumer:

> There is substantial overlapping to be sure between marketing and eco-
> nomics but not identity. Economics proper is preoccupied with the
> allocation of means in the pursuit of any human purpose. Marketing begins
> with the manifold purposes, expectations and anxieties of the consuming
> unit and analyses the creation of assortments to satisfy these needs. The
> marketing analyst can make good use of the tools of economics but mar-
> keting has also developed its own techniques directed toward the expansion
> of demand and the efficiency of exchange transactions. Insatiable demand
> and the costless transaction are convenient notions for some purposes but
> they have no place in marketing.[62]

Marketing, he acknowledged, has much to learn from the manifold
schools of economic thought; most notably from the American institu-
tionalists like J.R. Commons, the monopolistic competition of E.H.
Chamberlin and the Austrian insights of von Mises and Boehn-Bawerk.

What's more, marketing can never hope to attain the rigour and eloquence of formal economic theory. But in order to solve the unique problems that it seeks to address, such as the conundrum of organizational survival – the fact that they hang on in demonstrably 'uneconomic' circumstances, marketing needs 'a broader and richer approach than is currently offered by any school of economics'.[63] To this end, Alderson argued, marketing theorists must be prepared to extract whatever they need from wherever they can find it and adapt the exogenous concepts to their particular problem-solving purposes:

> Marketing already has its own method of fact finding and analysis and its own standards of performance in scientific research. It must be ready to draw on any division of the social sciences that can contribute to the solution of marketing problems. Its need for theory is a need for the kind of perspective that can guide the selection of methods in specific problem situations and that can facilitate the integration of research findings into a growing body of scientific marketing principles.[64]

That said, Alderson's competitive desire to differentiate the discipline isn't solely directed at marketing's academic antecedents. It also applies to himself and is demonstrated through readily identifiable discursive devices. In other words, Wroe's prose rhetorically reinforces his scholarly dissimilarity and distinctiveness. It has an Olympian tone that effectively sets him above the issues he's addressing and thereby intimates that we are in the presence of a marketing master, an original thinker, someone whose weighty words of wisdom are worth attending to ('It is well to remember', 'To use a technical term', 'Such distinctions are not without importance in business and in marketing'; 'The accumulating elements for at least a rudimentary theory of marketing are scattered throughout the literature of the social sciences').

Imperious though this textual tone sometimes appears to us (fifty years after the event), our Ur-guru's insinuation of effortless superiority is achieved in three main ways. First, by his citation of, comments on and comparisons with a compendious catalogue of celebrated thinkers from Adam Smith and Alfred Marshall to René Descartes and Francis Bacon:

> Descartes was not the first to emphasise the need for getting rid of preconceptions. In fact, this was the main burden of the *Novum Organum*, written a few years earlier by his great contemporary, Sir Francis Bacon.[65]

> Admittedly this version of marketing theory is speculative and in that sense is similar to the successive versions of economic theory from Adam Smith to Alfred Marshall.[66]

Bertrand Russell, in one of his gentler jibes at the pragmatists, says that this
school would obviously prefer Othello, the man of action to Hamlet, the
man of thought. This figure is singularly inept since Hamlet brought about
the death of six people through violent action.[67]

Second, by his constant recourse to highfalutin language – 'effectuate',
'propinquitous', 'abnegation', 'shibboleth' – and equally ostentatious
euphemisms like 'the experienced household purchasing agent' (for
housewife) or 'once a meritorious product obtains a foothold, it gains
momentum from the contagion of favourable reactions' (for 'success
breeds success'). So extravagant is Alderson's vocabulary in fact that it is
fair to say he never utilizes a diminutive word when a gargantuan one
will suffice ('procrastination', 'attenuated', 'inculcation', 'serendipity').

Third, and most effectively, by occasional use of the opposite rhetorical
device, the low-falutin ruse of ridicule. He repeatedly skewers marketing's
academic forebears by humorously highlighting the absurd assumptions,
quixotic conjectures and manifest wrong-headedness of mainstream economics, marketing's allegedly illustrious intellectual ancestor ('Received
competitive theory seems to embody the myth of the Garden of Eden and
the fall of man. Man and markets having once been in a state of perfection
have fallen from grace so that only imperfect markets are found in the real
world today'). Admittedly, he metes out the same rough-and-tumble treatment to putative rivals within the marketing discipline, which is rather less
than edifying.[68] What's more, his differentiation-driven contention that
marketing was theoretically bereft before functionalism appeared on the
scene, is somewhat parsimonious with the facts, to put it politely; in literary terms, Alderson would be deemed an 'unreliable narrator'.

Such lapses on the road to differential advantage, however, are more
than made up for by Wroe's occasional flashes of acerbic wit. Consider his
riposte to the rhetorical question 'Do you really expect the head of an
organization to take a shot of survival every morning along with his
orange juice?' ('One might reply that he would not expect the executive to
take a short of profit maximization either'). Consider also his faux-
apologetic exposé of E.H. Chamberlin's manifest otherworldliness:

> At our first meeting in 1933 Chamberlin was amused by questions about his
> sales experience and how he had acquired his remarkable knowledge of
> marketing. In the perspective of some thirty-odd years it appears that the
> most serious limitation in Chamberlin's achievements stemmed from the
> fact that his knowledge of marketing minutiae was purely academic.[69]

To add insult to injury, he concludes this demolition of a rival claimant to
his concept of differential advantage by disingenuously stating: 'There is

no intention to minimize the enormous impact Chamberlin has had on marketing thought over this period'.

Disorganized Belief System: As far as Wroe Alderson is concerned, there are two main organized behaviour systems, the family and the firm. The former faces the dilemma of decision-taking in a epoch of abundance, which stands in marked contrast to economists' traditional concern with the allocation of scarce resources. The latter is driven by a desire to maximize its revenue stream, which again stands in marked contrast with the profit-maximizing assumptions of economics.

Analogously, the organized behaviour system that is Alderson's body of thought is nothing if not abundant, the conceptual equivalent of a torrential income stream. His prose may be placid – flat calm, if deceptively deep and dangerous – but the cascade of concepts is almost overpowering. Indeed, the decision-taking difficulties faced by family units are not dissimilar to the difficulties facing readers of *Marketing Behavior and Executive Action* or *Dynamic Marketing Behavior*. The raging revenue stream of his thought is difficult to harness and control. This difficulty is compounded by the fact that his corpus is closer to a disorganized belief system than an organized behaviour system. Alderson's ideas, to put it bluntly, are all over the place. Or so it seems. Closer examination, however, reveals that this ostensible disorganization is quite deliberate.[70] There is method in the master marketer's madness.

In this regard, contemporary readers of Wroe's prose cannot help but be struck by his constant recourse to three distinctive literary devices, *excursus*, *anachrony* and *ellipsis*, all of which convey a sense of seeming textual disorganization. Excursus is the technical term for digressions and analogous rhetorical tacks away from the main line of argument. Now, most would concede that, whatever else it is, Wroe's writing is full of digressions (as he openly acknowledges and occasionally 'apologises' for). Again and again, he introduces a topic, goes off on a tangent and returns unannounced to the original topic several lengthy paragraphs later. What's more, the tangential material is almost always theoretical – as opposed to, say, an empirical illustration of his basic point – and by the time Wroe's thesis gets back on track the reader has lost touch with the overall arc of the argument and, on occasion, the very will to live:

> This sketch for a theory of economic interaction may appear to have ranged far beyond the boundaries of marketing.[71]

> In recent years market analysts have talked about the process of 'diffusion', which is a term borrowed from anthropology. Incidentally, some

anthropologists are evolutionists and emphasize the way in which a new product or a new culture trait may originate independently in many separate areas.[72]

From a reader's perspective, the obvious solution to this digressive difficulty is simply to reread the offending passage, irritating though this can prove. Backtracking, however, not only compounds the feeling of dislocation and diffuseness, but it is further compounded by Alderson's fondness for *anachrony* in both *analeptic* and *proleptic* variants (flashbacks and flashforwards, in other words). Instead of a simple linear narrative, where A is followed by B, with C in hot pursuit, he repeatedly refers back to earlier sections, prior paragraphs and previously posited points ('Let us now return', 'Some years ago the author asserted', 'As indicated in the preceding chapter', 'Returning to the *Discourse on Method* by Descartes').

Conversely, he constantly defers the current discussion to some unspecified passage or chapter still to come and which one has completely forgotten about by the time it hoves into view ('the above factors will be discussed more fully later', 'The question of completeness . . . can only be answered after the development of an acceptable list of theorems'). In fact, it is not unusual to encounter an expression or concept that is not defined or elucidated for hundreds of pages (in *Marketing Behavior and Executive Action*, for instance, the notion of monostasy and systasy is introduced on page 136, but it is not explained until page 325). On one immortal occasion, he employs analepsis and prolepsis in the same sentence: 'We are still at the beginning of the informational revolution referred to earlier – the most remarkable developments still lie ahead'. In these discombobulating circumstances, it is not surprising that library copies of Alderson's texts are often heavily annotated by past readers, valiantly trying to impose a modicum of order on the author's confusing conceptual congeries.

Making work for marketing marginaliatists, as it were, may not have been the foremost functionalist's original intent, but his obsessive *ellipsis* is suggestive of design rather than accident. Ellipses draw attention to absences and, in Alderson's case, this means research that is not to hand or can't be incorporated for some reason. Time and again, Wroe alludes to proprietary findings, confidential consultancy exercises, unpublished research reports and the bulging archives of his consultancy firm, which contain the necessary empirical proof of his current theoretical contentions ('These charts will not be reproduced here', 'our results, as reported in various places', 'hundreds of projects for individual clients, manufacturers, wholesalers and retailers, and for public agencies at all levels have helped to shape the view of marketing reality reported here'). Very little of this hard evidence, however, is allowed to sully the maestro's magniloquent prose, since 'it is not germane to the present discussion' or 'lies beyond the scope of this article' or 'space does not permit detailed discussion' (even though there's always ample room for a theoretical excursus or two). Now, this is not to suggest that Alderson withheld the scholarly evidence with malice aforethought. On the contrary, his corpus contains a number of fairly straightforward empirical articles, such as his comprehensive study of retail competition in Philadelphia,[73] though excursus, anachrony and ellipsis are much to the fore. In fact, the Philly article is a classic example of off-stage argument, where almost every hard fact is tantalisingly withheld, yet it still comes across as a solid empirical study.

On top of the complexities of Professor Alderson's chronotope – that is, the temporal and spatial alignment of his rhetorical trajectory – the basic organization of his textual material is anything but straightforward. The books in particular lack a clear-cut structure, lacking the sense of one chapter leading logically on to the next and the next. They flit, rather, from topic to topic and, even within the chapters, the headings are either misplaced (often a paragraph too late or too early) or are worded slightly differently from the information that follows. Subheadings, furthermore, are conspicuous by their absence, as are figures, tables, scholarly citations and, of all things, punctuation marks, commas especially:

> The direction for advance which is indicated here is an analysis of the process of price negotiation and the conditions for a balance of economic forces achieved through bargaining. Ordinarily there are limits observed by either side and principles by which their bargaining activities are guided which may result in a long-run outcome with respect to process which is not too different from the long-run outcome under the supposition of pure competition. In a mass production economy the central consideration in negotiation may generally be expected to be the endeavor to balance access to markets through diversified channels against the need for enough volume to reach the breaking point in production costs.[74]

> Of the total number of establishments in the wholesale trades about half were accounted for by service and limited wholesale functions alone while goods handling intermediaries number approximately 160,000 or two-thirds of all firms engaged in wholesale trade. For all wholesale trade the average volume of business in 1948 was about 780 thousand dollars as compared with approximately 275 thousand in 1939. For all goods handling intermediaries the average figure for 1948 was approximately 500 thousand as compared with 200 thousand in 1939.[75]

Yet, for all the discursive disarray, it is important to appreciate that the disorganization is quite deliberate (or if accidental, brilliantly so). Akin to the tantalizing jumble of olde-tyme antique dealers or the here-be-bargains dishabille of department stores at sales time, Alderson's seemingly unsystematic prose performs an important rhetorical function. It is difficult because readers *expect*, and to some extent *require*, it to be. Important ideas and concepts are often presented in a recondite manner, as any reader of Jacques Lacan, Fredric Jameson, Judith Butler or, God help us, Guattavari Spivak, will concede. Lucidity can be an impediment to acceptance when serious theoretical matters are being disseminated. Like it or not, convoluted prose carries connotations of profundity, sagacity and scholarly perspicacity. As Alderson admits in his very last publication, unsophisticated readers are intimidated, indeed overawed, by displays of apparent erudition.[76] They blame themselves for failing to get the point and mistake the author's incomprehensibility for insightfulness.

Thus, far from being examples of bad writing, Alderson's impenetrable articles are models of intellectual intimidation and carefully calculated obfuscation. They represent organized disorganisation. They digress to impress. They flit to flummox. They withhold empirical evidence, not because there is no empirical evidence to support the argument, but because it operates more powerfully in absentia. In the decades since Alderson's death, many commentators have condemned his unsystematic style and failure to operationalize his concepts.[77] It is equally arguable that it is this very unsystematicity that continues to attract readers – intrigued readers, bemused readers, eager readers – and that operationalizing his ideas would be the death of them. Alderson is the Everest of marketing scholarship, something difficult, dangerous and demanding which draws people because it's there. He was on a mission to mystify and most would agree that he succeeded triumphantly.

Heterogeneous Hypotheses: Just as Wroe Alderson can reasonably claim to be marketing's most distinctively difficult thinker – his school of thought is nothing if not *sui generis* – so too he is one of the most heterogeneous. In truth, if the seminal thinker's corpus had to be summarized in a single word, that word would probably be heterogeneous. It is heterogeneous, furthermore, on both sides of the scholarly market. His inputs are heterogeneous, his outputs are heterogeneous, his content is heterogeneous, his style is heterogeneous, he supplies heterogeneous ideas to meet the heterogeneous demands of heterogeneous audiences of executives, academics, students and, to some extent at least, the general reading public.

Be that as it may, by far the most striking thing about Alderson's body of work is the wealth, diversity and sheer catholicism of his source material. With the possible exception of Russell Belk, another cite-heavy scholar who browbeats readers with his bionic erudition, no one in the history of marketing thought can claim to be so widely read. Whether it be mathematics or military history, whether it be game theory or gestalt psychology, whether it be particle physics or pragmatist philosophy, whether it be systems theory or Shakespearean tragedy, whether it be institutional economics or information technology, whether it be cultural anthropology or Parsonian sociology, Wroe Alderson was grounded in them all, and more besides:

> Russell has suggested elsewhere that philosophers can be classified according to a tripartite division based on whether their chief interest is a theory of knowledge, a theory of action, or a theory of value. He places himself in the first category and points to Dewey and his fellow pragmatists as prime examples of the second. Actually in some of its versions pragmatism is a theory of knowledge promulgated by thinkers who are impressed with the importance of action. When philosophers really make action primary they are inclined to emphasize its irrational character, whether they end up by deploring it like Schopenhauer or glorifying it like Nietzsche and Bergson. A theory of rational action which would provide an adequate perspective for the executive and policy-maker has yet to be formulated.[78]

In addition to the heterogeneity of Alderson's input, his output is equally polymorphic. He writes what can only be described as heterogeneous prose. Instead of the standard subject–verb–object construction, beloved by advocates of plain English, he often includes two or more contrasting ideas in a single sentence and, as often as not, incorporates a couple of tangential sub-clauses, for good measure. This propensity accounts for the inordinate length of many Aldersonian paragraphs and sentences, some of which are Faulknerian in their interminability, as well as the high incidence of and/or conjunctions in the great man's syntax. When added to his penchant for approximations ('sometimes', 'generally', 'usually', 'commonly', 'roughly', 'vaguely', 'on the average', 'something resembling'), it is more or less easy to understand why certain readers occasionally find Wroe's writing somewhat dense and/or vaguely disorientating:

> In order to measure some aspects of effort expended and work done, reliance can best be put upon concepts of movement or flow through some one or more varieties of space and time against the resistance of some one or more varieties of obstacle. To use these concepts effectively, clear definitions will be required of distributive space and time, location or position, and flow or movement.[79]

The Aldersonian brain forest, in keeping with his preferred ecological conceit, is a jungle of jumbled ideas and expressions. His books and articles are teeming with life but difficult to penetrate. Yet, just as he was much more than an apologist for Talcott Parsons, the early postwar ecological analogist nonpareil (and the single biggest influence on Alderson's thought),[80] so too Wroe's rota of metaphors is much more heterogeneous than he is given credit for. Granted, the great man makes frequent reference to mutation, adaptation, parasitism, succession, survival, hypertrophy, habitability, evolution, niche and analogous ecological figures of speech. Across Alderson's corpus as a whole, however, ecological references are vastly outnumbered by his deployment of military metaphors, corporeal conceits, agricultural similes, travelling tropes and, occasionally, unfortunate admixtures of the above:

> Thus competition presents an analogy to a succession of military campaigns rather than to the pressures and attrition of a single battle. A competitor may gain ground through a successful campaign based on new product features or merchandizing ideas. It may lose ground or be forced to fall back on its core position because of the successful campaigns of others.[81]

> Finding the source of the difficulty in a marketing system is something like diagnosing the factors in a case of human illness or the malfunctioning of a mechanism such as an automobile.[82]

> It is difficult to measure their separate contributions to productivity since this is a clear case of multiple causation like the contributions of the sun and the rain to a crop of wheat.[83]

> The executive is in a position something like the driver on a hazardous road. He must always concentrate on taking the next step successfully even though this may involve some sacrifice in breadth of perspective. The planner can give uninterrupted study to the route as a whole because he does not have his hand on the wheel.[84]

> In the simpler and more homogeneous type of competition, a leading firm might be able to rest on its oars if it felt that it was the best in the field. . . . The firms themselves may not always survive the storm and may have to cut loose from earlier commitments in order to have a fighting chance.[85]

Although there's much more about Hannibal than habitat in Alderson, the key point about his verdant metaphors and disconcerting sentences is that they are quite deliberate. They perform an important function. They are verisimilitudinous. In their labyrinthine way, they reflect the heterogeneity, the plurivalence, the out-and-out complexity of the phenomena he writes about. Marketing, for Alderson, is not the 'grubby country cousin of economics which pokes around in the soil of human behavior'.[86] On the contrary, it is an extremely elaborate, carefully coordinated, smoothly integrated system, involving all manner of intricate sorts and transformations. The complexity of Alderson's style captures the complexity of the marketing system. The syntactic doubling parallels the double search process of buyers and sellers in heterogeneous markets. The mixture of metaphors is a stylistic manifestation of the mixing and matching activity that takes place as merchandise is transhipped, transposed, transvected. Anyone inclined to dismiss or disdain 'the complex and wondrous mechanism by which goods and services move from producer to ultimate consumer'[87] is quickly disabused, as in this compelling description of the complexities of competition in a small corner of the flour-milling business:

> For ease of reference, consider local millers in Alabama and Kansas, blenders in Alabama, and national millers in Minneapolis. The national miller competes with the Kansas miller in selling flour to the blender in Alabama, and also in selling packages products to Alabama consumers. The national miller also competes with the Alabama miller both in sales to blenders and in sales to the consumer. He competes with the blender as well as with other national millers in sales to the consumer. Here are six competitive fronts facing the national miller, even though only three types of competitors are involved. To complete the network, all the competitive relations involving the other types, but not involving the national miller would have to be listed. The Kansas miller competes with the blender as well as supplying him, and also competes with the Alabama mill. The Alabama mill also competes with the blender as well as supplying him. Altogether there are nine competitive relations which serve to integrate supply and demand throughout the market. Thus the competitive network is far more complicated and far more effective in transmitting competitive pressures than is immediately apparent from the conception of multilevel competition.[88]

Scholarly Sorting: To be sure, Wroe's writing doesn't simply reflect the complexity of his subject matter, significant though that is. The mirroring also applies to his key conceptual contributions. That is to say, the great guru is engaged, above all else, in an act of scholarly sorting. The building up and breaking down process of sorts and transformations – the very essence of the marketing system, according to Alderson – is exactly what he engaged in on an intellectual plane. Our evangelical ecologist practised what he preached. He provided time, space and form utility for a clientele of concept consumers. He interposed himself between supply and demand and, in line with functionalist precept, reduced the total number of conceptual exchanges that are otherwise necessary (I mean, how many marketers, then or now, *really* have time to read Marx or Freud?). In so doing, he placed himself in an important position as marketing's principal principles supplier and this, in turn, helped him dominate and direct the market in marketing theory. Or, as he himself observed 'one way in which a firm can gain differential advantage is by organizing the market in a way that is favorable to its own operations'.[89]

Although Professor Alderson is unsurpassed in his role as an academic conduit – none of the others in *Writing Marketing* comes close – he is more than a past captain and coordinator of the channel of conceptual distribution. He transforms as well as transports the theoretical material. Many of these transformations, I grant you, are fairly minor, such as his translation of Cannon's and Commons's terminology into marketing idiom (the former's 'homeostasis' becomes 'internal balance' and the latter's 'collective action' is renamed 'group behavior'). But, the essential point is that he almost always altered, adapted or added to the original assortment, whether it be Margaret Mead, Chester Bernard or Adam Smith:

> The thirteen tribes covered in this study were scattered over an immense area in North America, Africa and the South Pacific. . . . The editor [Margaret Mead], in the manner of a field anthropologist, stresses individual differences and anomalies which blur the distinction suggested by the classification. Yet, there seems to be more room for generalization in the summary of material than was fully utilized by the editor.[90]

> Chester Bernard, a distinguished student of the executive function, has said that the head of a large company should not assume that he is running the organization. He should regard his role as that of keeping the organization tuned up. . . . This statement of Bernard's expresses a philosophy but does not describe a procedure. The concept of keeping an organization tuned up involves a variety of possible activities.[91]

> The father of economics held that specialization and consequent division of labor was a good thing up to a point. Beyond that point there would be no further savings from specialization and costs would actually increase. The analysis does not quite work out that way, however, if we assume that heterogeneous demand is preexistent.[92]

In addition to his self-appointed role as scholarship's sorter-in-chief, Wroe Alderson is an inveterate rearranger of his own prose. His very sentences are shrines to the sorts-and-transformation process. Consider the following, far from atypical syntactical outpourings:

> Sorting is reclassification resulting in the creation of subsets from a set and sets from subsets. Earlier treatments have identified four aspects of sorting, one of which is allocation, possibly the most fundamental concept for

economics. It now seems possible to compress these types of sorting from four to two to achieve greater simplicity. Most characteristically, sorting suggests sorting out, which means breaking down a heterogeneous set into homogeneous subsets. Sorting out can also be called assignment, since it means assigning each member of a set to the appropriate subset. Assignment is the more general term, while allocation can still be employed to designate the special case in which the original set is regarded as homogeneous.[93]

Exchangeability would be what is called in logic 'an equivalence relationship' and would have the qualities of being reflexive, transitive, and symmetrical. This discussion is only intended to illustrate the process of building up a logical vocabulary and analytical framework suitable for a formal theory of marketing.[94]

Logophile though he was, it is fair to say that Wroe Alderson loved words well rather than wisely. Whereas he set great store by the efficiency and effectiveness of the marketing system he so painstakingly described – how many sorts, he once asked, is too many? – the self-same rules do not apply to his own intellectual transvection. He ceaselessly sifts, shifts, shapes and sorts his published output. The same basic ideas constantly recur throughout his corpus, albeit in slightly different packaging or significantly modified forms. What's more, each iteration or turn of his intellectual inventory almost always involves locutional logistics of some kind. Thus *componency* morphs into *seriality*, which becomes *circularity*, spawns *concurrence*, begets *divergence*, sires *convergence* and eventually extrudes *centrality*. In less than two pages![95]

Actually, there are just too many textual sorts and transformations. Alderson's corpus evolves, so to speak, from meaningless to meaninglesser. 'There is the danger', he aptly observed, 'of confusing the customer and losing the sale by presenting too many alternatives'.[96] Quite write.

In fairness to the textual titan, it should be acknowledged that his writing exhibited clear evidence of stylistic progression. Just as marketing is an activity that turns conglomerate resources into coherent assortments, so too Wroe's prose becomes increasingly accessible with the passage of time. The heavy theorizing, abstract arguments, impersonal approach, deadly seriousness, insufferable self-importance and complex, unpunctuated syntax of his early publications, slowly give way to amusing anecdotes, alliterative indulgence, feather-light turns of phrase, illuminating empirical examples, endearing self-deprecation and the occasional exclamation mark! It's hard to believe, for example, that the author who wrote, 'The direction for advance which is indicated here is an analysis of the process of price negotiation and the conditions for a balance of economic forces achieved through bargaining' also wrote 'And now, at last, the ultimate breakthrough the world has been waiting for – the electric toothbrush!' Or that the same person penned 'work habits are communicated by contagion rather than by precept' and 'She may be accustomed to trade at Wibbleton but there is no recourse if she suddenly decides to shift to Wobbleton'.[97]

All sorts of reasons can no doubt be advanced for this stylistic transformation: the contribution of co-authors, the editorial-cum-review process, advancing years, deteriorating health, acceptance by the academy in general and Wharton Business School in particular, which lessened his autodidactic desire to prove himself. Yet, regardless of the underlying reasons, the fact of the matter is that Wroe's prose itself evolved, in keeping with functionalist precept. True, the transformation was patchy and the keepers of the Aldersonian flame have not done him any posthumous favours, insofar as Wroe's most entangled articles are the ones that tend to be reprinted and anthologized. However, by the end of his life, the self-styled Puritan was no longer hiding his prodigious literary light under a bushel of abstruse academese:

> Marketing attempts to alter the patterns of contemporary culture and advertising is its primary instrument for this purpose. Some critics charge that advertising is an active agency in the debasement of public taste. It is more likely that advertising has contributed to cultural confusion. Advertising itself is a public art, and as an art it deserves and must expect criticism. . . . Who wants to live in a hypochondriac's world in which the greatest joy is quick relief from headache? Who wants to live in a fool's paradise in which smokers believe that they can indulge in nicotine and yet escape all the hazards of indulgence? Who really wants the dullard's cuisine in which bland and tasteless foods are touted as the gourmet's delight?[98]

Who indeed?

The Descent of Manuscripts

When the literary achievements of Wroe Alderson are weighed in the balance, one all-important question arises – why did this talented wordsmith write in the way that he did? Clearly, this question is impossible to answer, since the great man has long gone to the organized behaviour system in the sky, and even if he were available for interview, it is not certain he could fully articulate his literary rationale. As we noted in Chapter 1, studies of living authors often reveal that they find it difficult to make sense of their motivational mainsprings.[99] Be that as it may, biopoetic literary theory intimates that the environment might have had something to do with it, that the ecological context of Wroe's writings is a salient explanatory factor. To be sure, our memories of the fifties are grossly distorted by hindsight, nostalgia and media misrepresentations, the Hollywood studio stereotype of pearly picket fences, chrome-clad automobiles, ever-burgeoning suburbs and nuclear fallout-fearing nuclear families of 2.4 children and an unfailingly faithful canine. Historians, however, agree that the epoch in which Alderson penned his words of marketing wisdom was characterized by a progressive, onward-and-upward, science-will-provide worldview.[100] As Wroe himself acknowledges in one of his final published articles, 'at the time we were perhaps all a little hypnotized by faith in technological advance'.[101]

In marketing terms, the late fifties/early sixties cusp is remembered for many things such as the creative revolution, the 'modern' marketing concept, the much-vaunted managerial paradigm, the fashion for motivation research and the intellectual ferment that spawned several still-studied theoretical frameworks (for example, the 4Ps, marketing mix, channels theory, market segmentation, wheel of retailing, hierarchy of advertising effects and many more). In retrospect, nevertheless, it seems clear that these scholarly developments are part and parcel of, arguably subsumed by, the broader art-or-science debate. At a time when marketing was tarred by the Edsel fiasco, the Quiz Show and radio payola scandals, the highly critical Ford and Carnegie Reports, and the obloquy of prominent public intellectuals like J.K. Galbraith, Vance Packard, Rachel Carson and Betty Freidan, it was imperative that marketing demonstrated its scientific aspirations, scholarly credentials and unwavering commitment to objectivity, reliability, dispassion, truth and, ideally, the identification of law-like generalizations.[102]

It is arguable, then, that Professor Alderson was suppressing his natural literary instincts in order to write in a para-scientific manner, a manner which is characterized by flat, spare, neutral, unadorned prose, prose that sets more store by transparency than mellifluousness. True, he slips from time to time, especially in later years when he may have felt less need to man the minimalist barricades. But the bulk of his published work gives no real hint of the marketing maestro's rhetorical prowess. The telegraphic tone, the eschewal of adjectives, the compound sentences, the terminological tergiversation, the lengthy digressions, the elevated expressions, the avoidance of asinine alliteration, the nothing if not noetic vocabulary, the lack of sound bites, aphorisms or even boxes-and-arrows diagrams, all bespeak scientific rigour, scholarly propriety and absolute integrity. Casual readers of Wroe Alderson may smile wryly when they encounter his occasional exhortations to communicate clearly. The fact of the matter, however, is that Alderson *was* a brilliant communicator, who brilliantly communicated the complexity of marketing, the seriousness of scholarly purpose, the legitimacy of the subject area and the richness of its intellectual hinterland at a time when the discipline was considered an offshoot of economics at best or a lair of wily ne'er-do-wells at worst. Reading Wroe may be heavy sledding but heavy sledding has its place.

The utilitarian, hard-headed tenor of Alderson's pragmatic poetics is perfectly illustrated by his constant recourse to numerical discourse. Although Wroe was a talented mathematician (at one point, he immodestly claims to have solved the Goldbach conjecture) and his solo-authored publications are peppered with equations and formulae (Marketing Yield Ratio, Index of Productivity, Sortability Scale, Ratio of Advantage), he can hardly be described as a quants jock. Quite the opposite. Indeed, in line with Reavis Cox's[103] recommendation that when you're looking for a survey, 'hire a surveyor', Alderson was happy to subcontract his statistics to specialist suppliers, such as Paul Green, who contributed nine quantitative chapters to *Planning and Problem Solving in Marketing*.[104]

If, at most, Wroe was a wannabe number-cruncher, he was a brilliant exponent of mathematical rhetoric. He appreciated that big numbers are blessed with a gee-whiz, believe-it-or-not, Guinness Book of World Records quality, which is guaranteed to impress even the most innumerate reader or, for that matter, convince anyone who dares doubt the marketing master. Thus his model of consumer behaviour contains 24 stages (compared to the usual 4 or 5); his marketing planning procedure involves 14 steps and 80 tasks (instead of the normal 10 to 12); he is aware of 140 ways of setting prices (on electrical products alone); he claims to have identified no less than 600 customer motives (note, *exactly* 600, not approximately); his much-admired 'transvections' article includes an appendix with 72 definitions pertaining to three primitive concepts (sets, behaviour and expectations); and, most famously of all, the final chapter of *Dynamic Marketing Behavior* contains 150 'falsifiable propositions' for future functionalist researchers. To be sure, the merest glance at the list reveals that the vast majority are neither propositions nor falsifiable. Some of them are indistinguishable, others are incomprehensible and more than a few are inconsequential.[105] It is clear, then, that the *number* of putative propositions – precisely 150 – is the really important factor, not their falsifiability or otherwise. Accordingly, it is unsurprising that they remain untested, as many lachrymose, Woe-is-Wroe commentators point out. But, the *existence* of this theoretical treasure trove is an integral part of the Aldersonian legend, alongside his volcanic temper, superhuman scholarship and inscrutable literary style, what Smalley and Fraedrich aptly term 'his digressions, extensions and philosophic ramblings'.[106] The alleged hypotheses help keep Alderson's memory green, help him stand out from the scholarly crowd and help ensure that his theoretical transvection is still operating, still delivering, still cranking after all these years.

Now, the foregoing should not be taken to mean that Alderson's published work is misleading, or meretricious or a mischievous morass of marketing misinformation. On the contrary, the peerless pedagogue consistently stresses his commitment to science, went to great lengths to promote scientific procedures, imposed a theoretical tithe on the clients of his consultancy firm, was awarded a Ford Foundation Distinguished Professorship at New York University, found the first sponsor of the fledgling Marketing Science Institute and took pains to distinguish between proper scientific research and the action-orientated research typically required by executives.

At the same time, he is well aware of the 'marketability' of scientific method, the competitive advantage it confers upon its disciplinary distributors and, as his conceptual channel captaincy might lead one to expect, the opportunity it affords to steer the direction of the field. Accordingly, he pitches his published products at the 'scientific', theory-minded market segment. He adapts himself successfully to the prevailing scholarly environment. He carves out a rich niche in the extant academic ecosystem. He camouflages himself so successfully that to this very day most readers still think he lacks literary finesse. Perhaps Wroe Alderson's greatest stylistic accomplishment is that he convinces us he is stylistically unaccomplished.

Still, on reading Wroe's prose today, we cannot help but be struck by its 'experimental' character.[107] Far from being badly written, as conventional wisdom suggests, it is a remarkable example of avant-garde academese, an exercise in disciplinary defamiliarization, a veritable stream of scholarly consciousness. To be sure, Alderson didn't set out to write like James, or Joyce, or Faulkner, or Fitzgerald. However, the long, unpunctuated sentences are somewhat reminiscent of Kerouac's spontaneous prose. The detached tone has more than a touch of Surrealist 'automatic writing'. The interminable digressions are proto-Thomas Pynchon and the constant sorting of his sentences is akin to William Burroughs's cut-ups and collages.

In this regard, it is worth recalling that Wroe Alderson was a lifelong lover of art and literature (he also collected sculpture on a small scale). Furthermore, he lived through the entire period of modernist literary experimentation (he was fifteen when Mann wrote *Death in Venice*, twenty-five when *Ulysses* and *The Waste Land* appeared and in his prime as an author when the Beats were howling at the moon). Most importantly perhaps, he himself was a talented literary stylist, who endeavoured to write in a carefully controlled, suitably scientific manner. In so doing, he forged a difficult scholarly style, a style that has been disparaged, dismissed and disdained for decades, a style that, in accordance with the concept of differential advantage, is nothing if not distinctive. A style, I believe, that succeeds because of its difficulty. It is a literary style that exemplifies Alderson's own injunction, 'use the dramatic flair of the artist as well as tested principles of scientific technique'.[108]

6

The Anxieties of Morris Holbrook

Beware of people who dislike cats.

Old Irish Proverb[1]

He's the Most Tip-Top, Babadabap

Of all the writers in this book, the one I admire most is Morris Holbrook. Fantastic as Levitt's lexiconartistry is; prodigious as Kotler's powers of synthesis are; staggering as SDH's close reading abilities remain; and wonderful as Alderson's recondite wordsmithery was, the greatest of them all is Morris the Cat: aka Morris the Martyr, Morris the Epicurean, MoHo and Turtle – yep, Turtle. Morris is the foremost writer-in-residence of the marketing discipline.[2] When it comes to coining a quip, composing a sentence or constructing an argument, Morris is head and shoulders above everyone else. Reading his writing has sent more shivers down my spine than Stephen King and Bram Stoker combined. He is the only marketing scholar who consistently casts me, if not quite into paroxysms of Othelloesque jealousy, certainly into a slough of scholarly despond, where I wallow in my inability to write as well as the one and only MoHo.

I should perhaps declare a personal interest, since Morris has had more influence on me than any other marketing academic. As a deeply unhappy doctoral student, I was basically forced to 'unlearn' my natural writing style in order to get the damn degree and for eight or nine years thereafter I struggled to write in an alien mode of discourse. The only things that kept me (comparatively) sane during this painful period were my book reviews for *IMR*, such as the Kotler critique mentioned previously, and the wonderful published works of Morris B. Holbrook. I will never forget my first encounter with the Cat's peerless prose – a 1986 article in *JM* entitled 'A Note on Sado-masochism in the Review Process' – which completely blew me away, though it didn't encourage me to get in touch with my inner scribbler, curiously enough.[3] It was only after discovering postmodernism and realizing that the way marketing researchers write is not written in stone, as it were, that I sought to recapture the style that I'd reluctantly abandoned as a miserable PhD candidate – the style that Morris the Cat pioneered, the style that was staring me in the face while I was trying to do the write thing.

Since being released from stylistic servitude, I have basically followed in the tracks of the turtle (at a great distance, admittedly, and in the full knowledge that I'm falling further and further behind). In fairness to myself, I should point out that this imitative endeavour isn't deliberate on my part. It's just that I keep finding Morris the Cat's paw-prints on everything I'm interested in, or drawn towards. Whether it be postmodernism, introspection, retromarketing, romancing the market, the aesthetic imperative, the entertainment economy, space and place, writing books where each chapter has a marketing hero, or even tiny things like titular tomfoolery and biographical braggadocio, I usually discover that Morris has not only been there and done that, but been and done it much better than I ever could.[4] I hate him, really.

Miraculously, moreover, MoHo hasn't taken umbrage at my inept echoes of his signature style. On the contrary, he has been kindness itself. I have been invited to his plush apartment in the upper west side. I have met Sally, Chris and Rocky the cat; I have had the '25c tour' of his incredible record collection; I have seen the original artworks that pepper his papers; and I have even shared a frozen margarita at his favourite Mexican restaurant. (Readers familiar with the Holbrook oeuvre will appreciate the import of all this.) Edited volumes aside, I have never actually worked with the great man – he has to maintain some quality control, after all – but he's always been exceptionally supportive. Akin to the jazz greats who encouraged him in his early musical struggles, Morris is more than happy to help those who strive to follow in his footsteps.[5]

Be that as it may, the thing that makes MoHo great is the fecundity of his prose. Morris is one of those wonderful authors you can read, and reread, and find something new on each and every occasion. Prior to writing this chapter, for example, I reread his 1995 book *Consumer Research* and came across the following prescient passage, which resonates more now than it ever did:

> Prior to the mid-1980s, conventional research on consumer behavior had held fast to two basic tenets that served as the twin towers where members

of the field found their axiological and methodological homes. Tower 1 embodied our *axiology* – that is, our concept of value, based on the aims of the discipline – and erected its gleaming façade on a foundation of managerial relevance. Tower 2 embodied our philosophy of science and endorsed a neopositivistic perspective, which served as a methodological constraint on anyone wishing to undertake the study of consumption.

But during the mid-1980s, as I described in the previous chapter, members of the old guard in consumer research watched with horror as Tower 1 came tumbling down. Various free-spirited individuals had torn away the managerial bulwark of the discipline and had proclaimed the 'irrelevance of relevance' as a goal in studies of consumption. Many traditionalists took refuge in Tower 2 – namely, in a neopositivistic philosophy of science built on the hypothetico-deductive method.[6]

If the mark of a truly great writer is the ability to intrigue in perpetuity, then Morris B. Holbrook qualifies as a truly great writer. The Oracle Previously Known As Turtle (TOPKAT) is the best in our business. Bar none.

TOPKAT, however, isn't a one-off, much less in a league of his own. He too has his influences. Just as Philip Kotler is a faint echo of Karl Marx, so too Morris Holbrook owes an awful lot to Theodore Levitt. So much so, that Harold Bloom's 'anxiety of influence' thesis is applicable to our titanic textual twosome. Far from being positioned at opposite ends of the scholarly spectrum – one pure, the other applied – Theodore and TOPKAT are, in literary terms at least, precursor and ephebe, father and son, one and the same.

I kid you not.

Bloom With a View

By any reckoning Harold Bloom must be considered one of the foremost, if not *the* foremost, literary critics in the Western world.[7] Sterling Professor of the Humanities at Yale, he has written more than twenty-five books, edited approximately thirty anthologies and, as general editor of the Chelsea House literary criticism series, contributed over 350 introductory chapters. His meteoric academic ascent commenced at the comparatively early age of twenty-nine, when he published a radical reinterpretation of Percy Bysshe Shelley, a poet whose work was regarded by the then New Critical orthodoxy as unworthy of serious consideration, let alone canonization. This challenge to the critical elite was swiftly followed by a complete reassessment of the Romantic Movement, a torrent of theoretical texts during the drear deconstruction-dominated decades and, of late, a magisterial sequence of mature works, most notably *The Western Canon* and *Genius* which engage with the mainsprings of 'the great tradition', for example the Bible, Homer and Shakespeare.[8]

The principal reason for Bloom's singular status is that he has taken a commonplace of literary criticism – the notion that authors are influenced by the publications of their predecessors – and completely rethought, reimagined, reinvented and, not least, renamed its basic premises. Prior to Bloom's revolutionary reinterpretation, the standard assumption was that literary influence consisted of borrowings from or allusions to the work of earlier writers.[9] By means of close textual study, moreover, it was possible to identify and evaluate the influence of, say, Homer on Virgil, Spenser on Milton, Milton on Wordsworth and so on. The great tradition thus consisted of a progressive sequence of additions to and assimilations of poetic precursors, a cumulative standing on the shoulders of literary giants that attained its apogee in the Modernist movement of the present century. Drawing, however, upon an idiosyncratic admixture of Freudian psychology, Nietzschean nihilism and cabalistic codices – what Bruss terms 'the subterranean underside of western rationalism'[10] – Bloom formulated an agonistic, antagonistic, irredeemably antithetical interpretation of the forerunner–newcomer relationship.

In essence, this 'anxiety of influence' thesis posits that neophyte poets struggle to define themselves against the crushing weight of their 'strong' predecessors. Suffering the agonies of belatedness, a primal fear that their precursors have already said all that can be said, thereby leaving no room for literary laggards like themselves, the would-be poets engage in head-to-head conflict – a figurative life or death struggle – with the established, anxiety-inducing titans. Just as sons are oppressed by their fathers in the Oedipal triangle, and must be symbolically slain, so too the ephebe poet challenges his overshadowing antecedent by a process of radical 'misreading' or 'misprision' (literally mis-taking). This comprises an aggressive assimilation, a drastic distortion, a systematic remoulding of the predecessor's poems in the oeuvre of the novitiate. The newcomer, then, writes in a way that reshapes, reworks, recasts and ultimately *replaces* the achievements of the precursor. All poems, in other words, are misinterpretations of earlier poems, attempts to clear a space in the literary firmament for strong but anxiety-stricken arrivistes.[11]

For Bloom, the belated poet's bid to best his betters consists of six separate but sequential stages of development. Termed 'revisionary ratios', and aptly described by Baldick as 'full of abracadabras',[12] these comprise: *clinamen, tessera, kenosis, daemonization, askesis* and *apophrades*. Clinamen is a poetic misreading or misprision, where the ephebe endeavours to correct a perceived error in the predecessor's poem through a revisionary swerve or sidestep. Tessera requires the identification of something incomplete about the forerunner's corpus which is brought to antithetical fruition in the work of the newcomer. Kenosis comprises the tyro's attempt to break with the precursor by disavowing his own and, by implication, the father figure's poetic powers. This leads to daemonization, a movement towards a personalized counter-sublime, based upon a higher power than that employed by the antecedent poet. Askesis commences the return to the predecessor by means of a purgatorial period of isolation and retreat into the self. 'Burdened by an imaginative solitude that is almost a solipsism', the ephebe finally enters apophrades, where the progenitor is transcended and subsumed.[13] So much so, that it almost seems as if the earlier poet's work is a subset of the later's, as though the latter had actually composed, or made possible, the former's signature accomplishments.

Despite its terminological arabesques, Bloom's basic framework is comparatively straightforward and, as Bruss observes, appears to be predicated on the archetypal triadic pattern of glory–fall–recovery that is a staple of the western literary tradition from ancient myth and medieval fairy tale to television mini-series and blockbuster Hollywood movie.[14] Indeed, although the anxiety thesis concentrates on pugnacious inter-generational conflict, it is important to appreciate that the poets involved may not see it that way. The life or death struggle is not only metaphorical but unconscious, insofar as the creative efflorescence of the ephebe is *inspired* by the accomplishments of the precursor (the inchoate poetic impulse is *inside* the adept but it is precipitated by *outside* factors – Bloom describes this epiphanic sensation of discovery-cum-destiny as being 'flooded' or akin to a 'rebirth'). The neophyte's attitude to the father figure, furthermore, is essentially ambivalent, an uneasy amalgam of love, admiration and envy, coupled with undertones of rivalry and hate. Thus the belated poet unthinkingly palisades his own imaginative space by reading the parent poem in a revisionist manner or, strange though this may seem, by *not reading it at all*. However, since he cannot avoid the precursor's influence, not even by ignoring it, the best the ephebe can hope for is to write in such a strong manner that he assimilates the work of the forerunner and creates the illusion of primacy. In these admittedly counter-intuitive circumstances, where the meaning of any poem is, in effect, another poem, the place of the critic is to practise what Bloom terms 'antithetical criticism'. That is to say, literary critics must read each poem as its author's misreading of an earlier poem, or of poetry in general, and just as strong poets are doomed to misread, so too are strong critics. For Bloom, in fact, all criticism is prose poetry and all poetry versified criticism.

The anxiety of influence thesis is undoubtedly complex, unfailingly extravagant and utterly incomprehensible in places, albeit no more so than the perplexing ruminations of Wroe Alderson. Yet a moment's reflection suggests that it is not entirely irrelevant to the academic marketing context. The published reflections of our discipline's emeriti often draw attention to the inspiration provided by and debt of gratitude owed to an illustrious predecessor.[15] What is more, tyro marketing scholars are often beset by all sorts of anxieties concerning their likely contributions to the cerebral cause. As 'everything' has already been said on the subject of, say, brand choice, relationship marketing or the internationalization process, or so it seems, how can they possibly contribute to the conversation or clear a space for themselves in the great scholarly scheme of things?

In fact, some form of intellectual space clearing is a standard trope, arguably *the* standard trope, at the commencement of almost every published academic paper. Introductory paragraphs are replete with spatial-cum-positioning expressions like 'gap', 'lack', 'silence', 'situate', 'open up', 'lacunae', 'caesura', 'surprising omission', 'strangely neglected', 'curiously overlooked', 'contribute to body of knowledge' and so on and so forth. More importantly perhaps, *failure* to employ some form of space clearing literary device suggests that a contribution is *not* being made and, if that is the case, there is no compelling rationale for publication in the first place.

Excuse Me, While I Touch The Sky

Strictly speaking, of course, the anxiety thesis does not apply to arriviste academics (panic-stricken or otherwise). Nor, for that matter, is the influence apparent to the influenced (it is unconscious, after all).[16] The anxiety of influence thesis only applies to 'strong poets' – the stylists supreme of the discipline – and, in this regard, there are only two serious contenders for the strong poet accolade, Theodore Levitt and Morris Holbrook. The former, as we have seen, is routinely referred to as the voice, the spokesperson, the personification of marketing, the epitome of marketing and the marketing concept. Thanks to a string of seminal and much cited papers, an extended sequence of provocative editorials in the *Harvard Business Review* and a hefty back-catalogue of best-selling books and anthologies, Levitt is in a literary class apart.[17] For many practising managers, Theodore Levitt is more than a skilful advocate of the marketing cause, Theodore Levitt *is* marketing.

If Ted is the personification of marketing scholarship for numerous non-academics, TOPKAT is the personification of scholarship within the academic marketing community. W.T. Dillard Professor of Marketing at Columbia University, New York, MoHo is perhaps the discipline's most outspoken opponent of managerial orientation – the widely held belief that business schools exist to serve the perceived needs of business-people – and the most articulate advocate of marketing research, pure research, for its own sake.[18] His one-man campaign against the philistin-ism of marketing practitioners, as well as their manifold academic apologists and professorial patsies, has been waged in a series of mono-graphs, reviews, essays and books, most notably *Postmodern Consumer Research*, *The Semiotics of Consumption* and *Consumer Research: Introspective Essays on the Study of Consumption*.[19] True, his own arrestingly written accounts of these endeavours suggest that Holbrook has staggered from resounding defeat to resounding defeat. He frequently warns newcomers not to follow in his footsteps, but a long and distinguished record of pub-lication in the premier academic outlets suggests otherwise.[20] As one cynic has rightly observed, 'Morris has published more papers on the problems of getting published than most of us have publications'.[21]

On the surface at least, Levitt, a Jewish immigrant, and Holbrook, a mid-western WASP, couldn't be more different. Sheer productivity, illus-trious careers and the admiration of their peers aside, the former epitomizes the pragmatic end of the marketing spectrum. Despite his august academic base in possibly the world's most prestigious business school, Levitt writes short, punchy and largely citation-free articles for and about practising managers. His carefully crafted textual persona is that of a cracker-barrel management philosopher, a purveyor of wry, homespun, seat-of-the-pants, eminently implementable pearls of marketing *wisdom*. One almost imagines him in a rocking chair on a balmy southern porch, idly whittling, chewing tobacco and expectorating gobbets of practical advice to a circle of admiring practitioners.

Holbrook, by contrast, is not only an erudite exponent of the imprac-tical and unimplementable, but he is the author of long, learned, intellectually challenging, citation-strewn papers about abstruse philo-sophical, literary and aesthetic issues.[22] His equally carefully-crafted textual persona is that of the urbane urbanite – a widely read, if some-times less than worldly-wise, denizen of literary salons, art galleries, bijou restaurants, chic shops, fashionable therapists and avant-garde, off-off-Broadway productions. He is the archetypal east coast intellectual-cum-culture-vulture-cum-art-for-art's-sake aesthete. He is an élitist who takes pride in his élitism and is not reluctant to chastise the anti-élitist among us:

> In other words – beyond the rhetorical force of such epithets as racist or sexist, beyond the besmirching power of names like homophobic or ethno-centric, beyond the dismissive quality of such coinages as lookism or ageism, beyond phallocentric or xenophobic, beyond Orientalism or other neolo-gisms – the one handy-dandy, all-purpose, cut-and-dried, dyed-in-the-wool,

true-blue, and, indeed, indelible slur that we can all apply more or less indiscriminately to discredit any person or position with whom or which we happen to disagree is to call that object of our distastes elite, elitist or elitism.[23]

Awopbopaloobop Alopbamboom

Closer inspection, however, indicates that Ted and Morris are not in fact polar opposites but one and the same, precursor and ephebe, father and son. Interestingly, this parallel is nowhere better illustrated than in their respective textual personae. The important thing to appreciate about these presentations of self is that they are literary *constructs*. The real person may be quite different, albeit they may find it necessary to play the part for public consumption, but in both cases the authorial self is brilliantly constructed out of the most unpromising material. Professor Levitt is a leading academic authority in a leading academic institution yet he manages convincingly to portray himself as a practical man, an ordinary Joe, one-of-the-guys. This portrayal, paradoxically, is reinforced by the learned milieu from which he hails, thanks to his periodic denigration of woolly-headed academics and their impractical ilk. Professor Holbrook, conversely, has successfully donned the mantle of the cosmopolitan, high-browed man-of-letters, even though as a marketing academic from a business school he occupies a position that in cerebral circles would be considered irredeemably boorish, unspeakably philistine, the lowest of the literary low. Marketing may be a noble academic pursuit, with a long and distinguished record of conceptual achievements, but it is not perceived thus by the intellectual élite.[24]

Both Levitt and Holbrook are demonstrably creative writers – characterization is generally regarded as one of the hardest literary effects to achieve[25] – nevertheless their ostensibly contrasting authorial personae only serve to divert attention from their often astonishing stylistic similarities. Prominent among these is both authors' sheer love of language, incessant wordplay and, not least, vast vocabularies. Thus Levitt's papers are replete with alliteration ('complex congeries', 'producing properly promising packaging'); Oscar Wildean epigrams ('clothes may not make the man but they help make the sale', 'inaction is the only inexhaustible form of executive energy', 'leaders produce consent, others seeks consensus', 'the business of business is to stay in business'); and all sorts of arcane words ('protean', 'incubus', 'abjure', 'integument', 'munificent', 'crescive', 'Brobdignagian') – so much so, that he is quite capable of coining neologisms if the cadence of the sentence calls for it ('vendables', 'informational', 'ineffectualness', 'errorlessly', 'vertglomerate', 'hetero-consumer').

The same is true of Holbrook, where in addition to alliteration ('ego-centric eccentricity', 'complex concatenation', 'overt obeisance', 'patriarchal patois', 'semiotically shaky', 'materialistic metonymy', 'epi-grammatic encapsulations'); aphoristic inclinations ('like Ivory Soap, I hope to float', 'from intellectual liberty comes scholarly progress', 'ask not what semiotics can do for marketing but what marketing can do for semi-otics', 'the aim of the elite is to stay elite'); ceaseless sesquipedalianism ('adumbrate', 'sobriquet', 'ailurophobe', 'filiopeitistic', 'ascensive', 'melis-matic', 'contrapuntal', 'parsimonious', 'mien', 'propaedeutic', 'Sisyphean'); and sheer inventiveness ('catarche', 'ethology', 'antibanausic', 'kroywen', 'vendome', 'aerologic', 'politicorrectness', 'Cholbrookian chutzpah'), ety-mological considerations and subtle shades of linguistic meaning are a constantly recurring feature of his work. Not only is Merriam-Webster Morris's single most frequently cited source – or rather second to Columbia University's research fund – but one of these days he'll take it to the next level by looking up 'dictionary' in the dictionary and writing a learned disquisition on its philological antecedents. You read it here first.

In a similar vein, both Levitt and Holbrook are masters of metaphor. The latter's career-spanning passion for animalistic conceits is perhaps his principal stylistic tic, certainly the one for which he is best known. Among countless other symbolic creatures, TOPKAT alludes to and draws inspi-ration from elephants, birds, gorillas, fish, dogs, roaches, turtles and, naturally, cats.[26] Not only does he playfully portray himself as the afore-mentioned 'Morris the Cat', but he has written at length about purported personality differences between cats and dogs and the lessons these con-tain for marketing endeavour:

> I propose that those who pursue managerial relevance in their research as opposed to those who care mostly about academic scholarship reveal tem-peraments or orientations or perspectives that we might characterize as relatively more canine versus feline, respectively.
>
> In this, dogs resemble researchers who seek to pursue managerial rele-vance. Such researchers voluntarily take their direction or their directions – sort their priorities or respond to instructions – in a way that honors the interests of practitioners. Figuratively or even literally, they follow orders. They thereby please managers a great deal because managers are accus-tomed to giving directions and like it when their commands are obeyed.
>
> . . . By contrast, we all hold very different expectations of a cat. According to Hearne, 'most house cats would rather die than obey a direct order' . . . Herein, your cat resembles the academic researcher who will also refuse to retrieve the information you seek. Rather, like the cat, academic

researchers pursue the circuitous path to knowledge, more or less indifferent to the approval or disapproval of their masters (the marketing managers) and ready to starve – or at least dwell in dignified academic penury – before succumbing to the pressures implicit in the dictates of managerial relevance.[27]

Levitt is equally inclined to indulge in tropeography. Although animals don't loom large in his rhetorical roster – he alludes to Berlin's famous hedgehog–fox distinction, notes Napoleon's rabbit versus lion leadership analogy and refers to 'prowling packs' of lawyers and investment bankers – personification figures very prominently in the peerless professor's figurative armoury. He often makes insightful comparisons between business organizations and the human body, be it in terms of growth, development, nutrition, disease, mortality or interpersonal relationships ('the throbbing pulse of reality the data sought to capture', 'the industrialization of the service sector industries . . . is just now crawling out of infancy and seems on its way to adolescence', 'companies that don't metabolize information right will see small problems and discontinuities metastasize into major maladies'). Games and activities are another major source of Levittite allusion – chess, checkers, poker, bridge, dance, music and baseball – as indeed they are to Morris the Ephebe, whose plangent peroration in his principal philosophical proclamation was predicated upon a bathetic footballing analogy: 'One might recapture, however evanescently, that brief but boundless moment of ecstatic insight in which fleeting truth crashes in around us, arrested in mid-flight by the urgent grasp of our wildest lunging embrace'.[28]

As the above passage suggests, another literary trait that Levitt and Holbrook have in common is hyperbole. Both are such arresting stylists that their sheer writing ability sometimes seems to get the better of them.[29] This gives rise to passages of prose that, if not exactly purple, certainly contain more than a hint of mauve. Levitt routinely makes exaggerated comparisons between the lower-level employees of nondescript marketing organizations and the creative giants of Western civilization, as well as the occasional legendary figure (Cellini, Mozart, Michelangelo, Rubens, Handel, Prometheus, etc.). Likewise, the laudable achievements of hamburger vendors, insurance agencies, plastics extruders and steel sheet manufacturers are frequently compared, without the faintest trace of irony, to those of Copernicus, Bernoulli, Boyle, Lavoisier, Darwin or Newton. Indeed, during his more extreme passages of essayistic overdrive, Levitt teeters on the brink of tautology and alliterative absurdity ('the paradox that puzzles and perplexes: precisely as the marketing concept has advanced over the years, so, perversely, has the irritation it's produced, even among its practitioners').[30]

Holbrook is no less hyperbolic, if anything more so, and as someone who has made a convincing case for adopting increasingly lyrical modes of marketing expression, especially when emotional considerations are at stake, TOPKAT cannot be accused of letting the literary side down.[31] To cite but a few far from atypical examples:

> In an academic world dominated by marketing researchers preoccupied with buying, as opposed to consuming, consumer researchers face a lonely battle if they elect to sing about the tarnished vestiges of the perfect consumption that characterized lost innocence.[32]

> Informed by private experiential self-reflection, the introspective essay attempts to achieve a deep probing of the human condition and pursues broad suggestiveness, as opposed to narrow empiricism. Bathed in the ethos of romanticism, it aspires to an exaltation of ecstatic experience, rather than a resignation to inhibited rationality. In this, it moves toward the celebratory Wordsworthian vision of consumer behavior as consummation. Aware of suffering, it moves toward joy.[33]

> The constant oscillation in *Out of Africa* between conventional felicities and feral realities, between civilized pleasantries and nature red in tooth and claw, underscores the film's most central theme – namely, that all things fall apart, that everything runs down, that nothing endures, that no possession lasts forever, that no thing or person can be permanently owned, mastered, or loved. In short, no consumer durables exist in the African wilds of this movie.[34]

While some may consider such expositional effulgences to be as far from conventional social science reportage as it is humanly possible to be, they do not do justice to the supreme literary abilities of both scholars and, taken out of context, may conspire to give the impression that the authors are little more than bombastic propagandists. To some extent, of course, they are. Like many creative people Morris and Ted hold very strong views on a range of (marketing-related) issues and are not reluctant to express them.[35] But these opinionated excesses are leavened by their well-developed and immensely engaging senses of self-deprecatory humour. Holbrook often portrays himself as an uncoordinated, occasionally hapless, incompetent, whether it be in his capacity as a sportsman, scholar, handyman, traveller, musician, collector, cat wrangler, disburser of million dollar words, or a walking, talking, gum-chewing embodiment of WIMP culture (Western Imperialistic Materialistic Paternalism). What's more, he is ever prepared to proffer amusing asides about the absurdities of life in academia, or the Big Apple, or the unfettered joys of listening to his son's favourite rock bands ('somewhere between a wailing screech and a screeching wail').[36]

Ted Levitt's textual self is equally personable thanks to his redoubtable refusal to take himself or his gurudom too seriously. Hence he 'complains' about being an underpaid educator, even though his consultancy income must be astronomical ('as a certified academic, who is paid, however paltry the sum, to think, teach and advise'); he attacks professorial pro-lixity in prolix professorial prose ('literary obfuscation masquerading as wisdom'); he coins slogans about the mindless sloganising of manage-ment gurus ('man lives not by bread alone but mostly by catchwords'); he warns against 'the glittering plausibility of a well-turned phrase', itself a glitteringly plausible phrase that's been well and truly turned; and he simultaneously reinforces and ridicules his august academic position by maintaining 'firm control over any fleeting tendencies toward modesty'.[37]

Pure Panting Lupinity

Alongside hyperbole, humour and well-nigh heroic chutzpah, our literary duo share several other textual characteristics that some may find discon-certing, distasteful or indeed disingenuous. The first of these is *sexuality*. Again and again Levitt makes risqué remarks which may have been per-missible in decades past but are regarded with much less equanimity today ('The age of the blind date or the one-night stand is gone. Marriage is both more convenient and more necessary', 'not the cold figures in our intended's balance sheet but our warm feelings about our intended's figure', 'the middle-aged man today wants to believe that he still has a good fighting chance for the occasional conquest . . . he does it in part by dieting and by sartorial fastidiousness. The same is true of women. They feel forced to remodel themselves into grotesque apparitions of attractive youthfulness, if only to keep their restless husbands from roaming after more gamey prey'). In fairness, he frequently goes out of his way to ven-erate the 'housewife' and seeks to excuse his parasexism by asserting that the books are written for a predominantly masculine audience, which is true. Nevertheless, when Harvard Business School Press unleashed a Levitt anthology in the early 1990s, they prefaced the publication with a fulsome apology for the author's non-gender-neutral language.[38]

Holbrook, likewise, is nothing if not libidinous and in addition to his drawings of masturbating monkeys, incessant recitations of a bawdy lim-erick about an innocent young lady from Kent and self-confessed predilection for pornographic magazines, videos and websites, he has vol-unteered numerous detailed textual analyses of the relationship between consumption and concupiscence (for example, the Plumtree's potted meat episode in *Ulysses*), as well as a toe-curling retelling of his infantile Oedipal trauma.[39] He has also expatiated at astonishing length on his voyeuristic inclinations and, in keeping with his playful desire to drop the names of leading jazz musicians into learned academic articles, TOPKAT seems moved by a strange desire to mention as many 'bad' words as he possibly can. One can only wonder about the state of his Merriam-Webster.

Morris, of course, is sure to be piqued by such an insinuation, although in doing so he merely exhibits another of his and Theodore's less captivating textual characteristics. Call it what you will – undue sensitivity, touchiness, paranoia, narcissism, self-absorption, the artistic temperament, rampant egomania – but the personae of both Holbrook and Levitt come across as extremely *thin-skinned*.[40] MoHo repeatedly rails against his maltreatment at the hands of malicious reviewers, those conspiratorial individuals who have gone out of their way to thwart his intellectual ambitions (often quoting them at length).[41] What's more, he rarely misses an opportunity to berate those who fail to pay appropriate tribute to his manifold published papers (for example, Colin Campbell, a very distinguished British sociologist, for his unforgivable ignorance of Holbrook's hedonistic paradigm).[42] He even castigates the contributors to his own edited volume, *Consumer Value*, for having the temerity to criticize TOPKAT's creaky typology:

> In one way or another, several chapters suggest or imply a criticism of the Typology of Consumer Value that, in my opinion, represents a basic logical error. . . . I believe that all such concerns involve a basic philosophical mistake . . . they argue that X→Y; that Y→Z; so that, therefore, Y = Z. Stated in these terms, the argument entails an obvious fallacy. The more convoluted discussions that appear in some of the preceding chapters disguise this fallacy in part. But it lurks beneath the surface nonetheless . . . this does not mean . . . that any of the other confusions noted earlier have any logical validity whatsoever.[43]

Levitt, analogously, has pursued a long, bitter, almost libellous textual vendetta against Tom Peters, the management guru who usurped his conceptual USP of customer-orientated organizations ('sweaty evangelist', 'devout acquisitor', 'evangelical zealot'), though the snake-oil salesmen of motivational research were given equally slanderous treatment at an earlier stage of his career ('imprecise and artless', 'astrologers', 'untrustworthy', 'blind guessing', 'rudimentary', 'sheer pretentiousness and gross negligence').[44] As for an impertinent, Poland-bound do-gooder who made the mistake of wasting Professor Levitt's time one enchanted evening:

At seven P.M., Mr. Hubert answered his room call cheerfully. 'I'll be down in two minutes sharp,' he said. 'I'm tall, slim, and fully gray-headed.' All true. He was also full of easy congeniality. The tall, slim, fully gray head swiftly led the way to the mezzanine-floor restaurant.

At the table he spoke importantly of 'my book,' of his close friendships with various political eminences such as Pete and Mike and Henry and Jesse and Ben and so forth, of his business background, of his three prior trips to the Soviet Union, and of his 'eagerness' to do as much for the Polish people . . .

Until then the tall, slim, fully gray-headed missionary up-from-New-York, headed-for-Moscow, and eager-for-Warsaw, had not asked even a single question about his guest's Polish connections, interests, knowledge, activities or intentions. Nor did he ask later, which came soon indeed. Suddenly, the host was on his feet, extending a firm handshake for 'all the help and insight you've given me this evening.'

Full of wonderment outside the Meridien, the guest was stimulated by the newspaper headlines to more wondering. If all these years of Communist rule did not kill the spirit of people in Eastern Europe, nor entirely destroy the Soviet people's entrepreneurial instincts, surely they would recognize this different kind of snake-oil salesman?[45]

Another notable textual parallel between our dynamic duo is their inordinate fondness for *repetition*. Besides their anaphoric inclinations (that is, using the same words to start successive sentences: 'And it worked, like magic', 'Like Horton . . . Like Horton . . . Like Horton'), both authors ceaselessly recycle their own work, usually with minor editorial adjustments to suit the requirements of the situation. Part of this propensity is attributable to the anthologization process – each has produced a number of 'greatest hits' packages – but it also seems to reflect a shared belief that well-written passages are infinitely recyclable.[46] Thus Professor Levitt has a repertoire of stock phrases and aphorisms that he plunders with impunity ('fast history', 'the solution to a problem changes the problem', 'not everything that is possible is probable'). Professor Holbrook is equally promiscuous with his prose having rehashed his voluble remarks on romanticism, defence of subjective personal intro-spection, explanation of the stereoscopic viewing process and, needless to say, his celebrated cat-versus-dog comparison on copious occasions.[47]

So marked is this recapitulative inclination that both authors have developed signature textual stratagems, recognizable rhetorical devices which immediately signal the Holbrookian or Levittite presence. The former is characterized by striking titles, aestheticised epigraphs, poetic inserts and, above all, alliterative triplets ('fantasies feelings and fun', 'ads, artworks and aesthetics', 'bombs, burnouts and bigamists', 'make the

movie matter', 'titans of televisual titillation', 'congeries of consonant con-
cord'), whereas the latter typically employs a combination of catchy titles
('Marketing Myopia', 'Think Small', 'Business to Business Business', 'The
Youthification of Management', 'Differentiation – Of Anything', 'The
Sphinx that Thinks'), racy prose (achieved by the use of dynamic adjectives and adverbial clauses such as 'increasingly', 'escalating',
'relentlessly') and, when the mood takes him, newly-minted neologisms-
cum-gerundives ('pluralization', 'Chrystlerization', 'Tangibilization',
'Bureaucratization', 'Cosmopolitanization', 'Proletarianization').

The foregoing, it must be stressed, does not mean that our tumescent
textual twosome are indistinguishable. Far from it. There are several stylistic differences between them, some minor, some major. While both are
partial, shall we say, to penning extremely long sentences, Holbrook's
rarely exceed a hundred words. Levitt, however, is happy to go on for two
hundred words plus. MoHo, by contrast, is much more inclined to string
sequences of long sentences together and is less inclined to rely on semi-
colons – or similar 'breathing spaces' – that his role model turns to when
he's pushing the loquacious boat out. Metaphorically, moreover, Morris
has a weakness for environmental allusions, especially aquatic or estuar-
ine conceits, which Ted doesn't share (streams, tributaries, shoals, reefs,
tides, swamps, morasses, voyages of discovery, etc.):

> They have scraped away the barnacles of utilitarian concerns, have escaped
> the perilous flood of managerial relevance, and have explored fresh woods
> or new pastures by developing approaches to the study of consumption that
> they see as intrinsically worthwhile and even joyful.[48]

An equally important difference between father and son is that, struc-
turally speaking, Levitt's articles tend to have bold opening statements
and gradually peter out in keeping with standard journalistic precept.
Holbrook's articles, by contrast, start off in a fairly low key (they often
begin with banalities like 'This paper') and culminate in show-stopping,
spine-tingling climaxes:

> If nothing else, the AMA Task-Force report serves to call attention to this
> divergence in viewpoints. If nothing else, it reminds us that marketing aca-
> demics do pursue certain righteous if circuitous paths that deserve the
> respect of their more managerially inclined colleagues. And, if nothing else,
> it thereby justifies its own conclusion that we desperately need some sort of
> spiritual center to help us feel good about the kind of research we do and
> that, toward this end, we must find, elevate, and proclaim whatever is noble,
> worthwhile, and profound in the development of marketing thought.[49]

The structure of their individual sentences, interestingly, is just the opposite. Whereas Holbrook's are front-loaded (his repertoire of introductory conjunctions – 'Clearly', 'Herein', 'Surely', 'Yet', 'Hence', 'Thereby', 'Briefly', 'Further', 'In short', 'In other words', 'If nothing else' – is quite staggering) and characterized by a rise and fall cadence (indicated by 'bracketing' constructions or qualifiers like 'at best . . . at worst', 'in general . . . in particular', 'former . . . latter', 'aforementioned', 'versus'), Levitt's sentences tend to build and build and build thanks to the accumulation of adjectives and adverbs. As often as not, they finish with a slap in the face, occasionally a boom-boom punch line, or a climactic couplet presaged by the emphatic adverb 'even'. With its hint of surprise, and tincture of twist in the tail, 'even' is a signature Levitt word, one he employs repeatedly. Excessively, even. In one classic crescendo, he even uses even in three successive sentences:

> Suddenly, in the world's urban places the demand thrives for ethnic fast foods: pizza, hamburgers, sushi, frankfurters, Greek salad, Chinese egg rolls, pita bread, croissants, tapas, curry, bagels, chilli, doughnuts, French fries, and even Sacher torte. Everybody who can get them wants them, regardless of national residence, origin, religion, tradition, or even taboos. Suddenly everybody everywhere simultaneously occupies each of these product-market segments – often several on a given day, even at a given eating occasion.[50]

Precursor and Ephebe

Superb stylists though both scholars are, a parallel reading of their respective literary oeuvres leads to the inevitable critical conclusion that, word for word, Ted is better than Morris. Although TOPKAT is considered to be marketing academia's alpha author, there is nothing in the Holbrookian corpus to compare with Levitt's brilliantly evocative description of disgraced financier Ivan Boesky: 'paraded before the public with ill-gotten dollars dribbling from his pockets'; or his affectionate parody of the marketing utopia portrayed in travel brochures: 'gloriously glossy pictures of elegant rooms in distant resort hotels set by the shimmering sea'.[51] When set against Levitt's featherlite evocations, especially his magnificent, less-is-more epigrams ('success comes to those who attack each task with the passion of the scientist and the precision of the artist'), Holbrook's prose seems ever so slightly ponderous, pretentious, pompous and, on occasion, patronizing. Whereas Levitt wears his learning lightly and makes frequent allusion to works of scholarship, which his readership may or may not recognize ('The Marketing Imagination', 'Marketing and its Discontents', 'What Managers Want'), Holbrook feels obliged to explain *everything*, just in case the dullards in his audience don't get it (*'ceteris paribus* [all else being equal]', 'note that Campbell's title plays on Weber's *The Protestant Ethic and the Spirit of Capitalism'*). The inevitable upshot is a blizzard of citations, quotations and condescending commentary, which only serves to detract from his prodigious literary talents. True, even in his most poetic moments, Morris is prone to opt for a derivative image or clichéd expression ('as summer follows spring', 'dance with the angels', 'too hot to handle', 'in the land of the blind, the one eyed man is king') but, unlike Ted, who peaked early and trod literary water for the bulk of his career, MoHo has improved markedly with the passage of time and eventually eclipsed his poetic precursor.[52]

As a very gifted writer, Morris Holbrook must always have been aware – largely unconsciously, it must be stressed – of the immense creative shadow cast by Theodore Levitt. Indeed, there is ample evidence to suggest that TOPKAT suffers, or has suffered, from the anxiety of academic influence. Not only has he confessed to the classic symptoms of the anxiety-stricken arriviste,[53] but in describing his Presidential Address at the 1989 ACR conference (a speech, incidentally, which comprised the fullest expression of his aestheticized research agenda), he observes that 'the structure of the situation was perfectly calculated to give me heavy anxiety attacks, especially because, by the time I got my turn, almost every conceivably worthwhile thing had been said by my many distinguished predecessors'.[54] This is as clear a statement of the anxiety thesis as one could possibly imagine. Holbrook, furthermore, has offered a vivid account of the 'flooding' process (internal to the poet but brought to fruition by an external stimulus) that precedes the unrolling of Bloom's revisionary ratios. During a prolonged period of Freudian psychotherapy in the late 1970s, he relates that he felt deeply frustrated by his academic career, dedicated as it then was to positivistic path analyses of automobile purchasing behaviour. His ordinarily silent therapist asked why he didn't investigate musical consumption activities – at the time, a non-scholarly yet personally fulfilling sideline – and this proved to be the turning point in Holbrook's personal intellectual trajectory.[55]

While the above may be deemed indicative of Morris the Son's anxiety proneness, as does his repeated invocation of the structure, departure and reconciliation stages of the creative process (the same primordial triadic schema upon which Bloom's thesis rests), it does not establish an *explicit* connection with Theodore the Father. Granted, the anxiety model does not require a demonstrable association – the influence, to repeat, is unconscious – but it doesn't rule out a direct linkage either. And, in this regard, there is some corroborative evidence of an incipient precursor–ephebe relationship. When Holbrook completed his Harvard BA in 1965, he applied for a position on his Alma Mater's MBA programme, but was spurned by the Business School, a rejection that still rankles (Levitt was a lecturer at the time and shortly thereafter appointed head of Harvard's marketing division).[56] His very first publication was a vituperative review of one of Levitt's books on selling – an attack which prompted a mortifyingly amiable response from the unfairly maligned author. For years, furthermore, Holbrook taught a course on strategy which used Levitt's 'Marketing Myopia' as a starting point, but then went on to demonstrate that total customer orientation was a recipe for organizational disaster.[57]

More meaningfully perhaps, it is possible to discern *direct* textual connections between Levitt and Holbrook. Apart from the broad stylistic commonalities, it is noteworthy that Ted actually used the somewhat unusual noun 'consummation' (the terminological centrepiece of TOPKAT's aesthetic vision)[58] several years prior to his ambitious ephebe.[59] Similarly, they are both prone to press esoteric words such as 'paean', 'avatar', 'obeisance', 'adumbrate', 'unctuous', 'abjure', 'palpable', 'apotheosis', 'ratiocinated' and 'shibboleth' into stylistic service, all of which are comparatively rarely encountered in the mainstream marketing literature.[60] One of Levitt's signature stylistic devices (anadiplosis), which involves ending subsections with a word or phrase that provides the starting point for the next subsection, is also used by Holbrook, most notably in his landmark 'What is consumer research?' publication.[61] Levitt, likewise, led the way with aestheticized epigraphs, matrix thinking (another favourite of the arriviste) and, not least, the alliterative triplet ('faith, fantasy and new product failures', 'dramatically dissimilar and disproportionate', 'creating customers for customers', 'hard to hurt their heirs').

However, perhaps the most obvious correspondence between precursor and ephebe is their incessant utilization of the first person singular and plural. Although this is seldom found – indeed actively discouraged – in conventional social science writing, the prose of Levitt and Holbrook is replete with 'I' and 'we'.[62] The former, interestingly, makes much greater use of the second person than the latter; and it is this act of addressing 'you', the readership, that gives his textual persona the man-of-the-people aspect that Holbrook's conspicuously lacks.

You Talkin' Through Me?

Be that as it may, the essence of the ephebe–precursor relationship is found in the unfolding of the six revisionary ratios – clinamen, tessera, kenosis, daemonization, askesis, apophrades – which, as previously observed, are predicated on the primordial trichotomous schema of affiliation, denial and reaffiliation. The first two stages, clinamen and tessera, involve the identification of perceived shortcomings in the work of the precursor and the ephebe's attempt to bring things to antithetical completion. In the case of Morris 'n' Ted, these initial stages are very clearly marked. Notwithstanding his manifold publications on manifold marketing topics, if the life's work of Professor Theodore Levitt had to be synthesized, distilled and placed in a proverbial nutshell, that nutshell would probably contain the words: 'the customer is everything'. The Levittonian mantra, that 'the purpose of a business is to create and keep a customer', is chanted at one time or another in most – make that all – of his numberless articles. Granted, he tones the message down on occasion, but from first to last it is clear that Levitt considers the customer to be king. K-I-N-G.

Holbrook, on the other hand, has been highly critical of this notion of total customer orientation, actually going so far as to describe it as 'illogical', 'preposterous' and 'exaggerated'.[63] However, his own intellectual preoccupations are not only equally explicit, eminently epigrammatic and endlessly recycled, à la Levitt, but they represent an antithetical extension of the latter's intellectual agenda. Whereas Ted considers the customer to be everything, MoHo stoutly maintains that *everything is consumption*. As far as the ephebe is concerned, everything from chewing a candy bar, through contemplating works of art, to conceptualizing the deity's very act of cosmic Creation, represents a form of consumption activity. Indeed, he has actually posited a fifteen-point scale of consumer 'durables' which stretches from those that are consumed in less than a second (nano-durables) to those that last billions of years (mega-durables).[64]

It can, admittedly, be argued that although Holbrook's contention that 'everything is consumption' is analogous to Levitt's all-embracing customer orientation, it can hardly be described as *antithetical* (mind you, Morris maintains that it 'differs fundamentally').[65] Yet a detailed reading of the authors' respective oeuvres reveals that their stated stances, while broadly consonant, are ultimately oppositional. Thus Levitt frequently makes the point that, all other things being equal and even allowing for the occasional desire for novelty, consumer behaviour is basically motivated by *price*, by the prospect of picking up a bargain, by 'cash on the barrelhead'. What's more, he intones on numerous occasions that people don't so much buy products as solutions to perceived problems (people buy ¼-inch holes not ¼-inch drills, hope not perfume, transport not automobiles).

If, however, the basic premise of Holbrook's position had to be summarized in a couple of sentences, it would be that there are certain things *beyond* price, that there are products, services, consumption experiences and so on which are literally *priceless*, and which are *not* solutions to banausic, everyday problems but worthwhile, satisfying and uplifting in and of themselves. Consuming *Hamlet*, for Holbrook, is not a solution to the problem of an enjoyable evening's entertainment (though it can indeed be that), it is consuming *Hamlet*, and *Hamlet* alone, one of the incomparable artistic masterpieces of Western civilization.[66]

Despite this marked difference in emphasis, it is apparent that the 'consumer is everything' and 'everything is consumption' positions are broadly complementary, predicated as they are on some elemental notion of consumer orientation. In keeping with clinamen and tessera, the ephebe has performed a revisionary swerve and brought the precursor's work to an antithetical culmination. However, the second major phase of the anxiety of influence process, comprising kenosis and daemonization, is characterized by a complete repudiation of the forerunner's scholarly stance and the articulation of a personalized counter-sublime premised on a 'higher power' than that invoked by the antecedent author. This too is evident in the Levitt–Holbrook literary dyad. The former, perhaps more than anyone in the entire marketing discipline, has devoted his career to furthering the everyday lot of the marketing manager and, unlike many academic para-practitioners, can reasonably claim to have succeeded. Although Levitt has periodically published papers for scholarly consumption, he is the absolute embodiment of practitioner orientation. He never forgets that his readership mainly consists of people who have to meet a target, make a payroll, move the merchandise, or mind the store.[67]

By contrast, Holbrook's principal claim to fame, or rather notoriety, is his complete and unequivocal repudiation of the managerial cause. In a series of papers, panel discussions, personal appearances and op-ed pieces during the middle-to-late 1980s, the ephebe ostentatiously eschewed the hitherto sacrosanct managerial ethos, albeit he conspicuously failed to mention Levitt as the *primum mobile* of this particular intellectual position (an almost inconceivable yet, Oedipally speaking, unsurprising omission). Not only did the aspirant strong poet contend that the concerns of marketing practitioners were no concern of marketing academics, he actually revelled in his irrelevance and celebrated the fact that his research was totally impractical, unashamedly non-functional and, above all, utterly useless.[68] Indeed, it was this issue that stimulated Holbrook's seminal categorization of researcher types: obedient, managerially orientated *dogs* and free-spirited, unabashedly unbusinesslike *cats*.

Naturally, Holbrook's wanton abandon of the managerial paradigm did not end with kenosis. On the contrary, TOPKAT contended that a higher position was available to those happy few researchers of a feline temperament who were prepared to endure the disdain of their more prosaic peers. Primed by his extensive analyses of aesthetics, artworks and diverse forms of popular culture, which embraced everything from movies and Broadway productions to television game shows and the screeching wails/wailing screeches of rock music,[69] Morris announced that the most meaningful countermeasure to the reductive, narrow-minded managerialism of the marketing scientists lay in consumer research in general and *scholarship* in particular.[70] As far as he was concerned, the burgeoning subfield of consumer research was separate from, though related to, its parent discipline of marketing and that, by breaking the ancestral connection, consumer researchers would be free to develop their own academic interests, unfettered by the pragmatic demands of marketing practitioners. Above and beyond his perceived need for a named domain, MoHo championed a much more scholarly approach than had been apparent hitherto.[71] Taking its cue from the humanities or liberal arts rather than the physical sciences, this romantic vision of scholarship rested on the assumption that 'some truths may lie buried at a level of human experience too deep for science to penetrate'.[72] For Holbrook at least, science was characterized by rigour, detachment and rigid adherence to established methods, while scholarship was predicated upon imagination, involvement, insight and, above all, wisdom. In short, where science was narrow, scholarship was broad; where science was shallow, scholarship was deep; where marketing was scientific, consumer research was scholarly. Not everyone, admittedly, accepted this distinction – it seems excessive to insinuate that science cannot be practised in a scholarly fashion[73] – but, as far as daemonization is concerned, his suggested science/scholarship dichotomy is as clear as it gets.

Paradigmatic though Holbrook's denial of his domineering predecessor undoubtedly is, the quintessential instantiation of the anxiety thesis occurs in the third and final phase, which comprises askesis and apophrades. Askesis, as previously noted, involves a purgatorial period of isolation and retreat into the self; so much so, that it almost seems solipsistic. It doesn't take a great deal of imagination, let alone scholarship, to recognize that this is a perfect description of Morris's much-touted, and much-debated, technique of 'subjective personal introspection' (SPI).[74] Unlike established approaches to positivistic and post-positivistic marketing research, with their methodological safety nets of representative samples, member checks, standardized interview schedules and procedures, SPI requires the investigator to reflect on his or her own consumer behaviours and bring them together in the form of an extended autobiographical essay. To pluck a (resonant) passage at random:

> The result of my first queuing experience is a personal transfiguration from the qualitative status of human to the quantitative rank as numerical digit: Flight 483, Gate 6. Seat 39A. As I proceed toward the gate, I pass through a

transitional state as suspected alien intruder. My briefcase, hand luggage, shoulder bag, and overcoat must pass through an X-ray machine. My body must pass through metal detectors miraculously sensitive to the most minute amounts of pocket change or the smallest number of house keys, but apparently not able to detect arsenal-sized collections of handguns and grenades. Amazingly, as I am detained, or relieved of the contents of my pockets, and perhaps even frisked or strip-searched, I experience something approaching gratitude. Perhaps one instinctively interprets these security precautions as a sign of safety: 'If they treat *me* like this, then surely they would catch a vicious terrorist before he or she got onto the plane.' Naturally, we know that often they do not.[75]

Clearly, this procedure breaks all manner of 'good research practice' guidelines and it has been excoriated accordingly.[76] But for the purposes of the present chapter, the rights and wrongs of SPI are less important than the fact that it exemplifies the askesis stage of the anxiety thesis. While it can be argued that Holbrook's experiments in SPI commenced in the middle-to-late 1980s, and hence coincided with the 'denial' phase of the anxiety process, his nomination, articulation and justification of the technique, *qua* technique, dates from the early 1990s. Holbrook freely admits, what is more, the purgatorial, Morris-against-the-world character of his introspective ambitions and acknowledges that he has often been accused of solipsism or worse. Indeed, this preoccupation with the self is amply demonstrated by his reaction to Wallendorf and Brucks' critique of SPI[77] – they omitted to mention his contributions to the genre, which TOPKAT interpreted as a personal slight – even though their attack was primarily aimed at another marketing scholar, Stephen J. Gould.[78]

After the solitude and self-absorption of askesis, the culmination of the anxiety trajectory transpires. In apophrates, the ephebe not only surpasses the overshadowing forefather, and thereby takes his place in the pantheon of strong poets, but also succeeds in suggesting that the work of the predecessor is somehow posterior to that of the ephebe. Paradoxical, not to say antinomous, though this possibility appears, it is once again clearly demonstrated in the Levitt–Holbrook literary horn-lock. The latter's return to the former's fold began in the early 1990s, when he forsook his attempt to declare sub-disciplinary independence for consumer research and refocused on marketing matters, arguing that his 'scholarly' approach had as much place in marketing as it did in consumer research. Having failed, furthermore, to convince the sceptics that a cogent scientific case could be made for the SPI procedure, Holbrook effectively let the scientific mainstream go hang and produced by far the most beautifully written paper of his career, 'Loving and Hating New York', a paper that was short, straight from the heart and just like Theodore Levitt – *only better.*

Subsequent to 'Loving and Hating New York',[79] Professor Holbrook has published a series of papers from the 'margins' of the discipline, lengthy book reviews, chapters in edited volumes and non-US journals in the main (thereby paralleling Professor Levitt, who, despite his stature among marketing practitioners, is not really regarded as a scholar's scholar).[80] More to the point, and incredible though it seems, MoHo's latter-day intellectual obsession revolves around *stereoscopic photographs*.[81] Not only does this employ, exceed and eclipse Levitt's seemingly unsurpassable metaphor of marketing *myopia*, but Holbrook's stereoscopic photos appear most vivid to those who suffer from short-sightedness. Thus the precursor's single most significant contribution has been taken, transformed and transcended by the triumphant ephebe, the new strong poet, Morris the Catoptric.

Marketing Catoptrics

Catoptrics is the study of mirror images and it is arguable that this mirror-image quality is perfectly illustrated in our strong poets' finest literary moments, 'Marketing Myopia' and, as noted above, 'Loving and Hating New York'. 'Myopia' was written at a very early stage of Levitt's academic career and, according to several churlish commentators, it was never bettered.[82] In truth, Ted Levitt is occasionally, if unfairly, portrayed as a one-hit-wonder of management thought. Be that as it may, 'Myopia' is still considered a seminal contribution to postwar marketing scholarship (even if readers feel otherwise). It is an oft-cited, best-selling, frequently anthologized *classic*, one that was recognized as such at the time of publication and subsequently by the author himself.[83] Not only did it appear as the lead article in a leading American journal but it was also given the special, this-is-sure-to-prove-controversial-read-it-at-your-peril editorial treatment.[84]

'Loving and Hating New York', by contrast, was a fairly late addition to Holbrook's compendious literary corpus. Although it can reasonably be considered a significant milestone in TOPKAT's personal development, the paper cannot be regarded as a major contribution to the marketing literature, not by any stretch of the academic imagination. It is rarely cited, it has never been anthologized and even the author seems uncertain about the stature of the piece. While it is mentioned in passing, 'Loving and Hating' was not deemed important enough to merit inclusion in Holbrook's retrospective volume, *Consumer Research: Introspective Essays on the Study of Consumption*.[85] The paper, moreover, was published in the second of two special issues of a European academic organ, which is indicative of its less than elevated status, as is its position in the journal, neither lead article nor lauded by the guest editors.

'Marketing Myopia', then, is a classic 'classic', written by someone seemingly determined to pull out all the stops and make a definitive contribution to the field. In this respect, indeed, it is noteworthy that 'Myopia' is one of Levitt's longest and most heavily referenced papers (only six citations, admittedly, but the piece mentions several other supporting publications). 'Loving and Hating', by contrast, is a classic confessional, seemingly written for private consumption by someone weary of trying and failing to make the field pay attention to his aesthetic agenda. It is one of the shortest papers that Morris has ever published and, unlike his usual attempts to swamp the reader with argument-bolstering citation, the article is completely devoid of references. Whereas Levitt has everything to prove and proves it, Holbrook has nothing to prove and, for once, doesn't feel compelled to try too hard. Therein lies the secret of its greatness.[86]

This authorial antithesis is also apparent in the intended audiences, overall objectives and principal data sources of the respective papers. Consonant with his subsequent career trajectory and the then prevailing ethos concerning the overall purpose of marketing scholarship, Levitt is writing for an audience of practitioners or would-be practitioners. His article is a manifesto, a call to metaphorical arms, containing a simple, ostensibly implementable message: the customer is everything. Holbrook's paper, conversely, has nothing whatsoever to do with the mundane concerns of marketing managers nor, for that matter, the scientific aspirations of fellow marketing academics. It doesn't so much prescribe as describe. It is, in fact, the *outcome* of his previously stated 'pursuit of scholarship' agenda. Levitt's, on the other hand, is an ambitious statement of *intent*, one which he subsequently cashed out. Big time.

The irony, however, is that the great Harvardian's practitioner-orientated proclamation is largely predicated upon secondary sources such as Henry Ford's autobiography, Zimmerman's history of the supermarket and Schumpeter's celebrated notion of 'creative destruction'. As his condemnation of an entire industry on the basis of a single issue of the *American Petroleum Institute Quarterly* amply testifies, Levitt's landmark paper is actually the work of a bookish academic. By complete contrast, the great aesthete's non-managerially-orientated piece draws almost entirely upon the author's personal experiences, his own, real-world, anti-practitioner practices on the mean and not quite so mean streets of New York City (being mugged, encountering celebrities, the neighbourhood butcher who knows your name and the waitress who sets up 'the usual' slightly salted margaritas).

Fascinating as the thought of TOPKAT the down-to-earth artisan versus Theodore the ethereal academic undoubtedly is, another intriguing disparity between the papers is apparent in the underpinning root metaphors. Despite its title, 'Marketing Myopia' is predicated primarily upon a temporal trope, while 'Loving and Hating' is predominantly spatial. Thus Levitt commences with a discussion of the rise and fall of companies, draws salient lessons from business history in general and the petroleum, automobile and electrical industries in particular, and makes a number of confident predictions, all of which have failed to come to fruition. Set against this, Holbrook's essay is confined to a comparatively limited geographical area, though it takes in several other locations (Disneyland, Italy, Utah), and it is almost entirely made up of evocatively described street scenes ranging from the squalor and degradation of Times Square to the sweet smelling, freshly-hosed sidewalks of the Upper West Side. There is, admittedly, a spatial element to Ted's opus, principally its inside–outside dialectic (his contention that strangers and non-initiates precipitate change in self-absorbed, incestuous industries), and MoHo's paper contains several temporal allusions pertaining to personal memories, family holidays and the changing of the seasons, as well as recycled anecdotes and quasi-urban myths (such as the innocent marketing professor who had his bank account cleared out by fraudsters posing as policemen). Nevertheless, as its essentially linear overall structure suggests, the basic thrust of 'Marketing Myopia' is temporal (it has a clear beginning, middle and end), whereas the vivid, disconnected vignettes of 'Loving and Hating' combine to provide a powerful sense of place. Indeed, notwithstanding Levitt's much-lauded espousal of the - optical metaphor, Holbrook's paper is the much more visual of the two. At times it almost reads like the shooting schedule of a Manhattan based screenplay. So much so, that it throws 'Marketing Myopia's' complete lack of visual imagery into very sharp relief. Despite its title, the optical metaphor is comparatively rarely employed in Levitt's classic contribution.[87]

If metaphor, according to the prominent literary theorist Roman Jakobson, is one pole of a figural dialectic, metonymy is the other.[88] And metonymy, where the part stands for the whole, is manifest in both papers. Levitt, for instance, presents each of his often highly specific, historically contingent case studies as exemplars for businesses and managers *as a whole*. Just as the idiosyncratic contents of a single trade magazine are deemed indicative of the production-orientated mentality of a massive, presumably highly internally variegated, industry, so too he contends that his three calamitous case studies contain lessons for *all* companies, in *all* places, at *all* times (by any stretch of the imagination, this is an incredible stretch of the imagination). Likewise, 'Loving and Hating' seems to be very place specific – as localized as it gets – yet the essay also implies, and occasionally states, that New York is the be all and end all.

Everything that happens, happens in New York. Everyone who is anyone is found in New York. New York is more than the centre of the universe, it *is* the universe ('If New York contains everything bad, it is only because New York contains Everything').

Metonymy, to be sure, is not confined to the content of both papers. The authors themselves, or rather their authorial personae, perform in an essentially metonymical capacity. Holbrook attempts to present himself as an archetypal New Yorker and, in the world of the myopic, where the twenty–twenty visionary is king, Levitt endeavours to play the paradigmatic outsider, the sharp-eyed stranger capable of identifying any industry's short-sighted shortcomings. More to the point, it can be contended that, as all of their signature stylistic foibles are on show in 'Myopia' and 'Loving and Hating', these particular publications metonymically embody the entire literary corpuses of both men. Both articles, for instance, offer abundant examples of the authors' fondness for words and wordplay. Apart from his lexical elephantiasis ('vicissitudes', 'appellation', 'senescence') and alliterative-cum-neologistic inclinations ('aggressive ardor', 'primal position', 'vulgarize', 'pridefully product oriented'), Levitt's epigrammatic qualities are already apparent ('if thinking is an intellectual response to a problem, then the absence of a problem leads to the absence of thinking', 'they kept their pride but lost their shirts', 'words are cheap and deeds are dear'). Holbrook, similarly, succeeds in strutting his sesquipedalian ('omphalos', 'detrital'), aphoristic ('you really can get homesick for New York if New York happens to be your home') and, above all, alliterative stuff ('salacious salons', 'frightening felony', 'dangerous denizens', 'ceaseless curiosity', 'puzzling paradox', 'sweet sidewalks').

Metaphorically speaking, moreover, our strong poets are veritable titans of tropefication. The very first paragraph of 'Marketing Myopia' contains Levitt's trademark figure of personification (growth and demise of industries); variations on this pathetic fallacy are repeated throughout the paper (marketing as stepchild, gasoline on its 'last legs', the entire corporation as a 'customer-creating and customer-satisfying organism') and it concludes with the anthropomorphic suggestion that if organizations do not know where they are going, everyone else (that is, other organizations) will notice it soon enough. Holbrook, meanwhile, endows New York with human qualities in 'Loving and Hating' ('cold, unfriendly place', 'the city's vast energy'), superhuman qualities on occasion ('they implode toward the heart of the city, drawn by some sort of ungoverned centripetal force'), though he also indulges in some palpably preposterous pathetic patois ('fortress of equanimity', 'vicious thunderstorm', 'blossoming of charity').

Characteristically, of course, these metaphorical orchestrations segue seamlessly into hyperbole, as for example in Holbrook's imaginative insinuation that his appendages have minds of their own ('my legs follow the familiar path to my office uptown'); his fabulous postmodern parallel between being accosted by deranged panhandlers and the rides in a dystopian theme park ('Demented derelicts leer at you through toothless grins . . . experiences that resemble nothing so much as a carefully-crafted fantasy trip at Disneyland'), or indeed his depiction of *genius loci* which would not be out of place in the pages of Edgar Allan Poe or H.P. Lovecraft: 'I feel as if I have wandered onto a terrain that is absolutely pregnant with implications waiting to be plucked from the concrete slabs beneath my feet or from the brick edifices around my head'.[89]

Levitt, likewise, luxuriates in several passages of pixillated prose that hail from the lilac end of the textual spectrum ('the water wheel and the steam industry were cut to ribbons by the flexibility, reliability, simplicity and just plain easy availability of electric motors', 'unless an industry is especially lucky, as oil has been until now, it can easily go down in a sea of red figures'). By far the most arresting of these is Ted's final frenetic section, which in its call to managerial arms and its espousal of visceral entrepreneurial greatness, is the nearest thing to Friedrich Nietzsche this side of *Beyond Good and Evil*. For Levitt, at least, it appears that the *Übermenschen* of management are driven by the will to marketing power: 'No organization can achieve greatness without a vigorous leader who is driven onward by his own pulsating *will to succeed*. He has to have a vision of grandeur, a vision that can produce eager followers in vast numbers. In business, the followers are the customers'.[90]

Alongside hyperbole, humour is also much in evidence. Levitt tells the apocryphal tale of a Boston millionaire who insisted that his legacy be invested exclusively in electric streetcars (thereby condemning his heirs to pumping gas at filling stations); judiciously juxtaposes the 'insanity' of drinking martinis at 20,000 feet in a 100-ton tube of metal against the once equally 'insane' suggestion that the all-conquering railroads might one day decline; draws a witty anadiplotic parallel between the *Perils of Pauline* and the perils of petroleum; and makes an appropriately crude remark about the oil companies that 'pooh-poohed the potential of gas'. In a similar vein, Holbrook revels in pun-ditry ('if you have a sudden yen for Japanese cuisine'); takes comfort from the fact that, for all its faults, New York 'does not have avalanches, rock slides, falling boulders, floods, frequent earthquakes, seasonal tornadoes, scorpions, tarantulas, rattle snakes, boa constrictors, tsetse flies or Jesse Helms'; and regales his readers with an endearingly self-deprecating account of a post-conference encounter in 42nd Street, when a malodorous vagrant greeted him warmly by name ('Who could this person be? Someone from our congregation at Church? An old classmate from Harvard? A former student wishing to express his gratitude for my steering him away from the evils of managerial relevance?'). The answer to this metropolitan riddle, suffice it to say, is that Morris was still wearing his nametag from the conference earlier in the day.

Just as the eminently engaging sides of our duo's textual personae are on display, so too the less amiable aspects of Ted-and-Morris are manifest in 'Myopia' and 'Loving and Hating'. Levitt gives an early indication of his subsequent erotic preoccupations by means of a priapic allusion to Hollywood being 'ravished' by television, as well as his exaggeratedly mythical depiction of gas station attendants as 'a handsome Adonis or a seductive Venus'. Likewise, he contemptuously dismisses the ill-considered remarks of rival commentators, most notably Barzun's analysis of the travails of the railroad industry ('even an amateur like Jacques Barzun . . .') and his colleague J.K. Galbraith's then current thesis on the Affluent Society ('Galbraith has a finger on something real, but he misses the strategic point').[91] Holbrook's text is no less carnal ('I amused myself by browsing through several of the pornographic bookstores that line this particular thoroughfare'), refers yet again to Harvard, the one ostensible blot on his otherwise exemplary academic record, and makes condescendingly light of non-New Yorkers in general and other nationalities in particular. Not only does he regard New York as the centre of the universe where 'local events are virtually indistinguishable from the affairs of the world', but the glory that was Spain is spurned with the staggering stereotype: 'Undoubtedly, the Spanish know how to mount a memorable bull fight' (indeed it seems that Europe generally is full of thieves, extortionists, con-artists and, worst of all, Europeans).[92]

Last but not least, both papers are suffused with the tiny but quintessential stylistic quirks that we have come to associate with the authors. Thus Levitt treats his readership to a provocative opening statement ('Every major industry was once a growth industry. But some that are now riding a wave of growth enthusiasm are very much in the shadow of decline'), precociously racy prose ('explosive demand', 'galloping industry', 'spectacularly successful', 'extravagantly profitable'), nascent gerundives and anadiplosis akimbo ('dieselization', 'until it blew over. It never blew over', 'as the railroads have, as the buggy whip manufacturers have, as the corner grocery chains have, as most of the big movie companies have, and indeed as many other industries have'), not to mention several chants of his trademark 'customer creating' mantra. Holbrook, moreover, sets out his stall with a veritable cornucopia of aestheticised epigraphs (*nine* quotations from popular songs), proffers what can only be described as an alliterative triple-doublet ('limping and loitering, lunging and leaping, leering and lurching') and exhibits his catoptric qualities in the opening and closing paragraphs, which are sublime mirror images of one another ('I hate New York. I have lived in the City for over 25 years. Yet I feel that I hardly begin to understand it', 'Yet I know that I barely understand New York. I have lived in the City for over 25 years. And I love it').[93] Even Father Ted Levitt at his most brilliant never surpassed such heights of marketing poetics.

Holbrook, however, does more than merely exceed Levitt's literary ability in 'Loving and Hating New York'. He becomes him. This postmodern transmogrification is not simply a matter of stylistic devices, such as the statement, 'Tourism is downright dangerous. Everywhere', which is Levitt through and through, it is also inscribed in one small but vital difference between these two totemic papers and the remainder of the Holbrookian and Levittite literary oeuvres. Although precursor and ephebe both make use of the first person singular, in keeping with the remainder of their corpuses, it is Holbrook and *not* Levitt who repeatedly employs the second person. The outcome of this is that the textual persona of the former is much warmer, more personable, than that of the latter. MoHo, for once, actually comes across as Mr Average, a typical New Yorker, subject to the same pleasures and pains as every other inhabitant of the Big Apple, whereas Ted's brilliantly written but bookish slant on marketing practice, coupled with his lofty dismissal of uninformed commentators and often quite acidic denigration of practitioners, is suggestive of ivory tower arrogance (a regrettable trait that he excised thereafter).[94]

It is arguable, then, that Levitt and Holbrook metonymically represent the entire academic marketing community, with its antithetical orientations towards pure scholarship and applied practice. However, this parallel reading of the authors' emblematic papers and overall publication records, leads to the inevitable conclusion that Holbrook is the practitioner and Levitt the purist. Morris's aestheticized agenda is very much in keeping with contemporary management thought,[95] while Ted's confident prognostications on globalization, marketing orientation and so on have latterly been exposed as the essentially academic speculations that they always were. Holbrook, furthermore, has always been prepared to compromise with the marketing mainstream in order to have his traditional, quantitative, positivistic papers published in the premier journals, whereas Levitt has never shifted on his condemnation of undue quantification and supposedly 'rigorous' marketing research, even though this virtually guaranteed his exclusion from the premier academic outlets. Just as the son is in the father, so the father is in the son.

Take me home, daddy.[96]

7

The 3Rs of Marketing Writing

I think we ought to read only books that bite and sting us. If the book we are reading doesn't shake us awake like a blow on the skull, why bother reading it in the first place? What we need are books that hit us like a most painful misfortune, like the death of someone we loved more than ourselves, that make us feel as though we had been banished to the woods, far from any human presence, like a suicide. A book must be the axe for the frozen sea within us. That is what I believe.

Franz Kafka[1]

Starting Marketing

According to Jacques Derrida, the abstruse French philosopher, Western thought is characterized by logocentrism.[2] That is, an unending, unseemly and ultimately futile search for origins, the 'in the Beginning' where 'the Word' was, is, and presumably, will continue to be.

This logocentric quest may or may not be true of Western thought per se, but it is certainly true of marketing. Hardly a year goes by without some learned disquisition on the roots of our field. For some, marketing dates from the mid-1950s, when Peter Drucker stated that 'the customer is the foundation of a business'.[3] For others, marketing started at the turn of the twentieth century, when US university courses were offered in the subject and Arch Shaw published the inaugural academic article 'Some Problems in Market Distribution'.[4] For yet others, marketing's wellsprings lie in the Industrial Revolution of the early nineteenth century, when mass production demanded mass distribution and mass distribution demanded mass consumption and a self-perpetuating commercial cycle thus commenced.[5] And, for yet others, marketing's origins are co-terminous with the rise of urban civilization in the ancient Middle East, when long-distance trade routes were established and surpluses were exchanged between nascent city states such as Ur, Sumer and Akkad.[6]

Unending as it is, this ongoing quest for marketing's origins is pointless, since it is not a search for an ur-activity, as such, as a search for the meaning of a word. If, by marketing, we mean a customer-orientated philosophy of doing business, then Drucker is as good a starting point as any. If, by marketing, we mean an autonomous academic discipline, then the early twentieth century is when scholarship started to coalesce. If, by marketing, we mean an organizational undertaking or function, then something significant happened in the nineteenth century, albeit cause and effect are difficult to untangle. If, by marketing, we mean another word for exchange, then we can go right back to apple-for-innocence in the Garden of Eden and, naturally, the nugatory negotiations prior to that.

As literary meaning is impossible to pin down, or so serpentine post-structuralists like Derrida aver, the origins of marketing will always be beyond our grasp. The same is true of any learned buzzword – 'branding', 'relationships', 'convenience', 'value', or whatever – hence the perennial complaint by concerned scholars about the lack of agreed, clear-cut definitions of core marketing constructs. It is arguable, of course, that this very imprecision is what propels marketing scholarship forward, if only because the meanings academics attach to a construct, in order to measure it, can always be questioned and this, in turn, triggers additional research activity and this . . .[7] The process may be unending and inconclusive – some may even consider it a professorial Ponzi scheme – but all of this research has to be written up and foisted on the reading public (or the RAE assessment panels at least).

Writing Rudiments

Just as the meaning of marketing cannot be secured, so too writing is a slippery signifier.[8] Philologists spend many a happy hour debating the credentials of hieroglyphs, pictograms, knot records, notch records, message sticks, smoke signals, cave paintings, cat's cradles, cuneiform tablets and countless other communication devices. Are they writing or not? Do they qualify as proto- or incomplete-writing systems? What about Luba memory boards, or Azilian coloured pebbles, or Native Australian tally sticks, or indeed the clay tokens known as *bullae*, found throughout the ancient world, from southern Turkey to the Indus Valley? Take your philological pick.

If, however, 'complete' writing is defined as fulfilling three criteria – a system of graphic marks on a durable surface, which represent articulate speech, and function as a form of communication[9] – then writing was invented in the middle of the fifth millennium BCE by a Sumerian trader who was monitoring his stock of sheep, goats, textiles, cooking pots and wooden implements. *Writing was invented by marketers.* Indeed, many of the proto-writing methods, such as tallies and *bullae*, were marketing-related too. As Manguel observes:

> Writing was invented for commercial reasons, to remember that a certain number of cattle belonged to a certain family, or were being transported to a certain place. A written sign served as a mnemonic device: a picture of an ox stood for an ox, to remind the reader that the transaction was in oxen, how many oxen and perhaps the names of the buyer and seller. Memory, in this form, is also a document, the record of such a transaction.
>
> The inventor of the first written tablets may have realized the advantage these pieces of clay had over holding memory in the brain: first, the amount of information storable on tablets was endless – one could go on producing tablets ad infinitum, while the brain's remembering capacity is limited; second, tablets did not require the presence of the memory-holder to retrieve information. Suddenly, something intangible – a number, an item of news, a thought, an order – could be acquired without the physical presence of the message-giver; magically, it could be imagined, noted and passed on across space and beyond time. Since the earliest vestiges of prehistoric civilization, human society had tried to overcome the obstacles of geography, the finality of death, the erosion of oblivion. With a single act – the incision of a figure on a clay tablet – that first anonymous writer suddenly succeeded in all these seemingly impossible feats.[10]

The heavy hand of hyperbole notwithstanding, Manguel's ruminations on the origin of writing are testament to the interpenetration of marketing and writing. If not exactly made for each other, they are more than just good friends. The literati's legendary disdain for commercial life, summarized in Chapter 1, is not only misplaced but mistaken. It is an after-effect of the Romantic Movement of the nineteenth century, when avant-garde artists set their face against the industrialization, bureaucratization and commercialization of society, an aesthetic *volte-face* further reinforced by the *épater les bourgeois* ethos of the modernists and high culture vultures generally.[11]

It is clear, therefore, that the latter-day blurring of the culture–commerce distinction, noted by Brooks, Seabrook and White among others, is actually a *return* to pre-modern conditions of possibility, when writing and marketing were as close to incestuous as makes no difference.[12] Western culture, says Zaid, was born with the book business; the printing press presaged mass production; the Bible was an astutely marketed best-seller, long before the Reformation; and the roots of the French Revolution reside in the circulation and sale of encyclopedias.[13] Karl Popper, conversely, contends that Western culture began in classical Athens, with the establishment of a book market in the fifth century BCE.[14]

Today's marketing-savvy literati, it seems, are not selling out when they acknowledge, as Updike does, that every successful writer is a huckster at heart.[15] They are merely getting back to the position, forcefully articulated by Dr Johnson, that 'no man but a blockhead ever wrote, except for money'.[16] Anton Chekhov, Margaret Atwood argues:

> began his career by writing exclusively for money, and never for any other reason, in order to support his poverty stricken family. Does that make him ignoble? Shakespeare wrote for the stage, much of the time, and naturally he cranked out stuff he thought would appeal to his audience. Once he got his start, Charles Dickens tossed his day job and lived by the pen. Jane Austen and Emily Brontë didn't, though they wouldn't have minded some extra cash. But you can't say any one of these is a better or a worse artist simply because of the money factor.[17]

Nowadays, Atwood goes on:

> He who writes, and makes it pay,
> Will live to write another day.[18]

Chalk 'n' Cheese

Counter-pointing the penetration of writing by marketing, marketing is replete with writing. Writing marketing is not simply an academic affectation. The practice of marketing is permeated by prose. Advertising copywriters coin slogans that call down the years. Brand-naming consultants concoct noisome neologisms like FCUK or Viagra or, once the much-anticipated joint venture is announced, FCUK Viagra. Mission statement missionaries authorize missionary positioning strategies from a severely constricted palette of corporate platitudes – 'customers', 'commitment', 'conscience', 'compassion', 'community', 'charity', 'clarity', 'care' and others. Marketing planners write lengthy reports about the sanctity of the marketing planning process, which are promptly consigned to the I'll-get-round-to-it-sometime shelf. Marketing research departments write even lengthier reports about sophisticated consumers who are so marketing-savvy that they tell deliberate fibs to marketing researchers, especially those researching the marketer-baiting behaviours of sophisticated consumers. PR departments polish the perfect press release that will grab front pages the world over and deliver countless, deathless column inches for their ego-inflated, self-intoxicated, but endearingly modest with it, CEOs. Ghost-writers, meanwhile, slave in the executive autobiography sweatshop – sorry, scriptorium – churning out works of customer-consecrating fiction that make *Finnegans Wake* read like an instruction manual for flat-pack furniture.[19]

And then, of course, there's the marketing gurus, putative purveyors of fads, fashions, and buy-my-book buzzwords, who sell tall tales about storytelling, publish almost indistinguishable articles on differentiation and offer consultancy advice on Best Business Writing Practice (BBWP), as well as Alliterative Acronym Avoidance Assistance (AAAA – sign me up).[20] Roving cultural critic Jonathan Meades may exaggerate slightly when he contends that 'Business books are written by evangelical illiterates to convert the ambitiously gullible', but there's definitely something rotten in the business jargon business.[21] As David Brooks points out about the poor bloody business infantry, the people who have to put up with salvoes of this sub-literary stuff:

> Like the soldiers in Pickett's charge, they will march straight into the hail of bullet points. They will endure . . . valuable advice on how they can prioritize their cost-effective operational performance and increase network functionality whilst magnifying their brand power through strategic B-to-B partnering in ways that will leverage their competitive-advantage matrixes without sacrificing any of their core-competency components or their multiple-vendor, mission-critical supply-chain service-provider solution resources.[22]

The quality of marketing writing may be moot, but its quantity more than compensates. So rampant is writing about marketing – just think of all the memos, emails and text messages that get written by marketers day and daily – that it is akin to an infestation, the literary equivalent of kudzu or couch grass. Weed-killers, however, are now available. The best-known of these is Bullfighter, a computer programme developed by Deloitte Consulting that cuts out the corporate claptrap, excises unspeakable consultancy-speak and generally turns junk jargon-soused terminological inexactitudes into something resembling proper English.[23] No doubt an academic version of Bullfighter is already in the works (ArticleAssassin, perhaps, Papershredder, possibly?). And while I can feel its fetid breath on my back as I write, I cannot deny that there's a market for it. Academia, after all, represents the acme of writing marketing, or the nadir if you prefer. Academics are the proletariat of post-industrial society. They toil in the writing mines. The hours are long and the remuneration is risible. Publications are their currency, the journals their denominations. An article in a top-tier journal is worth its weight in gold and second-tier hits are worth a bob or two as well. A best-selling student text can make life comfortable, or so royalties-replete colleagues tell me, but it's completely worthless in the carefully-regulated bourse of cerebration. Big Fat Books About Marketing are the soft currency of scholarship, an academic equivalent of the zloty, the kwacha, the Weimar mark when inflation ran amok.[24]

Many marketing academics are research inactive, admittedly, though few confess to the fact or take pride in their penury. It can be contended, what is more, that there is a small but very important difference between *writing* and *publication*. As no one actually reads the articles in top-notch journals – though everyone takes note of their existence and authorship – the actual contents are neither here nor there. Appearance is all. Appointments committees, RAE panels and academic acquaintances are more impressed by the ranking of the journal than our article's gripping insights, sparking turns of phrase or show-stopping metaphors. Writing doesn't matter, compadre; publication is what counts, boyo.

There is some truth in this somewhat sceptical view. Many academic articles *are* written for cosmetic purposes. They are akin to collagen injections for sagging CVs, the botox of higher education. So much so that a little literary liposuction or colophonic irrigation mightn't go amiss.[25] Yet writing is far from irrelevant. Words on the page *do* count for something. Even the most research averse academics write their lecture notes anew on occasion or download the latest articles in order to update their reading lists, if only to keep their teaching scores ticking over. Arcane articles in highly regarded journals may reach a fairly circumscribed readership – and even then, most readers won't get past the abstract or, if it's particularly good, the introductory top and concluding tail – but they are minutely scrutinized by reviewers, editors and several other assorted gatekeepers at the prestigious publication's pearly portals (where's AAAA when you need it?).

Writing matters to marketers. As noted in Chapter 1, it is one of the few commonalities in a fragmented, multi-faceted field, which studies everything from the sales pitches of market stall-holders to the marketing outsourcing strategies of multinational corporations. Literature is the lingua franca of the marketing academy. We talk writing. We discuss publications. Our passport to professional status, the doctorate, is a hefty work of literature. Our MS is the message.[26]

The Gutenberg BOGOF

Literature may be our livelihood, but just as 'proper' authors and analogous literary types have been reluctant to acknowledge their trade's association with 'trade', so too marketing scholars are unwilling to get in touch with their inner scribbler. Most academics, if the eerie silence surrounding the process is any indication, consider writing a chore, a pain, an annoying but unavoidable obligation between the down 'n' dirty pleasures of doing research and the career enhancing appearance of the published article.[27] The construction of the book or article itself – the creative process of drafting, composing, polishing and repolishing, or indeed tearing it all up and starting again – is completely ignored, irrespective of its importance to the finished product and regardless of the fact that every single marketing scholar wrestles with writing issues. First and last, we are all grammar grapplers, word wranglers, lexicon lassoers, clause cowboys . . .

Clearly, some of this reticence is due to our discipline's scientific and pragmatic imperatives, as we observed at the outset. Yet even those foolhardy few who have taken up the tools and techniques of literary criticism typically apply them to non-literary texts, such as adverts, brands, shopping centres and similar marketplace phenomena.[28] Make no mistake, 'reading' supermarkets, service encounters or *Star Trek* fan-fests is all fine and dandy – fun, too – but our disinclination to use the lit-crit toolkit for its designated purpose seems perverse at best and perverted at worst. There are, I grant you, innumerable normative texts on best writing practice, all chock-a-block with handy hints, dos and don'ts and prescriptive proscriptions. Hell, I once wrote one myself, a ten-step guide to composing publishable marketing articles. However, as no one actually read the article in which my article writing rules appeared (ahem), and as I'm duty bound to draw some meaningful writing lessons before wrapping up (I did warn you), I'm happy to pass some of them on once again (who said pass them off?):

1. Your title *must* contain a colon (semi-colons are for wimps, whereas full stops connote incipient megalomania).
2. Your theoretical framework, and you must have a theoretical framework, should comprise not five, not four, not two, but precisely *three* stages or elements.
3. It's always prudent to include a diagram of a *pyramid* (matrices are passé, molecular-type things risible, and boxes-and-arrows the graphic equivalent of polyester tank tops).
4. A couple of tables always add a much-needed touch of class, but as no one ever reads them you can fill them up with any old rubbish.

5. It's sensible to concoct a few concluding limitations, because this gives you the opportunity to add the old reliable rider 'additional research is needed'. This 'need' for additional research can then be cited in your next paper, and the next and, hey presto, one successful academic career is made.[29]

Most would agree that paper-writing guidelines have their place. They are especially useful for neophyte academics, who need some notion of what's expected of them. However, the problem is that if everyone follows the same article-assembly rules, an extremely dull discursive formation soon ensues. This write-alike process, what's worse, is self-perpetuating inasmuch as reviewers, having internalized the expected scholarly schema, will (in)advertently penalize those who depart from the norm ('Where's your methodology section?', 'What about managerial implications?').[30] Top-tier journals are especially prone to the attack of the clones, if only because editors and reviewers can't be seen to risk the journal's hard-earned reputation for rigour, rectitude and all the redoubtable rest. Our writing, meantime, gets more and more constrained, contrived, conditioned, constricted, constipated (what's keeping those AAAA people?).

Writing Marketing has attempted to escape the identikit imperative. It has done so by eschewing the normative, how-to-do-it perspective that prevails in the existing writing literature and attending instead to the writings of five prominent pen-pushers, much-admired academics whose publications have had a significant impact on our field. The approach is descriptive rather than prescriptive. It is *positive* not *normative*.[31] Positive research approaches, as Shelby D. Hunt points out, are a necessary precondition for authentic scientific achievement (but let's not get into the scientific status of the present text, amigos). Positive approaches, furthermore, can provide the basis for normative prescriptions (whereas the reverse flow is disbarred, according to SDH).[32] It follows, therefore, that we can extract some general writing principles, or precepts, from our famous five, notwithstanding the negligible sample size, the arbitrary selection process and the sheer preposterousness of the foregoing literary analyses (preposterousness, remember, isn't necessarily a bad thing).

The 3Rs of Marketing Writing

When everything is taken into account, and at the risk of misrepresenting the nuances of each author's unique style, it is clear that our leaders' literary achievements are attributable to their complete command of the basics. The 'basics' in this case being the 3Rs of *Reading, Righting* and *Rhythmatic*.

Reading: The key to successful writing is reading, and more reading, and even more reading. Manners maketh man, or so the old, sexist saying goes, but writers are made by reading. Reading and writing are the recto and verso, systole and diastole, ebb and flow of literary endeavour. Almost every creative writer who takes the time to reflect on his or her craft, acknowledges the all-important part played by reading, voracious reading, incessant reading, reading to the point of addiction.[33] Stephen King, for instance, attributes his best-sellerdom, his total mastery of the schlock-horror genre, to his insatiable reading habit.[34] He takes a book wherever he goes and dips into it at every opportunity. 'Reading,' he comments, 'is the creative center of a writer's life.' So much so, that 'if you don't have time to read, you don't have the time (or the tools) to write. Simple as that.'[35]

Of course, every one of us *knows* that reading is important and, more to the point perhaps, we all do it. The merest glance at almost any academic marketing article reveals that the writer is well read, very well read. Copious citations striate our texts and the final few pages unfailingly provide an impressive inventory of our insatiable textual appetites. I appreciate, therefore, that telling you reading is really, *really* important is, well, superfluous, pointless, unnecessary. Reading, rather, is de rigueur, a prerequisite, an obligation, a must, not something that helps us stand out from the clamouring crowd.

This is true. But there is an important reading wrinkle. Namely, the distinction between depth and breadth of reading. Most run-of-the-mill marketing academics, the likes of you and me, are indubitably deeply read. We know everything that there is to know about impulse purchases, gift giving, brand personality, the Boston matrix, or whatever our specialist area happens to be. What we seem to lack is *breadth* of reading, the incisive insight that comes from reading writings far removed from the existing literature, the stuff that rarely features in the journals we typically subscribe to and contribute to on occasion. Literary myopia, admittedly, is an occupational hazard. So voluminous is 'the literature' these days, especially in a burgeoning discipline like marketing, that it is virtually impossible to keep up with what's being written in our own field, or even subfield, much less master the compendious contents of adjacent domains. When it comes to more and more 'distant' academic domains, let alone the ever-growing mound of novels, short stories and other must-read literary output, the seemingly impassable soon becomes the simply impossible.

Yet, for all that, one of the things *Writing Marketing*'s roster share is breadth of reading. They all draw upon extremely broad academic repertoires, whether it be Morris Holbrook's effervescent reflections on aesthetics, Shelby Hunt's prodigious grasp of Western philosophy, Philip

Kotler's amazing ability to absorb stuff from every conceivable cultural sphere, both high and low, Wroe Alderson's insatiable appetite for books, books and more books (he devoured three per night, apparently)[36] or, indeed, Theodore Levitt's legendary card file index, containing quotes, aphorisms, excerpts and paraphrases of key texts, which he assembled over the decades and dipped into as the scholarly occasion demanded.

The first lesson, then, is that if we want to become better writers *we must read more widely*. But does this mean sacrificing depth for breadth? Yes and no. According to Michael Baker's essay on writing literature reviews, reading should be guided by the EVPI (expected value of perfect information).[37] This is the point, around about the fifteenth pertinent paper, where additional reading on the topic of interest yields no new information. If the Pareto principle thus applies to our reading – 80 per cent of insight comes from 20 per cent of articles perused – the time saved by skipping second-rate publications can be devoted to other domains, intellectual uplift and left-field stuff generally.

Fine though this idea is in principle, it inevitably necessitates drawing the line in practice. It asks us to resist the next article on brand personality, or online retailing, or after-sales service or whatever. We are being denied the very papers that could solve the problem we're tackling, or could turn out to be the ones that our reviewers are most aware of (or, in light of Murphy's Law, actually wrote). Embracing EVPI, what is more, overlooks the benefits that come from reading the duff, the dross, the ho-hum, the substandard. For younger academics in particular, there's nothing like reading a poor paper to persuade them to give it a go. Just as one needs to be bowled over by the best of the best, so too we occasionally need to feel 'I can do better than that!'

Still, given the sheer difficulty of keeping tabs on what's being written in our area, and given our deep-seated desire to absorb it all, no matter how mediocre, perhaps the best we can hope for is *recognition* of the fact that we need to read more widely. The marketing magi do it and we must do it too if we want to improve our writing. Time set aside to take in the latest sex 'n' shopping novel or stirring sci-fi saga is not time wasted. Quite the opposite.[38] *Bridget Jones's Diary* says more about contemporary consumer behaviour than any number of scholarly publications in the *Journal of Consumer Research*.

Righting: Abandoning the *JCR* for Bridget Jones may seem like an heretical action, and so it is in certain academic respects. Heresy, however, has its place. As the phonic and philological connotations of the word 'righting' convey, one of the most striking characteristics of our five scholarly superstars is their desire to overturn convention, to upend the accepted and to ensure that things are the way they should be (or as they think things should be). Righting marketing is their modus operandi. Without exception, their signature scholarly achievements involve turning the tables in some way, shape or form.

Ted Levitt, as we discovered in Chapter 2, famously flipped the field on its head by claiming that the customer is the point of marketing departure, not the denouement of marketer activity. Phil Kotler challenged the myopic, if widely held, notion that marketing is confined to the for-profit sector and contended that it is in fact a universal verity. Morris Holbrook brought an aesthetic sheen to marketing and made a compelling case against base managerialism, the utilitarian ethos that many marketing faculty still subscribe to, if less forcefully than before. Shelby Hunt not only added philosophical lustre to an hitherto hands-on discipline, but brilliantly turned the tables on the table-turners, those trying to turn the discipline into a post-positivist paradise. Wroe Alderson, likewise, did something so radical that it seems almost inconceivable today. A self-taught farm boy without a PhD, or any serious scholarly credibility, Wroe rose from the grubby ranks of marketing consultancy to the very pinnacle of academic respectability. He finished up at Wharton, set the agenda for the entire field in the forties and fifties and, perhaps more than anyone before or since, demonstrated that intellectual might is marketing right.

This upending imperative, what is more, is not confined to our exemplars' overall contribution. It permeates their oeuvres, the lineaments of their arguments and the very organization of their sentences. Kotler's preferred prosodic ploy involves variations on the construction, 'you may think this, but it actually isn't so'. Levitt repeatedly rails against prolix professors and management gurus, thereby satirically subverting himself and everything he wryly represents. Alderson's written texts almost oscillate, insofar as they constantly refer to points discussed previously and allude to insights to come, which leaves the reader overwhelmed, over-awed, overturned and, ultimately, in no position to argue. Holbrook, meanwhile, is an absolute master of ironic inversion – turning textual turtle, if you will – as his rigorous statistical analysis of a short story, *Coastal Disturbances*, or his in-depth ethnographic investigation of his pedigree cat, Rocky, bear brilliant witness.[39]

Hunt, similarly, uses a form of 'judo strategy' where the strength of his opponents is used against them. Their semantic infelicities, syntactical failings, logical shortcomings or intellectual incongruities are incisively identified and duly employed against the antagonist. The most effective condemnation is self-condemnation, after all. There's no more powerful contradiction than self-contradiction.[40] SDH's critics, in effect, defeat themselves by dint of their own ill-considered statements:

Peter proposes: 'It is the *usefulness* of the theories that *accounts for* the success of science over the last four hundred years (p.14, italics added). However, this is rhetorical sleight-of- hand. To 'account for' implies answering *why* science has been successful. Because science can successfully explain and predict phenomena, it is useful. However, this usefulness is clearly a consequence of science's success, not its antecedent. Therefore, contra Peter, usefulness cannot 'account for' science's success.[41]

There's a very important lesson here for those of us who lack, and aspire to acquire, the write stuff. The conventional wisdom of academic marketing discourse, derived largely from the presumed norms of scientific endeavour, is that scholarship is a cumulative activity. We add to the ever-growing body of literature. We contribute our textual two-penny-worth to marketing's conceptual treasure chest. We stand on the shoulders of giants. We are building a shining scholarly city on a hill. The underlying ethos is progressive, linear, onward and upward, new and improved, washes whiter-than-white.[42] The acme of academic achievement is a replication experiment that formally confirms an empirical finding and thereby establishes a bone fide marketing axiom or, gasp, law-like generalization.

Our greats don't think or act like that, though they often espouse the cumulative model for argument's sake. In practice, they tend to operate on Ted Levitt's precept 'think opposite', or in terms of the Kotlero–Marxist–Hegelian dialectic, or in the MoHo mode of structure–departure–reconciliation, or with regard to Wroe Alderson's circles, seasons, gyres and eternal returns of 'cyclical time', rather than the slow but steady accretion that underpins conventional notions of 'linear time'.[43] Oppositionalism, outsiderdom and obversity, if there is such a word, are the rhetorical hallmarks of our textual tall poppies, strange though this may seem when Kotler's under consideration. Yet the venerable Phil, of all people, is a past master of recycling, repetition and strategic reversal. He has announced a 'new marketing' paradigm on at least eight separate occasions, each one a challenge to the prevailing approach (previously laid down by Kotler himself).

The lesson, then, is that if you want to get ahead in marketing letters, turn the page upside down before putting pen to paper.

Rhythmatic: Like obversity, rhythmatic is a word that doesn't exist. Until now. The neologism, nevertheless, combines 'rhythm', the essential characteristic of felicitous prose, with an intertextual allusion to 'rithmatic' of the original 3Rs. As such, it is singularly pertinent to our heroic handful. When all is said and done, the central trait that connects our poetic champions is a compelling literary style. On reading their works, one is instantly aware of an authorial presence, a distinctive textual persona that speaks to us in an inimitable manner, often mellifluous, always unique. Some of the passages in Levitt and Holbrook are breathtaking in their brilliance. They send shivers down our collective spine, raise the hairs on our neck and walk over our grave. It may not be marketing science, but with writing of this standard, who needs science?

Appropriately, moreover, our principal peers' peerless prose is replete with neologisms, wordplay, linguistic excesses and, as often as not, extreme sesquipedalianism. Kotler has generated more jargon than you can shake a stick at (meta-marketing, turbo-marketing, demarketing and many more). Alderson is no slouch in the locution foundry either (transvection, blaze, hedonomics). Levitt is always ready to riff rhetorically or practise his lexical scales ('the paradox that puzzles and perplexes', 'what needs to happen for that to happen?'). Holbrook seems to work on the premise that assonance is good, alliteration is better, and alliterative assonance is best of all ('onerous, odious, and even odoriferous', 'rules, restrictions, rituals, repetitions, rigidities, redundancies, and regularities'). Even Hunt, who conveys the impression of being above base rhetorical concerns is blessed with a repertoire of quasi-quips, semi-catchphrases and nearly-refrains, which he is never reluctant to unleash ('there is much work to be done', 'alone among extant theories of competition', 'the long-run success of a theory gives reason to believe that something like the entities and structures posited by the theory actually exist').

So incessant, indeed, is their wordplay that the arteries of our titans' texts are, frankly, clogged, sclerotic and in serious need of bypass surgery. They don't so much suffer from writer's block as blocked writing. Their books and papers are near-enough unreadable, if truth be told.[44] Hunt and Alderson are especially stricken, as any postgraduate student will attest. Holbrook and Kotler are heavy sledding on some occasions and very heavy sledding on others. Levitt's scintillating style is marred, bizarrely by its scintillation, inasmuch as the brilliance of the individual words is so dazzling that we can't quite see what he's getting at (the myopic among us, excepted).

The reading difficulty that some people have when grappling with the greats again contains an important lesson for would-be writers of distinction. Clarity is not strictly necessary. Lucidity is a barrier to entry. KISS is the kiss of death. This contention, needless to say, runs completely counter to everything that is said about writing, academic writing especially.[45] We are constantly exhorted to keep it plain and simple, to avoid big words, long sentences, unnecessary adverbs, or anything than detracts from getting the facts across in a clear, concise, coherent manner. The prevailing philosophy of marketing writing is predicated on the George Orwell school of thought, which famously made the case for plain prose, simply put.[46]

The crucial thing to appreciate, however, is that Orwell was expressing an opinion, not issuing an order. He was expressing an opinion, furthermore, that reflects the 'social realist' literary style that was then in vogue, as well as the minimalist mode of high modernism.[47] It was a credo that Orwell's equally gifted contemporaries did not subscribe to in many cases – for example, the magic realism of Borges and Márquez[48] – and one that promptly evaporated when the linguistic excesses of postmodernism burst on to the literary scene.[49] This is not to suggest that lucid writing is wrong, or that we should aspire to obscurantism, albeit incomprehensibility can be helpful in a strictly scholarly sense, since it carries connotations of depth, sagacity, learnedness and suchlike. Alderson and Hunt, certainly, owe at least some of their eminence to the if-it's-difficult-it-must-be-profound mental model that readers bring to their texts. The essential point is that there is more to writing than plain and simple, though you'd never know this from the academic marketing literature.

Great writing, lest we forget, is not necessarily easy writing. Theodor Adorno, the notoriously ascetic aesthete, regarded accessibility as an abomination, the mark of the mere journeyman, the proficient artisan, the unspeakable philistine.[50] John Updike, in an acidic if apt assessment of Tom Wolfe, draws a distinction between *literature* and *entertainment*.[51] Leading literary critic Valentine Cunningham makes a compelling case for 'pleasurable pain', the delicious bewilderment that great writing often brings.[52] Or, in the words of the imperishable Harold Bloom: 'the strongest, most authentic motive for deep reading of the now much-abused traditional canon is the search for a difficult pleasure . . . pleasurable difficulty seems to me a plausible definition of the Sublime'. Reading well, he concludes, 'returns you to otherness'.[53]

In this regard, it is important to appreciate that by refusing to countenance anything other than plain and simple prose, the proselytizers for plain and simple fail to appreciate that plain and simple is itself a literary style, a literary style that is hard to master.[54] It is very difficult to write in a plain and simple way; write well, that is. Orwell's oft-cited encomium to the joys of plain and simple is a sublime example of the essayist's art. Marketing's plain and simple imperative encourages us to think that writing plain and simple is something that is plain and simple to do. This is nonsense, and the outcome of this nonsensical misconception is the plethora of poorly written, pseudo-plain, sham-simple marketing articles that atrophy our principal academic organs. Plain and simple is the *epitome* of creative writing, one of the hardest literary effects to achieve. Most marketing academics aren't good enough to write plain and simple.[55] And I can't put it more plain and simply than that.

Three More Rs

Although *Reading, Righting* and *Rhythmatic* are central to our redoubtables' writing endeavours, the Rs don't stop there. No siree. To the contrary, they all exhibit at least three more Rs, albeit compared to the capital Rs these can be considered lower case characteristics.

The first of these is *regularity*, the sheer volume of output. Our famous five don't just issue a couple of papers per annum and the occasional text-book or monograph. It's a non-stop, no-holds-barred, year-in-year-out operation. They appear to work at two speeds: flat out and flatter out. Their textual torrent is incessant, unstoppable, overwhelming. Philip Kotler, for example, is now in his early seventies and his reputation as one of the world's foremost marketing thinkers is unassailable. Yet he not only continues to publish several new books a year but constantly updates his manifold old ones, for good measure. Impressive as his industry is, how-ever, the really important writing point is that he practises more than the rest of us. Writing is a craft, to some extent at least, and craftpersons improve with experience. There is a learning-curve effect that can't be cir-cumvented or short-circuited. Part of the reason that Kotler and Co. are better than us is because they write more than us. The more we write, the better our writing becomes.[56]

The second R is *repetition*. Although our heroes write a lot, a lot of what they write is repetitive. They make the same basic points again and again. And then again, in case we didn't get it last time. Recapitulation, admit-tedly, isn't necessarily a bad thing, as every ad executive knows.[57] Things have to be restated to get through and our literary leaders can't be accused of failing to get through. True, I've made this point several times already in *Writing Marketing* – merely repeating the point about repetition, dear reader – but it is apparent, indeed prominent, in all five cases. Wroe Alderson, to cite an instance not cited earlier, consistently churned his corpus. *Marketing Behavior and Executive Action* was assembled from the newsletters that his consultancy firm issued in the mid-1950s; *Dynamic Marketing Behavior* was a rewrite of *Marketing Behavior and Executive Action*; and *Men, Motives, and Markets* was itself a popularization of his previous publications. In fairness, Wroe's repetitions almost always involved a modicum of modification, adaptation and, as often as not, the creation of a completely new term for an old idea (thus the essence of marketing was variously attributed to 'assorting', 'differential advantage', 'balanced potencies', 'group behavior', 'handling information', 'skilful direction of effort' and 'status'). It is clear, however, that these terminological twists and turns represent attempts to keep the message fresh. Just as the mes-sage must be repeated, ringing the changes must also be repeated.

The third R is *robbery*. All authors are thieves. Stealing is a tool of the trade.[58] 'Whatever is well said by others,' says Seneca, 'is mine'.[59] According to T.S. Eliot's famous formulation, 'immature poets imitate, mature poets steal'.[60] For Harold Bloom, plagiarism can be condoned in authors, since it is unavoidable, if only at an unconscious level. What cannot be condoned, he contends, is plagiarism from badly written originals.[61] The history of literature not only shows that 'strong poets,' such as Chaucer and Shakespeare, misappropriated everything that moved – as indeed do today's writers[62] – but that 'borrowing' is a vitally necessary component of the creative process. Clearly, this stance runs counter to scientific custom and practice, where draconian penalties are imposed on plagiarists or suspected plagiarists.[63] However, the relationship between research and robbery is less clear-cut in the literary sphere. And while I'm not for a moment suggesting that our learned luminaries are marketing miscreants – though Ted Levitt openly acknowledges that when writing 'Marketing Myopia' he stole (his word) from Joseph Schumpeter[64] – there is something of the marketing magpie about them. Without exception, they are moulders of ideas not manufacturers of them. They seize, shape, synthesize and sprinkle stardust on extant concepts or bodies of thought. They take pigs ears, the poorly written scratchings of the rest of us, and turn them into silk scholarly purses. And there's nothing wrong with that.

Rs Longa Vita Brevis

There may be nothing wrong with writerly robbery, but that doesn't mean there's nothing wrong with the writings of our famous five. To the contrary, there are three further Rs worth noting, the first two of which are double jeopardous. *Restraint*, for example, is a vitally important literary talent. Novelists and creative writers generally are ruthless with their writings.[65] They edit, excise and extirpate (alliterative excesses especially) or work with people who are prepared to help them 'kill their children', as Stephen King puts it.[66] The problem with literary greats in disciplines like marketing is that they are allowed to overindulge, possibly because book and journal editors are reluctant to take the blue pencil to them, or possibly because our field lacks literary cowpokes, the kind of people who keep creatives under strict style control.[67] The upshot is that all of our exemplars suffer from the 'professors' disease' of textual elephantiasis.[68] Morris Holbrook, in particular, is now in a position where he can publish extremely lengthy articles, which are brilliantly written but dreadfully self-indulgent. He badly needs an editor, just as Ted Levitt did in his empurpled period in the early eighties and Phil Kotler did when he was publishing ever more massive marketing textbooks. But whereas Levitt was saved by the editorship of *HBR* (his late period papers are short and sharp, primarily because they started life as editorials for the journal), and whereas Kotler has been pushed by his publisher toward short, sizzling books for the marketing executive market (when Ted retired, the management seer 'mantle' inevitably fell to Phil), Morris is increasingly enwrapped in a 'serpentine nexus' of professorial prolixity (as Levitt put it at the apotheosis of his purple patch).[69]

Remonstration is another ambivalent one. By dint of their heroic endeavours to challenge convention and turn the field on its head, our intellectual iconoclasts inevitably run into opposition from scholarly stick-in-the-muds. All five have found themselves embroiled in controversy. Their writing careers are punctuated with comments, rejoinders, manifestoes, denunciations, head-buttings and similar cerebral exchanges. It sometimes seems that they are not simply putting the rest of us to right, but severely chastising anyone who demurs from their disciplinary dictat. Shelby Hunt's rebarbative responses to his critics are classics of the genre. They are the academic equivalent of car wrecks, from which SDH emerges unscathed and casually strolls off to find another turbo-charged theoretical vehicle, which will be put through its paces in a forthcoming MASCAR rally (Marketing Academia's Serial Clashes And Remonstrations). MoHo, meantime, has scratched countless clueless scholars who foolishly thought they were tangling with a pussycat. Ted, Phil and Wroe could mix it up too and, while many may regard this pugilistic propensity as an affront to the purportedly cooperative ethos of the academic community, their intellectual belligerence brings benefits as well.[70] There's nothing like a little argy-bargy to raise one's professional profile. Scholarly slugfests certainly draw the crowds. It's mud-wrestling of the mind. Whatever else they are, then, our serial subversives are ever ready, willing and able to resort to literary fisticuffs. The pen may be mightier than the sword but it is necessary to use the pen *as* a sword from time to time.

Reflexivity, as noted in the Wroe Alderson chapter, involves the application of academic precepts to the academic concerned.[71] Alderson, of course, was an absolute master of Alderson-mongering. His newsletters, conferences and conceptual channel captaincy were second to none. However, all of our marketing maestros are superlative self-promoters.[72] Aside from the aforementioned kerfuffles, which are nothing if not good publicity, they make full use of established marketing methods such as segmentation (focusing on specific sectors, for example executives, students, fellow scholars), differentiation (no one else writes like Shelby Hunt or Morris Holbrook, not even remotely) and, as noted earlier, repetition, repetition, repetition, repetition (there are so many academic 'brands' out

there, all clamouring for attention, it is necessary to self-advertise incessantly).[73] Each of our exemplars, what is more, markets himself in a
slightly different way, in a way that parallels the archetypal patter patterns
of the marketing/advertising profession. Theodore Levitt is the ace
slogan-coiner, the king of the catchphrase, the limpid one-liner, the killer
quip. Philip Kotler is the model of consistency, the long-running, happy-
clappy campaign that is constantly convivial, constantly congenial,
constantly constant. SDH, possibly because of his background in the
plastics and automotive industries, is the hard-sell, foot-in-the-door,
won't-take-no-for-an-answer type, the Rosser Reeves of marketing
research. Wroe Alderson is the fast talking, pitch perfect spielmeister, who
has an answer to every objection and spins a web of disorientating words
around his scholarly marks from which it is impossible to escape.
TOPKAT, by contrast, sells by not selling, by Bill Bernbach style ironic
inversion, where an anti-marketing stance and insult-the-product attitude
are brilliantly effective ways of moving the marketing merchandise.[74]

Fryes With That

Actually, this archetypal allusion is less extreme than it appears. Indeed,
it seems to me that archetypal literary criticism, or myth-crit as it is sometimes known, can help us make sense of the bigger writing picture.
Myth-crit is the brainchild of Northrop Frye, the architectonic literary theorist we encountered in Chapter 1. Like many celebrity thinkers, Frye is
best remembered for a single show-stopping idea that he recycled for the
remainder of his long and distinguished career. His barnstorming book,
Anatomy of Criticism, was published in 1957, to considerable popular
acclaim, and it instantly propelled him to the top of the critical list.[75] In a
homage to Robert Burton's *Anatomy of Melancholy* (anatomies are ordinarily characterized by detailed examination and exhaustive erudition),
Frye's opus comprised a synoptic taxonomic system that enwrapped all
of Western literature in its capacious coils. These coils consisted of four
archetypal narrative forms – comedy, romance, tragedy, and satire – which
followed each other in sequence, akin to seasonal *mythoi* of the natural
world, spring, summer, autumn and winter respectively. Each individual
narrative form was further subdivided into six sequential symmetrical
stages, all linked into a recursive whole of twenty-four separate phases,
analogous to the circle of fifths in music.[76]

By any reckoning, Frye's symphonic system was a massively ambitious
conception. He regarded his procedure as somewhat similar to stepping
back from an individual artwork in order to better see and thereby grasp

the underlying organizational principle (as one does with a painting in a gallery). Unlike many of his lit-crit contemporaries, furthermore, Frye refused to look outside literature for insight. That is, he refused to explain literary accomplishments in terms of historical circumstances, authorial intentions or psychological drives. Literature was treated as an autonomous entity, a single 'order of words', where literary works are forged from foregoing literary works and foregoing literary works forged from foregoing literary works, and so on ad infinitum.

Although Frye is best remembered for his calendrical conception of narrative forms, the *Anatomy of Criticism* didn't end there. On the contrary, it contains another conceptual schema, derived from Aristotle, which is directly relevant to *Writing Marketing*. In the opening essay of his magisterial monograph, Frye posits an evolutionary 'theory of modes'.[77] This focuses on the asymmetric relationship between ourselves as readers and the protagonist of a particular fictional modality. In *myth*, the hero is a divine being, superior in kind to the environment and almost everyone else, ourselves included. In *romance*, all manner of fantastical events occur but the hero is recognizably human, albeit he or she is superior in degree to the environment and the rest of us. In *high mimetic* modes, such as tragedy or epic, the hero is significantly better than the average Joe, though his (or her) actions are beholden to and buffeted by uncontrollable circumstances. In *low mimetic* literary modes, like the realist novel and most comedies, the hero is one of us, subject to the stresses, strains and environmental vicissitudes of daily existence. In *ironic* or *satirical* modes, finally, the protagonist is positioned on a lower plane than the average reader, an anti-hero in effect. The upshot is that 'we have a sense of looking down on a scene of bondage, frustration or absurdity'.[78]

This descending sequence of narrative forms, Frye further contends, characterizes the history of European literature, from the myths of the Celtic and early Christian period, via the knights errant and courtly love-ins of medieval times, through the Shakespearean and Miltonian epics of the Renaissance, en route to the realist and comic novels of the eighteenth and nineteenth centuries, exemplified by Austen, Dickens and Balzac, only to terminate with the ironic anti-heroes of the twentieth century, such as Leopold Bloom, J. Alfred Prufrock, Mr K, Willy Loman, Winston Smith, Holden Caulfield and Homer Simpson. The framework, of course, is not hard and fast. As with so much of Northrop Frye, there are countless subdivisions, sub-subdivisions and sub-sub-subdivisions, to say nothing of inter-category parallels and echoes. Thus each of the five main modes is split into the naïve and the sentimental, which are further split into the thematic and the fictional, where the hero is either isolated from or integrated into society. The overall effect, as Hamilton drolly notes, is like 'entering the sorting room of a busy post office, wondering into which slot a literary work may fall'.[79]

Anatomy of Marketing

Despite the great critic's taxonomic logorrhoea, Frye's overall pattern provides a plausible model of literary development, one that is 'generally accepted'.[80] More to the point perhaps, it is a pattern that is applicable to the history of modern marketing thought, from the 1960s to the present. It is a pattern that can help us place our literary lions in the great scholarly scheme of things – marketing's postwar evolutionary trajectory. It is a microcosmic marketing pattern, whereby each author embodies the signature scholarly achievement of the decade concerned. Thus Ted Levitt is the stellar legend who exploded onto the scene in the 1960s and whose customer-orientated, managerially-relevant ideas completely revolutionized the field. Phil Kotler is the questing romantic, who rose to the top of the tree in the 1970s and who broadened marketing's focus beyond for-profit organizations to the not-for-profit sphere of hospitals, schools, art galleries and so on. The magnificently tragic Shelby Hunt came to the fore in the 1980s and, while endowing the discipline with the philosophical depth that it previously lacked, his pro-positivist campaigning actually advanced the post-positivist cause he denounced. Wroe Alderson, the environmentally-influenced functionalist, may have died in 1964 but his ideas came to full fruition in the retrospectively-minded 1990s, when networks, relationships, eco-issues and e-tailing (anticipated by Alderson) held academic sway.[81] Morris Holbrook is the satirical ironist supreme, someone who will be seen, in future years, as the embodiment of the present decade – irreverent, anti-business, aesthetics-led, consumption- rather than consumer-orientated.

Naturally, this 'theory of marketing modes' is not without limitations. Apart from the fairly obvious fact that Frye formulated it with regard to 500 years of literary achievement (as opposed to the 50 years of modern marketing's academic arc), there is a basic biographical issue. With the exception of Alderson, all five founders of marketing discursivity have been active throughout much of the period under consideration. They aren't so much sequential as contemporaneous. The underpinning decadal premise is also debatable, since decade-by-decade perspectives are prone to stereotyping (the roaring twenties, the hungry thirties), suffer from boundary delimitation issues (when did the sixties *really* start?, what about seventies revivals?), and, for many professional historians, are redolent of old-fashioned, 'impositional' modes of explanation characterized by facile frameworks, puerile periodizations and historicist speculations about alleged 'cycles', 'epochs' and 'eras'.[82]

Historicism, however, has made a comeback, in literary circles at least. As noted in Chapter 1, the irredeemably textual nature of history – its narrative forms, storytelling propensities, emplotment procedures, the simple fact that history is writing – is central to the New Historicist school of thought. Indeed, the prototypical New Historicist approach is to take an item of literary ephemera, such as a playbill or promotional flyer for patent medicine, and use this marginal text to gain insight into the power/knowledge structures of society as a whole.[83] The macrocosm in the microcosm model rides again, albeit in a retro lit-crit context.

Be that as it may, marketing has always had a predilection for epoch-spotting and naming (production era, sales era, marketing era, etc.).[84] It is not averse to decade-by-decade deliberations on its own academic achievements (Bartels's *History of Marketing Thought* is the classic case in point).[85] It is characterized by a canonizing imperative (that is, the identification and lionization of classic articles, celebrity scholars and top-rank institutions).[86] And it is undeniable that individual academics are indissolubly associated with their key contribution to the discipline.[87] Professors are placed in a pigeonhole, regardless of their many and varied publications, pretty much as Frye anticipated.

For all its faults, Frye's model *does* capture the essence of marketing scholarship's postwar evolution. The Ted Levitt-led counter-revolution of the 1960s, the Phil Kotler-inspired broadening of the 1970s, the Shelby Hunt-precipitated deepening of the 1980s, the Wroe Alderson-refracted reinvention of the 1990s, and the Morris Holbrook-modulated catharsis of the here and now. MoHo, in fact, is an especially significant element of this schematic, insofar as his work simultaneously harks back to Ted Levitt, the founder of the modern marketing paradigm, and provides a possible model for the future of marketing research. Under the guise of book reviews, he is single-handedly reinventing the academic article. Since emerging from the shadow of Theodore the Father, TOPKAT has forged a distinctive scholarly style, one that foregrounds the visual (stereoscopic photos), the cultural (both high and low) and the contradictions of contemporary consumer society (people's love–hate relationship with the marketplace). True, on reading Morris's recent writings it is tempting to say 'this isn't marketing'. But that is exactly the kind of reaction that avant-garde artists always provoke. Morris's post-'Loving and Hating' articles, such as 'The Millennial Consumer in the Texts of our Times' (parts one and two), represent the future of the field, though in light of the entrenched attitude of the academic marketing mainstream, I fear that our discipline will either slide further and further into irrelevance or cede the subject area to others.[88]

Whither Writing Marketing?

The ceding, in fact, has already begun. A marketing writing revolution is under way, but it is not being prosecuted by marketing scholars. The foremost marketing commentator of the twenty-first century is a journalist, Naomi Klein. Her turn-of-the-century tract, *No Logo*, has done more to set the contemporary marketing agenda than any number of learned disquisitions in *Journal of Marketing*, *Journal of Marketing Research* or *Journal of Consumer Research*.[89] As the CSR movement attests, her journalism is having a greater impact in executive suites than even the best business best-sellers – how-to, twelve-step, seven-secret, whatever – and unlike the latter, Klein's work is being read by the consuming public at large.[90] Naomi Klein is just one journo among many, moreover. Felicity Lawrence, Thomas Frank, Eric Schlosser, George Monboit, Malcolm Gladwell, David Brooks, Joanna Blythman, Douglas Rushkoff, Paco Underhill and Thomas Hine, to name but a few, are today's pre-eminent spokespersons on marketing matters.[91] Not one of them is an academic.

Some in academia, admittedly, might draw comfort from Klein et al.'s lack of scholarly standing, since it debars them from the cerebral conversation. Such obdurate attitudes, however, are doomed to failure, because even within the academy marketing's territorial claims are being usurped. Anthropologists, sociologists, geographers, historians, literary critics and countless others are quite happy to write about marketing matters, as the cascade of books concerning consumption, shopping centres, credit cards, theme parks and so forth bear witness.[92] Rachel Bowlby, Mica Nava, Juliet Schor, Jackson Lears, Lizabeth Cohen, George Ritzer, Daniel Miller, Alan Bryman and the like are writing marketing nowadays, as is James Twitchell, a professor of English Literature at the University of Florida who has published several influential books on branding, advertising and the delicious, devilish dilemmas of our marketing-impregnated times.[93] Not only are these books better written than most academic marketing publications, but many don't even refer to the publications of marketing scholars. This neglect is undeniably frustrating for certain illustrious marketers, especially as some of the outsiders' insights are little more than Marketing 101.[94] Nevertheless, it is an inevitable consequence of the university caste system – Bourdieu's *homo academicus*[95] – inasmuch as B-school based faculty are irredeemably tainted by association with capitalist imperatives, no matter how brilliant their publications.

Is writing marketing dead? Have we, in effect, capitulated to Pulitzer Prize-coveting journalists and our academic elders and betters? Not necessarily. There are a few noteworthy writers who stand proud like mesas in the desertified marketing landscape. Indeed, just as English literature has been invigorated by the rise of post-colonial perspectives in the writings of Salman Rushdie, Vikram Seth, and Monica Ali among others,[96] so too the marketing empire is starting to write back to the United States. Evert Gummesson, Bernard Cova, Pauline Maclaran and Mark Ritson are especially worthy of note. The best of these is Nigel Piercy, who on a word-for-word basis is as good a writer as any of the famous five featured herein.[97] His writing not only engages with one of marketing's core constituencies – senior executives – but he has been published in many of the top-tier American journals, which means that he has serious scholarly credibility in the academic marketing heartland. Now, Piercy is not without fault. He scores highly on two of our three key Rs, *Righting* and *Rhythmatic*, however his lack of wider *Reading* lets him down. Thus he published a book entitled *Tales From the Marketplace*, yet made no reference whatsoever to the wider literature on narrative, storytelling and suchlike, which would have improved the volume enormously.[98] Still, there's no doubt that, in literary terms at least, Nigel Piercy is capable of ascending to the writing marketing immortals.

Nigel may be our best literary bet, but even if he fails and we bid a fond farewell to marketing managers and the wider university community, there's still another option. Ourselves alone. The marketing discipline is so enormous, and so entrenched, that we can quite contentedly write for and to each other, irrespective of what anyone else thinks. That's what we do already, let's be honest. Scholars and wannabe scholars excepted, who actually reads *JMR* or *MS*? Not managers, that's for sure. Not non-marketing scholars, that's for surer. Not anyone other than the authors of the articles, that's for surest (and I'm not even certain about the authors). This state of affairs, admittedly, is somewhat solipsistic not to say dangerously incestuous. It smacks of taking in each other's washing, eating our own young, and living off the fat we've accumulated during the years of plenty, when marketing was regarded as a discipline with something to say.[99] Let's not pretend it isn't happening, however. The fact of the matter is that there's a large and captive market for marketing writing – undergraduate, postgraduate, doctoral student, etc. – and it's likely to comprise our principal readership for the foreseeable future. Safely ensconced in our scholarly cocoon, we can continue writing to each other for years before anyone notices something's seriously amiss. Perhaps we're already there, scribbling away to ourselves in the *Truman Show* of thought . . .

In this regard, Martin Amis's brilliantly written book about book writing, *The Information*, reflexively reimagines Northrop Frye's 'modes of writing' framework:

'Literature,' Richard said (and it would be nice to write something like 'wiping the foam from his lips with his sleeve as the company fell silent'. But he was drinking cheap red wine and eating pork scratchings and Gina and Gilda were talking about something else) – literature, Richard said, describes a descent. First, gods. The demigods. Then epic became tragedy: failed kings failed heroes. Then the gentry. Then the middle class and its mercantile dreams. Then it was about *you* – Gina, Gilda: social realism. Then it was about *them*: lowlife. Villains. The ironic age. And he was saying, Richard was saying: now what? Literature for a while can be about *us*: about writers. But that won't last long. How do we burst clear of all this? And he asked them: whither the novel?[100]

Uroboros Unbound

It is arguable, then, that marketing is entering the writing about writing epoch.[101] The idea seems absurd, I must confess. Who on earth would waste their time writing about writing marketing? Who on earth would take the time to read it? Not a discerning intellectual like you, that's for sure. Nevertheless, it can't be denied that there's considerable scope for writing about marketing writing. Apart from all the prominent academics whose writings are ripe for reading and rereading – for example, Beth Hirschman, Barbara Stern, Sid Levy, Russ Belk, John Sherry and Stan Hollander – there's the serried ranks of journalists, consultants and non-marketing scholars whose marketing-related works can be critiqued from a literary perspective (that'll show 'em!). Similarly, the marketing tactics of anti-marketing literary critics, such as Terry Eagleton, Fredric Jameson and analogous self-publicists, can also be exposed for what they are (that'll show 'em, too!). While we're at it, the lit-crit larder can be raided for all the tools and techniques that haven't been considered herein and these can be applied to our famous five, as well as all of the above. There's no end to the writing marketing possibilities.

Nah, it'll never happen . . .

The Appendix of Stephen Brown

> Knowledge only comes in lightning flashes.
> The text is the roll of thunder that follows.
>
> Walter Benjamin, *The Arcades Project*[1]

Writing Marketing is my fourteenth book, or thereabouts, and writing it has been an interesting experience. It is the book I've always wanted to write. For as long as I can remember, I've been more interested in the construction of writing (how it's put together) than the content (what it's trying to say). Well, OK, OK, that's a bit of an exaggeration. But even as a bookish adolescent, when I was guzzling genre fiction by the bucketful, I was just as interested in 'how they do that?' than 'what happens next?'

For example, I often found myself reading and rereading P.G. Wodehouse to see if I could figure out how he constructed his superlative sentences (such as Gussie Fink-Nottle's imperishable prize-giving speech in *Right Ho, Jeeves*) and the thing I loved most about H.P. Lovecraft's sci-fi shockers was his wonderfully arcane vocabulary, which gave his horror stories their eerie, otherworldly flavour ('ululation', 'mephitic', 'chthonic'). It actually got to the point where, on picking up an Agatha Christie, I knew within the first couple of chapters who dun it. I don't know how I knew who Christie's culprit was – peeking at the last page helped, mind you – but familiarity with her oeuvre gave me a feel for the formula. Indeed, I well remember working out *Who Killed Roger Ackroyd?*, her breakthrough book, before finishing the first sentence.[2]

Most well-adjusted people, I suppose, set aside their textual obsessions on reaching adulthood. And I too spent the first ten years of my academic career writing nondescript scholarly articles on nondescript marketing matters. However, the how-they-do-that urge didn't go away. I once had the nerve to write a 'Disgusted of Tunbridge Wells' letter to Morris

Holbrook, chastising him for changing the concluding paragraph of his impeccable 'Bird Lives!' paper. (When MoHo recycled this piece as Chapter 2 of his greatest hits textbook *Consumer Research*, he refused to leave well enough alone and, unfortunately, tried to tinker with perfection. I was not amused; I told him so. I'm nice like that.)

What's more, the book that impressed me most during my postmodern conversion wasn't by Derrida, Foucault, Barthes, Jameson or even Baudrillard. It was *Works and Lives* by Clifford Geertz. Although he was far from the first to write about anthropological writing (much less the inaugural commentator on social science writing per se), here was a guy who not only wrote about writing but whose writings about writing were beautifully written.[3] Geertz is rightly renowned for his brilliant bon mots on Balinese cock fighting. For me, however, he'll always be the scholar who made mock of those who make mock of those who 'lounge about in libraries reflecting on literary questions' (and, yes, I 'borrowed' this line in Chapter 1, in accordance with the sixth 'R' of marketing writing).[4]

* * *

If on the one hand *Writing Marketing* is the book I've long longed to write, the inevitable other hand is that writing *Writing Marketing* has been particularly tough going. It's not the sheer amount of preparatory reading that each of the individual chapters required. On the contrary, I usually found that the nooks and crannies of my chosen authors' corpuses contained the most revealing material. Writers appear to let their guards down in footnotes, appendices and other marginal places where readers rarely venture (a point, incidentally, that's noted somewhere by – wouldn't you know it – babadabap TOPKAT). The big problem, rather, was deciding who to include. Marketing academics may not be renowned for the 'limpid pellucidicity of their mellifluous prose', as a pretentious so-and-so once put it.[5] However, there is an awful lot of good writing going on, writing that is worthy of careful study. Russ Belk, John Sherry, Nigel Piercy, Sid Levy, Stan Hollander and Craig Thompson are just some of the scholars I seriously considered studying. For a long time, in fact, Russ Belk was part of my *Writing Marketing* roster but, given the basic structure of the book, it boiled down to a choice between Russ and Morris. Now, Russ is a superb writer. His depth of scholarship is astounding. He pens the best opening and closing paragraphs in the business. All too often, however, the middle bit of his papers is unremarkable. Russ, it seems to me, is always prepared to compromise his writing in order to get published in a top-tier journal, whereas Morris at least tries to find a way around editorial constraints in an attempt to ensure that his published writing is as pure and untainted as possible. Word for word they are equally gifted writers, but Morris is the artist, Russ is the artisan.

In addition to sorting out the writing rans from the also rans, I also ran the literary slide rule over several 'quasi-marketing scholars' such as Peter Drucker, Henry Mintzberg, Paul Lazarsfeld, and a number of 'non-scholar marketers', such as Edward Bernays, Tom Peters and Howard Gossage. At one stage, I contemplated the possibility of a much larger scale, if necessarily shallower, approach to marketing writing. While this angle had merit, not least because it provided an opportunity to apply Bourdieu's notions of 'field' and 'habitus' to the marketing academy, I concluded that close reading, tight focus and less rather than more is the hallmark of literary criticism. Precision is preferable to panorama. Discrimination is the better part of valour.

That said, I'm acutely aware that none of my famous five is female, or of colour, or non-American, or hails from any other marginalized authorial constituency. I realize that there's a great white male element to *Writing Marketing*. I wish it were otherwise. Beth Hirschman was a very serious candidate at one stage, as was Barbara Stern. But I felt that Beth, albeit bedazzling on *Reading* and *Righting*, fell down slightly on the third key 'R' of *Rhythmatic*. It is no accident, I suspect, that her best-written papers were co-authored with Morris Holbrook and, now that the two have gone their separate scholarly ways, it's clear that Morris's style hasn't suffered as a consequence of the split. Barbara Stern, by contrast, is more of a critic than a creative. She writes very well (as do all our nearly-but-no-cigars) and she has done more than anyone to make the case for literary approaches to marketing research. However, I feel that her impact has been confined to a comparatively small corner of the field. For all her impressive academic achievements, Stern hasn't really made the marketing earth move, the way Levitt, Kotler, Hunt, Alderson and Holbrook have.

Despite the above, and notwithstanding the danger of coming across as a supercilious hypocrite, I firmly believe that the future of marketing writing is female. Naomi Klein is a harbinger in this regard. Some of the best of the younger generation of marketing writers are female (Pauline Maclaran, Hope Schau, Lorna Stevens spring to mind) and feminine writing styles are increasingly evident among the great white male contingent (Holbrook is the classic case in point, though Thompson, Sherry and Piercy qualify too). Granted, there is much debate about what exactly constitutes a feminine mode of writing – discursive as opposed to direct, corporeal rather than clinical, fantastic instead of factual – however Holbrook et al. are closer to the feminine end of the spectrum than most of the marketing mainstream.

* * *

Selecting the scholars was one thing, selecting the schools of thought was something else again. As with the potential analysands, the putative analyst is faced with a cornucopia of critical methods to choose from. The five schools actually employed in the present volume are just a tiny fraction of the lit-crit spectrum. Within each tradition, what is more, all sorts of theoretical options are available. Indeed, one of the most frustrating aspects of *Writing Marketing* was that innumerable alternative angles presented themselves to me while I was writing. Wouldn't a reader-response approach to Wroe Alderson be enlightening?[6] What about a Marxist take on Ted Levitt, especially the aestheticized neo-Marxist version developed by Walter Benjamin?[7] I wonder if a feminist interrogation of Shelby D. Hunt would be as fascinating as I suspect it might be?[8] Phil Kotler's corpus is just begging for a post colonial critique, isn't it?[9] And so the internal debate went on.

Sometimes, however, the first idea is the best one. Several years back, I wrote an article on Morris Holbrook and used Harold Bloom's anxiety thesis to try and make sense of his oeuvre. Accordingly, I intended to tackle Morris from a different angle in *Writing Marketing*. As an alternative psychoanalytical perspective (Jungian, say, or Lacanian) would have been too obvious, I thought about adopting a narratological approach. There's a strong storytelling component to Holbrook's writing – the quest motif appears again and again – so I reckoned a narratological stance might prove productive.

On rereading Morris's body of work, however, it became increasingly clear to me that Bloom's anxiety of influence is still the one. I'm more convinced than ever that it is applicable to our extraordinary ephebe and his peerless precursor (though the Proppian folk-tale schema or Greimas's semiotic square definitely had potential). More importantly, the anxiety model also fit neatly from a narrative perspective, my own narrative perspective, the narrative of *Writing Marketing*. Morris simultaneously transports us back to the first subject under study and points the way forward for marketing writing generally. Regardless of the insights that a narratological approach to TOPKAT would have generated, and still could since there is no limit to this kind of thing, the narrative of *Writing Marketing* had to take precedence, I'm afraid.

The irony, however, is that my intended narrative for the present volume changed significantly as the writing progressed. The original plan was to foreground the historical dimension. Northrop Frye's model of modes comprised the basic structure of the text and each individual chapter represented a decade in modern marketing's fifty-year history. Ted Levitt epitomized marketing in the 1960s, Phil Kotler the seventies and so on throughout the whole of the modern marketing era. So prominent was this historical approach that the original subtitle for the book was 'A Literary History'.

This approach, I should record, was defensible from a lit-crit perspective.

The idea that individual authors somehow capture the zeitgeist (or represent an epoch) is a standard, if controversial, assumption. Marketing historians, admittedly, dislike evolutionary models and 'impositional' prescriptions, popular though they are in our discipline (Product Life Cycle, Wheel of Retailing Theory). Nevertheless, the latter-day advent of postmodern history, which foregrounds narrative, and the rise of New Historicist schools of literary theory, ensured that any such critique could be covered.[10] Indeed, there's no doubt in my mind that Wroe Alderson was rediscovered in the 1990s. Shelby Hunt's general theory of competition – and the relationships and networks paradigm generally – owes an enormous amount to Alderson. Likewise, I'm convinced that Morris Holbrook is currently reinventing the academic marketing article for the twenty-first century. His so-called 'book reviews' are a form of commercial cultural criticism that take their cue from Western society's ironic, irreverent and increasingly visual ethos.

My original decadal structure, in sum, had narrative merit. As things progressed, however, I discovered that it was causing me problems. Not me personally, as an author, but me personally, as a presenter. When I 'test-marketed' my ideas in seminars and discussions, I found that although the feedback was quite positive overall, the decadal element met with considerable scholarly resistance. People could see the merit of a book about writing marketing, but why was the history necessary? How come Levitt represents the sixties, much less Alderson the nineties? Justifiable or not, the historical subplot made the book seem too busy, too cluttered, too much. It was inhibiting the suspension of disbelief and, in fact, leading to the suspension of the suspension of disbelief.

From my perspective, I must make clear, the Frye model was merely a framing device. It helped me tell the story. It provided a potentially disparate book with a degree of structural coherence. However, that is not how my likely readership saw it and, while I suppose I could have ignored the feedback, it was clear that the decadal element was distracting at best and detracting at worst. I found that most of the post-seminar/round-table discussion focused on what, to my mind, was a comparatively minor component of *Writing Marketing*. So I decided to save the Frye framework for the final chapter, where it is supposed to function as an Agatha Christie-style twist in the tale. Ah, you thought this book was about writing, and so it is, but it's also about the history of thought! Eat your heart out, Hercule!!

* * *

Above and beyond the basic structure of the book, I wrestled with three issues when writing *Writing Marketing*. The first of these is – brace yourselves – writing. Yes, writing. As you might expect, I was very conscious that writing a book about writing inevitably invites scrutiny of one's own writing. Can it possibly do justice to the greats under consideration? Who on earth am I to write about them? Will my penmanship measure up? The funny thing is that, on hearing about this project, several people suggested I include a chapter on myself. Real people, mind you, not just figments of my fevered imagination. Honest! Part of me, I must confess, was very tempted by this prospect. I mean, I have written reviews of my own books before (and given them negative notices, naturally). I could see how a chapter on myself might work from a how-not-to-do-it angle. I further reckoned that a bit of light relief might not go amiss, especially in a book unavoidably weighed down by the minutiae of close reading. What's more, I have a bunch of pseudonyms on retainer, which I could have employed – possibly in a hidden chapter, unlisted in the contents – rather than commit the monumentally egotistical act of including a chapter on Stephen Brown in a book by Stephen Brown.

A moment's reflection, however, disabused me of this lunatic fantasy. Even if written in a self-deprecating or pseudonymous manner, any such chapter would still come across as rampant egomania (as does mentioning the possibility in an appendix). This book is about *great* writers, people who have made a major impact on marketing. It has *excluded* titans like Russ Belk and Beth Hirschman. It most certainly has no room for the likes of me, not even as a joker in the pack. Actually, any such inclusion would also undermine one of my justifications for writing *Writing Marketing* in the first place – namely, that authors aren't the best judges of themselves. Worst of all, it would mean that I'd have to read everything I've written in order to write about myself. Truly, a fate worse than death.

So, I decided to write an appendix instead.

* * *

The second matter I've meditated on – well, OK, thought about a bit – is irreverence. I've been conscious of how readers might react to my occasionally irreverent remarks about the gurus under scrutiny. Striking the right balance between admiration and admonition isn't easy. Make no mistake, I greatly admire all of the scholars featured in the present volume. I wouldn't have spent so much time studying their writings if I didn't think they were worth studying. *Writing Marketing* is a work of literary appreciation and the wider meanings of 'appreciation' ought to be respected, after a fashion. However, I don't think hagiography or sycophancy or unctuousness is particularly helpful. It's not good for our field, which is beset by good-ole-boy bonhomie (what someone once described as 'you scratch my back catalogue, I'll scratch yours').[11] It's especially unhelpful in a book that uses the tools of literary criticism to identify writing dos and don'ts. Criticism is, after all, *critical* and critique is what this book's about.

Therefore, I have tried to pitch it somewhere between approbation and opprobrium. While I recognize that there may be too much of the latter for American taste – the US academy, in my experience, is obscenely obsequious towards its superstars – I can only say that the present version is a lot less irreverent than the first draft. In that version, each of our literary exemplars was christened with an impudent sobriquet, which was liberally scattered throughout the chapter concerned. Only TOPKAT made the cut and only because I know that Morris will appreciate the acronym.

Although I yield to no one in my admiration for Levitt, Kotler, Hunt, Alderson and Holbrook, my appreciation of them changed in the course of writing *Writing Marketing*. None went down in my estimation, though I now think of them differently. To my mind, Morris Holbrook is the best in our business and I'm not the only one who subscribes to this view. His was the name that always came up when I was market-testing my material. Everyone, it seems, considers him a great writer. What's more he keeps getting better and better. Because of his brilliance, however, slack editors let him get away with things that he shouldn't be allowed to get away with.[12] He's becoming his own worst enemy, unfortunately.

Ted Levitt is the master of the aphorism, the snappy sound bite, the breathtaking turn of phrase. Reading Ted is a blessed relief, especially after struggling with the typically turgid texts of common-or-garden marketing academics. He really is the proverbial breath of fresh air in what is a pretty mephitic marketing atmosphere. Nevertheless, the more you read of Ted, the more you realize that he relies on a limited repertoire of literary tricks. They are fantastic tricks, excellently executed, but as he himself puts it, 'Too much of a good thing can be a bad thing'. Even Ted Levitt.

My changing feelings towards Philip Kotler, however, surprised even me. Although I'd always admired his writing enormously, I was under the impression that he wrote very little of it himself. I'd always thought of Kotler as akin to a brand name, an elaborate publishing operation with teams of gifted ghost-writers who actually cranked out the stuff on demand. This is not so. He writes it himself. I know this because he attended a presentation I gave at Kellogg and later that same day – to my amazement – he emailed me a 200-word précis of my argument, with a view to including it in the latest edition of *Marketing Management*.[13] In the space of a couple of hours he had not only slotted my (admittedly modest) thoughts into the Kotlerite cosmology but he'd also explained them more clearly and far, far better than I ever could. The guy is prodigiously talented. He got to the top on merit. It's as simple as that.

Wroe Alderson is an interesting one. I first read his stuff many years ago, when I was working on the Wheel of Retailing theory. At that time,

I found his writings somewhat inaccessible, not to say utterly insufferable. I reckoned he was totally overrated, one of those thinkers that everybody cites but no one actually reads. To my mind, he was the marketing equivalent of Proust or Tolstoy, rather more written about than read, if you see what I mean. However, just as marketing rediscovered his ideas in the retrotastic 1990s, I too found myself going back to this fount of wisdom. As *Writing Marketing* started to cohere in my mind, he seemed like an interesting subject, if only because he is renowned for his 'difficulty'. Was he really as bad a writer as I remembered? The strange thing is that, having spent most of the early nineties wrestling with Derrida, Jameson, Lacan and others, reading Wroe was a breeze. Now, don't get me wrong, he is indeed difficult. But when you see how well he could write when he put his mind to it, the intriguing question is *why* he wrote in the way that he did? I suspect that the disciplinary context – the scholarly environment – had a lot to do with it.

Shelby D. Hunt surprised me most of all. He's one of those writers where there's a striking contrast between the real person and the textual persona. The real person, I'm reliably informed, is as kind and supportive a marketing scholar as one could hope to meet. However, his textual persona is, well, hard to warm to. He comes across as Professor Pedantic, the nitpicker's nitpicker, an indomitably dogmatic, I'm-right-you're-wrong kind of guy. But, and this is a big but, the more you read of SDH, the more you can't help admiring his eye for detail, his critical facility, his adroit construction of antagonist-defeating arguments and, not least, his downright industriousness, thoroughness, doggedness. While I disagree with much, practically all, of what Shelby says, I can see that he is a very gifted critic. He's a far better critic than he is a theorist. Rest assured, this is not an attempt to damn him with faint praise, because I believe that the critical function is vitally important, particularly in a bogus, back-slapping discipline like marketing. Perhaps the best way to put it, I guess, is that reading Hunt is a bit like reading micro-economics. I disagree with the basic premises and *homo economicus* assumptions, but the logic, precision and, yes, eloquence of the argument is outstanding in its own way.

I can't believe I just wrote that.

* * *

The final issue that exercised me in the writing of *Writing Marketing* is what can be called the bigger picture, the fact that marketing writing is not confined to academia. Granted, writing is of paramount importance to academics, careers depend on it, but writing is pretty important outside the cloistered greensward and sylvan groves of the ivied ivory tower. Marketing practice involves a lot of pen-pushing too. Whether it be lifestyle trend-spotters who invent neat names for the market segments they're studying (BoBos, Sad Bastards and so forth), whether it be management consultants who run short courses on, and write at length about, creative writing (John Simmons's *The Invisible Grail* is a good example of the genre), or whether it be the veritable swarm of buzzwords and Management Acronym Disorders that afflict our field, writing marketing is something that goes way, way beyond academia.[14] Jeez, I feel a sequel coming on. Time to call a halt, lie down in a darkened room and slip on the padded straightjacket. Again.

My telling tale is almost over. I'd like to thank all those who listened to my ramblings on *Writing Marketing* and gave me invaluable feedback, to say nothing of an occasional rap on the knuckles. I'm particularly grateful to Evan Alderson, George Fisk, Paul Green, Morris Holbrook, Philip Kotler, Stan Shapiro and Robert Tamilia. Many thanks also to SAGE, especially Delia Alphonso and Sharika Sharma. Above all, however, I'd like to thank my wife Linda and daughters, Madison, Holly and Sophie, for putting up with my tantrums. I call it the artistic temperament. They call it the bear with a sore head. The Brown bear with a very sore head. Grrrr.

The Endnotes of the Exercise

1   The ABCs of Writing Marketing

1 Fred Metcalf, 'Writing', in *The Penguin Dictionary of Humorous Quotations* (London: Penguin, 1986), p. 273.

2 Johny Johansson, *Global Marketing: Foreign Entry, Local Marketing and Global Management* (New York: McGraw-Hill, 1999); Stephen Brown, *Free Gift Inside* (Oxford: Capstone, 2003).

3 Adamantios Diamantopoulos and Judy A. Siguaw, *Introducing LISREL: A Guide for the Uninitiated* (London: Sage, 2000); Robert V. Kozinets, 'The Field Behind The Screen: Using Netnography For Marketing Research in Online Communities', *Journal of Marketing Research*, 39 (February), 2002, pp. 61–72.

4 Shelby D. Hunt, *Controversy In Marketing Theory: For Reason, Realism, Truth, and Objectivity* (Armonk, NY: M.E. Sharpe, 2003); Stephen Brown, *Postmodern Marketing* (London: Routledge, 1995).

5 Christopher Hackley, *Marketing and Social Construction: Exploring the Rhetorics of Managed Consumption* (London: Routledge, 2001).

6 My point here is that most, if not all, of these 'alternatives' ultimately rest on the written word. We write our lecture notes, presentation transcripts, literature reviews and what have you; our scatter graphs are based on questionnaires that involved written responses, ticking boxes and all the rest; our discussion groups are transcribed word-for-word and we analyse the written text with the aid of NUDIST, or whatever. You see what I'm getting at?

7 In light of the UK's Research Assessment Exercises, this citing/ranking carry-on has become something of a mini-industry. Fairly typical of the breed is: Geoff Easton and D.M. Easton, 'Marketing Journals and the Research Assessment Exercise', *Journal of Marketing Management*, 19 (1–2), 2003, pp. 5–24.

8 For example, Chris Hart, *Doing a Literature Review: Releasing the Social Science Research Imagination* (London: Sage, 2002); Rowena Murray, *How to Write a Thesis* (Buckingham: Open University Press, 2002); Zina O'Leary, *The Essential Guide to Doing Research* (London: Sage, 2004); Skillpath, *Business Writing and Grammar Skills Made Easy and Fun!* (Oxted: Skillpath Seminars promotional flyer, 2004).

9 Again typical examples are: HBSP, *Harvard Business Review on Marketing* (Cambridge, MA: Harvard Business School Press, 2002); Russell W. Belk, 'ACR Fellows' Bookshelf', *ACR News* (Spring) 2003, pp. 10–13; Bodo B. Schlegelmilch, 'Special Symposium on Shelby D. Hunt's "A General Theory of Competition: Resources, Competencies, Productivity, Economic Growth" Part 1. Comments', *Journal of Marketing Management*, 18 (1–2), 2002, pp. 221–7; Robin Wensley, 'Special Symposium on Shelby D. Hunt's 'A General Theory of Competition: Resources, Competencies, Productivity, Economic Growth' Part 2. Marketing for a New Century', *Journal of Marketing Management*, 18 (1–2), 2002, pp. 229–37.

10 There's a huge literature on the peer review process. I review some of it in 'The Eunuch's Tale: Reviewing Reviewed', *Journal of Marketing Management*, 11 (7), 1995, pp. 681–706.

11 Stephen Brown, 'Art or Science? Fifty Years of Marketing Debate', *Journal of Marketing Management*, 12 (4), 1996, pp. 243–67.

12 Ibid.

13 This by-line has been in use for a very long time. See Roger A. Kerin, 'In Pursuit of an Ideal: The Editorial and Literary History of the *Journal of Marketing*', *Journal of Marketing*, 60 (January), 1996, pp. 1–13.

14 Douglas Brownlie and Mike Saren, 'Beyond the One-Dimensional Marketing Manager: The Discourse of Theory, Practice and Relevance', *International Journal of Research in Marketing*, 14 (2), 1997, pp. 147–62.

15 Ah, yet another happy hunting ground for twenty-first century management researchers. These days, it's not so much a case of 'go west young man' as 'go CSR young fellow'. A good example of the genre is Malcolm McIntosh, *Raising a Ladder to the Moon: The Complexities of Corporate Social Responsibility* (Basingstoke: Palgrave, 2003). Enjoy.

16 Peter Doyle, *Value-based Marketing: Marketing Strategies for Corporate Growth and Shareholder Value* (Chichester: Wiley, 2000).

17 Take your pick: Naomi Klein, *No Logo: Taking Aim at the Brand Bullies* (London: HarperCollins, 2000); Noreena Hertz, *The Silent Takeover: Global Capitalism and the Death of Democracy* (London: Heinemann, 2001); Alex Callinicos, *An Anti-capitalist Manifesto* (Cambridge: Polity, 2003); Paul Kingsworth, *One No, Many Yesses: A Journey to the Heart of the Global Resistance Movement* (London: Free Press, 2003); Thomas Frank, *One Market Under God: Extreme Capitalism, Market Populism and the End of Economic Democracy* (London: Secker & Warburg, 2001); Kalle Lasn, *Culture Jam: How to Reverse America's Suicidal Consumer Binge – And Why We Must* (New York: Quill, 1999).

18 Clifford Geertz, *Works and Lives: The Anthropologist as Author* (Stanford, CA: Stanford University Press, 1988).

19 Deirdre McCloskey, *The Rhetoric of Economics* (Madison, WI: University of Wisconsin Press, 1998).

20 A.J. Soyland, *Psychology as Metaphor* (London: Sage, 1994).

21 Barbara Czarniawska, *Narrating the Organization: Dramas of Institutional Identity* (Chicago: University of Chicago Press, 1997); David Grant and Cliff Oswick, *Metaphor and Organizations* (London: Sage, 1996); David M. Boje, Robert P. Gephart, Jr., and Tojo Joseph Thatchenkery, *Postmodern Management and Organization Theory* (Thousand Oaks, CA: Sage, 1996); John Hassard and Martin Parker, *Postmodernism and Organizations* (London: Sage, 1993); David

M. Boje, *Narrative Methods for Organizational and Communication Research* (Thousand Oaks, CA: Sage, 2001).

22 For example, Stephen W. Hawking, *The Universe in a Nutshell* (London: Bantam, 2001); Stephen Jay Gould, *The Hedgehog, the Fox, and the Magister's Pox: Mending the Gap Between Science and the Humanities* (London: Jonathan Cape, 2003); Stephen Pinker, *The Blank Slate* (London, Penguin, 2003). On the writing of science generally, see David Locke, *Science as Writing* (New Haven: Yale University Press, 1992); Alan G. Gross, *The Rhetoric of Science* (Cambridge, MA: Harvard University Press, 1990).

23 C.J. McKenzie, S. Wright, F.D. Ball and P.J. Baron, 'The Publications of Marketing Faculty – Who Are We Really Talking To?', *European Journal of Marketing*, 36 (11/12), 2002, pp. 1196–1208.

24 Ibid.

25 This principle even applies to things such as our methodologies. After all, no one actually comes round and checks the coding of our questionnaires, or our focus group transcripts, or our reams and reams of SPSS output. The work is taken on trust, by and large, and that 'trust' is conveyed, indeed *earned*, by means of the written word. It's not unusual for journal reviewers to point out that, say, the methodology section of a manuscript needs to be fuller, or clearer, or more detailed. This can only be achieved through writing, by better explanations of what we did during our data-gathering phase. In short it's a rhetorical issue not a methodological issue. It all boils down to text. Note also, this is not just a marketing/social science matter. It's true of all research, even that undertaken in the 'hard sciences'. As the recent controversy over the publication of false findings in *Nature* amply demonstrates, experimental results are usually taken on trust by the premier scientific journals. No one recalculates the stats, for example since doing so would cause inordinate delays and clog up the entire system. It's less about the execution of research than the representation of research in other words. See 'Sloppy Stats Shame Science', *The Economist*, 5 June, 2004, pp. 78–9.

26 The number of introductions to literary theory is almost beyond measure. Examples include, Stephen Bonnycastle, *In Search of Authority: An Introductory Guide to Literary Theory* (Orchard Park, NY: Broadview Press, 1996); Jonathan Culler, *Literary Theory: A Very Short Introduction* (Oxford: Oxford University Press, 1997); Valentine Cunningham, *Reading After Theory* (Oxford: Blackwell, 2002). Still the best, however, is Terry Eagleton, *Literary Theory: An Introduction* (Oxford: Blackwell, 1983).

27 Terry Eagleton, *Literary Theory: An Introduction* (Oxford: Blackwell, 1983).

28 Imre Lakatos, 'Falsification and the Methodology of Scientific Research Programmes', in I. Lakatos and A. Musgrave (eds), *Criticism and the Growth of Knowledge* (Cambridge: Cambridge University Press, 1970), pp. 91–196.

29 Matthew Arnold, *Culture and Anarchy and Other Writings* (Cambridge: Cambridge University Press, 1993 [1869]).

30 Patrick Murray (ed.), *Reflections on Commercial Life: An Anthology of Classic Texts From Plato to the Present* (New York: Routledge, 1997).

31 John Blundell, 'Introduction', in A. Pollard (ed.), *The Representation of Business in English Literature* (London: Institute of Economic Affairs, 2000), p. viii.

32 Graham Thompson, *The Business of America: The Cultural Production of a Post-War Nation* (London: Pluto, 2004, pp. 4–5).

33 John Blundell, 'Introduction', op. cit., p. viii.

34 Jonathan Franzen, 'Why Bother?', in *How To Be Alone: Essays* (London: Fourth Estate, 2002), pp. 63–4.

35 Hardy Green, 'Selling Books Like Bacon', *Business Week*, 16 June 2003, pp. 60–1; Sonoo Singh, 'Searching For Text Appeal', *Marketing Week*, 13 May, 2004, pp. 24–7.

36 See note 17 above.

37 John Seabrook, *Nobrow: The Culture of Marketing – The Marketing of Culture* (New York: Knopf, 2000).

38 David Brooks, *BoBos in Paradise: The New Upper Class and How They Got There* (New York: Simon & Schuster, 2000).

39 Jim Collins (ed.), *High Pop: Making Culture into Popular Entertainment* (Malden, MA: Blackwell, 2002).

40 Curtis White, *The Middle Mind: Why Americans Don't Think for Themselves* (London: Allen Lane, 2003).

41 Ibid., p. 200.

42 Tom Wolfe, 'Hooking Up: What Life Was Like at the Turn of the Second Millennium: An American's World', in *Hooking Up: Essays and Fiction* (London: Jonathan Cape, 2000), p. 3.

43 Paul Delany, *Literature, Money and the Market: From Trollope to Amis* (New York: Palgrave, 2002).

44 Catherine Gallagher and Stephen Greenblatt, *Practicing New Historicism* (Chicago: University of Chicago Press, 2000); John Brannigan, *New Historicism and Cultural Materialism* (Basingstoke: Macmillan, 1998); Kiernan Ryan, *New Historicism and Cultural Materialism: A Reader* (London: Arnold, 1996).

45 Walter Benn Michaels, *The Gold Standard and the Logic of Naturalism: American Literature at the Turn of the Century* (Los Angeles: University of California Press, 1987), which deals with literary representations of consumerism during the Gilded Age, is an archetypal New Historicist exercise.

46 Catherine Gallagher and Stephen Greenblatt, *Practicing New Historicism* (Chicago: University of Chicago Press, 2000), pp. 1–19.

47 Richard Florida, *The Rise of the Creative Class: And How It's Transforming Work, Leisure, Community and Everyday Life* (New York: Basic Books, 2002).

48 Michael J. Wolf, *The Entertainment Economy: How Mega-media Forces are Transforming Our Lives* (London: Penguin, 1999).

49 David James, 'We Must Learn From the Music Industry', *The Business*, 30 May, 2004, p. 11; Stephen Brown, *Free Gift Inside* (Oxford: Capstone, 2003).

50 Stephen Brown, 'On Madonna's Brand Ambition: Presentation Transcript', in D. Turley and S. Brown (eds), *All Changed – Changed Utterly?* (Provo, UT: Association for Consumer Research, 2004).

51 So popular has literature become among practising marketing types, according to Collins (note 39) that an 'Ernest Hemingway Collection' is now available from friendly neighbourhood furniture stores. No doubt the Tom Sawyer paint range, George Orwell rat-trap and William Burroughs brand pharmaceuticals are on their way. The less said about the Hunter S. Thompson package tour of Las Vegas, the better!

52 Robert A. Brawer, *Fictions of Business: Insights on Management From Great Literature* (New York: John Wiley, 1998).

53 Stephen Brown, 'I Can Read You Like A Book! Novel Thoughts on Consumer Behaviour', *Qualitative Marketing Research: An International Journal*, in press.

54 Quoted in Colin Roberts, 'On the Other Hand There's a Fist,' *Uncut*, 53 (October), 2001, pp. 88–90.

55 Elizabeth Young and Graham Caveney (eds), *Shopping in Space: Essays on American 'Blank Generation' Fiction* (London: Serpent's Tail, 1992), p. viii.

56 Jen Webb, Tony Schirato and Geoff Danaher, *Understanding Bourdieu* (London: Sage, 2002), p. 151.

57 Barbara B. Stern, 'Literary Criticism and Consumer Research: Overview and Illustrative Analysis', *Journal of Consumer Research*, 16 (December), 1989, pp. 322–34; Barbara B. Stern, 'Other-speak: Classical Allegory and Contemporary Advertising', *Journal of Advertising*, 19 (3), 1990, pp. 14–26; Barbara B. Stern, 'Deconstructive Strategy and Consumer Research: Concepts and Illustrative Exemplar', *Journal of Consumer Research*, 23 (September), 1995, pp. 136–47; Barbara B. Stern, 'Consumer Myths: Frye's Taxonomy and the Structural Analysis of Consumption Text', *Journal of Consumer Research*, 22 (September), 1995, pp 165–85.

58 Linda M. Scott, 'The Bridge From Text to Mind: Adapting Reader-Response Theory to Consumer Research', *Journal of Consumer Research*, 21 (December), 1994, pp. 461–80; Lorna Stevens, *The Joy of Text* (University of Ulster: unpublished PhD dissertation, 2003).

59 Edward F. McQuarrie and David Glen Mick, 'Figures of Advertising Rhetoric', *Journal of Consumer Research*, 22 (March), 1996, pp. 424–38.

60 Benôit Heilbrunn, 'In Search of the Hidden Go(o)d: A Philosophical Deconstruction and Narratological Revisitation of the Eschatological Metaphor in Marketing', in S. Brown, J. Bell and D. Carson (eds), *Marketing Apocalypse: Eschatology, Escapology and the Illusion of the End* (London: Routledge, 1996), pp. 112–32.

61 Jean-Marie Floch, 'The Contribution of Structural Semiotics to the Design of a Hypermarket', *International Journal of Research in Marketing*, 4 (2), 1988, pp. 233–52; Jean-Marie Floch, *Semiotics, Marketing and Communication: Beneath the Signs, the Strategies* (Basingstoke: Palgrave, 2001).

62 Stephanie O'Donohoe, 'Leaky Boundaries: Intertextuality and Young Adult Experiences of Advertising', in M. Nava, A. Blake, I. MacRury and B. Richards, *Buy This Book: Studies in Advertising and Consumption* (London: Routledge, 1997), pp. 257–75.

63 Stephen Brown, Lorna Stevens and Pauline Maclaran, 'I Can't Believe It's Not Bakhtin: Literary Theory, Postmodern Advertising and the Gender Agenda', *Journal of Advertising*, 28 (1), 1999, pp. 11–24; Stephen Brown, Elizabeth C. Hirschman and Pauline Maclaran, 'Always Historicize! Researching Marketing History in a Post-historical Epoch', *Marketing Theory*, 1 (1), 2001, pp. 49–89; Stephen Brown, Robert V. Kozinets and John F. Sherry, Jr, 'Teaching Old Brands New Tricks: Retro Brands and the Revival of Brand Meaning', *Journal of Marketing*, 67 (July), 2003, pp. 15–30.

64 I discuss some of this in Stephen Brown, *Postmodern Marketing Two: Telling Tales* (London: ITBP, 1998). The literature has burgeoned considerably since 1998, mind you.

65 The ZMET research program – no, I didn't say 'rip-off program', you must have misheard me – is ably summarized in Gerald Zaltman, *How Customers*

Think: Essential Insights into the Mind of the Market (Cambridge, MA: Harvard Business School Press, 2003). You may be wondering who described it as, ahem, the 'mutant methodological love-child of Ernest Dichter and Walt Disney'. My lips are sealed.

66 Barbara B. Stern, 'Literary Criticism and the History of Marketing Thought: A New Perspective on "Reading" Marketing Theory', *Journal of the Academy of Marketing Science*, 18 (4), 1990, pp. 329–36; Jeffrey F. Durgee, 'Interpreting Dichter's Interpretations: An Analysis of Consumption Symbolism' in *The Handbook of Consumer Motivations* ', in H.H. Larsen, D.G. Mick and G. Alsted (eds), *Marketing and Semiotics: Selected Papers From the Copenhagen Symposium* (Copenhagen: Nyt Nordisk Forlag Arnold Busck, 1991), pp. 52–74.

67 Craig J. Thompson, 'Modern Truth and Postmodern Incredulity: A Hermeneutic Deconstruction of the Metanarrative of "Scientific Truth" in Marketing Research', *International Journal of Research in Marketing*, 10 (3), 1993, pp. 325–38.

68 Daragh O'Reilly, 'On the Precipice of a Revolution with Hamel and Prahalad', *Journal of Marketing Management*, 16 (1–3), 2000, pp. 99–109.

69 Avi Shankar and Maurice Patterson, 'Interpreting the Past: Writing the Future', *Journal of Marketing Management*, 17 (5–6), 2001, pp. 481–501.

70 Chris Hackley, '"We Are All Customers Now . . ." Rhetorical Strategy and Ideological Control in Marketing Management Texts', *Journal of Management Studies*, 40 (4), 2003, pp. 1325–52.

71 Ryan Mathews and Watts Wacker, *The Deviant's Advantage: How Fringe Ideas Create Mass Markets* (New York: Crown, 2002).

72 John F. Sherry, Jr, 'The Soul of the Company Store: Nike Town Chicago and the Emplaced Brandscape,' in J.F. Sherry, Jr.. (ed.), *Servicescapes: The Concept of Place in Contemporary Markets* (Lincolnwood, IL: NTC Books, 1998), pp. 109–50.

73 Russell W. Belk, 'A Cultural Biography of My Groucho Glasses', in Stephen Brown and Anthony Patterson (eds), *Imagining Marketing: Art, Aesthetics and the Avant-garde* (London: Routledge, 2000), pp. 249–59.

74 Elizabeth C. Hirschman, 'The Consciousness of Addiction: Toward a General Theory of Consumption', *Journal of Consumer Research*, 19 (September), 1992, pp. 155–79.

75 Craig J. Thompson, 'Going Out in a Blaze of Glory: Southern White Trash Retrospections on my Personal Relationship with Jesus, Hank Williams, Elvis Presley and a Pentecostal-Elvis-Impersonating-Professional-Wrestling-Snake-Handling-Minister-who-Sang-Hank-Williams'-Songs' in S. Brown and A. Patterson (eds), *Imagining Marketing: Art, Aesthetics and the Avant-garde* (London: Routledge, 2000), pp. 214–31.

76 Hope Jensen Schau, 'Suburban Soundtracks', in S. Brown and A. Patterson (eds), *Imagining Marketing: Art, Aesthetics and the Avant-garde* (London: Routledge, 2000), pp. 232–9; A. Patterson and S. Brown, 'Marketers Wake! A Portrait of the Artist as a Marketing Man', in S. Brown and A. Patterson (eds), *Imagining Marketing: Art, Aesthetics and the Avant-garde* (London: Routledge, 2000), pp. 73–85; Robert Grafton Small, 'Beyond the Pleasure Principle: The Death Instinct of Pioneer Studies in Marketing', in S. Brown and A. Patterson (eds), *Imagining Marketing: Art, Aesthetics and the Avant-garde* (London: Routledge, 2000), pp. 281–90.

77 Valentine Cunningham, *Reading After Theory* (Oxford: Blackwell, 1983).

78 See Fredric Jameson, *Postmodernism: Or, the Cultural Logic of Late Capitalism* (London: Verso, 1991).

79 Michel Foucault, 'What is an Author?', in D.F. Bouchard (ed.), *Language, Counter-Memory, Practice: Selected Essays and Interviews* (Ithaca: Cornell University Press, 1977), pp. 113–38.

80 Roland Barthes, 'Écrivains et écrivants', in S. Sontag (ed.), *Selected Writings* (London: Fontana, 1983).

81 Harold Bloom, *The Anxiety of Influence: A Theory of Poetry* (New York: Oxford University Press, 1973).

82 Terry Eagleton, *Literary Theory: An Introduction* (Oxford: Blackwell, 1983).

83 Christopher Norris, *Deconstruction* (London: Routledge, 2002), p. xii.

84 Harold Bloom, *The Western Canon: The Books and School of the Ages* (Basingstoke: Papermac, 1994), p. 3.

85 Ibid.

86 See Philip Rice and Patricia Waugh (eds), *Modern Literary Theory: A Reader* (London: Arnold, 1992), pp. 17–24.

87 Curtis White, *The Middle Mind: Why Americans Don't Think for Themselves* (London: Allen Lane, 2003), p. 85. Although this is a musical example, White makes exactly the same case about literature. Artistic innovation of any kind, he argues, involves attempts to abandon, complicate or subvert conventional formal expectations.

88 John Guillory, *Cultural Capital: The Problem of Canon Foundation* (Chicago: Chicago University Press, 1994).

89 Erich Auerbach, *Mimesis: The Representation of Reality in Western Literature* (Princeton, NJ: Princeton University Press, 1953).

90 A good discussion of Benjamin's micrological method can be found in John McCole, *Walter Benjamin and the Antimonies of Tradition* (Ithaca: Cornell University Press, 1993).

91 Roland Barthes 'Studium and Punctum', in *Camera Lucida* (London: Vintage, 1993), pp. 25–7.

92 Bloom, mind you, was a marketer and you know what they say about marketers, especially Irish marketers . . .

93 Anthony C. Grayling, *The Mystery of Things* (London: Weidenfeld & Nicolson, 2004), pp. 56–7.

94 Northrop Frye, *Anatomy of Criticism: Four Essays* (Princeton, NJ: Princeton University Press, 1957).

95 Ibid., pp. 117–18.

96 Sven Birkets, the literary critic, has a nice term for this. In *My Sky Blue Trades* (New York: Penguin, 2002), he calls it 'the jinxing power of hubris'.

97 Tobias Wolff, *Old School* (London: Bloomsbury, 2004), p. 136. Note, although *Old School* is a work of fiction, Wolff's novel is deeply autobiographical, as are all his writings. Irrespective of whether Hemingway's 'advice' is invented, it certainly has the ring of truth. On the inability of authors to critique their own works, see the first chapter of Northrop Frye's *Anatomy of Criticism*, op. cit.

98 Terry Eagleton, *Literary Theory*, op. cit.

99 Northrop Frye, *Anatomy of Criticism*, op. cit., pp. 17–18. Note Frye's use of a scientific metaphor to describe literary criticism ('the absurd quantum formula of criticism'). Others who argue along the same line include Rene Wellek

and Austin Warren, *Theory of Literature* (San Diego: Harcourt Brace, 1956), p. 42; David Lodge, *Consciousness and the Novel* (London: Secker & Warburg, 2002), especially Chapter 2.

100 Roland Barthes, 'The Death of the Author', in *Image Music Text* (New York: Hill and Wang, 1977), pp. 142–8. On the 'death of the author' debate, see H.L. Hix, *Morte d'Author: An Autopsy* (Philadelphia, PA: Temple University Press, 1990).

101 Roland Barthes, 'The Death of the Author', ibid, p. 146.

102 To pluck a tiny but typical example from my own experience, I once wrote a paper on Michael Jackson, whom I described as a 'mulatto moonwalker'. I quite liked this construction, which captured the singer's steady evolution from ebony to ivory, or so I thought. The copy editor wouldn't have it, however, insisting that the word mulatto refers to someone of mixed black and white parentage, which Jackson most definitely wasn't. It was also a tad un-PC, though not officially proscribed. I countered with the suggestion that Michael is a sort of postmodern mulatto, but she again demurred and replaced the locution with 'musical moonwalker'. Naturally, I wasn't very happy with that, so I suggested 'metamorphic moonwalker' as a possible compromise, which she finally accepted. Regardless of the outcome of this admittedly trivial example, it is clear that the content of 'my' article was negotiated. Did I write it? Did the copy editor write it? Just who is the author here?

2   The Antinomies of Theodore Levitt

1 Okay, okay, it's not an *HBR* haiku. It's an S.B. haiku – are there no limits to my talentlessness?

2 Theodore Levitt, 'The Globalization of Markets', in *The Marketing Imagination: New Expanded Edition* (Free Press: New York, 1986), pp. 20–49.

3 Richard Tomkins, 'Happy Birthday Globalization', *Financial Times*, 6 May, 2003, p. 14.

4 Alan Mitchell, 'Why Ted Levitt Wasn't Wrong About Globalization', *Marketing Week*, 26 June, 2003, pp. 26–7.

5 John Quelch, 'The Return of the Global Brand', *Harvard Business Review*, 81 (8), 2003, pp. 22–3.

6 Alan Mitchell, op. cit., p. 27.

7 John Quelch, op. cit., p. 22.

8 Richard Tomkins, op. cit., p. 14.

9 Robert Bartels, 'Theodore Levitt', in *The History of Marketing Thought*, 3rd edn (Columbus, OH: Publishing Horizons, 1988), p. 268.

10 See for example: Theodore Levitt, 'Retrospective Commentary', in B.M. Enis and K.K. Cox (eds), *Marketing Classics: A Selection of Influential Articles* (Boston: Allyn and Bacon, 1975), pp. 17–20; Theodore Levitt, 'Preface to the New Expanded edition', in *The Marketing Imagination*, op. cit., pp. xi–xix. Also Robert Bartels, 'Theodore Levitt', ibid.; David Clutterbuck and Stuart Crainer, 'Theodore Levitt', in *Makers of Management* (London: Macmillan, 1990), pp. 158–63.

11 Theodore Levitt, 'Retrospective Commentary', ibid., p. 19.

12 Theodore Levitt, 'Communications Bottlenecks', in *Innovation in Márketing* (New York: McGraw-Hill, 1962), p. 213.

13 Theodore Levitt, 'Retrospective Commentary', op. cit., p. 19.

14 Martin Gray, 'Antinomy', in *A Dictionary of Literary Terms* (Harlow: Longman, 1992), pp. 26–7.

15 John McCole, *Walter Benjamin and the Antinomies of Tradition* (Ithaca: Cornell University Press, 1993).

16 Walter Benjamin, *The Arcades Project*, trans. H. Eiland and K. McLaughlin (Cambridge, MA: Belknap, 1999).

17 Alex Shakar, *The Savage Girl* (London: Schribner, 2001).

18 Ibid., pp. 69–84.

19 Although all of Ted's writings reflect this propensity, a particularly fine selection is found in Theodore Levitt, *Thinking About Management* (New York: Free Press, 1991).

20 Robert Bartels, 'Theodore Levitt', op. cit.; David Clutterbuck and Stuart Crainer, 'Theodore Levitt', op. cit.

21 Theodore Levitt, *The Marketing Imagination*, op. cit.; *Thinking About Management*, op. cit.; *Innovation in Marketing* (New York: McGraw-Hill, 1963); *The Marketing Mode: Pathways to Corporate Growth* (New York: McGraw-Hill, 1969); *The Third Sector: New Tactics for a Responsive Society* (New York: Amacom, 1973); *Marketing for Business Growth* (New York: McGraw-Hill, 1974); *Levitt on Marketing: A Harvard Business Review Paperback* (Boston: Harvard Business School Press, 1992).

22 Carol Kennedy, *Guide to the Management Gurus* (London: Business Books, 1991).

23 Theodore Levitt, 'Thinking Ahead', in *The Marketing Mode: Pathways to Corporate Growth* (New York: McGraw-Hill, 1969), p. 316.

24 Theodore Levitt, 'Communications Bottlenecks', in *Innovation in Marketing*, op. cit., p. 224.

25 For example, when a second edition of *The Marketing Mode* was published in 1974, under the more executive-friendly title of *Marketing for Business Growth*, the preface freely acknowledged that the first edition lacked the sharpness, structure, snap and salience that its managerial audience demanded (or, to be more precise, that Ted presumed it demanded). Happily, he reverted to type in his next best-seller, *The Marketing Imagination*, a unstructured assemblage of old and new, that was translated into 11 languages and reprinted in a new and expanded edition three years later. Second editions and reprints, I should perhaps also add, are themselves sifted, shifted and shuffled. Slice and dice, in short, is the marketing magus's modus operandi or as he memorably puts it 'never leave well enough alone'.

26 Tom Wolfe, *The New Journalism* (London: Picador, 1975).

27 Theodore Levitt, 'The Marketing Chief and the Chief Executive', in *The Marketing Mode*, op. cit., p. 255.

28 Theodore Levitt, 'The Globalization of Markets', in *The Marketing Imagination*, op. cit., p. 23.

29 Theodore Levitt, 'Futurism and Management', in *Thinking About Management* (New York: Free Press, 1991), p. 93.

30 Theodore Levitt, 'The Globalization of Markets', in *The Marketing Imagination*, op. cit., p. 21.

31 Theodore Levitt, 'Think Small', in *The Marketing Mode: Pathways to Corporate Growth* (New York: McGraw-Hill, 1969), p. 102.

32 Theodore Levitt, 'The Marketing Imagination', in *The Marketing Imagination*, op. cit., p. 129.

33 Theodore Levitt, 'Futurism and Management', in *Thinking About Management*, op. cit., p. 91.

34 Ibid, p. 95.

35 Theodore Levitt, 'The Limits of the Marketing Concept', in *The Marketing Mode: Pathways to Corporate Growth* (New York: McGraw-Hill, 1969), p. 242.

36 Theodore Levitt, 'Thinking Ahead', in *The Marketing Mode*, op. cit., p. 286.

37 Terry Eagleton, *Literary Theory: An Introduction* (Oxford: Blackwell, 1983).

38 According to Eagleton in *Literary Theory*, the history of Western literary criticism can be divided into three broad phases, each focused on a different constituent of what may be termed the literary triumvirate. The first, dating from the Romantic Movement of the early nineteenth century, concentrated on the *author*. The second, comprising the New Critics of the mid-twentieth century, attended primarily to the *text*. The third, which emerged in the late-1960s and still holds sway, is preoccupied with the *reader*.

39 For a fine overview of reader-response criticism, see Todd F. Davis and Kenneth Womack, *Formalist Criticism and Reader-Response Theory* (Basingstoke: Palgrave, 2003). Also useful, if a bit dated, is Jane P. Tompkins, *Reader-Response Criticism: From Formalism to Poststructuralism* (Baltimore: Johns Hopkins University Press, 1980).

40 Norman N. Holland, *The Dynamics of Literary Response* (New York: Norton, 1968).

41 David Bleich, *Subjective Criticism* (Baltimore: Johns Hopkins University Press, 1978).

42 Stanley Fish, *Is There a Text in This Class? The Authority of Interpretive Communities* (Cambridge: Harvard University Press, 1980).

43 Roland Barthes, *S/Z*, trans. R. Miller (Oxford: Blackwell, 1990).

44 Umberto Eco, *The Role of the Reader: Explorations in the Semiotics of Texts* (London: Hutchinson, 1981).

45 Wolfgang Iser, *The Implied Reader* (Baltimore: Johns Hopkins University Press, 1974).

46 Ibid.

47 Harold Bloom, *Shakespeare: The Invention of the Human* (New York: Scribner, 2000).

48 Hans R. Jauss, *Aesthetic Experience and Literary Hermeneutics* (Minneapolis: University of Minnesota Press, 1982).

49 The issue of introspection has been much debated in marketing. I summarize the main strands in (much as the title mortifies me) Stephen Brown 'The Wind in the Wallows: Literary Theory, Autobiographical Criticism and Subjective Personal Introspection', in J.W. Alba and J.W. Hutchinson (eds), *Advances in Consumer Research*, Vol. 25 (Provo, UT: Association for Consumer Research, 1998), pp. 25–30. See also Stephen Brown and Rhona Reid, 'Shoppers on the Verge of a Nervous Breakdown', in S. Brown and D. Turley (eds), *Consumer Research: Postcards From the Edge* (London: Routledge, 1997), pp. 79–149.

50 Elizabeth A. Flynn, 'Gender and Reading', in E.A. Flynn and P.P. Schweickart (eds), *Gender and Reading: Essays on Readers, Texts, and Contexts* (Baltimore: Johns Hopkins University Press, 1986), pp. 267–88.

51 Caroline, female, 20s.

52 Sinead Q., female, 20s.
53 Nicola K., female, 20s.
54 Catherine, female, 30s.
55 Adele, female, 40s.
56 Emma-Jane, female, 20s.
57 Theodore Levitt, 'Retrospective Commentary', in B.M. Enis and K.K. Cox
    (eds), *Marketing Classics: A Selection of Influential Articles* (Boston: Allyn and
    Bacon, 1975), pp. 17–20.
58 Deborah, female, 40s.
59 Lisa, female, 30s.
60 Andrew, male, 40s.
61 Caroline, female, 20s, op. cit.
62 William, male, 30s.
63 Leanne, female, 20s.
64 Stephen, male, 30s.
65 Jonathan, male, 30s.
66 Denise, female, 30s.
67 Nicola K., female, 20s, op. cit.
68 Jennifer, female, 20s.
69 Shauna, female, 20s.
70 Paul C., male, 20s.
71 Nicola D., female, 20s.
72 Sinead C., female, 20s.
73 Stephen, male, 20s.
74 Paul C., male, 20s, op. cit.
75 Paul G., male, 20s.
76 Ian, male, 40s.
77 Jacqueline, female, 30s.
78 Sinead Q., female, 20s, op. cit.
79 Julie, female, 40s.
80 Julie, ibid.
81 Sabrina A., female, 20s, op. cit.
82 Catherine, female, 30s, op. cit.
83 I consider these issues further in Stephen Brown 'Reading Ted Levitt: Myopia
    Or Misogyny?', in C. Thompson and L. Scott (eds), *Proceedings of the Gender
    and Marketing Conference* (Madison, WI: University of Wisconsin, 2004).
84 That said, there are national, cultural and ethnic differences as well. My
    American readers found Professor Levitt's bombast much more to their taste.
    Of the four US essayists, not one had anything critical to say about 'Marketing
    Myopia'. The honeyed words of Harvard's finest were accepted without
    demur. Clearly, we are dealing with a very tiny proportion of the 208 con-
    tributors (who said small sample? – how dare you!). Therefore, care must be
    taken when drawing inferences. Nevertheless, their uncritical reaction does
    indicate that readers' nationality may be a factor here. At a time of widespread
    anti-Americanism – the essays were written in the months immediately prior
    to the second Gulf War – US nationals are perhaps less critical of a fellow
    American than they otherwise might be. Further research, as they say, is
    clearly necessary.
85 Mark, male, 20s.

86 Margaret, female, 30s.

87 Sabrina F., female, 20s.

88 Hans R. Jauss, *Aesthetic Experience and Literary Hermeneutics* (Minneapolis: University of Minnesota Press, 1982).

89 Emma-Jane, female, 20s, op. cit.

90 William, male, 30s, op. cit.

91 Sinead C., female, 20s, op. cit.

92 William, male, 30s, op. cit.

93 Catherine, female, 30s, op. cit.

94 Andrew, male, 40s, op. cit.

95 Tim, male, 50s.

96 Lyndsey, female, 40s.

97 Caroline, female, 20s, op. cit.

98 Curtis White, *The Middle Mind: Why Americans Don't Think for Themselves* (London: Allen Lane, 2003).

99 Declan, male, 50s, op. cit.

100 Mark, male, 20s.

101 Quoted in H.L. Hix, *Morte d'Author: An Autopsy* (Philadelphia, PA: Temple University Press, 1990), p. 175.

102 Ibid, p. 175.

3 The Spectres of Philip Kotler

1 Alan Smithee, *Postmodern Marketing Two: Telling Tales* (London: International Thomson, 1998).

2 Philip Kotler, *Marketing Management: Analysis, Planning and Control*, 4th edn (Englewood Cliffs, NJ: Prentice Hall, 1980); Philip Kotler, Liam Fahey and Somkid Jatusripitak, *The New Competition* (Englewood Cliffs: Prentice Hall, 1985); Irving Rein, Philip Kotler and Martin Stoller, *High Visibility* (New York: Dodd, Mead and Co., 1987); Philip Kotler, Dipak C. Jain and Suvit Maesincee, *Marketing Moves: A New Approach to Profits, Growth, and Renewal* (Cambridge, MA: Harvard Business School Press, 2002); Philip Kotler, *Marketing Insights From A to Z: 80 Concepts Every Manager Needs to Know* (New York: Wiley, 2003); Philip Kotler, *Ten Deadly Marketing Sins: Signs and Solutions* (New York: Wiley, 2004).

3 Michael Chung, 'Philip Kotler Ranked Among World's Most Influential Gurus,' *Kellogg World*, Spring, 2001, p. 11; Stuart Crainer, 'Philip Kotler,' in *The Ultimate Book of Business Gurus: 110 Thinkers Who Really Made a Difference* (New York: American Management Association, 1998), pp. 115–20.

4 Carol Kennedy, 'Philip Kotler,' in *Guide to the Management Gurus: Shortcuts to the Ideas of Leading Management Thinkers* (New York: Century Business, 1998), p. 109. To give you some idea of what we're talking about here, Phil Kotler's *very first* published article won a major best paper award ('Elements in a Theory of Growth Stock Valuation', *Financial Analysts Journal*, May–June, 1962, pp. 3–10, winner of the Graham and Dodd award for best article of the year).

5 Stephen Brown, 'Coca Kotler: Over-wrought, Over-rated and Over Here', *Irish Marketing Review*, 8, 1995, pp. 134–39.

6 Stephen Brown, 'Kotler is Dead!' *European Journal of Marketing*, 31 (2/3), 1997, pp. 315–25 (written under the pseudonym Alan Smithee).

7 Stephen Brown, 'Once Upon a Marketplace' in S. Brown and J.F. Sherry, Jr. (eds), *Time, Space, and the Market: Retroscapes Rising* (Armonk, NY: M.E. Sharpe, 2003), pp. 293–310.

8 See for example, Terry Eagleton, *Literary Theory: An Introduction* (Oxford: Blackwell, 1996); Moyra Haslett, *Marxist Literary and Cultural Theories* (Basingstoke: Macmillan, 2000); Fredric Jameson, *The Cultural Turn: Selected Writings on the Postmodern 1983–1998* (London: Verso, 1998). On Marxist literary theory generally, see Terry Eagleton and Drew Milne, *Marxist Literary Theory: A Reader* (Oxford: Blackwell, 1996); Francis Mulhern, *Contemporary Marxist Literary Criticism* (London: Longman, 1992); Raymond Williams, *Marxism and Literature* (Oxford: Oxford University Press, 1977).

9 Fredric Jameson, *Postmodernism: Or, the Cultural Logic of Late Capitalism* (London: Verso, 1991), p. 188.

10 Useful overviews of Marx's life and work can be found in: Terry Eagleton, *Marx* (London: Routledge, 1999); Peter Singer, *Marx: A Very Short Introduction* (Oxford: Oxford University Press, 2000); Francis Wheen, *Karl Marx: A Life* (New York: Norton, 2000).

11 As Perry Anderson notes in *Considerations on Western Marxism* (London: Verso, 1979), p. 26. 'Lukács was the son of a banker; Benjamin of an art dealer; Adorno of a wine merchant; [and] Horkheimer of a textile manufacturer.' The famous Frankfurt School, furthermore, was funded by a fabulously wealthy grain merchant. See Martin Jay, *The Dialectical Imagination: A History of the Frankfurt School and the Institute of Social Research* (London: Heinemann, 1973).

12 Shelby D. Hunt is especially resistant to Marxist perspectives, as his contributions to the 'reification debate' reveal (see also Chapter 4, Note 64).

13 For example, Dawn Burton, 'Critical Marketing Theory: The Blueprint?', *European Journal of Marketing*, 35 (5/6), 2001, pp. 722–43. A. Fuat Firat and Nikhilesh Dholakia, *Consuming People: From Political Economy to Theaters of Consumption* (London: Routledge, 1998); Elizabeth C. Hirschman, 'The Ideology of Consumption: A Marxist and Feminist Critique', *Journal of Consumer Research*, 19 (March), 1993, pp. 537–55; Jeff B. Murray and Julie L. Ozanne, 'The Critical Imagination: Emancipatory Interests in Consumer Research', *Journal of Consumer Research*, 18 (September), 1991, pp. 129–44; Barbara B. Stern, 'Feminist Literary Criticism and the Deconstruction of Ads: A Postmodern View of Advertising and Consumer Responses', *Journal of Consumer Research*, 19 (March), 1993, pp. 556–66.

14 The literature in this area is compendious to put it mildly. The following treatments are a fair reflection of the genre: Jean Baudrillard, *The Consumer Society: Myths and Structures* (London: Sage, 1998); Roger Burrows and Catherine Marsh, *Consumption and Class: Divisions and Change* (London: Macmillan, 1982); Haidar Eid, 'White Noise: A Late-Capitalist World of Consumerism,' *Consumption, Markets and Culture*, 3 (3), 1999, pp. 215–38; Ben Fine and Ellen Leopold, *The World of Consumption* (London: Routledge, 1993); Don Slater and Fran Tonkiss, *Market Society: Markets and Modern Social Theory* (London: Polity, 2001).

15 See Ronald Aronson, *After Marxism* (New York: Guildford Press, 1995); Marshall Berman, *Adventures in Marxism* (Oxford: Verso, 1999); Richard Sakwa, *Postcommunism* (Milton Keynes: Open University Press, 1999).

16 Francis Fukuyama, *The End of History and the Last Man* (New York: Free Press,

1992); Shelby D. Hunt, *A General Theory of Competition: Resources, Competences, Productivity, Economic Growth* (Thousand Oaks, CA: Sage, 2000), especially Chapter 7.

17 Tom Wolfe, 'In the Land of Rococo Marxists', in *Hooking Up* (New York: Farrar, Straus and Giroux, 2000), pp. 113–30.

18 Take your pick: Alex Callinicos, *An Anti-Capitalist Manifesto* (Cambridge: Polity, 2003); Alexander Cockburn, Jeffrey St Clair and Alan Sekula, *Five Days that Shook the World: Seattle and Beyond* (London: Verso, 2000); Noreena Hertz, *The Silent Takeover: Global Capitalism and the Death of Democracy* (London: Heinemann, 2001); Paul Kingsworth, *One No, Many Yesses: A Journey to the Heart of the Global Resistance Movement* (London: The Free Press, 2003).

19 Naomi Klein, *No Logo: Taking Aim at the Brand Bullies* (London: HarperCollins, 2000); Stephen Brown, 'Marketing to Generation ®', *Harvard Business Review*, 81 (6), 2003, pp. 10–11.

20 Stephen Brown, 'The Laugh of the Marketing Medusa: Men are from Marx, Women are from Veblen,' in M. Catterall, P. Maclaran and L. Stevens (eds), *Marketing and Feminism* (London: Routledge, 2000), pp. 129–42.

21 Francis Wheen, *Karl Marx: A Life* (New York: Norton, 2000).

22 Philip Kotler, 'Behavior Models for Analyzing Buyers', *Journal of Marketing*, 29 (October), 1965, pp. 37–45. Although Veblen is best-remembered today for his 1899 classic *Theory of the Leisure Class*, his scholarly reputation was established with a devastating critique of Marx's labour theory of value. See John P. Diggins, *Thorstein Veblen: Theorist of the Leisure Class* (Princeton, NJ: Princeton University Press, 1999).

23 Mark J. Arnold and James E. Fisher, 'Counter-culture, Criticisms and Crisis: Assessing the Effect of the Sixties on Marketing Thought', *Journal of Macromarketing*, 16 (Spring), 1996, pp. 118–32.

24 Philip Kotler, 'Humanistic Marketing: Beyond the Marketing Concept', in A. Fuat Firat, Nikhilesh Dholakia and R.P. Bagozzi (eds), *Philosophical and Radical Thought in Marketing* (Lexington, MA: Lexington Books, 1987), pp. 271–88.

25 Philip Kotler, *Marketing Management: Analysis, Planning and Control* (Englewood Cliffs, NJ: Prentice Hall, 1967). See also the second, fifth and seventh editions published in 1971, 1984 and 1991 respectively.

26 Philip Kotler, *Kotler on Marketing* (New York: Free Press, 1999), p. 4. I should perhaps add that there's a second-order influence as well, though I don't have the space to address this in detail. However, consider 'A Generic Concept of Marketing', the third of Kotler's three great Alpha Kappa Psi-winning articles. The basic framework for the paper is Charles A. Reich's 'Three Consciousness Model'. Now almost forgotten, albeit a best-selling sensation in its time, Reich's *The Greening of America* (New York: Random House, 1970) postulated that a new social dispensation was dawning. Whereas 'Consciousness One' was characterized by buccaneering robber-barons and 'Consciousness Two' by bureaucratic conformity of the grey flannel suit variety, 'Consciousness Three' was shaping up to be an epoch of peace, love and understanding. Con. III specifically eschewed the corporate state and the attendant apparatus of big science, which had only resulted in resource depletion, environmental despoliation, the threat of thermo-nuclear immolation and the Big Mac. Philip Kotler, in other words, was basing his axiom- and corollary-bandoleered

model of Con. III Marketing on a conceptual framework that was itself based on Karl Marx's five-stage (but really three-stage) theory of historical materialism, as Reich's acknowledgements make perfectly clear (see *The Greening of America*, p. 397). Phil Kotler's single-most celebrated, solo-authored article was predicated on the published works of Karl Marx.

27 It has often been said that Marx founded a new religion, notwithstanding his disdain for religiosity (see for example, Paul Strathern, *Marx in Ninety Minutes* (Chicago: Ivan R. Dee, 2001)). Kotler too has been deified, albeit in a much less egregious manner. *Marketing Management*, for example, is regularly described as the Bible of our discipline. What is more, in Kellogg Graduate School of Management there is a mural depicting the great and good of the past and present Marketing Department. Above them all, sitting on a cloud, is none other than Saint Philip himself.

28 Peter Singer, *Marx: A Very Short Introduction* (Oxford: Oxford University Press, 2000).

29 See Karl Marx, 'Preface to *A Contribution to the Critique of Political Economy*', in R. Tucker (ed.), *The Marx-Engels Reader* (New York: Norton, 1978), pp. 594–617. See also Allan G. Johnson, 'Mode of Production', in A.G. Johnson (ed.), *The Blackwell Dictionary of Sociology* (Oxford: Blackwell, 1995), pp. 198–9.

30 See for example, Susan Himmelweit, 'Forces and Relations of Production', in T. Bottomore (ed.), *A Dictionary of Marxist Thought* (Cambridge, MA: Harvard University Press, 1983), pp. 178–80.

31 In *Marketing for Non-Profit Organizations* (Englewood Cliffs, NJ: Prentice Hall, 1975), for instance, he identifies sixteen separate relationships that are integral to the marketing of a university and those that prevail in today's networked economy are more elaborate still (see also Note 32 below).

32 Mohanbir Sawhney and Philip Kotler, 'Marketing in the Age of Information Democracy', in D. Iacobucci (ed.), *Kellogg on Marketing* (New York: John Wiley, 2001), pp. 386–408.

33 Jagdish N. Sheth, David M. Gardner and Dennis E. Garrett, *Marketing Theory: Evolution and Evaluation* (New York: Wiley, 1988).

34 Karl Marx, 'Preface to *A Contribution of the Critique of Political Economy*', op. cit., p. 7.

35 Moyra Haslett, *Marxist Literary and Cultural Theories* (Basingstoke: Macmillan, 2000).

36 Fredric Jameson, *Late Marxism* (London: Verso, 1990).

37 See for example Philip Kotler, 'The Use of Mathematical Models in Marketing', *Journal of Marketing*, 27 (October), 1963, pp. 31–41; Ravi S. Achrol and Philip Kotler, 'Marketing in the Network Economy', *Journal of Marketing*, 63 (Special Issue), 1999, pp. 146–63.

38 Philip Kotler and Sidney J. Levy, 'Broadening the Concept of Marketing', *Journal of Marketing*, 33 (January), 1969, pp. 10–15.

39 To cite but a few: Philip Kotler and Paul N. Bloom, *Marketing Professional Services* (Engelwood Cliffs, NJ: Prentice Hall, 1984); Philip Kotler and Roberta N. Clarke, *Marketing for Health Organizations* (Englewood Cliffs, NJ: Prentice Hall, 1987); Philip Kotler and Karen Fox, *Strategic Marketing for Educational Institutions* (Englewood Cliffs, NJ: Prentice Hall, 1985); Philip Kotler, Donald H. Haider and Irving Rein, *Marketing Places: Attracting Investment, Industry and Tourism to Cities, States and Nations* (New York: Free Press, 1993).

40 However, it is interesting to note that having exhausted the cultural super-structure, Kotler is increasingly turning his attention to the economic base at a time of rapid technological change. See for instance, Philip Kotler and Francoise Simon, *Marketing Biotechnology: Building and Sustaining Global Biobrands* (New York: Simon and Schuster, 2003).

41 Perry Anderson, *Considerations on Western Marxism* (London: Verso, 1979).

42 A cogent review of the broadening controversy is contained in Dennis Rook's 'Introduction' to his anthology of Sid Levy's writings, *Brands, Consumers, Symbols and Research: Sidney J. Levy on Marketing* (Thousand Oaks: Sage, 1999), pp. 32–3.

43 Philip Kotler and Gerald Zaltman, 'Social Marketing: An Approach to Planned Social Change', *Journal of Marketing*, 35 (July), 1972, p. 12.

44 Georg Lukács, *History and Class Consciousness* (Cambridge, MA: MIT Press, 1971). See also Allan G. Johnson, 'Reification', in A.G. Johnson (ed.), *The Blackwell Dictionary of Sociology* (Oxford: Blackwell, 1995), p. 258.

45 Karl Marx, *Capital: A Critique of Political Economy*, in E. Kamenka (ed.), *The Portable Karl Marx* (New York: Penguin, 1983), pp. 444–5.

46 Philip Kotler and Sidney J. Levy, 'Broadening the Concept of Marketing', *Journal of Marketing*, 33 (January), 1969, pp. 10–15.

47 Philip Kotler, 'Phasing Out Weak Products', *Harvard Business Review*, 43 (November–December), 1965, p. 108.

48 Irving Rein, Philip Kotler and Martin Stoller, *High Visibility* (New York: Dodd, Mead and Co., 1987).

49 Ibid., p. 23.

50 Tom Peters, *The Brand You: Fifty Ways to Transform Yourself From an Employee into a Brand that Shouts Distinction, Commitment, and Passion!* (New York: Knopf, 1999); Rachel Greenwald, *The Program: Fifteen Steps to Finding a Husband After Thirty* (London: TimeWarner, 2004).

51 Terry Eagleton, *Ideology: An Introduction* (London: Verso, 1991) and *Ideology* (Harlow: Longman, 1994); David Hawkes, *Ideology* (London: Routledge, 1996).

52 Karl Marx, *The German Ideology*, in E. Kamenka (ed.), *The Portable Karl Marx* (New York: Penguin, 1983), pp. 162–95.

53 Antonio Gramsci, *Selections From Prison Notebooks* (London: Lawrence and Wishart, 1971).

54 Kotler, of course, makes this point on many occasions (see for example his *Kotler on Marketing* (New York: Free Press, 1999), Chapter 2). A somewhat different, but complementary, stance is taken by Douglas Brownlie and Mike Saren, 'The Four Ps of the Marketing Concept: Prescriptive, Polemical, Permanent and Problematical', *European Journal of Marketing*, 26 (4), 1992, pp. 34–47.

55 Philip Kotler and Joanne Scheff, *Standing Room Only: Strategies for Marketing the Performing Arts* (Boston: Harvard Business School Press, 1997); Neil Kotler and Philip Kotler, *Museum Strategies and Marketing* (San Francisco: Jossey-Bass, 1998).

56 Curtis White, *The Middle Mind: Why Americans Don't Think for Themselves* (London: Penguin, 2004).

57 Stephen Brown and Anthony Patterson, 'Figments for Sale: Marketing, Imagination and the Artistic Imperative', in S. Brown and A. Patterson (eds),

Imagining Marketing: Art, Aesthetics and the Avant-Garde (London: Routledge, 2000), pp. 4–32.

58 See Stephen Brown, 'Trinitarianism, the Eternal Evangel and the Three Eras Schema', in S. Brown, J. Bell and D. Carson (eds), *Marketing Apocalypse: Eschatology, Escapology and the Illusion of the End* (London: Routledge, 1996), pp. 23–43.

59 Philip Kotler, *Marketing Management: Analysis, Planning and Control*, 4th edn (Englewood Cliffs, NJ: Prentice Hall, 1980) Philip Kotler and Gerald Zaltman, 'Social Marketing: An Approach to Planned Social Change', *Journal of Marketing*, 35 (July), 1972, p. 12. Philip Kotler and Fernando Trias de Bes, *Lateral Marketing: New Techniques for Finding Breakthrough Ideas* (New York: Wiley, 2003).

60 Karl Marx, 'Preface to *A Contribution to the Critique of Political Economy*', in R. Tucker (ed.), *The Marx-Engels Reader* (New York: Norton, 1978), pp. 594–617. Friedrich Engels, 'Engels's Speech at the Graveside of Karl Marx', in E. Kamenka (ed.), *The Portable Karl Marx* (New York: Penguin, 1983), pp. 68–71.

61 Karl Popper, *The Poverty of Historicism* (London: Ark, 1957). The marketing angle is covered by Ronald Fullerton, 'Historicism: What It Is and What It Means for Consumer Research', in M. Wallendorf and P.F. Anderson (eds), *Advances in Consumer Research*, Vol. 14 (Provo, UT: Association for Consumer Research, 1987), pp. 431–4.

62 Frank E. Manuel, *A Requiem for Karl Marx* (Cambridge, MA: Harvard University Press, 1995). See also, Peter Burke, *History and Social Theory* (Oxford: Polity, 1992) and Gordon Graham, *The Shape of the Past: A Philosophical Approach to History* (Oxford: Oxford University Press, 1997). Marketing historians' take on the topic is considered by Terence Nevett, 'Historical Investigation and the Practice of Marketing', *Journal of Marketing*, 55 (July), 1991, pp. 13–23.

63 David Harvey, 'Introduction to the Verso Edition', in *The Limits to Capital* (London: Verso, 1999), pp. xiii–xxviii; Edward Reiss, *Marx: A Clear Guide* (London: Pluto, 1997); Peter Singer, *Marx: A Very Short Introduction* (Oxford: Oxford University Press, 2000).

64 Philip Kotler, *Marketing Management: Analysis, Planning and Control*, 5th edn (Englewood Cliffs, NJ: Prentice Hall, 1984).

65 Richard P. Bagozzi, 'Marketing as Exchange', *Journal of Marketing*, 39 (October), 1975, pp. 32–9; Ben Fine and Ellen Leopold, *The World of Consumption* (London: Routledge, 1993); Don Slater and Fran Tonkiss, *Market Society: Markets and Modern Social Theory* (London: Polity, 2001).

66 Philip Kotler, *Kotler on Marketing* (New York: Free Press, 1999), p. 40.

67 Karl Marx, 'Critique of the Gotha Programme', in E. Kamenka, *The Portable Karl Marx* (New York: Penguin, 1983), p. 550.

68 Philip Kotler, *Marketing Management: Analysis, Planning and Control* (Englewood Cliffs, NJ: Prentice Hall, 1967), unpaged.

69 Philip Kotler, *Kotler on Marketing*, op. cit., p. xii.

70 Stephen Brown, 'Art or Science? Fifty Years of Marketing Debate', *Journal of Marketing Management*, 12 (4), 1996, pp. 243–67.

71 Carol Kennedy, *Guide to the Management Gurus: Shortcuts to the Ideas of Leading Management Thinkers* (New York: Century Business, 1998).

72 Robert Bartels, 'Philip Kotler', in *The History of Marketing Thought* (Columbus, OH: Publishing Horizons, 1988), pp. 255–6.

73 Philip Kotler, *Marketing Management: Millennium Edition* (Englewood Cliffs, NJ: Prentice Hall, 2000), p. xxvii.

74 Paul Strathern, *Marx in Ninety Minutes* (Chicago: Ivan R. Dee, 2001).

75 On Benjamin, see Richard Wolin, *Walter Benjamin: An Aesthetic of Redemption* (New York: Columbia University Press, 1982). The work of marketing word-mongers is described by Alex Frankel, *Word Craft: The Art of Turning Little Words into Big Business* (New York: Crown, 2004).

76 Philip Kotler, 'Reconceptualizing Marketing: An Interview with Philip Kotler', *European Management Journal*, 12 (December), 1994, pp. 353–61; Philip Kotler, 'Preface', in D. Iacobucci (ed.), *Kellogg on Marketing* (New York: Wiley, 2001), pp. xiii–xvi; Philip Kotler and Ravi Singh, 'Marketing Warfare in the 1980s', *Journal of Business Strategy*, (Winter), 1981, pp. 30–41; Philip Kotler, Liam Fahey and Somkid Jatusripitak, *The New Competition* (Englewood Cliffs, NJ: Prentice Hall, 1985); Philip Kotler, *Marketing Management*, 1967, op. cit.; Philip Kotler, *Kotler on Marketing*, op. cit.; Philip Kotler, *Ten Deadly Marketing Sins: Signs and Solutions* (New York: Wiley, 2004).

77 Jacques Derrida, *Specters of Marx* (London: Routledge, 1994).

78 Terrell Carver, *The Postmodern Marx* (University Park: Pennsylvania State University Press, 1998), pp. 15–16.

79 Philip Kotler, Donald H. Haider and Irving Rein, *Marketing Places: Attracting Investment, Industry and Tourism to Cities, States and Nations* (New York, Free Press, 1993).

80 Stephen Brown, 'Trinitarianism, the Eternal Evangel and the Three Eras Schema', in S. Brown, J. Bell and D. Carson (eds), *Marketing Apocalypse: Eschatology, Escapology and the Illusion of the End* (London: Routledge, 1996), pp. 23–43.

81 Karl Marx and Friedrich Engels, *Manifesto of the Communist Party* in E. Kamenka (ed.), *The Portable Karl Marx* (New York: Penguin, 1983), p. 206.

82 Philip Kotler, 'Phasing Out Weak Products', *Harvard Business Review*, 43 (November–December), 1965, p. 118.

83 Philip Kotler and Sidney J. Levy, 'Broadening the Concept of Marketing', *Journal of Marketing*, 33 (January), 1969, p. 11.

84 Philip Kotler, *Kotler on Marketing* (New York: Free Press, 1999), p. 12.

85 Philip Kotler and Sidney J. Levy, 'Broadening', op. cit., p. 15.

86 Arthur A. Berger, *Blind Men and Elephants: Perspectives on Humor* (New York: Transaction, 1995) and *An Anatomy of Humor* (New York: Transaction, 1998).

87 Dominick La Capra, *Rethinking Intellectual History: Texts, Contexts, Language*, (Ithaca: Cornell University Press, 1983).

88 Philip Kotler, *Marketing Management: Analysis, Planning and Control* (Englewood Cliffs, NJ: Prentice Hall, 1967), p. 25.

89 Philip Kotler, 'A Generic Concept of Marketing', *Journal of Marketing*, 36 (April), 1972, p. 47.

90 The wryly ironic side of Kotler is neatly illustrated in the following excerpt from Philip Kotler, Donald H. Haider and Irving Rein, *Marketing Places*: 'The city of Wichita Falls, Texas, having lost its waterfalls in a flood in the 1890s, replaced them almost a hundred years later to stimulate tourism. The artificial falls have reignited city pride and have given residents a place to take friends and visitors, but the tidal wave of tourists has yet to appear' (p. 122).

91 Philip Kotler, *Marketing for Non-Profit Organizations* (Englewood Cliffs, NJ: Prentice Hall, 1975), p. 190.

92 Philip Kotler, *Kotler on Marketing* (New York: Free Press, 1999), p. 150.

93 Roy Bhaskar, *Dialectic: The Pulse of Freedom* (New York: Verso, 1993).

94 Karl Marx, *Economico-Philosophical Manuscripts of 1844*, in E. Kamenka (ed.), *The Portable Karl Marx* (New York: Penguin, 1983), p. 135.

95 Philip Kotler, *Marketing Management*, 1967, op. cit., p. 453.

96 Philip Kotler, *Ten Deadly Marketing Sins: Signs and Solutions* (New York: Wiley, 2004).

97 Philip Kotler, *Marketing Management*, 1967, op. cit., unpaged.

98 Strictly speaking, 'negative capability' refers to writers' ability to empathize. That is, to set aside their own personality and imaginatively enter into the mind, existence and behaviour of other people, be they characters in a novel, biographical subjects, or whatever. Although I am using the term to refer specifically to Kotler's dialectical-style reasoning, I am also thinking of his amazing ability to absorb the ideas of those around him and incorporate them into the Kotlerite cosmology. At Northwestern University, they call it the Kotler 'mindsuck'. I, myself, have experienced the mindsuck – didn't take long, as you might imagine – and, believe me, it's an extraordinary experience (see S. Brown, 'Once Upon a Marketplace', in S. Brown and J.F. Sherry, Jr. (eds), *Time, Space, and the Market: Retroscapes Rising* (Armonk, NY: M.E. Sharpe, 2003), pp. 293–310).

99 Eugene Kamenka, 'Introduction', in E. Kamenka (ed.), *The Portable Karl Marx* (New York: Penguin, 1983), pp. xxxii–xxxiii. In this regard, consider the following (thirty-year-old) assessment of Kotler's contribution to marketing thought: 'A man having a broad interdisciplinary range would ordinarily be expected to be intellectually restless and dissatisfied. Professor Kotler has discovered, as have most scholars, that for every question answered several more appear. Yet unlike some scholars he is undaunted by the encounter of an ever expanding body of unanswered questions and unsolved problems. On the contrary, he seems to thrive on them' (Gerald Zaltman, 'Leaders in Marketing: Philip Kotler', *Journal of Marketing*, 36 (October), 1972, pp. 60–1).

100 Frank E. Manuel, *A Requiem for Karl Marx* (Cambridge, MA: Harvard University Press, 1995), p. 138.

101 Morris Holbrook possibly excepted. See Chapter 6.

102 Quoted in Carol Kennedy, *Guide to the Management Gurus: Shortcuts to the Ideas of Leading Management Thinkers* (New York: Century Business, 1998), p. 114.

103 Frank E. Manuel and Fritzie P. Manuel, *Utopian Thought in the Western World* (Cambridge, MA: Belknap, 1979). For a marketing perspective on utopianism, check out Stephen Brown and Pauline Maclaran, 'The Future is Past: Marketing, Apocalypse and the Retreat From Utopia', in S. Brown, J. Bell and D. Carson (eds), *Marketing Apocalypse: Eschatology, Escapology and the Illusion of the End* (London: Routledge, 1996), pp. 260–77.

104 Quoted in Carol Kennedy, *Guide to the Management Gurus*, op. cit., p. 111.

4 The Deconstruction of Shelby D. Hunt

1 First line quoted by Shelby D. Hunt in 'Positivism and Paradigm Dominance in Consumer Research: Toward Critical Pluralism and Rapprochement', *Journal of Consumer Research*, 18 (June), 1991, p. 32. Second line excerpted from Robert Frost's 'Mending Wall' (line five in the original poem).

2 Shelby D. Hunt, *A General Theory of Competition: Resources, Competences, Productivity, Economic Growth* (Thousand Oaks, CA: Sage, 2000), p. 1.

3 There are many examples of SDH's anti-rhetoric rhetoric. To pick one at random: 'Although I have restricted my examples to those in this volume from Ozanne and Hudson, similar rhetorical devices seem all too commonplace throughout the literature . . . The use of these rhetorical devices may serve well when "preaching to the committed." However, such techniques are unlikely to gain "converts."' Example taken from 'Naturalistic, Humanistic, and Interpretive Inquiry: Challenges and Ultimate Potential', in E.C. Hirschman (ed.), *Interpretive Consumer Research* (Provo, UT: Association for Consumer Research, 1989), p. 186.

4 Shelby D. Hunt, 'The Influence of Philosophy: Philosophers and Philosophies on a Marketer's Scholarship', *Journal of Marketing*, 65 (4), 2001, pp. 117–22.

5 I was tempted to write 'It's a long way from Tupperwarey' and I would have done had it not been for the fact that SDH worked on the B2B side of the plastics-selling fence (autos and appliances, mainly). It's not like me to deny myself a punning opportunity. Consider yourselves very lucky!

6 Lawrence B. Chonko and Patrick M. Dunne, 'Marketing Theory: A Status Report', in R.F. Bush and S.D. Hunt (eds), *Marketing Theory: Philosophy of Science Perspectives* (Chicago, IL: American Marketing Association, 1982), pp. 43–6. The fact that both Chonko and Dunne were based at Texas Tech University had no influence whatsoever on the results of their survey.

7 Shelby D. Hunt, 'The Nature and Scope of Marketing', *Journal of Marketing*, 40 (July), 1976, pp. 17–28.

8 A cogent summary of this controversy is contained in Donncha Kavanagh, 'Hunt versus Anderson: Round Sixteen', *European Journal of Marketing*, 28 (3), 1994, pp. 26–41.

9 Shelby D. Hunt and Robert M. Morgan, 'The Resource-Advantage Theory of Competition: Dynamics, Path Dependencies, and Evolutionary Dimensions', *Journal of Marketing*, 60 (October), 1996, pp. 107–14.

10 I'm not being catty here, since I firmly believe that SDH is a great writer. This is SDH's own assessment. He frequently refers to the difficulty of his prose, as for example in the opening pages of *Modern Marketing Theory* where he expounds on the problems students have with his recondite philosophical writings (*Modern Marketing Theory: Critical Issues in the Philosophy of Marketing Science* (Cincinnati, OH: South-Western Publishing, 1991), pp. 1–4).

11 Ibid., p. 110.

12 Many of these are collected in Shelby D. Hunt, *Controversy in Marketing Theory: For Reason, Realism, Truth, and Objectivity* (Armonk, NY: M.E. Sharpe, 2003).

13 Edward Blair and George M. Zinkhan, 'The Realist View of Science: Implications for Marketing', in P.F. Anderson and M.J. Ryan (eds), *Scientific Method in Marketing* (Chicago, IL: American Marketing Association, 1984), p. 26.

14 A useful, if extremely critical, overview of the relationship between science and postmodernism is found in Alan Sokal and Jean Bricmont, *Intellectual Impostures* (London: Profile Books, 1998). For a more sympathetic slant, see Steven Best and Douglas Kellner, *The Postmodern Adventure: Science, Technology, and Cultural Studies at the Third Millennium* (New York: Guilford Press, 2001).

15 'The Nature and Scope of Marketing', op. cit.; *Modern Marketing Theory*, op. cit.; 'Naturalistic, Humanistic, and Interpretive Inquiry', op. cit. See also, Shelby D. Hunt, 'On Rethinking Marketing: Our Discipline, Our Practice, Our Methods', *European Journal of Marketing*, 28 (3), 1994, pp. 13–25.

16 I suppose I should explain this one. If SDH's body of work is set against the scientific demarcation criteria that *he himself* sets out – empirical testing, intersubjective certification and a positive rather than normative approach – then our hero flunks the science test. SDH's scholarly corpus is an empirical-free zone, near enough. Similarly, his oeuvre has not been intersubjectively certified; that is, unequivocally endorsed by fellow academics. On the contrary, every stage of his career has been punctuated by disparagement, disagreement, disputation and diatribe. Many of his statements, what's more, are more normative than positive. His books and articles, in effect, lay down the law on how marketing *should* proceed if it wishes to attain the 'nirvana position' of scientific respectability, philosophical propriety or esteem in the eyes of equilibrium-obsessed economists. They are normative, to all intents and purposes. Granted, SDH makes innumerable positive statements – 'No marketing academician would dispute this assertion', 'By the 1970s, most philosophers of science had adopted some version of scientific realism', and so on – but very few of these claims are supported by solid empirical evidence, let alone intersubjective certification.

17 See for example, Z. Seyda Deligönül and S. Tamer Çavuşgil, 'Does the Comparative Advantage Theory of Competition Really Replace the Neoclassical Theory of Perfect Competition?', *Journal of Marketing*, 61 (October), 1997, pp. 65–73.

18 Shelby D. Hunt, 'The Morphology of Theory and the General Theory of Marketing', *Journal of Marketing*, 35 (April), pp. 65–8.

19 'Assume competition' is only the start of it. The paragraph continues: 'On thousands of occasions each day, in lectures, discussions, books and journals, one finds the expression *assume competition*. And on each such occasion, the expression is taken to mean that one is being asked to assume the foundational premises, structure, and implications of the theory of *perfect* competition. Good communication is economical; to place the adjective 'perfect' before the noun 'competition' is simply redundant. That it frames the language, hence the discourse, of mainstream economics testifies as to the dominance of the theory of perfect competition.' Is SDH a marketing literatus, or what?

20 Shelby D. Hunt, 'A General Paradigm of Marketing: In Support of the Three Dichotomies Model', *Journal of Marketing*, 42 (April), 1978, p. 109.

21 Gerald Graff, *Clueless in Academe: How Schooling Obscures the Life of the Mind* (New Haven, CT.: Yale University Press, 2003).

22 Elizabeth George, *Write Away: One Novelist's Approach to Fiction and the Writing Life* (London: Hodder & Stoughton, 2004).

23 Shelby D. Hunt and Robert M. Morgan, 'The Comparative Advantage Theory of Competition', *Journal of Marketing*, 59 (April), 1995, p. 13.

24 Shelby D. Hunt, 'For Reason and Realism in Marketing', *Journal of Marketing*, 56 (April), 1992, p. 101.

25 Shelby D. Hunt, *Modern Marketing Theory: Critical Issues in the Philosophy of Marketing Science* (Cincinnati, OH: South-Western Publishing, 1991); Shelby

D. Hunt, *Marketing Theory: The Philosophy of Marketing Science* (Homewood, IL: Richard D. Irwin, 1983).

26 Shelby D. Hunt, 'On Rethinking Marketing: Our Discipline, Our Practice, Our Methods', *European Journal of Marketing*, 28 (3), 1994, p. 19.

27 *A General Theory of Competition: Resources, Competences, Productivity, Economic Growth* (Thousand Oaks, CA: Sage), p. 103.

28 When Chapter 9 of *Modern Marketing Theory* became Chapter 3 of *Controversy in Marketing Theory*, the title changed from 'The Development of the Discipline of Philosophy of Science' to 'The Development of the Philosophy of Science Discipline'. The subtitle of a 1997 article in the *Journal of Economic Issues* evolved (at the editor's insistence, apparently) from 'An Evolutionary Theory of Competition' to 'An Evolutionary Theory of Competitive Firm Behavior'. A statement in his classic 1976 article 'The Nature and Scope of Marketing', 'the major purpose of science is to discover laws and theories', was replaced with 'the major purpose of science is to develop laws and theories' when it was incorporated into *Modern Marketing Theory*. This one word alteration may not seem particularly significant, but from a philosophy of science perspective there is a world of difference between 'discovering' and 'developing' theories.

29 Shelby D. Hunt, 'Marketing Research: Proximate Purpose and Ultimate Value', in R.W. Belk et al. (eds), *Marketing Theory* (Chicago, IL: American Marketing Association, 1987), p. 212.

30 Shelby D. Hunt, 'Naturalistic, Humanistic, and Interpretive Inquiry: Challenges and Ultimate Potential', in E.C. Hirschman (ed.), *Interpretive Consumer Research* (Provo, UT: Association for Consumer Research, 1989), p. 192.

31 Shelby D. Hunt, 'Truth in Marketing Theory and Research', *Journal of Marketing*, 54 (July), 1990, p. 8.

32 Shelby D. Hunt, 'On the Rhetoric of Qualitative Inquiry: Toward Historically Informed Argumentation in Management Inquiry', *Journal of Management Inquiry*, 3 (September), 1994, pp. 221–34.

33 Shelby D. Hunt, *Controversy in Marketing Theory: For Reason, Realism, Truth, and Objectivity* (Armonk, NY: M.E. Sharpe, 2003), p. 218.

34 Shelby D. Hunt and Anil Menon, 'Metaphors and Competitive Advantage: Evaluating the Use of Metaphors in Theories of Competitive Strategy', *Journal of Business Research*, 33 (1), 1995, pp. 81–90.

35 Shelby D. Hunt, 'Should Marketing Adopt Relativism?', in P.F. Anderson and M.J. Ryan (eds), *Scientific Method in Marketing* (Chicago, IL: American Marketing Association, 1984), p. 34.

36 Shelby D. Hunt, '1989 Postscript to "Should Marketing Adopt Relativism"', in Shelby D. Hunt, *Modern Marketing Theory: Critical Issues in the Philosophy of Marketing Science* (Cincinnati, OH: South-Western Publishing, 1991), p. 411. Lest there is any misunderstanding, moreover, SDH goes on: *'this writer in no way implies that others in the debate over the appropriateness of relativism in marketing and consumer behavior advocate the monstrous world of Orwell's 1984'*, albeit this elaborate apologia only serves to reinforce the connection (see also Note 59 below). Nevertheless, for those who still don't get it, he follows up with, 'Yet, the message is clear to be gleaned from both the *hypothetical* world of Orwell and the *actual* world of contemporary societies . . . scientists and

philosophers of science must assume some measure of responsibility for their knowledge claims'. Now, that's what I call crushing one's opponents!

37 Shelby D. Hunt, 'Positivism and Paradigm Dominance in Consumer Research: Toward Critical Pluralism and Rapproachement', *Journal of Consumer Research*, 18 (June), 1991, pp. 32–44.

38 Shelby D. Hunt, *Modern Marketing Theory*, op. cit., pp. 222–3.

39 *Modern Marketing Theory*, op. cit., p. 94. The source of this I-S argument (Jones is a black; Jones drinks alcoholic beverages; 90 percent of all black drinkers drink Scotch; [very likely] Jones drinks Scotch) is a little bit unclear. It seems to be Carnap but could just as easily be Hempel. The example is repeated in the 1991 edition, *Modern Marketing Theory*, though there's a change in the most recent edition of his marketing theory text, where SDH substitutes a whisky-swilling Scottish-American (Shelby D. Hunt, *Foundations of Marketing Theory: Toward a General Theory of Marketing* (Armonk, NY: M.E. Sharpe, 2002), p. 97).

40 A.S. Byatt, *On Histories and Stories: Selected Essays* (London: Chatto & Windus, 2000), p. 5.

41 'I offer the reader the following long passage from Bradley's book . . . [193-word quote follows] . . . Note the obtuseness of the preceding argument', *Modern Marketing Theory*, op. cit., p. 249.

42 Geoffrey M. Hodgson, 'The Marketing of Wisdom: Resource-Advantage Theory', *Journal of Macromarketing*, 20 (June), 2000, pp. 68–72, Shelby D. Hunt, 'A General Theory of Competition: Too Eclectic or Not Eclectic Enough? Too Incremental or Not Incremental Enough? Too Neoclassical or Not Neoclassical Enough?', *Journal of Macromarketing*, 20 (June), 2000, pp. 77–81.

43 Alan Watkins, 'Mr Heseltine May Get His Secret Wish', *The Observer*, October 20, 1991, p. 21.

44 Stephen Brown, *Postmodern Marketing* (London: Routledge, 1995).

45 For example: 'His very thorough approach, detailed to a degree that it reaches the pain barrier', Bodo B. Schlegelmilch, 'Special Symposium on Shelby D. Hunt's "A General Theory of Competition: Resources, Competences, Productivity, Economic Growth" Part 1. Comments', *Journal of Marketing Management*, 18 (1/2), 2002, p. 226.

46 Shelby D. Hunt, *Controversy in Marketing Theory: For Reason, Realism, Truth, and Objectivity* (Armonk, NY: M.E. Sharpe, 2003), p. 135.

47 Shelby D. Hunt, *A General Theory of Competition: Resources, Competences, Productivity, Economic Growth* (Thousand Oaks, CA: Sage, 2000), pp. 227–8.

48 Lynne Truss, *Eats, Shoots & Leaves: The Zero Tolerance Approach to Punctuation* (London: Profile Books, 2003).

49 Shelby D. Hunt, *A General Theory of Competition*, op. cit., pp. 101–2.

50 Ibid, p. 12.

51 Curiously, he doesn't much care for exclamation marks, the standard stress-conveying screamer. When he does deign to use one, moreover, he deploys it in an unorthodox, almost ironic, way. To say, in effect, 'What an idiot!'

52 Shelby D. Hunt, *A General Theory of Competition*, op. cit., p. 125.

53 Actually, *Mr Wordsmith Goes to Washington* might be a closer to the mark.

54 Stephen Brown, *Postmodern Marketing* (London: Routledge, 1995).

55 Ron Popeil, the self-appointed 'Salesman of the Century' is the guy behind Ronco, famous for its cheesy infomercials featuring slice 'n' dice, chop-o-matic kitchen implements and analogous superfluous products, such as the

unforgettable 'pocket fisherman', 'in-egg scrambler' and 'spray-on hair'. The immortal marketer's autobiography is priceless: Ron Popeil, *The Salesman of the Century* (New York: Delacorte Press, 1995).

56 Z. Seyda Deligönül and S. Tamer Çavuşgil, 'Does the Comparative Advantage Theory of Competition Really Replace the Neoclassical Theory of Perfect Competition?', *Journal of Marketing*, 61 (October), 1997, pp. 65–73.

57 S.D. Hunt, 'The Influence of Philosophy, Philosophers and Philosophies on a Marketer's Scholarship', *Journal of Marketing*, 65 (4), 2001, p. 118.

58 Jamie Whyte, *Bad Thoughts: A Guide to Clear Thinking* (London: Corvo Books, 2003), p. 61.

59 Besides basking in this reflected semantic glory, SDH has a syntactic trick up his stylistic sleeve. Somewhat akin to celebrity endorsement, where brands benefit by association with an exceedingly famous or otherwise highly regarded individual, SDH positions his position, as it were, where it is guaranteed to look good. The most ostentatious example of this confirmation by contiguity is found in his oft-repeated insinuation that CAT is equivalent to the Copernican revolution in astronomy. Note, SDH does not claim that CAT is on a par with Copernicus – though he comes close on occasion – he simply places them in close proximity, which is more than enough for persuasive purposes. This brilliant ability to blur distinctions also works in reverse. SDH not only aligns himself with 'the good guys', such as Galileo and Copernicus, but he repeatedly portrays his relativist/social constructionist opponents as being in league with mystics, Marxists, nihilists, new agers, flat earthers, flaky feminists, religious fundamentalists, repressive regimes, Holocaust deniers, hallucinogenic drug addicts, and assorted benighted opponents of peace, progress and scientific achievement. Of course, he doesn't actually say they espouse such beliefs, but he doesn't have to because simple juxtaposition is quite sufficient. Furthermore, condemnation by contiguity is extremely difficult to argue against since the arguer is obliged to mention the connection when contesting it, thereby affirming the original alleged association. As Whyte (Ibid., p. 47) rightly puts it in his primer on persuasive arguments, 'Hitler . . . is like a reverse Einstein. If you can associate someone's opinion with Hitler, or the Nazis more generally, then goodbye to that idea.'

60 Stephen Brown, *Postmodern Marketing*, op. cit.

61 For an overview of the salient historical literature, see Stephen Brown, Elizabeth C. Hirschman and Pauline Maclaran, 'Always Historicize! Researching Marketing History in a Post-historical Epoch', *Marketing Theory*, 1 (1), 2001, pp. 49–89.

62 Shelby D. Hunt and Jerry Goolsby, 'The Rise and Fall of the Functional Approach to Marketing: A Paradigm Displacement Perspective', in T. Nevett and R.A. Fullerton (eds), *Historical Perspectives in Marketing: Essays in Honor of Stanley C. Hollander* (Lexington, MA: Lexington Books, 1988), pp. 35–51.

63 For SDH to employ such a flagrant framing device in such a scrupulous scholarly setting is undeniably bold, shall we say, but hardly guaranteed to endear him to those whose party he pooped. Stan the Man excepted, I suspect.

64 Shelby D. Hunt, 'Reification and Realism in Marketing: In Defense of Reason', *Journal of Macromarketing*, 9 (Fall), 1989, p. 9.

65 This omission is somewhat surprising given the great scholar's penchant for the minutiae of philosophical method and the history thereof. History, like economics, is chock-a-block with disputatious research traditions, which are meat and drink to someone of SDH's scholarly sensibilities. To my knowledge, however, his sole methodological citation is Marilyn Lavin and Thomas J. Archdeacon, 'The Relevance of Historical Method for Marketing Research', in E.C. Hirschman (ed.), *Interpretive Consumer Research* (Provo, UT: Association for Consumer Research, 1989), pp. 60–8.

66 Stephen Brown et al., 'Always Historicize!', op. cit.

67 Shelby D. Hunt, *Modern Marketing Theory: Critical Issues on the Philosophy of Marketing Science* (Cincinnati, OH: South-Western Publishing, 1991), p. 248. The connotations here are pretty crude, it has to be said. See Note 59 above on guilt by association.

68 For an excellent, and extremely enlightening, discussion of Kuhn's context, see Steve Fuller, *Kuhn vs Popper: The Struggle for the Soul of Science* (Cambridge: Icon Books, 2003).

69 If you don't believe me about the 'naying', I crave the fragrant reader's forgiveness and humbly invite you, forsooth and egad, to peruse *Controversy in Marketing Theory*, op. cit., p. 281.

70 Stephen Brown, *Marketing: The Retro Revolution* (London: Sage, 2001).

71 Shelby D. Hunt, *A General Theory of Competition: Resources, Competences, Productivity, Economic Growth* (Thousand Oaks, CA: Sage, 2000), op. cit., p. 61.

72 Stephen Brown, *Postmodern Marketing* (London: Routledge, 1995).

73 Shelby D. Hunt, 'Positivism and Paradigm Dominance in Consumer Research: Toward Critical Pluralism and Rapprochement', *Journal of Consumer Research*, 18 (June), 1991, p. 38.

74 Ibid., p. 39.

75 Ibid., p. 32.

76 Ben Agger, *Reading Science: A Literary, Political, and Sociological Analysis* (Dix Hills, NY: General Hall Inc., 1989).

77 Nameless well-wishers (*Controversy in Marketing Theory*, op. cit., p. 252); precocious student (*Foundations of Marketing Theory*, op. cit., p. 82); unknown foot-soldiers (*Modern Marketing Theory*, op. cit., p. 90); Professor John Does ('The Comparative Advantage Theory of Competition', op. cit., p. 1); bewildered RA (*Modern Marketing Theory*, op. cit., p. 25); even more bewildered conference delegate (*Modern Marketing Theory*, p. 210).

78 The 'space limitations' remark is particularly intriguing, since SDH even employs it in 500-page books, for example *Modern Marketing Theory*, where space limitations are presumably minimal (they can't be that serious if he has room for 651 citations). However, there's an important rhetorical aspect to 'space limitations', inasmuch as it intimates that the extremely well-read author has much more scholarly ammunition in reserve (and, not coincidentally, sends 'are you tough enough?' signals to would-be critics-cum-antagonists).

79 See for example, Ronald Savitt, 'A Philosophical Essay About *A General Theory of Competition: Resources, Competences, Productivity, Economic Growth*', *Journal of Macromarketing*, 20 (1), 2000, pp. 73–6; Robin Wensley, 'Special Symposium on Shelby D. Hunt's *A General Theory of Competition: Resources, Competences, Productivity, Economic Growth*, Part 2. Marketing For a New Century', *Journal of Marketing Management*, 18 (1/2), 2002, pp. 229–37.

80 Stephen Brown, *Postmodern Marketing*, op. cit.

81 Analogously, if there is one statement by SDH that surpasses the 'much mischief' done to marketing, it is the 'wrong turning' taken by economics. Although our hero is quoting Joan Robertson's critical assessment of General Equilibrium Theory, he cites her 'wrong turning' remark on at least eight separate occasions in *A General Theory of Competition*, op. cit. We GET the picture, Shelby!

82 In *Postmodern Marketing* (op. cit., p. 144), I compare this propensity to a fastest-epistemologist-in-the-west face-off.

83 Christopher Norris, *Deconstruction* (London, Routledge, 2002), p. 8.

84 Jamie Whyte, *Bad Thoughts: A Guide to Clear Thinking* (London: Corvo Books, 2003), p. 63.

85 FYI, the Jerry Lee Lewis allusion is tucked away in the 'Questions' section of the first chapter of Shelby D. Hunt, *Modern Marketing Theory* (op. cit., p. 81).

86 Unlisted papers ('Snake Swallowing Tail', p. 79, Footnotes 8 and 9); parentheses and quotation marks (*Controversy in Marketing Theory*, op. cit., p. 132, 163, 'Naturalistic, Humanistic', op. cit., p. 190); queue shortening (*A General Theory of Competition*, op. cit., p. 158); subsection misinformation (*Controversy in Marketing Theory*, op. cit., p. 296, there is no section 8.3.1); epigraph placement (*Foundations in Marketing Theory*, op. cit., p. 46, question 12 erroneously directs readers to the epigraph in Chapter 6, which was replaced between editions, that is, *Modern Marketing Theory*, Chapter 5, p. 121); non-existent italics ('Comparative Advantage Theory', op. cit., p. 5, Footnote 6, claims 'italics added' to a statement that doesn't contain italics); commodity fetishism ('Positivism and Paradigm Dominance', op. cit., p. 36, contra-SDH, commoditization and commodity fetishism are *not* synonymous); misrepresented dialectic (*Controversy in Marketing Theory*, op. cit., p. 42, the dialectic's 'contradictions' are not equivalent to 'polar opposites'); misspelled Comte (ibid., p. 7), Evans-Pritchard (*Modern Marketing Theory*, op. cit., p. 340), Barzun ('Objectivity in Marketing Theory and Research', p. 87, footnote 15), Isaac Newton (*Modern Marketing Theory*, op. cit., p. 241 and *Controversy in Marketing Theory*, op. cit., p. 35); Stephen Hawking ('Positivism and Paradigm Dominance', op. cit., p. 35; Hawking was not the 'originator' of the Big Bang theory, as SDH claims, the originator was Fred Hoyle); mislabelled matrix (*Foundations of Marketing Theory*, op. cit., p. 251); entelechy comment (*Controversy in Marketing Theory*, op. cit., p. 64, in philosophy, entelechy refers to actuality or realization, as opposed to potentiality); deathless abstract ('Truth in Marketing Theory and Research', op. cit., p. 1, final sentence – a philosophical paraprax if ever there was one!).

87 Martin McQuillan, *Deconstruction: A Reader* (Edinburgh: Edinburgh University Press, 2000).

88 Christopher Norris, *Deconstruction*, op. cit., p. 33.

89 See for example, Jonathan Culler, *On Deconstruction: Theory and Criticism After Structuralism* (London: Routledge, 1983); Catherine Besley, *Poststructuralism: A Very Short Introduction* (Oxford: Oxford University Press, 2002).

90 'Positivism and Paradigm Dominance in Consumer Research', op. cit., p. 36.

91 Shelby D. Hunt, *Controversy in Marketing Theory: For Reason, Realism, Truth, and Objectivity* (Armonk, NY: M.E. Sharpe, 2003), p. 207.

92 Ibid, p. 190.

93 Shelby D. Hunt and Robert M. Morgan, 'Resource-Advantage Theory: A Snake Swallowing its Tail or a General Theory of Competition?', *Journal of Marketing*, 61 (October), 1997, p. 81.

94 Shelby D. Hunt, *Modern Marketing Theory: Critical Issues in the Philosophy of Marketing Science* (Cincinnati, OH: South-Western Publishing, 1991), p. 340.

95 Shelby D. Hunt, 'For Reason and Realism in Marketing', *Journal of Marketing*, 56 (April), p. 94.

96 For instance, when Leong suggested that his four 'fundamental explanada' comprised the Lakatosian 'hard core' of marketing thought, SDH stressed their fallibility, provisionality and strictly conjectural status. See Siew Meng Leong, 'Metatheory and Metamethodology in Marketing: A Lakatosian Reconstruction', *Journal of Marketing*, 49 (Fall), 1985, pp. 23–40; Shelby D. Hunt, 'General Theories and the Fundamental Explananda of Marketing', *Journal of Marketing*, 47 (Fall), 1983, pp. 9–17; Shelby D. Hunt, *Controversy in Marketing Theory*, op. cit., p. 155.

97 Shelby D. Hunt, *Controversy in Marketing Theory*, op. cit., p. 92.

98 Terry Eagleton, *Literary Theory: An Introduction* (Oxford: Blackwell, 1996), p. 112.

99 Shelby D. Hunt, 'The Nature and Scope of Marketing', *Journal of Marketing*, 40 (July), 1976, p. 17.

100 Shelby D. Hunt, 'The Influence of Philosophy, Philosophers and Philosophies on a Marketer's Scholarship', *Journal of Marketing*, 65 (4), 2001, p. 118.

5   The Biopoetics of Wroe Alderson

1 This, admittedly rich, quote is attributed to Alderson by Hugh G. Wales and Lyndon E. Dawson, Jr., 'The Anomalous Qualities Between Present-day Conferences and Alderson's Marketing Theory Seminars', in O.C. Ferrell, S.W. Brown and C.W. Lamb, Jr. (eds), *Conceptual and Theoretical Developments in Marketing* (Chicago, IL: American Marketing Association, 1979), p. 224.

2 W. Alderson, S.G. Cary, W.B. Edgerton, H.W. Moore, C.E. Pickett, E. Clarence and E. Zelliot, *Meeting the Russians: American Quakers Visit the Soviet Union* (Philadelphia, PA: American Friends Service Committee, 1956).

3 Ibid., pp. 42–3.

4 Ibid., pp. 74–5.

5 See for example, Hiram C. Barksdale, 'Wroe Alderson's Contributions to Marketing Theory', in C.W. Lamb, Jr. and P.M. Dunne (eds), *Theoretical Developments in Marketing* (Chicago, IL: American Marketing Association, 1980), pp. 1–4; Edward Blair and Kenneth P. Uhl, 'Wroe Alderson and Modern Marketing Theory', in C.C. Slater (ed.), *Macro-Marketing: Distributive Processes From a Societal Perspective* (Boulder, CO: Business Research Division, University of Colorado, 1977), pp. 66–84; Jagdish N. Sheth, David M. Gardner and Dennis E. Garrett, *Marketing Theory: Evolution and Evaluation* (New York: John Wiley, 1988); Robert Tamila, *Aldersonian Marketing Thought and Functionalism* (unpublished research report and bibliography, 2001).

6 He 'couldn't express himself clearly', says Morris Holbrook, 'Wroe Alderson (1957) Marketing Behavior and Executive Action', *ACR News*, Winter, 2001, p. 37. Shelby D. Hunt is equally critical of his 'nonlucid articulation' (Shelby D. Hunt, *Modern Marketing Theory: Critical Issues in the*

Philosophy of Marketing Science (Cincinnati, OH: South-Western Publishing, 1991), p. 150). See also Shelby D. Hunt, James A. Muncy and Nina M. Ray, 'Alderson's General Theory of Marketing: A Formalization', in B.M. Enis and K.J. Roering (eds), *Review of Marketing 1981* (Chicago, IL: American Marketing Association, 1981), pp. 267–72.

7 Tim K. Hostiuck and David L. Kurtz, 'Alderson's Functionalism and the Development of Marketing Theory', *Journal of Business Research*, 1 (2), 1973, p. 141.

8 Wendell R. Smith, 'Leaders in Marketing – Wroe Alderson', *Journal of Marketing*, 30 (January), 1966, pp. 64–5.

9 Wroe Alderson and Paul E. Green, *Planning and Problem Solving in Marketing* (Homewood, IL: Richard D. Irwin, 1964), p. 5.

10 Alderson, in fairness, published a number of very short articles prior to World War II, including one in the inaugural issue of the *Journal of Marketing*, but the vast bulk of his output dates from the 1945–65 period.

11 Wroe Alderson, *Marketing Behavior and Executive Action: A Functionalist Approach to Marketing* (Homewood, IL: Richard D. Irwin, 1957); Wroe Alderson, *Dynamic Marketing Behavior: A Functionalist Theory of Marketing* (Homewood, IL: Richard D. Irwin, 1965).

12 Robert Bartels, *The History of Marketing Thought*, 2nd edn (Columbus, OH: Publishing Horizons, 1988), p. 238.

13 Ben Wooliscroft, 'Wroe Alderson's Contribution to Marketing Theory Through His Textbooks', *Journal of the Academy of Marketing Science*, 31 (4), 2003, p. 482.

14 Paul E. Green, 'The Vagaries of Becoming (and Remaining) a Marketing Research Methodologist', *Journal of Marketing*, 65 (July), 2001, p. 105.

15 Wroe Alderson, *Dynamic Marketing Behavior*, op. cit. By the way, I have a hypothesis about these hypotheses . . .

16 In addition to his six-year stint at Wharton, Alderson was a visiting professor at Massachusetts Institute of Technology during 1953 and ten years later served in a similar visiting capacity at New York University. Wroe also studied at George Washington University and the University of Pennsylvania, though he did not possess a PhD.

17 Arno J. Rethans, 'The Aldersonian Paradigm: A Perspective for Theory Development and Synthesis', in O.C. Ferrell, S.W. Brown and C.W. Lamb, Jr. (eds), *Conceptual and Theoretical Developments in Marketing* (Chicago, IL: American Marketing Association, 1979), pp. 197–209.

18 For a cogent discussion of the functional paradigm, see J.N. Sheth, D.M. Gardner and D.E. Garrett, *Marketing Theory: Evolution and Evaluation* (New York: John Wiley, 1988). Also useful is Alf H. Walle, 'Alderson's Functionalism: A Phoenix Rising From its Own Ashes', in P.F. Anderson and M.J. Ryan (eds), *Scientific Method in Marketing* (Chicago, IL: American Marketing Association, 1984), pp. 78–80.

19 Francesco M. Nicosia, 'Marketing and Alderson's Functionalism', *Journal of Business*, 35 (October), 1963, p. 404.

20 For example: Edward A. Duddy and David A. Revzan, *Marketing: An Institutional Approach* (New York: McGraw-Hill, 1947); George Fisk, *Marketing and the Ecological Crisis* (New York: Harper and Row, 1974); Mary Lambkin and George S. Day, 'Evolutionary Processes in Competitive Markets:

Beyond the Product Life Cycle', *Journal of Marketing*, 53 (July), 1989, pp. 4–20; Gerard Prendergast and Pierre Berthon, 'Insights from Ecology: An Ecotone Perspective of Marketing', *European Management Journal*, 18 (2), 2000, pp. 223–32.

21 An extremely lucid summary of Alderson's principal concepts is contained in Shelby D. Hunt, *A General Theory of Competition: Resources, Competences, Productivity, Economic Growth* (Thousand Oaks, CA: Sage, 2000), especially Chapter 3.

22 Sheth, Gardner and Garrett, *Marketing Theory: Evolution and Evaluation*, op. cit.

23 The biological analogy is not accidental, since Alderson considered trans-vections semi-sentient entities.

24 Wroe Alderson, *Marketing Behavior and Executive Action: A Functionalist Approach to Marketing* (Homewood, IL: Richard D. Irwin, 1957), p. 54.

25 Wroe Alderson, *Dynamic Marketing Behavior: A Functionalist Theory of Marketing*, p. 26.

26 See Wroe Alderson and Miles W. Martin, 'Toward a Formal Theory of Transactions and Transvections', *Journal of Marketing Research*, 2 (May), 1965, pp. 117–27.

27 C.P. Snow, *The Two Cultures* (Oxford: Oxford University Press, 1993 [1959]).

28 Indeed, the decidedly blurred boundary between art and science is exempli-fied by the present situation, where best-selling, blockbuster books are being written by physical scientists (for example, Stephen Hawking, Stephen Pinker, Steven Weinberg) and cutting-edge creative artists are engaging with the aes-thetics of emergence – fractals, chaos theory and the self-organizing system that is the internet. Useful considerations of these issues are found in: Melvyn Bragg, *On Giants' Shoulders: Great Scientists and their Discoveries from Archimedes to DNA* (London: Hodder and Stoughton,1998); John Carey, *The Faber Book of Science* (London: Faber and Faber, 1995); Peter Conrad, *Modern Times, Modern Places: Life and Art in the 20th Century* (London: Thames and Hudson, 1998); Sian Ede, *Strange and Charmed: Science and the Contemporary Visual Arts* (London: Calouste Gulbenkian Foundation, 2000); Steven Johnson, *Emergence: The Connected Lives of Ants, Brains, Cities and Software* (London: Allen Lane, 2001); Stephen Wilson, *Information Arts: Intersections of Art, Science, and Technology* (Cambridge, MA: MIT Press, 2002). The 'scientists should think like poets' quote is taken from Ivan Tolstoy, *The Knowledge and the Power: Reflections on the History of Science* (Edinburgh: Canongate, 1990).

29 Brett Cooke and Frederick Turner, *Biopoetics: Evolutionary Explorations in the Arts* (Lexington: ICUS, 1999).

30 Brett Cooke, 'Biopoetics: The New Synthesis', in B. Cooke and F. Turner (eds), *Biopoetics: Evolutionary Explorations in the Arts* (Lexington: ICUS, 1999), p. 6.

31 Eric S. Rabkin, 'The Descent of Fantasy,' in B. Cooke and F. Turner (eds), *Biopoetics: Evolutionary Explorations in the Arts* (Lexington: ICUS, 1999), pp. 47–57.

32 Karl Kroeber, *Ecological Literary Criticism: Romantic Imagining and the Biology of Mind* (New York: Columbia University Press, 1994).

33 Gordon E. Slethaug, *Beautiful Chaos: Chaos Theory and Metachaotics in Recent American Fiction* (Albany, NY: State University of New York Press, 2000).

34 Edward O. Wilson, *Sociobiology: The New Synthesis* (Cambridge, MA: Harvard University Press, 1975).

35 Edward O. Wilson, *Consilience: The Unity of Knowledge* (New York: Knopf, 1998), see especially pp. 233–64.

36 Frederick Turner terms this 'natural classicism'. See his *Natural Classicism: Essays on Literature and Science* (New York: Paragon, 1986).

37 Wilson, *Consilience*, op. cit., p. 237.

38 Stephen Jay Gould, 'More Things in Heaven and Earth', in H. Rose and S. Rose (eds), *Alas Poor Darwin: Arguments Against Evolutionary Psychology* (London: Vintage, 2001), pp. 85–105.

39 See for example, Janet Radcliffe Richards, *Human Nature After Darwin: A Philosophical Introduction* (London: Routledge, 2000). The collection edited by Hilary Rose and Steven Rose is no less illuminating (*Alas Poor Darwin: Arguments Against Evolutionary Psychology*, London: Vintage, 2001). The heinous marketing-orientated accusations are made in Andrew Ross, 'The Chicago Gangster Theory of Life', *Social Text*, 35, 1993, pp. 93–112. Don't all rush at once.

40 If you can't be bothered wading through the originals, check out Frederick Crews, *Postmodern Pooh* (New York: North Point Press, 2001), Chapter 7 in particular.

41 J. Hillis Miller, *Black Holes* (Stanford, CA: Stanford University Press, 1999).

42 Daniel Rancour-Laferriere, 'Preliminary Remarks on Literary Memetics', in B. Cooke and F. Turner (eds), *Biopoetics: Evolutionary Explorations in the Arts* (Lexington: ICUS, 1999), pp. 59–70.

43 N. Katherine Hayles, *Chaos Bound: Orderly Disorder in Contemporary Literature and Science* (Ithaca, NY: Cornell University Press, 1990). See also N. Katherine Hayles, *Chaos and Order: Complex Dynamics in Literature and Science* (Chicago, IL: University of Chicago Press, 1991).

44 Joseph Carroll, *Evolution and Literary Theory* (Columbia: University of Missouri Press, 1995), p. 1. Also useful is Carroll's *Literary Darwinism: Evolution, Human Nature and Literature* (New York: Routledge, 2004).

45 See Frederick Turner, *Natural Classicism: Essays on Literature and Science* (New York: Paragon, 1986). Also Frederick Turner, *Beauty: The Value of Values* (Charlottesville: University Press of Virginia, 1991); *The Culture of Hope: A New Birth of the Classical Spirit* (New York: Free Press, 1995).

46 Frederick Turner, 'An Ecopoetics of Beauty and Meaning', in B. Cooke and F. Turner (eds), *Biopoetics: Evolutionary Explorations in the Arts* (Lexington: ICUS, 1999), p. 127.

47 Ibid.

48 Helpful overviews of reflexive social science include: Mats Alvesson and Kaj Skoldberg, *Reflexive Methodology: New Vistas for Qualitative Research* (London: Sage, 2000); Frederick Steier, *Research and Reflexivity* (London: Sage, 1991); Steve Woolgar, *Knowledge and Reflexivity: New Frontiers in the Sociology of Knowledge* (London: Sage, 1988).

49 Especially so, I'd have thought, in an academic environment where environmental issues are high on the agenda. For example: George Fisk, 'Reflection and Retrospection: Searching for Visions in Marketing', *Journal of Marketing*, 63 (January), 1999, pp. 115–21; William Kilbourne, Pierre McDonagh and Andrea Prothero, 'Sustainable Consumption and the Quality of Life: A Macromarketing Challenge to the Dominant Social Paradigm', *Journal of Macromarketing*, 17 (Spring), 1997, pp. 4–24.

50 Wroe Alderson, *Dynamic Marketing Behavior: A Functionalist Theory of Marketing* (Homewood, IL: Richard D. Irwin, 1965), p. 86.

51 Reavis Cox, 'Introduction', in R. Cox, W. Alderson and S.J. Shapiro (eds), *Theory in Marketing* (Homewood, IL: Richard D. Irwin, 1964), pp. 1–14.

52 J.M. Sheth, D.M. Gardner and D.E. Garrett, *Marketing Theory: Evolution and Evaluation* (New York: John Wiley, 1988), p. 93.

53 Hiram C. Barksdale, 'Wroe Alderson's Contributions to Marketing Theory' in C.W. Lamb, Jr. and P.M. Dunne (eds), *Theoretical Developments in Marketing* (Chicago, IL: American Marketing Association, 1980), pp. 1–4; Arno J. Rethans, 'The Aldersonian Paradigm: A Perspective for Theory Development and Synthesis', in O.C. Ferrell, S.W. Brown and C.W. Lamb, Jr. (eds), *Conceptual and Theoretical Developments in Marketing* (Chicago, IL: American Marketing Association, 1979), pp. 197–209.

54 Reavis Cox, 'Introduction', op. cit., p. 13.

55 Robert F. Lusch, 'Alderson, Sessions and the 1950s Manager', in C.W. Lamb, Jr. and P.M. Dunne (eds), *Theoretical Developments in Marketing* (Chicago, IL: American Marketing Association, 1980), pp. 4–6.

56 *Dynamic Marketing Behavior*, op. cit., pp. 5, 24.

57 I am grateful to Professor Paul W. Green (Wharton Business School), who furnished me with this example of Alderson's personal correspondence.

58 Wroe Alderson, 'Survival and Adjustment in Organized Behavior Systems', in R. Cox and W. Alderson (eds), *Theory in Marketing: Selected Essays* (Homewood, IL: Richard D. Irwin, 1950), p. 79.

59 Alderson, *Dynamic Marketing Behavior*, op. cit., p. 99.

60 He espoused this position from start to finish of his academic career, see for example: Wroe Alderson, 'A Marketing View of Competition', *Journal of Marketing*, 1 (January), 1937, pp. 189–90; Wroe Alderson and Michael H. Halbert, *Men, Motives, and Markets* (Englewood Cliffs, NJ: Prentice Hall, 1968).

61 Charles Goodman, *The Transformation of the Marketing Discipline 1946–1986* (Philadelphia, PA: Wharton Working Paper # 88–010R, 1988).

62 Wroe Alderson, 'Basic Research and the Future of Marketing', in F.M. Bass (ed.), *The Frontiers of Marketing Thought and Science* (Chicago, IL: American Marketing Association, 1957), pp. 170–8.

63 Alderson, 'Survival and Adjustment', op. cit., pp. 66–7. On the antecedents and descendants of Alderson's thought, see: Donald F. Dixon, 'Some Late Nineteenth-Century Antecedents of Marketing Theory', *Journal of Macromarketing*, 19 (December), 1999, pp. 115–25; Richard L. Priem, Abdul M.A. Rasheed and Shahrzad Amirami, 'Alderson's Transvection and Porter's Value System: A Comparison of Two Independently-Developed Theories', *Journal of Management History*, 3 (2), 1997, pp. 145–165; W. Duncan Reekie and Ronald Savitt, 'Marketing Behaviour and Entrepreneurship: A Synthesis of Alderson and Austrian Economics', *European Journal of Marketing*, 16 (7), 1982, pp. 55–66; Ronald Savitt, 'Pre-Aldersonian Antecedents to Macromarketing: Insights from the Textual Literature', *Journal of the Academy of Marketing Science*, 18 (Fall), 1990, pp. 293–301.

64 Alderson, 'Survival and Adjustment', op. cit., p. 67.

65 Wroe Alderson, *Marketing Behavior and Executive Action: A Functionalist Approach to Marketing* (Homewood, IL: Richard D. Irwin, 1957), p. 388.

66 Alderson, *Dynamic Marketing Behavior*, op. cit., p. 4.

67 Wroe Alderson, 'A Systematics for Problems of Action', *Philosophy of Science*, 18 (January), 1951, p. 16.

68 I have no desire, rest assured, to cast aspersions on Alderson's memory. A condescending tone, nevertheless, clearly enters his prose when discussing putative rivals within the marketing academy, such as Michael Halbert (see for example, Alderson, *Marketing Behavior and Executive Action*, op. cit., pp. 16, 96). What's more, although Wroe is lionized for furthering the cause of marketing theory, he was not averse to dissuading ambitious academicians, as the epigraph of this chapter idicates. The Ur-guru, clearly, was a very competitive man, but until such times as a biographical study of his life and work is undertaken, the jury must remain out on his attempts to differentiate the Alderson brand.

69 Alderson, *Dynamic Marketing Behavior*, op. cit., p. 184.

70 Some readers might be inclined to challenge this assertion, since there is no hard evidence that Alderson deliberately wrote in a disorientating manner. This, of course, is correct. However, the present chapter's point of departure is that Alderson was a talented literary stylist, not the inarticulate academic of legend. It follows, therefore, that he knew what he was doing. The very fact, for example, that he apologizes for his (lengthy) digressions is clear evidence that he was aware he was digressing. What's more, he could quite easily have edited them out to improve the readability of the article or book. But chose not to do so. More fundamentally perhaps, the basic premise of functionalism is that *everything has a purpose* and, if functionalist precepts are applied to Alderson's functionalism, then it is appropriate to assume that Wroe's digressions perform in a purposeful manner.

71 Alderson, *Dynamic Marketing Behavior*, op. cit., p. 249.

72 Wroe Alderson and Michael H. Halbert, *Men, Motives, and Markets* (Englewood Cliffs, NJ: Prentice Hall, 1968), pp. 53–4.

73 Wroe Alderson and Stanley J. Shapiro, 'Towards a Theory of Retail Competition', in R. Cox, W. Alderson and S.J. Shapiro (eds), *Theory in Marketing* (Homewood, IL: Richard D. Irwin, 1964), pp. 190–212.

74 Wroe Alderson and Reavis Cox, 'Towards a Theory of Marketing', *Journal of Marketing*, 13 (October), 1948, pp. 137–52.

75 Wroe Alderson, 'Scope and Place of Wholesaling in the United States', *Journal of Marketing*, 14 (September), 1949, pp. 145–55.

76 Alderson and Halbert, *Men, Motives, and Markets*, op. cit.

77 Hiram C. Barksdale, 'Wroe Alderson's Contributions to Marketing Theory', in C.W. Lamb, Jr. and P.M. Dunne (eds), *Theoretical Development in Marketing* (Chicago, IL: American Marketing Association, 1980), pp. 1–4; Shelby D. Hunt, *Modern Marketing Theory: Critical Issues in the Philosophy of Marketing Science* (Cincinnati, OH: South-Western Publishing, 1991); J.M. Sheth, D.M. Gardner and D.E. Garrett, *Marketing Theory: Evolution and Evaluation* (New York: John Wiley, 1988).

78 Wroe Alderson, 'A Systematics for Problems of Action', *Philosophy of Science*, 18 (January), 1951, p. 16.

79 Wroe Alderson and Reavis Cox, 'Towards a Theory of Marketing', op. cit., p. 150.

80 David D. Monieson and Stanley J. Shapiro, 'Biological and Evolutionary Dimensions of Aldersonian Thought: What he Borrowed Then and What he

Might Have Borrowed Now', in C.W. Lamb, Jr. and P.M. Dunne (eds), *Theoretical Developments in Marketing* (Chicago, IL: American Marketing Association, 1980), pp. 7–12.

81 Wroe Alderson, 'The Analytical Famework for Marketing,' in D. Duncan (ed.), *Proceedings: Conference of Marketing Teachers from Far Western States* (Berkeley, CA: University of California, 1958), pp. 15–28, reprinted in Ben M. Enis and Keith K. Cox, *Marketing Classics: A Selection of Influential Articles*, 5th edn (Boston: Allyn and Bacon, 1985), p. 23.

82 Wroe Alderson, 'Marketing and the Computer: An Overview', in W. Alderson and S.J. Shapiro (eds), *Marketing and the Computer* (Englewood Cliffs, NJ: Prentice Hall, 1963), p. 10.

83 Wroe Alderson, 'A Formula for Measuring Productivity in Distribution', *Journal of Marketing*, 13 (April), 1948, p. 445.

84 Wroe Alderson and Paul E. Green, *Planning and Problem Solving in Marketing* (Homewood, IL: Richard D. Irwin, 1964), p. 374.

85 Wroe Alderson, *Marketing Behavior and Executive Action: A Functionalist Approach to Marketing* (Homewood, IL: Richard D. Irwin, 1957), pp. 121–2, 137.

86 Wroe Alderson, 'A Marketing View of the Patent System', in W. Alderson, V. Terpstra and S.J. Shapiro (eds), *Patents and Progress: The Sources and Impact of Advancing Technology* (Homewood, IL: Richard D. Irwin, 1965), p. 225.

87 Wroe Alderson and Michael H. Halbert, *Men, Motives, and Markets* (Englewood Cliffs, NJ: Prentice Hall, 1968), p. 1.

88 Alderson, *Marketing Behavior and Executive Action*, op. cit., p. 122.

89 Wroe Alderson, 'The Analytical Famework for Marketing', op. cit., p. 27.

90 Alderson, *Dynamic Marketing Behavior*, op. cit., p. 241.

91 Alderson, *Marketing Behavior and Executive Action*, op. cit., p. 367.

92 Alderson, *Dynamic Marketing Behavior*, op. cit., p. 187.

93 Wroe Alderson and Miles W. Martin, 'Toward a Formal Theory of Transactions and Transvections', *Journal of Marketing Research*, 2 (May), 1965, p. 123.

94 Alderson, *Marketing Behavior and Executive Action*, op. cit., p. 227.

95 Wroe Alderson, 'Survival and Adjustment in Organized Behavior Systems', in R. Cox and W. Alderson (eds), *Theory in Marketing: Selected Essays* (Homewood, IL: Richard D. Irwin, 1950), pp. 68–9. Similarly, sorts and transformations are apparent in, to cite but three examples, Wroe's descriptions of himself (which included 'gestalt psychologist', 'marketing economist', and 'management researcher'), the name of his consultancy firm (from Wroe Alderson and Company, through Alderson and Sessions, to Alderson Associates), and the most single important component of marketing endeavour (variously 'assorting', 'differential advantage', 'balanced potencies', 'group behavior', 'handling information', 'skilful direction of effort' and 'status').

96 Wroe Alderson, *Marketing Behavior and Executive Action: A Functionalist Approach to Marketing* (Homewood, IL: Richard D. Irwin, 1957), p. 153.

97 Quote sources: 'The direction for advance' from Alderson and Martin, Towards a Theory of Marketing', op. cit., p. 145; 'the electric toothbrush!' from Alderson, *Dynamic Marketing Behavior*, op. cit., p. 232; 'work habits are communicated' from Alderson, *Marketing Behavior and Executive Action*, op. cit., p. 371; 'Wibbleton . . . Wobbleton' from Alderson, *Dynamic Marketing Behavior*, op. cit., p. 45.

98 Wroe Alderson and Paul E. Green, *Planning and Problem Solving in Marketing* (Homewood, IL: Richard D. Irwin, 1964), p. 104.

99 Will Blythe, *Why I Write: Thoughts on the Craft of Fiction* (Boston: Little Brown, 1998).

100 See, for example: David Halberstam, *The Fifties* (New York: Ballantine, 1993); Thomas Hine, *Populuxe: From Tailfins and TV Dinners to Barbie Dolls and Fallout Shelters* (New York: MJF Books, 1999); Gary Cross, *An All-Consuming Century: Why Commercialism Won in Modern America* (New York: Columbia University Press, 2000).

101 Wroe Alderson, 'A Marketing View of the Patent System', op. cit., p. 232.

102 Stephen Brown, *Marketing – The Retro Revolution* (London: Sage, 2001), especially Chapter 2. On this point, I have a strong suspicion that *Marketing Behavior and Executive Action* was actually written for a mainstream readership, in the tradition of contemporary public intellectuals like Packard, Galbraith and Riesman. There is no hard evidence to support this contention, admittedly. In the preface, it is described as a book for graduate students. However, Alderson was an 'unreliable narrator' and this prefatorial statement shouldn't be taken at face value. Who, except the most egomaniacal, would claim that their book is a best-seller waiting to happen? In the event, the market for Wroe's prose must have been somewhat discrepant, inasmuch as the product was available but not in widespread demand. Presumably, the heterogeneity of the writing impeded Wroe's heroic attempt to appeal to the marketing-minded masses. Meowwww!

103 Reavis Cox, 'Introduction', in R. Cox, W. Alderson and S.J. Shapiro (eds), *Theory in Marketing* (Homewood, IL: Richard D. Irwin, 1964), p. 12.

104 Wroe Alderson and Paul E. Green, *Planning and Problem Solving in Marketing*, op. cit.

105 Neither propositions nor falsifiable (e.g. 28. *The transvection concept when fully developed will become one of the most powerful tools of system planning*; 114. *Design principles for planning facilities were stated in* Planning and Problem Solving in Marketing). Indistinguishable (e.g. 4. *Competition by problem-solvers in heterogeneous markets is necessarily dynamic*; 88. *Competition among problem-solvers in heterogeneous and discrepant markets is inherently dynamic*). Incomprehensible (15. *All information transmitted by means other than direct perception of the product is coded*; 59. *Congenial behavior is presumably the goal sought by instrumental behavior*). Inconsequential (86. *Proliferation of opportunity for enterprise is based on response to consumer needs and the needs of the firm*; 115. *Storage and display facilities must be adapted to the nature of the product*). The Wroe-is-Wonderful brigade claim that these 'propositions' could (and should) form the basis of numberless PhD dissertations. God help the poor doctoral students, I say!

106 Roger Smalley and John Fraedrich, 'Aldersonian Functionalism: An Enduring Theory of Marketing', *Journal of Marketing Theory and Practice*, 3 (Fall), 1995, p. 2.

107 Yes, I know this sounds a bit weird. I can only suggest that you reread some of Alderson's work without prejudice. You might be pleasantly surprised.

108 Alderson, *Marketing Behavior and Executive Action*, op. cit., p. 442.

6   The Anxieties of Morris Holbrook

1 Or so says Morris B. Holbrook in 'On Eschatology, Onanist Scatology, or Honest Catology? Cats Swinging, Scat Singing, and Cat Slinging as Riffs, Rifts, and Writs in a Catalytic Catechism for the Cataclysm', in S. Brown, J. Bell and D. Carson (eds), *Marketing Apocalypse: Eschatology, Escapology and the Illusion of the End* (London: Routledge, 1996), pp. 237–59. It's news to me, mind you. The nearest things we have to proverbs in my part of Ireland are 'Kick the Pope' and 'Tiocfaidh ár Lá'.

2 See Morris B. Holbrook, *Consumer Research: Introspective Essays on the Study of Consumption* (Thousand Oaks, CA: Sage, 1995). 'MoHo' isn't one of Morris's own inventions, I should add, though he has adopted it on occasion. It was actually coined by Richard Elliott (in an *IMR* book review) and I commandeered it for *Postmodern Marketing Two: Telling Tales* (London: International Thomson, 1998).

3 Morris B. Holbrook, 'A Note on Sadomasochism in the Review Process: I Hate When That Happens', *Journal of Marketing*, 50 (July), 1986, pp. 104–8.

4 He's even done things I'm thinking of doing! For some time now I've been toying with the idea of writing something on mirrors and marketing (don't ask). On rereading MoHo's corpus for this chapter, I only went and discovered that he has gone and done it already ('Mirror, Mirror on the Wall, What's Unfair in the Reflections on Advertising', *Journal of Marketing*, 51 (July), 1987, pp. 95–103). Give me a break, why don't you?!

5 Morris B. Holbrook, 'The Retailing of Performance and the Performance of Service: The Gift of Generosity with a Grin and the Magic of Munificence with Mirth', in J.F. Sherry, Jr. (ed.), *Servicescapes: The Concept of Place in Contemporary Markets* (Chicago, IL: NTC Books, 1998), pp. 487–513.

6 Holbrook, *Consumer Research, op. cit.*, p. 183.

7 Variously described as a Deconstructionist, a neo-Gnostic, a Nietzschean, an exponent of psychoanalytical criticism and many more besides, Harold Bloom is all of these things and none. According to Terry Eagleton, who is no fan, Bloom is 'daringly original' (Eagleton, *Literary Theory: An Introduction* (Oxford: Blackwell, 1996), p. 183) and, according to another antagonist, Frank Lentricchia, he is 'the bright particular star of our critical heavens' (*After the New Criticism* (Chicago: IL, Chicago University Press, 1980), p. 345). There are many more paeans along these lines. The New York Times encapsulates him thus on the blurb of one of his books: 'A colossus among critics . . . with an encyclopedic intellect, exuberant eccentricity, a massive love of literature. The legend of his genius spans four decades'.

8 See for example, Harold Bloom, *The Western Canon: The Books and School of the Ages* (Basingstoke: Papermac, 1994); *Shakespeare: The Invention of the Human* (London: Fourth Estate, 1999); *Genius: A Mosaic of One Hundred Exemplary Creative Minds* (London: Fourth Estate, 2002).

9 Louis A. Renza, 'Influence' in F. Lentricchia and T. McLaughlin (eds), *Critical Terms for Literary Study* (Chicago: University of Chicago Press, 1995), pp. 186–202.

10 Elizabeth W. Bruss, *Beautiful Theories: The Spectacle of Discourse in Contemporary Criticism* (Baltimore: The Johns Hopkins University Press, 1982), p. 285.

11 Harold Bloom, *The Anxiety of Influence: A Theory of Poetry* (New York: Oxford University Press, 1973).

12 Chris Baldick, *Criticism and Literary Theory: 1890 to the Present* (London: Longman, 1996), p. 177.

13 Harold Bloom, *The Anxiety of Influence*, op. cit., p. 15.

14 Elizabeth W. Bruss, *Beautiful Theories*, op. cit. However it's not *that* straightforward. In the series of books that swiftly followed *Anxiety of Influence*, for example, Bloom effectively remade, remoulded and remodelled his revisionary schema to produce a framework of labyrinthine, almost impenetrable complexity. Parallels were drawn between the six original ratios and the six key rhetorical tropes of *irony, synecdoche, metonymy, hyperbole, metaphor* and *matalepsis,* as well as the Freudian defence mechanisms of *reaction–formation, reversal, regression, repression, introjection* and *projection.* What's more, the complete schema was placed within a larger six-phase movement termed (after Freud and Derrida) 'The Scene of Instruction' and applied not only to poetic oeuvres, individual poems and the creative life cycle of strong poets, but to works of criticism and writing generally. As if that weren't enough, key concepts have been elided, glossed and massaged to such an extent that they comprise nothing less than an amorphous terminological pudding into which Bloom periodically dips his critical thumb and pulls out a lexical plum. See his *A Map of Misreading* (New York: Oxford University Press, 1975); *Kabbalah and Criticism* (New York: Seabury Press, 1975); *Agon: Towards a Theory of Revisionism* (New York: Oxford University Press, 1982).

15 Ted Levitt, for example, acknowledges his intellectual debt to Malcolm P. McNair; Philip Kotler mentions Wroe Alderson in dispatches; Shelby D. Hunt singles out Bud LaLonde; and Morris B. Holbrook cites John Howard as a major mentor (see Bartels, *The History of Marketing Thought*, 3rd edn (Columbus, OH: Publishing Horizons, 1988); 'The Influence of Philosophy', op. cit.; Morris B. Holbrook, *Consumer Research: Introspective Essays on the Study of Consumption* (Thousand Oaks, CA: Sage, 1995); Alderson, likewise, was clearly indebted to E.H. Chamberlin and Talcott Parsons, though I have no recollection of him acknowledging that fact.

16 Hence, from a Bloomian perspective, the above, openly acknowledged influences 'don't count'.

17 David Clutterbuck and Stuart Crainer, *Makers of Management* (London: Macmillan, 1980); Stuart Crainer, *The Financial Times Handbook of Management* (London: FT, 1995); Carol Kennedy, *Guide to the Management Gurus: Shortcuts to the Ideas of Leading Management Thinkers* (New York: Century Business, 1998).

18 Morris B. Holbrook, 'Why Business is Bad for Consumer Research: The Three Bears Revisited', in E.C. Hirschman and M.B. Holbrook (eds), *Advances in Consumer Research*, Vol. 12 (Provo, UT: Association for Consumer Research, 1985), pp. 145–56.

19 Holbrook, Consumer Research, op. cit.; Elizabeth C. Hirschman and Morris B. Holbrook, *Postmodern Consumer Research: The Study of Consumption as Text* (Newbury Park: Sage, 1992); Morris B. Holbrook and Elizabeth C. Hirschman, *The Semiotics of Consumption: Interpreting Symbolic Consumer Behavior in Popular Culture and Works of Art* (Berlin: de Gruyter, 1993).

20 On Morris's malign reviewers, check out *The Semiotics of Consumption*, op. cit.,

Chapter 1; and 'A Note on Sadomasochism in the Review Process: I Hate When That Happens', *Journal of Marketing*, 50 (July), 1986: 104–8.

21 Stephen Brown, *Postmodern Marketing Two: Telling Tales* (London: International Thomson, 1988), p. 275.

22 For example, Morris B. Holbrook, 'Theory Development is a Jazz Solo: Bird Lives', in P.F. Anderson and M.J. Ryan (eds), *Scientific Method in Marketing* (Chicago, IL: American Marketing Association, 1984), pp. 48–52; Morris B. Holbrook, 'The Role of Lyricism in Research on Consumer Emotions: Skylark, Have you Anything to Say to Me?', in M. Goldberg, G. Gorn and R. Pollay (eds), *Advances in Consumer Research*, Vol. 17 (Provo, UT: Association for Consumer Research, 1990), pp. 1–18; Morris B. Holbrook, 'Romanticism and Sentimentality in Consumer Behavior: A Literary Approach to the Joys and Sorrows of Consumption', in E.C. Hirschman (ed.), *Research in Consumer Behavior*, Vol. 5 (Greenwich, CT: JAI Press, 1991), pp. 105–80.

23 Morris B. Holbrook, 'The Three Faces of Elitism: Postmodernism, Political Correctness, and Popular Culture', *Journal of Macromarketing*, 15 (2), 1995, p. 130.

24 Though this is changing, as we discovered in Chapter 1.

25 Janet Burroway, *Writing Fiction: A Guide to Narrative Craft* (New York: HarperCollins, 1996).

26 Holbrook, *Consumer Research*, op. cit.

27 Morris B. Holbrook, 'Aftermath of the Task Force: Dogmatism and Catastrophe in the Development of Marketing Thought', *ACR Newsletter*, September, 1989, pp. 3–4.

28 Holbrook, *Consumer Research*, op. cit., p. 368.

29 Both Ted and Morris are prone to the occasional mixed metaphor. But I'll spare their blushes.

30 Theodore Levitt, 'Marketing and its Discontents' in *The Marketing Imagination*, 2nd edn, 1986, p. 220.

31 Morris B. Holbrook, 'The Role of Lyricism in Research on Consumer Emotions', op. cit.

32 Holbrook, *Consumer Research*, op. cit., p. 103.

33 Ibid., p. 210.

34 Morris B. Holbrook and Mark W. Grayson, 'The Semiology of Cinematic Consumption: Symbolic Consumer Behavior in *Out of Africa*', *Journal of Consumer Research*, 13 (December), 1986, p. 377.

35 As Ernest Gellner rightly observes, 'dogmatism is not uncommon among creative intellectuals, even or especially among those who preach liberalism' (*The Psychoanalytic Movement* (London: Fontana, 1993), p. 215.

36 Morris B. Holbrook, *Consumer Research: Introspective Essays on the Study of Consumption* (Thousand Oaks, CA: Sage, 1995), p. 335.

37 Theodore Levitt, 'Marketing and the Corporate Purpose' in *The Marketing Imagination*, 2nd edn, 1986, p. 1.

38 Theodore Levitt, *Levitt on Marketing* (Boston, MA: HBSP, 1992), p. iv.

39 Morris B. Holbrook, 'The Psychoanalytical Interpretation of Consumer Research: I Am An Animal', in E.C. Hirschman and J.N. Sheth (eds), *Research in Consumer Behavior*, Vol. 3 (Greenwich, CT: JAI Press, 1988), pp. 149–78.

40 See for example, Mihaly Csikszentmihalyi, *Creativity: Flow and the Psychology of Discovery and Invention* (New York: HarperCollins, 1996); Hans Eysenck,

Genius: The Natural History of Creativity (Cambridge: Cambridge University Press: 1995); Howard Gardner, *Extraordinary Minds* (London, Weidenfeld & Nicolson, 1997).

41 Morris B. Holbrook, 'The Four Faces of Commodification in the Development of Marketing Knowledge', *Journal of Marketing Management*, 11 (7), 1996, pp. 641–54.

42 Morris B. Holbrook, 'Romanticism, Introspection and the Roots of Experiential Consumption: Morris the Epicurean', in R.W. Belk, N. Dholakia and A. Venkatesh (eds), *Consumption and Marketing: Macro Dimensions* (Cincinnati, OH: South-Western Publishing, 1996), pp. 20–82.

43 Morris B. Holbrook, *Consumer Value: A Framework for Analysis and Research* (London: Routledge, 1999), pp. 184, 185, 187. Incidentally, I think Morris actually means X = Z in the passage quoted (and not Y = Z) but, hey, who am I to argue with TOPKAT?

44 Theodore Levitt, 'The M–R Snake Dance', *Harvard Business Review*, 38 (6), 1960, pp. 76–84.

45 Theodore Levitt, 'Entrepreneuring Eastern Europe', in *Thinking About Management* (New York: Free Press, 1991), pp. 78–9.

46 So marked is Ted's recycling tendency, that even his recycled papers (as gathered in *The Marketing Mode*) are themselves recycled (the least commercially successful of his books when it was published in 1969, *The Marketing Mode* was reissued with a new title, *Marketing For Business Growth*, in 1974).

47 This list, what's more, could be extended considerably. He has recycled his work on consumer values, perceptions of beauty, expert versus popular taste, his grandfather's logbook and so on, on several occasions. Holbrook is a serial recycler.

48 Holbrook, *Consumer Research*, op. cit., p. 24. Incidentally, if Morris is preoccupied with his waters, metaphorically speaking, Ted is inordinately fond of his figurative vittels, everything from juicy apples and lobster thermidor to frozen pizza and sizzling steak.

49 Morris B. Holbrook, 'Aftermath of the Task Force: Dogmatism and Catastrophe in the Development of Marketing Thought', *ACR Newsletter*, September, 1989, p. 11.

50 Theodore Levitt, 'The Pluralization of Consumption', in *Levitt on Marketing* (Boston, MA: HBSP, 1992), p. 51.

51 Theodore Levitt, 'The Mixed Metrics of Greed', in *Thinking About Management* (New York: Free Press, 1992), p. 40.

52 Ted evolved too, it must be said, but once he stumbled upon his signature style (with 'Marketing Myopia'), he pretty much stuck to it thereafter.

53 Holbrook, *Consumer Research*, op. cit., p. 79.

54 Ibid., p. 260.

55 Morris B. Holbrook, 'The Psychoanalytical Interpretation of Consumer Research: I Am An Animal', in E.C. Hirschman and J.N. Sheth (eds), *Research in Consumer Behavior*, Vol. 3 (Greenwich, CT: JAI Press, 1988), pp. 149–78.

56 Holbrook, *Consumer Research*, op. cit., p. 62.

57 Personal correspondence (which is a euphemism for 'Morris mentioned this to me once').

58 Morris B. Holbrook, 'What is Consumer Research?', *Journal of Consumer Research*, 14 (June), 1987, pp. 128–32.

59 Ironically, in his celebrated 1983 paper on 'globalization', a piece that Holbrook has since excoriated ('Marketing Across or Beyond, Without or Among, and At or On the Borders: Some Literal, Littoral and Literary Ideas Whose Times Definitely Have, Probably Have Not and Maybe Might Have Come', paper presented at Marketing Academy Conference, July, 1997, Manchester, England).

60 This 'use of weird words' argument may seem like a tenuous link, but it is an argument that TOPKAT employs himself (in an even more extreme form). In his cat-versus-dog paper, for example, he recruits A. Bartlett Giametti to his cat-cause on the basis that his book uses a lot of words beginning with the letter C. (And MoHo once had the gall to challenge my 'consummation' connection!)

61 Morris B. Holbrook, 'What is Consumer Research?', op. cit.

62 As is the prose of *Writing Marketing*'s roster, with the exception of Wroe Alderson. However, it's most strongly marked in Ted 'n' Mo.

63 Morris B. Holbrook, 'Marketing Across or Beyond', op. cit.

64 Morris B. Holbrook, 'O, Consumer, How You've Changed: Some Radical Reflections on the Roots of Consumption', in A.F. Firat, N. Dholakia and R. Bagozzi (eds), *Philosophical and Radical Thought in Marketing* (Lexington, MA: Lexington Books, 1987), pp. 156–77.

65 Morris B. Holbrook, *Consumer Research: Introspective Essays on the Study of Consumption* (Thousand Oaks, CA: Sage, 1995), p. 173.

66 Morris B. Holbrook, 'The Role of Lyricism in Research on Consumer Emotions: Skylark, Have You Anything to Say to Me?', in M. Goldberg, G. Gorn and R. Pollay (eds), *Advances in Consumer Research*, Vol. 17 (Provo, UT: Association for Consumer Research, 1990), pp. 1–28.

67 For more on Ted's 'pragmatism', see Stephen Brown, 'Theodore Levitt: The Ultimate Writing Machine', *Marketing Theory*, in press.

68 Morris memorably describes the 'great debate' with his managerially-inclined marketing brethren in *Consumer Research*, op. cit., pp. 298–300.

69 For example, Morris B. Holbrook, 'I'm Hip: An Autobiographical Account of Some Musical Consumption Experiences', in R.J. Lutz (ed.), *Advances in Consumer Research*, Vol. 13 (Provo, UT: Association for Consumer Research, 1986), pp. 614–18; Morris B. Holbrook, 'Consumption, Symbolism and Meaning in Works of Art: A Paradigmatic Case', *European Journal of Marketing*, 22 (7), 1988, pp. 19–36; Morris B. Holbrook, *Daytime Television Gameshows and the Celebration of Merchandise: The Price is Right* (Bowling Green: Bowling Green State University Popular Press, 1993).

70 Holbrook, *Consumer Research*, op. cit., pp. 255–9.

71 Morris B. Holbrook, Stephen Bell, and Mark W. Grayson, 'The Role of the Humanities in Consumer Research: Close Encounters and Coastal Disturbances', in E.C. Hirschman (ed.), *Interpretive Consumer Research* (Provo, UT: Association for Consumer Research, 1989), pp. 29–47.

72 Holbrook, *Consumer Research*, op. cit., p. 256.

73 Morris B. Holbrook, 'Holbrook's Reply to Pechmann: Prelude and Poem', *ACR Newsletter*, September, 1990, p. 4.

74 Morris B. Holbrook, 'Romanticism, Introspection and the Roots of Experiential Consumption', op. cit.

75 Elizabeth C. Hirschman and Morris B. Holbrook, *Postmodern Consumer Research*, op. cit., p. 97.

76 SPI has been much-debated. Key contributions include: Melanie Wallendorf

and Merrie Brucks, 'Introspection in Consumer Research: Implementation and Implications', *Journal of Consumer Research*, 20 (December), 1993, pp. 339–59; Stephen J. Gould, 'Researcher Introspection as a Method in Consumer Research: Applications, Issues and Implications', *Journal of Consumer Research*, 21 (March), 1995, pp. 719–22; Colin Campbell, 'Romanticism, Consumption and Introspection: Some Comments on Professor Holbrook's Paper', in R.W. Belk, N. Dholakia and A. Venkatesh (eds), *Consumption and Marketing: Macro Dimensions* (Cincinnati, OH: South-Western Publishing, 1996, pp. 96–103.

77 Morris B. Holbrook, 'On Reading Wallendorf and Brucks' (this is a 22-stanza poem, with A–B rhyme scheme, which was rejected by the *Journal of Consumer Research* and published in TOPKAT's 'autobiography', *Consumer Research*, op. cit., pp. 252–4).

78 Stephen J. Gould, 'The Self-manipulation of my Pervasive, Perceived Vital Energy Through Product Use: An Introspective-praxis Perspective', *Journal of Consumer Research*, 18 (September), 1991, pp. 194–207.

79 Morris B. Holbrook, 'Loving and Hating New York: Some Reflections on the Big Apple', *International Journal of Research in Marketing*, 11 (4), 1994, pp. 381–5.

80 MoHo, of course, still gets published in the top journals, on a regular basis. However, these increasingly tend to be his mainstream, quants-orientated articles. The creative stuff, so to speak, is largely confined to the margins. Jeez, he's even published in books edited by me. You can't get much more marginal than that.

81 See for example, Morris B. Holbrook, 'On Eschatology, Onanist Scatology, or Honest Catology? Cats Swinging, Scat Singing, and Cat Slinging as Riffs, Rifts, and Writs in a Catalytic Catechism for the Cataclysm', in S. Brown, J. Bell and D. Carson (eds), *Marketing Apocalypse: Eschatology, Escapology and the Illusion of the End* (London: Routledge, 1996), pp. 237–59; Morris B. Holbrook, 'Marketing Across or Beyond, Without or Among, and At or On the Borders: Some Literal, Littoral and Literary Ideas Whose Times Definitely Have, Probably Have Not and Maybe Might Have Come', paper presented at Marketing Academy Conference, July, 1997, Manchester, England; Morris B. Holbrook, 'Feline Consumption: Ethography, Felologies and Unobtrusive Participation in the Life of a Cat', *European Journal of Marketing*, 31 (3/4), 1997, pp. 214–33; Morris B. Holbrook, 'Walking on the Edge: A Stereographic Photo Essay on the Verge of Consumer Research', in S. Brown and D. Turley (eds), *Consumer Research: Postcards From the Edge* (London: Routledge, 1997), pp. 46–78; Morris B. Holbrook, 'Journey to Kroywen: An Ethnoscopic, Auto-auto-auto-driven Stereographic Photo Essay', in B.B. Stern (ed.), *Representing Consumers: Voices, Views and Visions* (London: Routledge, 1998), pp. 231–63.

82 Stuart Crainer, *The Financial Times Handbook of Management* (London: Pitman, 1995); John Micklethwait and Adrian Wooldridge, *The Witch Doctors: Making Sense of the Management Gurus* (New York: Times Books, 1996).

83 Theodore Levitt, 'Retrospective Commentary', in B.M. Enis and K.K. Cox (eds), *Marketing Classics: A Selection of Influential Articles* (Boston: Allyn and Bacon, 1975), pp. 20–3.

84 Edward C. Bursk, 'Marketing Myopia', *Harvard Business Review*, 38 (4), 1960, p. 2.

85 Actually, Morris has since bettered 'Loving and Hating New York'. I unreservedly recommend: Morris B. Holbrook, 'Time Travels in Retrospace: Unpacking My Grandfather's Trunk – Some Introspective Recollections of

Life on the Brule', in S. Brown and J.F. Sherry, Jr. (eds), *Time, Space, and the Market: Retroscapes Rising* (Armonk, NY: M.E. Sharpe, 2003), pp. 171–98.

86 Wouldn't you know it, Morris makes a very similar argument in 'The Role of the Humanities in Consumer Research: Close Encounters and Coastal Disturbances', in E.C. Hirschman (ed.), *Interpretive Consumer Research* (Provo, UT: Association for Consumer Research, 1989), pp. 29–47. As I said, TOPKAT's always one step ahead. Several steps, come to think of it.

87 See Stephen Brown, *Marketing – The Retro Revolution* (London: Sage, 2001), especially Chapter 2.

88 David Lodge, *The Modes of Modern Writing: Metaphor, Metonymy, and the Typology of Modern Literature* (London: Edward Arnold, 1977).

89 Morris B. Holbrook, 'Loving and Hating New York: Some Reflections on the Big Apple', *International Journal of Research in Marketing*, 11(4), 1994, p. 385.

90 Yes, I know this runs counter to my thesis that Levitt's papers start off strongly and slowly peter out. However, this orotund climax is an exception rather than the rule with Father Ted. I strongly suspect that it was an afterthought, or possibly included at the insistence of a *Harvard Business Review* editor. It doesn't really cohere with the rest of the paper, in my opinion.

91 Along with Tom call-me-crazy Peters and assorted motivation researchers, J.K. Galbraith is one of Ted's favourite hate figures. He lambastes him on a regular basis. Incredibly, however, Galbraith penned a puff for Levitt's 1973 text, *The Third Sector: New Tactics for a Responsive Society* (New York: Amacom, 1973).

92 Artiste that he is, Morris had the nerve to publish this stuff in a European journal.

93 Morris B. Holbrook, 'Loving and Hating New York', op. cit., pp. 381, 385.

94 Well, not entirely. There's a slight air of hauteur throughout Levitt's oeuvre. See Stephen Brown, 'Theodore Levitt: The Ultimate Writing Machine', *Marketing Theory*, in press, for more detail.

95 One of Morris's colleagues at Columbia, Bernd Schmitt, has successfully cannibalized TOPKAT's corpus for a managerial audience, which is somewhat ironic given MoHo's hostility to the great executive unwashed.

96 In case you're wondering, this is not some kind of Oedipal howl on my part. It's a homage to Morris's menagerie by way of a quote from Baloo the Bear in Disney's classic cartoon, *The Jungle Book*.

7 The 3Rs of Marketing Writing

1 Quoted in Alberto Minguel, *A History of Reading* (London: HarperCollins, 1996), p. 93.

2 An excellent selection of Derrida is available in Derek Attridge (ed.), *Acts of Literature* (New York: Routledge, 1992).

3 Mind you, Drucker's was a throwaway remark in the midst of a lengthy textbook, *The Practice of Management* (Oxford: Butterworth-Heineman, 1954), so perhaps it shouldn't count.

4 Mind you, German universities got into the marketing act long before the US, so perhaps America's originary claims should be discounted. See for example, Brian Jones and David Monieson, 'Early Development of the Philosophy of Marketing Thought', *Journal of Marketing*, 54 (January), 1990, pp. 102–13.

5 Mind you, Fullerton's 'complex flux' model shows that this industrio-marketing eruption had copious precursors, antecedents and harbingers, so perhaps this 'revolutionary' rhetoric should also be set aside. Ronald Fullerton, 'How Modern is Modern Marketing? Marketing's Evolution and the Myth of the "Production Era"', *Journal of Marketing*, 52 (January), 1988, pp. 108–25.

6 Mind you, stone axes were traded over extremely long distances in the Neolithic and Palaeolithic periods, so perhaps marketing is even older than we think. Stephen Brown, *Postmodern Marketing* (London: Routledge, 1995), Chapter 2.

7 I'm not sure if this counts as perpetual motion or infinite regress. Certainly, there's more than a touch of William James's 'turtles all the way down'.

8 Steven R. Fischer, *A History of Writing* (London: Reaktion, 2001).

9 Ibid., p. 12.

10 Alberto Manguel, *A History of Reading*, op. cit., pp. 178–9.

11 Martin Travers, *An Introduction to Modern European Literature: From Romanticism to Postmodernism* (Basingstoke: Macmillan, 2001).

12 David Brooks, *BoBos in Paradise: The New Upper Class and How They Got There* (New York: Simon & Schuster, 2000); John Seabrook, *NoBrow: The Culture of Marketing – The Marketing of Culture* (New York: Knopf, 2000); Curtis White, *The Middle Mind: Why Americans Don't Think For Themselves* (London: Allen Lane, 2003). Note, the traditional distinction hasn't disappeared completely. Not every literatus has got in touch with their inner capitalist. One noteworthy hold-out is Dubravka Ugresic, *Thank You For Not Reading: Essays on Literary Trivia* (Normal, IL: Dalkey Archive Press, 2003).

13 Gabriel Zaid, *So Many Books: Reading and Publishing in an Age of Abundance* (Philadelphia: Paul Dry Books, 2003).

14 Ibid., p. 17.

15 Quoted in Nicholson Baker, *U and I: A True Story* (London: Granta Books, 1991), p. 156.

16 Peter Kemp (ed.), *The Oxford Dictionary of Literary Quotations* (Oxford: Oxford University Press, 2003), p. 78.

17 Margaret Atwood, *Negotiating With the Dead: A Writer on Writing* (Cambridge: Cambridge University Press, 2002), p. 69.

18 Ibid., p. 65.

19 Instruction manuals have to be written as well, come to think of it. The joys of this literary task are described in David Flusfeder's novel, *The Gift* (London: Fourth Estate, 2003). On the importance of writing in business life generally, see Andrew Cracknell, 'A Complete Write Off', *FT Magazine*, 22 May, 2004, pp. 24–6.

20 For example, Sonoo Singh, 'Jargon-Mongers', *Marketing Week*, 6 February, 2003, pp. 22–5.

21 Jonathan Meades, 'Shop Nation', *Times Magazine*, 27 September, 2003, p. 19.

22 David Brooks, *On Paradise Drive: How We Live Now (And Always Have) In the Future Tense* (New York: Simon & Schuster, 2004), p. 241.

23 Nicola Graydon, 'Who's Talking a Load of Bull?', *Mail on Sunday*, 29 June, 2003, pp. 60–1.

24 For further details on Big Fat Books About Marketing, see Stephen Brown, *Postmodern Marketing Two: Telling Tales* (London: ITBP, 1998).

25 Sorry about the pun on 'colophonic', but I couldn't resist it. A colophon is a printer's mark, as well as an inscription that appeared at the end of many medieval manuscripts, somewhat akin to today's acknowledgements. Writerly, no?

26 Apologies again, this one is another stretch. I'm thinking here of Marshall McLuhan's famous book, *The Gutenberg Galaxy*, crossed with Buy One Get One Free. It's a bad sign when you have to start explaining your puns. I shall desist forthwith.

27 The same can't be said about authors. There's substantial literature on writers on writing. See John Darnton, *Writers on Writing: Collected Essays from the New York Times* (New York: Times Books, 2001); Jane Smiley, *Writers on Writing: More Collected Essays From the New York Times* (New York: Times Books, 2003); David Lodge, *The Art of Fiction* (London: Penguin, 1992); David Lodge, *The Practice of Writing* (London: Secker & Warburg, 1996).

28 Particularly good examples are Jean-Marie Floch, 'The Contribution of Structural Semiotics to the Design of a Hypermarket', *International Journal of Research in Marketing*, 4 (2), 1988, pp. 233–52; Robert V. Kozinets, 'Utopian Enterprise: Articulating the Meanings of *Star Trek*'s Culture of Consumption', *Journal of Consumer Research*, 28 (June), 2001, pp. 67–88.

29 No, don't thank me, it's all part of the scholarly service. The full how-to inventory can be found in Stephen Brown, *Postmodern Marketing Two*, op. cit., pp. 205–6.

30 Stephen Brown, 'The Eunuch's Tale: Reviewing Reviewed', *Journal of Marketing Management*, 11 (7), 1995, pp. 681–706.

31 In all senses of the word 'positive'. Hopefully.

32 Shelby D. Hunt, *Foundations of Marketing Theory: Toward a General Theory of Marketing* (Armonk, NY: M.E. Sharpe, 2002).

33 See for example, Margaret Atwood, *Negotiations With the Dead: A Writer on Writing* (Cambridge: Cambridge University Press, 2002); A.S. Byatt, *On Histories and Stories: Selected Essays* (London: Chatto & Windus, 2000); Norman Mailer, *The Spooky Art: Some Thoughts on Writing* (London: Little, Brown & Co., 2003); V.S. Naipaul, *Reading & Writing: A Personal Account* (New York: New York Review Books, 2000); Susan Sontag, *Where the Stress Falls: Essays* (London: Vintage, 2001); Jeanette Winterson, *Art Objects: Essays on Ecstasy and Effrontery* (London: Vintage, 1996).

34 Stephen King, *On Writing: A Memoir of the Craft* (London: Hodder & Stoughton, 2000).

35 Ibid., p. 167.

36 Ben Wooliscroft, 'Wroe Alderson's Contribution to Marketing Theory Through His Textbooks', *Journal of the Academy of Marketing Science*, 31 (4), 2003, p. 482.

37 Michael J. Baker, 'Writing a Literature Review', *The Marketing Review*, 1 (2), 2000, pp. 219–47.

38 In this regard, see Warren Smith, Matthew Higgins, Martin Parker and Geoff Lightfoot (eds), *Science Fiction and Organizations* (London: Routledge, 2001).

39 Morris B. Holbrook, Stephen Bell, and Mark W. Grayson, 'The Role of the Humanities in Consumer Research: Close Encounters and Coastal Disturbances', in E.C. Hirschman (ed.), *Interpretive Consumer Research* (Provo, UT: Association for Consumer Research, 1989), pp. 29–47; Morris B. Holbrook,

'Feline Consumption: Ethography, Felologies and Unobtrusive Participation in the Life of a Cat', *European Journal of Marketing*, 31 (3/4), 1997, pp. 214–33.

40 As SDH himself puts it, 'the principle of noncontradiction, is . . . a minimum desideratum for any academic discourse, including marketing'.

41 Shelby D. Hunt, 'For Reason and Realism in Marketing', op. cit., p. 94.

42 This notion of progress is not confined to marketing, of course. It is one of the reigning Western meta-narratives that postmodernists have attacked.

43 Compare with the quotation from Alderson's personal letter on pp 125–6.

44 There is no contradiction here, although it might look that way. Telling writing, as Graff notes in *Clueless in Academe: How Schooling Obscures the Life of the Mind* (New Haven, CT: Yale University Press, 2003), often involves a judicious mixture of clarity and opacity. There's a 'diamonds in the rough' element to all our literary exemplars.

45 Pick up any guide to good writing and you'll come across countless clarion calls for clarity (there's lots on avoiding alliteration as well, the literary rule I live by). Check out: Joseph M. Williams, *Style: Toward Clarity and Grace* (Chicago: University of Chicago Press, 1995); Marc McCutcheon, *Damn! Why Didn't I Write That?* (Clovis, CA: Quill Driver Books, 2001); Claire KelLwald Cook, *Line By Line: How to Edit Your Own Writing* (Boston: Houghton Mifflin, 1985).

46 George Orwell's golden rules of good writing are: (i) never use a metaphor, simile or other figure of speech which you are used to seeing in print; (ii) never use a long word where a short one will do; (iii) if it is possible to cut out a word, always cut it out; (iv) never use the passive where you can use the active; (v) never use a foreign phrase, a scientific word or a jargon word if you can think of an everyday English equivalent; (vi) break any of these rules sooner than say anything outright barbarous. See George Orwell, 'Politics and the English Language', in *Inside the Whale and Other Essays* (London: Penguin, 1962), pp. 143–57.

47 Michael Alexander, *A History of English Literature* (Basingstoke: Macmillan, 2000).

48 See Simon Beesley and Sheena Joughin, *History of 20th-Century Literature* (London: Hamlyn, 2001).

49 Martin Travers, *An Introduction to Modern European Literature: From Romanticism to Postmodernism* (Basingstoke: Macmillan, 2001).

50 Theodor Adorno, 'The Essay as Form', in Brian O'Conner (ed.), *The Adorno Reader* (Oxford: Blackwell, 2000), pp. 91–111.

51 Quoted in Stephen Bailey, 'Notes and Theories', *Independent on Sunday*, 16 June, 2004, p. 5.

52 Valentine Cunningham, *Reading After Theory* (Oxford: Blackwell, 2002), p. 40.

53 Harold Bloom, *How To Read and Why* (New York: Touchstone, 2000), pp. 29, 19.

54 See Ben Agger, *Reading Science: A Literary, Political, and Sociological Analysis* (Dix Hills, NY: General Hall Inc., 1989).

55 There's a wonderful line attributed to Antoine de Saint Exupery, he of *The Little Prince*, which just about sums things up: 'Perfection is achieved, not when there is nothing more to add, but when there is nothing left to take away'.

56 On the subject of wonderful lines, there's a great passage in Tobias Wolff's semi-autobiographical book, *Old School*, where Ernest Hemingway is disbursing literary advice to wannabe writers. The whole passage is worth

quoting, but the pertinent part to this endnote is: 'Get up at first light and work like hell. Let your wife sleep in, it'll pay off later . . . Work like hell and make enough money to go someplace else, some other country where the fucking Feds can't get at you' (London: Bloomsbury, 2004), p. 136.

57 I hate to repeat myself on marketing matters, but the need for repetition was first noted by the one and only P.T. Barnum. See Stephen Brown, *Marketing – The Retro Revolution* (London: Sage, 2001).

58 Peter Kemp (ed.), *Oxford Dictionary of Literary Quotations* (Oxford: Oxford University Press, 2003), p. 208.

59 Ibid., p. 207.

60 Ibid., p. 208.

61 Harold Bloom, 'Plagiarism – A Symposium', *Times Literary Supplement*, 9 April 1982, pp. 413–15.

62 The Tobias Wolff novel cited in Note 56 above hinges on a case of literary plagiarism.

63 See H.L. Hix, *Morte d'Author: An Autopsy* (Philadelphia, PA: Temple University Press), especially Chapter 10.

64 This is an interesting one. In the first chapter of *The Marketing Imagination*, Ted confesses to misappropriating Schumpeter's concept of 'creative destruction' for 'Marketing Myopia' ('Creative destruction, I called it, stealing that ringing phrase from Joseph Schumpeter, who was safely in his grave'). In the 1975 'Retrospective Commentary' on 'Marketing Myopia', moreover, he acknowledges his intellectual debt to Alderson, McKitterick, Drucker and others (none of whom were cited in the original article). Curiously, however, he fails to mention the two greatest influences on his thinking, Malcolm 'wheel of retailing' McNair and David 'lonely crowd' Riesman. The latter, in particular, was a very significant influence on Levitt. He actually wrote an article on Riesman's best-seller a couple of years prior to 'Marketing Myopia' and you only have to peruse the text to see how it affected Ted's thinking. He was also influenced by Packard's *The Hidden Persuaders*, but that's another story (see Stephen Brown, *Marketing – The Retro Revolution*, op. cit.).

65 I suspect most marketers don't appreciate just how much 'creative writers' actually cut out. Jeanette Winterson, to cite but one example, claims to write 9,000–10,000 words for every 1,000 that actually survive her editorial cull. I don't know if this is an exaggeration – others I've come across mention a ratio of four or five to one – but there's no doubt that an awful lot gets left on the cutting room floor, as it were. I think we need to learn from this. I know I do.

66 Stephen King, *On Writing: A Memoir of the Craft* (London: Hodder & Stoughton, 2000).

67 As, say, Ezra Pound did for W.B. Yeats, T.S. Eliot and others.

68 Gabriel Zaid, *So Many Books: Reading and Publishing in an Age of Abundance* (Philadelphia: Paul Dry Books, 2003).

69 A good example is his elephantine two-fer: Morris B. Holbrook, 'The Millennial Consumer Enters the Age of Exhibitionism – A Book Review Essay, Part 1', *Consumption, Markets and Culture*, 4 (4), 2001, pp. 345–437; and Morris B. Holbrook, 'The Millennial Consumer Enters the Age of Exhibitionism – A Book Review Essay, Part 2', *Consumption, Markets and Culture*, 5 (2), 2002, pp. 113–51.

70 I try too, gentle reader, I try too, but no one ever rises to the Brownian bait (and, let's be honest here, can you blame them?).

71 Mats Alvesson, *Postmodernism and Social Research* (Buckingham: Open University Press, 2002).

72 Phil Kotler, for example, recently provoked a debate in *Marketing Week*, which ran for weeks and weeks (articles, editorials, letters). Regardless of the rights and wrongs of the controversy, it was fantastic publicity for the guru's latest publication.

73 We academics like to think of ourselves as unique and that the world is hanging on our every learned word. The truth is that there's very little difference between our scholarly articles. They're so generic and stereotyped it's not true. Hence, our self-marketing endeavours are somewhat akin to selling soap-powder, where the heaviest advertiser wins.

74 In this regard, Morris advises wannabe feline researchers *not* to follow in his footsteps. Nothing's more guaranteed to encourage them!

75 Northrop Frye, *Anatomy of Criticism: Four Essays* (Princeton, NJ: Princeton University Press, 1957).

76 Ibid., pp. 131–239.

77 Ibid., pp. 33–67.

78 Ibid., p. 34.

79 Albert C. Hamilton, *Northrop Frye: Anatomy of his Criticism* (Toronto: University of Toronto Press, 1990), p. 65.

80 Ibid., p. 62.

81 Consider the following from Wroe Alderson, *Marketing Behavior and Executive Action: A Functionalist Approach to Marketing* (Homewood, IL: Richard D. Irwin, 1957), p. 318: 'The time may come when two-way television and other electronic developments will make it possible to conclude many transactions without either buyer or seller leaving his regular location'.

82 The postmodern history debate is reviewed in Stephen Brown, Elizabeth C. Hirschman and Pauline Maclaran, 'Always Historicize! Researching Marketing History in a Post-historical Epoch' *Marketing Theory*, 1(1), 2001, pp. 40–89.

83 See for example, John Brannigan, *New Historicisism and Cultural Materialism* (Basingstoke: Macmillan, 1998).

84 The three eras schema and similar historical periodisations are covered in Stephen Brown, 'Trinitarianism, The Eternal Evangel and the Three Eras Schema', in S. Brown, J. Bell and D. Carson (eds), *Marketing Apocalypse: Eschatology, Escapology and the Illusion of the End* (London: Routledge, 1996), pp. 23–43.

85 Robert Bartels, *The History of Marketing Thought* (Columbus, OH: Publishing Horizons, 1988). Another good example is, Roger A. Kerin, 'In Pursuit of an Ideal: The Editorial and Literary History of the *Journal of Marketing*', *Journal of Marketing*, 60 (January), pp. 1–13.

86 The ACR Newsletter, for example, includes an ongoing inventory of classic articles selected by star scholars such as Morris Holbrook and Russ Belk. The *Journal of Marketing*, likewise, is running a series of retrospectives by leading academic luminaries. As for institutional rankings, well, you don't need me to tell you about that.

87 Pigeonholing is unavoidable in academic life, I guess. Even nonentities like me get pigeonholed. I still get letters on the subject of retail location, more than ten years after I last wrote about the subject.

88 This propensity is reinforced by Morris's continuing refusal to converse with the marketing mainstream. Would that he'd swallow his pride and write a book for managers. It could be a barnstormer.

89 Naomi Klein, *No Logo: Taking Aim at the Brand Bullies* (London: HarperCollins, 2000).

90 It's also generating a substantial 'defence of globalization' literature. See for example, Alan Shipman, *The Globalization Myth* (Cambridge: Icon, 2002).

91 See, Felicity Lawrence, *Not on the Label* (London: Penguin, 2004); Thomas Frank, *One Market Under God: Extreme Capitalism, Market Populism and the End of Economic Democracy* (London: Secker & Warburg, 2001); Eric Schlosser, *Fast Food Nation* (London: Penguin, 2002); George Monbiot, *Captive State* (Basingstoke: Macmillan, 2000); Malcolm Gladwell, *The Tipping Point* (London: Little, Brown & Co., 2000); David Brooks, *On Paradise Drive: How We Live Now (And Always Have) In the Future Tense* (New York: Simon & Schuster, 2004); Joanna Blythman, *Shopped* (London: Fourth Estate, 2004); Douglas Rushkoff, *Coercion* (London: Little, Brown, 2000); Paco Underhill, *Call of the Mall* (New York: Simon & Schuster, 2004); Thomas Hine, *I Want That!* (New York: HarperCollins, 2002).

92 Rachel Bowlby, *Carried Away: The Invention of Modern Shopping* (London: Faber & Faber, 2000); Mica Nava, A. Blake, I. MacRury and B. Richards, *Buy This Book* (London: Routledge, 1997); Juliet B. Schor, *The Overspent American* (London: HarperCollins, 1999); Jackson Lears, *Something For Nothing* (New York: Viking, 2003), Lizabeth Cohen, *A Consumers' Republic* (New York: Knopf, 2003); George Ritzer, *Enchanting A Disenchanted World* (Thousand Oaks, CA: Pine Forge, 1999); Daniel Miller, *The Dialectics of Shopping* (Chicago: University of Chicago Press, 2001); Alan Bryman, *The Disneyization of Society* (London: Sage, 2004).

93 The best of them is, James B. Twitchell, *Adcult USA: The Triumph of Advertising in American Culture* (Columbia: Columbia University Press, 1996).

94 Ritzer's work in particular is pure Principles of Marketing.

95 Pierre Bourdieu, *Homo Academicus*, trans P. Collier (Cambridge: Polity Press, 1988).

96 Post-colonial literary theory is covered in most lit-crit primers, such as the ones cited in Note 26, Chapter 1. Also useful is Bill Ashcroft, Gareth Griffiths and Helen Tiffin, *The Post-Colonial Studies Reader* (London: Routledge, 1995).

97 Nigel Piercy, *Market-Led Strategic Change* (Oxford: Butterworth-Heinemann, 2002).

98 Nigel Piercy, *Tales From the Marketplace* (Oxford: Butterworth-Heinemann, 2001).

99 Hey, if we're expected to 'kill our children', we might as well eat them, right?

100 Martin Amis, *The Information* (London: Flamingo, 1996), pp. 435–6.

101 The Uroboros, in ancient mythology, is a symbol of eternal recurrence. It is usually depicted as a serpent biting its own tail (though sometimes dragons or long-necked birds are used instead). It is thus analogous to the Amphisbaena, described by Sidney J. Levy in his classic article, 'Stalking the Amphisbaena', *Journal of Consumer Research*, 23 (3), 1996, pp. 163–76.

The Appendix of Stephen Brown

1 Quoted in Peter Ackroyd, *The Collection* (London: Vintage, 2002), p. 309.

2 The rule is that when Agatha Christie writes in the first person, the first person dun it! She uses the same ruse several times in her late writings. I read the books out of sequence, as one does, and by the time I got round to Ackroyd, I'd twigged that 'I' is always the baddie.

3 Clifford, Fischer, Marcus and many more got there before him. McCloskey's pioneering (and very well written) analyses of economic rhetoric also predated *Works and Lives* by several years.

4 Clifford Geertz, *Works and Lives: The Anthropologist as Author* (Stanford, CA: Stanford University Press), p. 1.

5 Yes, friends, I am that soldier. Modesty forbids that I cite the source.

6 Actually, the reaction might surprise us.

7 You know, Benjamin's thoughts on 'mechanical reproduction' might be just the critical ticket regarding Ted's self-recycling tendencies.

8 Shelby's style is so masculine that scholarly sparks can't fail to fly, I feel.

9 The glocalization of his textbooks – Canadian versions, European versions, Asian versions, Australasian versions and so on – is manna from lit-crit heaven.

10 See Note 44, Chapter 1.

11 Modesty again forbids . . .

12 But not prepositions at the end of sentences, surely!

13 I never checked to see if he included it or not. Be my guest.

14 A useful source on segmentation is Joseph Turow, *Breaking Up America* (Chicago: University of Chicago Press, 1997). John Simmons has written several fine books on writing. The best of them is probably *The Invisible Grail* (London: Texere, 2003). They have very nice production values too.

Index

References to major mentions of topics are in **bold** print.